D1599828

A Fairytale in Question

A Fairytale in Question:
Historical Interactions between Humans and Wolves

Edited by

Patrick Masius and Jana Sprenger

The White Horse Press

Copyright © 2015

The White Horse Press, 10 High Street, Knapwell, Cambridge, CB23 4NR, UK

Set in 10 point Adobe Garamond Pro
Printed by Lightning Source

British Library Cataloguing in Publication Data
A catalogue record for this book is available from the British Library

ISBN   978-1-874267-84-3 (HB)

Contents

Preface
    Manfred Jakubowski-Tiessen vii

Introduction: Wolves and Humans in History
    Patrick Masius and Jana Sprenger 1

1.   War-Time, Wolf-Time. Material–Semiotic Knots
    in the Chronicles of the Thirty Years' War
    Alexander Kling 19

2.   The Belief in Werewolves and the Extermination
    of Real Wolves in Schleswig-Holstein
    Martin Rheinheimer 39

3.   The Wolf War in Sweden during the Eighteenth Century –
    Strategies, Measures and Leaders.
    Roger Bergström, Karin Dirke and Kjell Danell 57

4.   The Story of a Man-Eating Beast in Dauphiné, France
    (1746–1756)
    Julien Alleau and John D.C. Linnell 79

5.   Where is the Big Bad Wolf?
    Notes and Narratives on Wolves in Swedish Newspapers
    during the Eighteenth and Nineteenth Centuries
    Karin Dirke 101

6.   Reconstructing the Extermination of Wolves in Germany.
    Case Studies from Brandenburg and Rhineland-Palatinate
    Patrick Masius and Jana Sprenger 119

7.   Historical Decline (and Persistence) of the Grey Wolf in Spain
    José María Fernández-García. 141

8.   British Programmes for the Extermination of the Indian Wolf,
    c. 1870–1915
    Steven Rodriguez. 163

9.   Writing the Wolf: Canine Tales and North American
     Environmental-Literary Tradition
          Karen Jones 175

10. The Shifting Iconography of Wolves over the Twentieth Century
          Linda Kalof 203

11. Alaska Wild? Wolves in America's Last Frontier
          Lydia A. Dixon 229

12. Not an Easy Road to Success: The History of Exploitation
     and Restoration of the Wolf Population in Poland
     after World War Two
          Robert W. Mysłajek and Sabina Nowak 247

13. If You Wander in Winter, They Will Eat You:
     Local Knowledge, Wolves and Justice in Central Asia
          Adam Pérou Hermans 259

14. Hierarchy, Intrusion and the Anthropomorphism of Nature:
     Hunter and Rancher Discourse on North American Wolves
          Jessica Bell. 282

Author Biographies 305

Index 309

PREFACE

... and just as Little Red-Cap entered the wood, a wolf met her. Red-Cap did not
know what a wicked creature he was, and was not at all afraid of him.

(Grimm's Household Tales 1823, trans. by Edgar Taylor)

Everybody knows of Little Red Cap's Wolf, while the real wolf is hardly understood.
Creating knowledge about the latter is a far more challenging task. The fairytale wolf
has only a few attributes: he is hungry, cunning and dangerous, in particular for
children. The other wolf outside Grimm's storytelling is considerably more complex;
the sources to trace his character and his performances are harder to find and once
discovered they need to be interpreted very carefully. The authors of this book have
mastered this task beautifully. They have portrayed many different wolves, ranging
from werewolves and war-wolves to newspaper and iconic wolves, leading us on
a journey around the world. For the historian, wolves appear in various shapes: as
ideas, as hunters' prey, as criminals or as a trigger of political communication and
action. In the end, all these wolves can be brought together in a distinct picture
that overshadows the fairytale-wolf.

More than a decade after their return to eastern Germany, wolves are currently recolonising the north-eastern area of Lower Saxony. It is only a matter of
time until the population spreads to suitable habitats around Göttingen, one of the
centres of environmental history in Germany. I am delighted that two scholars from
Göttingen University, both former members of the research group 'Interdisciplinary
Environmental History', pursued the goal of editing a historical volume concerning
the interactions of humans and wolves. Following the Göttingen tradition of research
in the field of environmental history, the authors come from different disciplines,
including the natural sciences as well as the humanities, and consequently focus on
varying aspects of human–wolf interactions. They provide valuable orientational
knowledge for a topic of pressing concern in today's politics. Conflicts in current
predator management can only be successfully mitigated by taking into account
not only the present human dimension so often referred to, but also culturally and
ecologically influenced historical developments.

Manfred Jakubowski-Tiessen
Professor of History
University of Göttingen

Introduction: Wolves and Humans in History

Patrick Masius and Jana Sprenger

Since prehistoric times, large carnivores have played a prominent role in societies around the world. Various types of interactions have shaped the living conditions of both humans and predators, and have created innumerable discursive concepts of the animals. Large predators serve as symbols for a multitude of ideas. They have inspired imaginations, and found their way into stories and legends in a way quite unlike any other wild animal. Current predator management and conservation increasingly demand the inclusion of various human dimensions.[1] There is no doubt about the importance of economic, social, cultural, political and legal perspectives alongside the ecological context.[2] Perceptions influencing attitudes towards predators are strongly dependent on the animals' historical contacts with humans. Thus, analyses of historical interactions contribute significant insight into present-day relationships.[3]

The most widely-distributed large carnivore has been the wolf. Prior to extensive extermination efforts, wolves ranged throughout the northern hemisphere, resulting in various and varied encounters with human societies. The 'wolf-human relationship ... has taken so many forms, depending on time and place, that generalizations are impossible'.[4] A plethora of images and texts have portrayed the wolf in many different shapes around the world. Wolves have been feared and hated, adored and admired. They have been considered malicious and evil as well as associated with pristine wilderness. Even at the same historical moment, different cultural and social groups have upheld widely diverging ideas. Up to the present, in many regions, wolf management remains a controversial topic, accompanied by the strong emotions of various supporting and opposing groups. The image of the fairytale wolf is deeply rooted in our cultural consciousness and fear of wolves is still common, although dominant political discourses draw mainly on scientific data. Wolves are seen as keystone elements for functioning ecosystems or once more as pests threatening rural life and thus to be exterminated.[5] The history of the wolf will show that somewhere underneath the rational surface hides a wolf in our subconscious that is sometimes misapprehended as real.

---

1. E.g. Decker et al. 2012.
2. On wolves, see for example Bath 2009.
3. See Ritvo 2002.
4. Fritts et al. 2003, p. 289.
5. See Musiani et al. 2009, p. 7.

Patrick Masius and Jana Sprenger

~

For ages, human societies have created images and ideas of wolves.[6] Paintings in the cave of Lascaux date back to 17,000–15,000 BC and show wolves besides other wild animals of the time.[7] Since then, representations of the predator may be found in many cultures in all historical periods. It appears in most major mythological belief systems. Ancient Greek fables as well as biblical stories use metaphors of the wolf attacking flocks of sheep, and Roman mythology tells of a she-wolf nourishing Romulus and Remus.[8] The Romans also associated the God Mars with the wolf and in Germanic mythology the god Odin is accompanied by two wolves, Geri and Freki.[9] In ancient Japanese Ainu Culture, the (White) Wolf Gods were worshipped.[10] The North American Indian cultures respected and admired wolves as skilled hunters as well, in particular in the North-west, and included them in certain rituals.[11]

Medieval sources reveal the wolf as a fierce outcast that is even fought by Jesus himself.[12] In Barry Lopez's evaluation, the Middle Ages were a time when ideas about wolves occupied minds more than ever. Anything threatening was called 'wolf'. Real wolves transmitted an incurable disease: rabies. Dream wolves spread terror as hellhounds and werewolves. In his fourteenth-century epic poem *Divina commedia*, Dante associated the wolf with seducers and hypocrites, magicians, thieves and liars who will burn in the eighth circle of Hell, condemned for 'the sins of the wolf'.[13] In the Thirty Years' War (1618–1648), wolves became an icon for the horrors of war (see Kling, this volume). In general, wolves flourished during wars, following the battles and devouring the dead (see Masius and Sprenger, this volume).[14] The connections between the wolf as Death himself and the miseries of war are not difficult to draw. It appears that war transforms the land into a realm where Death howls with the voices of wolves. Subsequently, in times of peace, wolves were addressed as the Evil that could turn the world into a miserable place. Against this background, the wolf was included in many fairytales, of which *Little Red Riding Hood* is the most famous. For most parts of Europe, Russia and the United States it can be stated that negative connotations prevailed until the twentieth century (see Dirke, this volume). For instance, in nineteenth century Russia wolves were demonised by the media and politics concerning wolves were

---

6. See Lopez 2004 [1978], p. 5.
7. Schulz 2011, pp. 18–19.
8. For example, Marvin 2012 , pp. 38–43, pp. 127–31.
9. Koschorreck 1952, pp. 2–3.
10. Walker 2005, ch. 2.
11. Marvin 2012, pp. 122–4; compare also Robisch 2009, pp. 233–46.
12. Zimen 1990, p. 391.
13. Lopez 2004 [1978], p. 205.
14. Okarma 1997, p. 130.

deeply hostile.[15] Only recently did the perception of the wolf shift toward its being a noble authentic wild animal (see Jones and Kalof, this volume).

Human concepts of wolves are closely connected to the idea of wilderness. The predators not only physically ranged the wild lands outside of civilisation, but symbolised the threatening, uncontrollable world beyond human culture.[16] In the wolves' habitats, such as remote forests and swamplands, 'prescientific imagination could place a swarm of demons and spirits'.[17] These were 'eerie areas' associated with death (see Rheinheimer, this volume). Supported by Judeo-Christian tradition, in Western cultures, wilderness was predominantly considered the antipode to paradise.[18] Alongside creating economic damage, wolf attacks on livestock or people implied an intrusion of this wilderness, possibly causing a destabilisation of the social order. The idea culminated in wolves breaching the perceived secure walls of a city.[19] In early modern Central Europe, increasing attempts to exterminate wolves must be seen in the wider context of a growing interest in controlling (wild) nature. Cultivation of so-called wastelands, river engineering and wetland drainages – in short the transformation of wilderness areas – accompanied the economisation of agricultural production.[20] Combating natural hazards, such as destructive animals, was an integral part of these efforts. Particularly in the eighteenth century, numerous German governments frequently released decrees for controlling various animal pests. Prussian edicts against locusts, caterpillars, sparrows or field hamsters follow a similar rhetoric and structure to ordinances for the extermination of wolves.[21] During early colonial times, European settlers transported their traditional wilderness perceptions, together with their concepts of wolves as terrifying beasts and pests, to the North American colonies.[22]

Advancing science as well as the Romantic Movement formed the basis for changing attitudes towards wild nature in Europe and in the New World.[23] But it was not before expanding civilisation threatened to displace the last uncultivated landscapes that ideas of a wilderness to be appreciated gained broader acceptance. In the young United States, the individual pioneer's fight for survival beyond the western frontier developed into a prominent founding myth, defining national

---

15. Helfant 2010, pp. 63–4.
16. Compare for example, Marvin 2012, pp. 38–43.
17. Nash 2001 [1967], p. 8.
18. Ibid., pp. 13–20.
19. See Siemer 2003, pp. 364–5. On the importance of human placements of animals, as well as animals transgressing such boundaries, compare Philo and Wilbert 2000.
20. Beck 2003; Blackbourn 2007; for economisation of nature see also Bayerl 1994; Meyer 1999.
21. See Sprenger 2011.
22. For example, Coleman 2004, pp. 37–51.
23. Nash 2001 [1967], pp. 44–66.

4

character.[24] Thus, around the end of the nineteenth century, wilderness landscapes became worth preserving.[25] However, wild predators were not included in these early protection strategies.

~

Historiography has only recently focused on the relationships between humans and other species. Pioneering work in the 1980s, such as Keith Thomas' *Man and the Natural World* (1983) or Harriet Ritvo's *Animal Estate* (1987), set the starting point for an increasing number of historical studies analysing reciprocal influences. It is argued that animals have played a major role in history. As the history of ideas shows, the category 'animal' functions as the 'other' which contrasts with human beings and defines their nature. Rational and willing human beings have overcome the 'animal' and therefore many modern philosophers have declared this construction as central to a modern understanding of human nature.[26] Some, like Derrida, have proposed to deconstruct the term 'animal' altogether.[27] Others believe animals are good to think with and help humans to 'develop their own moral identities'.[28]

Writing a history of animals and human–animal interactions inevitably adopts a human perspective: we can never *experience* the world of an animal, as Nagel showed in his famous article 'What is it like to be a bat?'[29] The biological wolf represented in historical sources is 'clothed in culture',[30] 'colored by our individual, cultural, or social conditioning'.[31] Still, it possesses a certain character independent of our cultural interpretations, which we can never fully comprehend. As humans, to grasp the essence of the wolf, we can only try to construct a net of 'material-semiotic knots'. In this context, it appears that 'bodies and meaning coshape one another' and that a critical revision of the nature–culture divide would be desirable.[32] From this and related perspectives, Human–Animal Studies questions the notion that humans and animals belong to two fundamentally different categories, which only developed in European thinking during the Enlightenment. Instead, humans belong to nature, as evolutionary theory has shown, and all models of anthropocentric superiority are based on unreasonable arrogance. Against this background, the rejection of anthropomorphic narratives of animals needs to be reconsidered. If it is true that humans and animals do not belong to different categories, as sug-

24. In today's Alaska, America's 'last frontier', as nowhere else, the influences of different aspects of the pioneer ideas are apparent in present-day wolf management (see Dixon, this volume).
25. Cronon 1995, p. 7.
26. See Chimaira 2011, pp. 8–10, 32; Agamben 2003, p. 100; Brantz 2010, p. 11.
27. Chimaira 2011, p. 8.
28. Levi-Strauss, in Philo and Wilbert 2000, p. 24.
29. Nagel 1974. For the idea of *epistemic anthropocentrism*, compare also Krebs 1999.
30. Marvin 2010, p. 59.
31. Fritts et al. 2003, p. 290; compare also Jones 2002, p. 5; Jones, this volume.
32. Haraway 2008, p. 4.

Introduction

gested by alternative world views and post-modern philosophers, then it would not automatically be a category mistake to talk about animals in human terms.[33]

It seems that one animal which has suffered greatly under anthropomorphic narratives is the wolf. The wolf's behaviour was interpreted as evil and cunning and humans therefore treated him like a criminal. 'The wolf is the only animal with a criminal reputation and record that has lasted for centuries and resulted in so many legal acts putting a price on its head'.[34] The connection between criminals and wolves can be shown in many instances, where the punishment of a criminal was connected with wolves. In the Middle Ages, King Edgar (reg. 959–75), for instance, commuted the punishment of some criminals to a payment of wolf tongues.[35] In the thirteenth century, the German law collection *Sachsenspiegel* declared the wolf an outlaw which was allowed to be killed by everyone.[36] Travellers feared highwaymen as much as the wolf and the two often fused in the contemporary minds: 'Wolf and outlaw were one'.[37] The attributes of criminals were found in the behaviour of the wolf and *vice versa*. When wolves attacked and harmed people, they were often identified as humans (dead or alive) and punished henceforth by hanging them at the gallows. There were even cases where such an animal was hanged dressed up in human clothes and wearing a human mask. That way the criminal wolf was transformed back into an evil human, supporting the idea of werewolf. With the *werewolf* this idea became embodied, and people believed for centuries in evil humans transforming into werewolves and back into human form. In this mythical worldview, inner and outer nature were not separated (see Rheinheimer, this volume). Many regional werewolf legends have been preserved until today.[38]

Marvin has shown how attitudes towards wolves in Albania can only be comprehended by analysing the moral universe of the society and the people's treatment of human strangers as guests or enemies. By transgressing the boundaries of the village and the house, the wolf comes as a stranger but fails to fulfil the complex rules to merit treatment as a guest. 'It comes without announcing itself, it keeps weapons, it takes rather than waits to be served ... and it is a destroyer within the domestic space'.[39] These real wolves are seen through the cultural lens of an Albanian village society as rude intruders and, by breaking the code of hospitality, violate the honour and integrity of the family.

~

---

33. Philo and Wilbert 2000, p. 19.
34. Marvin 2012, p. 92.
35. Ibid., p. 81.
36. Landau 1849, p. 213.
37. Lopez 2004 [1978], p. 208.
38. See for example Scherf 2001, p. 75–9.
39. Marvin 2010, p. 70.

Patrick Masius and Jana Sprenger

Historical research focusing on human–animal interactions is based on the idea of a 'symmetry of powers',[40] in which the potential to act is not exclusively attributed to humans. Following Bruno Latour's *actor–network theory*, intentionality may not be considered a necessary premise for (historical) acting. Instead, a wide network of manifold influences on the acting entity is acknowledged. An actor 'is *made* to act by many others'[41] and, thus, an action should be seen as a 'conglomerate of … agencies'.[42] Subsequently, non-human entities, such as other organisms, and even inanimate objects or discursive structures, receive the power to act in continually changing *actor-networks*.[43] Within this theoretical framework, the complex historical relationships and reciprocal actions between humans and animals can be analysed.

Most animals do not communicate their intentions precisely through language, but we have to account for them, at least in a very basic way. Even natural scientists do this, when they consider the actions of a wolf in terms of increasing personal fitness and reproduction rate; or when they study the behaviour of a certain animal by looking at its search for food, shelter, sexual partners or flight in face of an enemy. Whether these actions are transmitted by processes which we might ascribe to intelligence on the one hand, or instinct on the other, seems to us of secondary importance. Even without knowing the exact mechanisms that lead to an action, we can analyse animal behaviour in terms of goals and obstacles.[44] When we narrate a story including animals in the same way as a human story, we take the risk of interpreting too much information from the animal's actions. Not doing so leaves us with the risk of misunderstanding animals by treating them analogously to machines. By sharing the experiences of life and death, in some way, it seems that we are closer to animals than animals are to machines.[45] According to Ingold, 'it would be quite wrong to conclude from our inability to penetrate the experience of other species that we are uniquely endowed with subjective will'.[46] Every caring dog-owner will be as sure of the intentions of his dog as a mother is of the intentions of her baby. Both are unable to talk, but they can still signify their feelings and longings. Historical writing often has the problem that the historian cannot reconstruct the thoughts and intentions of central actors in certain important historical situations. They have two options: either to ignore them, which means to imply that there were none; or to deduct them from the personality, the context and the circumstances as best as possible, in order to present a complete narrative.[47]

40. Philo and Wilbert 2000, p. 17.
41. Latour 2007, p. 46 (emphasis in original).
42. Ibid., p. 44.
43. See Belliger and Krieger 2006, p. 23.
44. Compare Ingold 1987, p. 16–39. Compare for research on animal intelligence Meyer 2000, pp. 509–13.
45. Hüppauf 2011, p. 30.
46. Ingold 1987, p. 19.
47. See Mann 1987.

Introduction

Animals have been used to fulfil material needs in society and, as domesticates, have been included in our social networks. Daily interactions with these animals should be included in our understanding of historic societies.[48] Whereas interdependencies between humans and other species are most evident in relation to pets and livestock, the relationship with wild beasts is often less apparent. They have always lived at a distance from human societies, but the rare moments of interaction have influenced human thinking and human action nevertheless. In urban societies, wild animals have been brought into human life through zoos, circuses and television recordings. The physical distance is neutralised and people are able to see wild animals close. However, with iron bars or TV-screens, there remain unsurpassable boundaries between human and animal which suggest they belong to two very different worlds. At the same time, these visions of animals caught in cages or in front of a camera imply that humans have mastered the other world and are in control of its dangers. Of course, such relations are very specific to late modern western culture and wild animals have interacted with human beings for millennia. Many wild species live hidden and rarely encounter humans. Interactions through habitat changes, food webs and material cycles are nonetheless evident. Wolves and other large carnivores are indirectly as well as directly connected with humans. Throughout history, wolves have regularly preyed on livestock and, less commonly, killed people. On the other hand, humans have modified the predators' habitats and pursued them to regional extinction. With expanding settlements, predator conflicts increased. Each species has been repeatedly prompted to alter its behaviour due to the actions of the other. The animals adapted to new landscape conditions as well as prey availability and increasingly learned to avoid capture. Humans improved hunting methods and invented livestock protection measures.

Wolves have continually challenged human claims to control nature. Despite an often age-old hunting tradition, the opportunistic predators persisted in many areas or were able to recover during times of war. They were known as mobile and wary. A great deal of time and effort was invested into the construction of hidden trapping devices as well as unnoticeable pre-arrangements for public drives. In the United States, during the last period of wolf eradication in the late nineteenth and first half of the twentieth century, individual wolves like Lobo, Bigfoot and Old Three Toes became renowned by temporarily resisting capture.[49] When dealing with wild animals, resistance to human influences is recurrently used as a topos to portray animal actions.[50] However, most wolf populations could not withstand when early-modern government-funded and state-wide systems of collective persecution developed, as can be seen in several European countries as well as in the contiguous United States.

48. Pearson and Weismantel 2010, pp. 390–9.
49. Coleman 2004, ch. 9.
50. For example, Barrow 2010, Masius 2014.

~

One of the most controversial topics concerning the wolf is its potential to attack and kill humans. On the one hand, fictional reports, fear and mythical beliefs might have unjustifiably contributed to the image of the wolf as a man-eater; on the other hand, reports of wolf attacks might have been rejected too easily as being based on an irrational world view. Most wolf activists have always conceded that rabid wolves were dangerous for humans. Recently, experts on wolf biology have come to regard attacks by non-rabid wolves in certain regions at certain times to be a historical reality.[51] For a comprehensive overview of wolf attacks, see Linnell et al. (2002). One problem was to distinguish fact from fiction in historical documents and find verified reports. Research in the last thirty years has discovered historic evidence for deadly attacks from non-rabid wolves in Europe and Asia.[52] For example, Cagnolaro et al. (1996) reconstructed that in northern Italy about 500 people were killed by wolves between 1400 and 1825.[53] Similar results exist for France.[54] And extraordinarily dangerous wolves, like the beasts of Dauphiné and Gevaudan, have become cultural icons of their local areas and are still remembered (see Alleau and Linnell, this volume). In Germany, there are currently only two verified historical cases from the sixteenth and seventeenth centuries of healthy wolves killing humans.[55] Reports from before 1700 need to be inspected with great care, however, since the public and judiciary still believed in werewolves. Therefore, human murderers and man-eating wolves were not always distinguishable (see Rheinheimer, this volume). For Russia there exists a multitude of cases but it is often close to impossible to evaluate the accuracy of the documentation. However, some cases during World War Two appear to be authentic.[56] Occasionally, through official investigations, historical records proved false shortly after their emergence.[57] Recent reports of wolves attacking and taking away children come mainly from India.[58] India has been one of the countries where wolves have been most prone to attack humans throughout history (see Rodriguez, this volume). Although difficult to verify, Asia seems to be the only continent where wolf attacks occur regularly even today (see Hermans, this volume). In the western world (North America and Europe) the widespread use of firearms might have taught wolves to keep some distance from

---

51. Fritts et al. 2003, pp. 302–4.
52. Linnell et al. 2002, p. 10.
53. Fritts et al. 2003, p. 303.
54. Moriceau 2011. These results are not prejudiced by the interests of hunters or anti-wolf groups. The Italian report even appeared in a WWF volume on wolves.
55. Butzeck in Linnell et al. 2002, p. 20, App. 4.
56. Pavlov in Graves 2007, p. 175–81.
57. See for example, Main State Archive Koblenz, Best. 403, No. 2371, 3 Feb. 1836.
58. Fritts et al. 2003, p. 303.

Introduction

humans and could be a reason why attacks occur very rarely.[59] It seems historical analyses of wolf attacks mostly refer to specific situations where individual predators or packs adapted to preying on vulnerable humans such as child-shepherds. The attacks usually stopped after killing the responsible animals or changing human behaviour (see Alleau and Linnell, this volume). If wolves had been a continuous threat to unarmed children herding livestock, such practices would most likely have been employed less frequently.[60]

~

Throughout the world, resource conflicts and adverse perceptions have eventually led to extensive wolf killings, often resulting in the regional or even state-wide eradication of the predators. The state associated violence and disorder with the wolf. Wolves were either treated as severe criminals or as evil enemies, and consequently combatted with police measures or military campaigns. European history provides numerous examples of wide-ranging extermination programmes. For the authorities, combatting wolves has always functioned as a means of control, since they actually could persecute wolves, while they were helpless in face of other hazards such as floods, famines or war. In many areas, wolf persecution was an inherent part of attempts to improve animal husbandry and general security. Alleau and Linnell (this volume) explore hunting efforts as reactions to wolf attacks on humans in eighteenth-century south-eastern France. Governmentally-organised as well as regionally-initiated hunting was common for centuries throughout the country.[61] In response to the potential threat from wolves, a national institution, the *Louveterie*, was supported. Its roots originated in the reign of Charlemagne in the ninth century.[62] Bergström, Dirke and Danell (this volume) examine the less known role of *Jägeristaten*, an early modern organisation that played a prominent role in the Swedish war on wolves which was conducted not only as a battle against predators but also as a fight against foreign intruders, since the wolves were believed to originate from neighbouring countries. After centuries of intensive persecution, wolves in Germany finally vanished in the second half of the nineteenth century. Throughout early modern times, an increasing number of ordinances informed about the implementation of different hunting methods and regulated the hunting duties of foresters alongside the population's obligations to take part in public drive hunts. Rheinheimer (this volume) analyses the extirpation of the predators in Schleswig-Holstein in the eighteenth century; Masius and Sprenger (this volume) focus on Brandenburg in the eighteenth century and the Prussian Rhine Province

---

59. Ibid., p. 304.
60. Eles 1986 in Kardell and Dahlström 2014, p. 187.
61. See also for example, Delort 1987; Beaufort 1988; Moriceau 2011.
62. Delort 1987, p. 268–9.

in the nineteenth century.[63] In today's Poland, where wolves were never fully eradicated, an extensive extermination programme was launched after World War Two, and was in practice until 1975 (see Mysłajek and Nowak, this volume). On the Iberian Peninsula, in less populated areas, wolves also survive up to the present day. However, in many regions, hunting efforts had already caused population declines in the eighteenth and especially in the second half of the nineteenth century, when the use of strychnine became rife. Additionally, declines in game and livestock caused prey shortages, illustrating the significance of ecological conditions for the population's ability to resist intensive hunting (see Fernández-García, this volume). Also in the United States, intensive killing efforts are traceable back to at least the seventeenth century. Wolves were persecuted with a bounty system that resembled the way human criminals were pursued.[64] In stages, wolf hunting expanded with proceeding colonisation from colonial New England, south- and westwards, from regional public and private actions to federal organisation.[65] Whereas at least the main currents of historical wolf persecution in Europe and North America have regularly been considered, far less attention has been given to wolf persecution beyond these regions. In India, in the late nineteenth and early twentieth centuries, the British colonial administration conducted an extensive extermination programme (see Rodriguez, this volume). Originally targeting tigers, leopards and snakes, the authorities became aware of the threat from wolves through the predators' regular fatal attacks on children. In the Far East, Japanese wolves, once worshipped as gods protecting crop farmers against large herbivores and even other threats such as fire and disease, turned into 'noxious animals' over the eighteenth and nineteenth centuries and became extinct at the turn of the twentieth century.[66]

~

Our current relationship with predators is highly influenced by culturally shaped scientific, social and ethical discourses.[67] Through a major shift in perception caused by vanishing populations and advancing ecological research, the idea of the wolf as dangerous predator has been widely replaced by the view of an endangered species. In Europe, as well as by the Washington Convention (1973), wolves are protected by the Berne Convention on the Conservation of European Wildlife and Natural Habitats (1979) and the resulting Habitats Directive (1992). In June 2014, the European Union launched the Platform on Coexistence between People and Large Carnivores to support dialogue between various stakeholders. In the contiguous

---

63. On wolf extermination in Germany, see also Butzeck et al. 1988; Ott 2004; Masius and Sprenger 2012a, 2012b.

64. Marvin 2012, pp. 89–111.

65. On wolf extermination in the US, see, for example, Lopez 2004 [1978]; McIntyre 1995; Emel 1998; Coleman 2004; Marvin 2012.

66. See Walker 2005.

67. Lynn 2010.

United States, grey wolves are federally listed as an endangered species under the Endangered Species Act, ESA (1973/74). However, after a perceived successful recovery, they were recently delisted in the northern Rocky Mountains and the western Great Lakes region, transferring management to the affected states.[68] Attempts to fully remove the wolf from ESA protection in 2013 and 2014 were opposed by an independent review by the National Center for Ecological Analysis and Synthesis in early 2014.[69] In contrast to the lower 48 states, in Alaska state-controlled wolf populations have continuously been considered stable, resulting in an absence of protection. The regularly conducted aerial shootings to minimise wolf numbers are intensively criticised by numerous stakeholder groups (see Dixon, this volume).

As mentioned before, predator management shows a growing demand for research into the human dimensions of wolf conservation.[70] An increasing number of studies research 'wolves in context',[71] focusing on recent attitudes depending on different cultural backgrounds and social affiliations. In a meta-analysis of 38 studies conducted in different countries between 1972 and 2000, 61 per cent of the general population had positive attitudes, whereas only 35 per cent of ranchers and farmers – groups traditionally opposed to predators (compare Bell, this volume) – were in favour of the animals.[72] People living distant from wolf habitats often showed more support for the predators than those living close to them.[73] However, a study of print news media in the US and Canada indicated significantly more negative expressions in wolf-related articles in states with newly established wolf populations (as well as in areas with anticipated populations) in comparison to states with permanent populations.[74] Negative attitudes in the general population may at first increase with the return of a large carnivore but often decrease over time, as coexistence proves possible.[75]

According to numerous studies, people's position within the controversies strongly depends on rural or urban residency. One of many examples is the Adirondack Mountains in the north-eastern United States. Based on historically-rooted controversies between urban and rural areas, rather than on representations of actual wolves, local inhabitants oppose a possible wolf reintroduction as an 'urban-based conservation ideology' dictating 'local landscape meaning and, subsequently, land

---

68. US Fish and Wildlife Service, http://www.fws.gov/mountain-prairie/species/mammals/wolf/ (Accessed 26 May 2014).

69. National Center for Ecological Analysis and Synthesis, http://www.fws.gov/home/wolfrecovery/ pdf/Final_Review_of_Proposed_rule_regarding_wolves2014.pdf (Accessed 26 May 2014).

70. For example, Bath 2009.

71. Skogen and Thrane 2008.

72. Williams et al. 2002; among others, see also review in Fritts et al. 2003, pp. 295–7.

73. Williams et al. 2002.

74. Houston et al. 2010.

75. See Zimmerman et al. 2001.

use and property rights'.[76] Human–wolf conflicts become thereby 'embedded in broader patterns of cultural and economic divergence'.[77] Research in rural Norway has shown how it is not necessarily negative representations of wolves that lead to adverse opinions about their presence but rather the belief that they do not belong in cultivated landscapes.[78] Opposing positions in carnivore conflicts are supported by 'differences in space perception'.[79] The present habitat uses of wolves clearly demonstrate that the animals are not dependent on remote areas, and can even enter cities to search for food, mostly unnoticed by human inhabitants.[80] Diverging human views may see the same region either as managed land, thus prevented from overgrowing with 'impenetrable and monotonous bush', or as a 'lost paradise' to be restored.[81] Though wild nature is no longer commonly seen as a threat, a divide between wilderness and civilisation persists. For example, wolves approaching human communities in Norway is 'interpreted as a transgression of the symbolic boundary between the wild and the socialized'.[82] Through hard work, generations of farmers cultivated the wilderness and transformed it into useful land, achievements that may now be at risk. Opposing hegemonic pro-wolf attitudes may be seen as cultural resistance to changes in a generations-old way of life.[83] However, growing research shows that 'what is ... frequently presented as radically polarized attitudes towards wolves are rather nuanced viewpoints and ambivalent feelings'.[84] A qualitative analysis of opinions of young people in rural Norway shows that attitudes in perceived groups (here rural residents) are much more diverse than often (publicly) anticipated.[85] Similarly, in anti-wolf dominated hunter and rancher internet forums, alternative discourses exist (see Bell, this volume).

Along with livestock depredation, the fear of wolves, still prevalent in human societies, is a significant reason for people opposing wolf presence.[86] In France, current fear of the predators has seemingly been supported by over-estimates of characteristics such as the wolves' size and weight, numbers of individuals in a pack and actual numbers of wolves in the country.[87] In Sweden, about one third

---

76. See Brownlow 2000, p. 154.
77. Figari and Skogen 2011, p. 318.
78. Figari and Skogen 2011.
79. Campion-Vincent 2005, pp. 106–7.
80. See Fritts et al. 2003, p. 300–1.
81. Campion-Vincent 2005, pp. 106–7.
82. Figari and Skogen 2011, p. 324.
83. For example, Skogen et al. 2008; Campion-Vincent 2005; compare also Scarce 2005.
84. Figari and Skogen 2011, p. 325.
85. Skogen 2001.
86. Fritts et al. 2003, p. 302.
87. Bath 2000, p. 124. When asked to identify the most dangerous animal out of bear, lynx and wolf, only 4.7% of participants chose the wolf (10.6% lynx, 35.1% bear). However, 32% considered all these predators a threat; only 17.6% did not fear any of them (pp. 57–8).

Introduction

(mainly female and elderly) of subjects interviewed at the turn of the twenty-first century, stated that they were afraid of meeting a wolf in the wild.[88] In contrast to recently recolonised areas in central and northern Europe, people in southern and eastern Europe, in regions where wolves have survived throughout the nineteenth and twentieth centuries, are less concerned about potential attacks on humans.[89] Teenagers in wolf regions in rural Spain were considerably less afraid of the predators (35 per cent) than teenagers from the mainland UK (48–53 per cent) and Northern Ireland (65 per cent).[90] The different stakeholder groups agree that modern wolf management needs to include human dimensions shaped by the local cultural and social conditions. Likewise, the wolf's position as a highly social animal with strong bonds between individuals should be considered where management intends to disrupt their families.[91] In the end, a successful cohabitation with wild animals will build upon a broad acceptance in large parts of the population. After more than one hundred years of biological research on wolf ecology and ethology, the narratives support coexistence of humans and wolves – at least in the West. Though the animals still occasionally prey on livestock or even attack humans, the interpretation of their intentions changed. The most probable explanation for these border crossings into the human world is not a journey from the realm of the dead or the personification of something evil but just a resourceful and adaptive strategy of the wolf in order to obtain adequate food.

Aldo Leopold's famous and often cited 1949 essay about his encounter with a dying wolf, describing his thoughts regarding interdependencies between vegetation, deer and wolves, marks a turning point in wildlife management, leading to a slowly increasing support for predators. 'I have lived to see state after state extirpate its wolves. I have watched the face of many a newly wolfless mountain, … I have seen every edible bush and seedling browsed, first to anaemic desuetude, and then to death.'[92] Already in the early 1940s, Leopold, among others, favoured a return of wolves to Yellowstone National Park.[93] In the second half of the twentieth century, increasing environmental awareness, alongside proceeding ecological research, altered the dominant discourse about wolves, which now values them as crucial components of ecosystems. At the same time, the evil fairytale-wolf has remained a very stable character in popular culture and perseveres through today.

~

---

88. See review in Brännlund et al. 2010, p. 3.
89. Boitani and Ciucci 2009, p. 33.
90. Bath 2009, p. 190–1.
91. For an inclusion of ethics see, Fox and Bekoff 2009, here p. 125.
92. Leopold 1949, p. 130.
93. Jones 2002, p. 47.

Patrick Masius and Jana Sprenger

Whereas present human dimensions are increasingly included in wolf management, historical case studies remain underrepresented. In this volume, we aim to reflect actual interactions between the two species in modern history as well as main currents of thought about human–wolf relationships. We focus on perceptions, interactions and dependencies, and include cultural and social analyses as well as biological aspects. Many have observed that writing about animals implies recapitulating and generating representations, as 'humans create their animals'.[94] However, the animals, whose actions continuously reassure or dissent representations, are essential authors themselves.[95] For a comprehensive understanding of human–animal relations, biological data and historical analyses need to be combined in order to reveal as much of the stories as possible. Coming from different disciplinary backgrounds including the humanities as well as the natural sciences, the contributing authors approach wolves and their contacts with humans from various perspectives. The intention of this history of humans and wolves is to strengthen exchange between different disciplines, aiming at a better understanding of cultural habits towards wolves and, in consequence, the opportunity for a better-grounded wolf policy. Our way of dealing with wolves throughout history far exceeds any isolated concern of an individual interest group but rather is embedded into our particular relationship with wild nature in general.[96]

BIBLIOGRAPHY

Agamben, G. 2003. *Das Offene: Der Mensch und das Tier* (Frankfurt a. M.: Suhrkamp).

Barrow, M.V. 2010. 'The Alligator's Allure: Changing Perceptions of a Charismatic Carnivore', in D. Brantz (ed.) *Beastly Natures: Animals, Humans, and the Study of History* (Charlottesville, London: University of Virginia Press) pp. 127–45.

Bath, A.J. 2000. 'Human Dimensions in Wolf Management in Savoie and Des Alpes Maritimes, France: Results Targeted toward Designing a more Effective Communication Campaign and Building better Public Awareness Materials'. *LIFE-Nature Project 'Le retour du loup dans les Alpes Françaises' and Large Carnivore Initiative for Europe.*

— 2009. 'Working with People to Achieve Wolf Conservation in Europe and North America', in M. Musiani, L. Boitani and P.C. Paquet (eds) *A New Era for Wolves and People. Wolf Recovery, Human Attitudes, and Policy* (Calgary: University of Calgary Press) pp. 173–99.

Bayerl, G. 1994. 'Prolegomenon der 'Große Industrie'. Der technisch-ökonomische Blick auf die Natur im 18. Jahrhundert', in W. Abelshauser (ed.) *Umweltgeschichte – Umweltverträgliches Wirtschaften in historischer Perspektive* (Göttingen: Vandenhoeck & Ruprecht) pp. 29–56.

---

94. Lopez 2004 [1978], p. 5.
95. See Benson 2011 ('Animal Writes').
96. See Musiani et al. 2009, p. 8.

Beaufort, F.G. de. 1988. *Ecologie historique du loup, Canis lupus L. 1758 en France*. (Dissertation: University of Rennes).

Beck, R. 2003. *Ebersberg oder das Ende der Wildnis – Eine Landschaftsgeschichte* (München: C.H. Beck).

Belliger, A. and D.J. Krieger. 2006. 'Einführung in die Akteur-Netzwerk-Theorie', in A. Belliger and D.J. Krieger (eds) *ANThology. Ein einführendes Handbuch zur Akteur-Netzwerk-Theorie* (Bielefeld: Transcript) pp. 13–50.

Benson, E. 2011. 'Animal Writes. Historiography, Disciplinarity, and the Animal Trace', in G. Montgomery and L. Kalof (eds) *Making Animals Meaning* (East Lansing: Michigan State University Press) pp. 3–16.

Blackbourn, D. 2007. *Die Eroberung der Natur – Eine Geschichte der deutschen Landschaft* (München: DVA).

Boitani, L. and P. Ciucci. 2009. 'Wolf Management across Europe: Species Conservation without Boundaries', in M. Musiani, L. Boitani and P.C. Paquet (eds) *A New Era for Wolves and People. Wolf Recovery, Human Attitudes, and Policy* (Calgary: University of Calgary Press) pp. 15–39.

Brantz, D. 2010. 'Introduction', in D. Brantz (ed.) *Beastly Natures: Animals, Humans, and the Study of History* (Charlottesville, London: University of Virginia Press) pp. 1–13.

Brännlund, R., M. Johansson, J. Karlsson and M. Sjöström. 2010. *Beware of the Wolf: Is Animal Fear Affecting Willingness to Pay for Conservation of Large Carnivores?* CERE Working Paper No. 2010:9. Available at SSRN: http://ssrn.com/abstract=1601847

Brownlow, A. 2000. 'A Wolf in the Garden', in C. Philo and C. Wilbert (eds) *Animal Spaces, Beastly Places: New Geographies of Human-Animal Relations* (London: Routledge) pp. 141–58.

Butzeck, S., M. Stubbe and R. Piechocki. 1988. 'Beiträge zur Geschichte der Säugetierfauna der DDR Teil 3: Der Wolf *Canis lupus* L., 1758'. *Hercynia N. F* 25 (3): 278–317.

Campion-Vincent, V. 2005. 'The Restoration of Wolves in France: Story, Conflicts and Use of Rumor', in A. Herda-Rapp and T.L. Goedeke (eds) *Mad About Wildlife: Looking at Social Conflict Over Wildlife* (Leiden, Boston: Brill) pp. 99–122.

Chimaira. 2011. 'Eine Einführung in Gesellschaftliche Mensch-Tier-Verhältnisse und Human-Animal Studies', in Chimaira (ed.) *Human-Animal Studies. Über die gesellschaftliche Natur von Mensch-Tier-Verhältnissen* (Bielefeld: Transcript) pp. 7–42.

Coleman, J.T. 2004. *Vicious. Wolves and Men in America* (New Haven, London: Yale University Press).

Cronon, W. 1995. 'The Trouble With Wilderness; or, Getting Back to the Wrong Nature'. *Environmental History* 1 (1): 7–28, URL: http://www.williamcronon.net/writing/Cronon_Trouble_with_ Wilderness_1995.pdf, pp. 1–24.

Decker, D.J., S.J. Riley and W.F. Siemer. 2012. Human Dimensions of Wildlife Management (Baltimore: John Hopkins University Press).

Delort, R. 1987. *Der Elefant, die Biene und der heilige Wolf. Die wahre Geschichte der Tiere* (München, Wien: Hanser) pp. 254–81.

Patrick Masius and Jana Sprenger

Emel, J. 1998. 'Are You Man Enough, Big and Bad Enough? Wolf Eradication in the US', in J. Wolch and J. Emel (eds) *Animal Geographies. Place, Politics, and Identity in the Nature-Culture Borderlands* (London, New York: Verso) pp. 91–116.

Figari, H. and K. Skogen. 2011. 'Social Representations of the Wolf'. *Acta Sociologica* 54 (4): 317–32.

Fox, C.H. and M. Bekoff. 2009. 'Ethical Reflections on Wolf Recovery and Conservation: A Practical Approach for Making Room for Wolves', in M. Musiani, L. Boitani and P.C. Paquet (eds) *A New Era for Wolves and People. Wolf Recovery, Human Attitudes, and Policy* (Calgary: University of Calgary Press) pp. 117–139.

Fritts, H.S., R.O. Stephenson, R.D. Hayes and L. Boitani. 2003. 'Wolves and Humans', in L.D. Mech and L. Boitani (eds) *Wolves. Behavior, Ecology, and Conservation* (Chicago, London: The University of Chicago Press) pp. 289–316.

Graves, W.A. 2007. *Wolves in Russia: Anxiety through the Ages* (Calgary: Detselig).

Haraway, D.J. 2008. *When Species Meet* (Minneapolis, London: University of Minnesota Press).

Helfant, I.M. 2010. 'That Savage Gaze – The Contested Portrayal of Wolves in Nineteenth-century Russia', in J. Costlow and A. Nelson (eds) *Other Animals – Beyond the Human in Russian Culture and History* (Pittsburgh: University of Pittsburgh Press) pp. 63–76.

Houston, M.J., J.T. Bruskotter and D.P. Fan. 2010. 'Attitudes Toward Wolves in the United States and Canada: A Content Analysis of the Print News Media, 1999–2008'. *Human Dimensions of Wildlife* 15 (5): 389–403.

Hüppauf, B. 2011. *Vom Frosch. Eine Kulturgeschiche zwischen Tierphilosophie und Ökologie* (Bielefeld: Transkript).

Ingold, T. 1987. *The Appropriation of Nature. Essays on Human Ecology and Social Relations* (Iowa City: University of Iowa Press).

Jones, K.R. 2002. *Wolf Mountains. A History of Wolves Along the Great Divide* (Calgary: University of Calgary Press).

Kardell, Ö. and A. Dahlström. 2014. 'Wolves in the Early Nineteenth-Century County of Jönköping, Sweden', in S. Johnson (comp.) *Animals* (Cambridge: The White Horse Press) pp. 185–214 (first published in *Environment and History* 19 (2013): 339–370).

Koschorreck, W. 1952. *Der Wolf. Eine Untersuchung über die Vorstellungen vom Verbrecher und seiner Tat sowie vom Wesen der Strafe in der Frühzeit* (Dissertation: Friedrich-Schiller-University Jena).

Krebs, A. 1997. 'Naturethik im Überblick', in A. Krebs (ed.) *Naturethik. Grundtexte der gegenwärtigen tier- und ökoethischen Diskussion* (Frankfurt a. M.: Suhrkamp) pp. 337–80.

Landau, G. 1849. *Beiträge zur Geschichte der Jagd und der Falknerei in Deutschland. Die Geschichte der Jagd und der Falknerei in beiden Hessen* (Kassel: Theodor Fischer).

Latour, B. 2007. *Reassembling the Social: An Introduction to Actor-Network-Theory* (London, Oxford, New York: Oxford University Press).

Leopold, A. 1949. *A Sand County Almanac. And Sketches Here and There* (London, Oxford, New York: Oxford University Press).

Introduction

Linnell, J.D.C., R. Andersen, Z. Andersone, L. Balciauskas, J.C. Blanco, L. Boitani, S. Brainerd, U. Breitenmoser, I. Kojola, O. Liberg, J. Løe, H. Okarma, H.C. Pedersen, C. Promberger, H. Sand, E.J. Solberg, H. Valdmannand P. Wabakken. 2002. *The Fear of Wolves: A Review of Wolf Attacks on Humans* (Trondheim: NINA Norsk institutt for naturforskning).

Lopez, B. 2004 [1978]. *Of Wolves and Men* (New York: Scribner).

Lynn, W.S. 2010. 'Discourse and Wolves: Science, Society, and Ethics'. *Society & Animals* **18** (1): 75–92.

Mann, G. 1987. *Wallenstein* (Frankfurt a. M.: S. Fischer).

Marvin, G. 2010. 'Wolves in Sheep's (and Others') Clothing', in D. Brantz (ed.) *Beastly Natures. Animals, Humans, and the Study of History* (Charlottesville, London: University of Virginia Press) pp. 59–78.

— 2012. *Wolf.* Animal Series (London: Reaktion Books).

Masius, P. 2014. *Schlangenlinien. Eine Geschichte der Kreuzotter* (Göttingen: Vandenhoeck & Ruprecht).

Masius, P. and J. Sprenger. 2012a. 'Die Geschichte vom bösen Wolf – Verfolgung, Ausrottung und Wiederkehr'. *Natur & Landschaft* **87** (1): 11–16.

— 2012b. 'Die Wolfsbestände des Regierungsbezirks Trier im 19. Jahrhundert'. *Dendrocopos – Faunistik, Floristik und Naturschutz in der Region Trier,* **39**: 49–57.

McIntyre, R. 1995. *War Against the Wolf. America's Campaign to Exterminate the Wolf* (Stillwater: Voyageur Press).

Meyer, H. 2000. '19./20. Jahrhundert', in P. Dinzelbacher (ed.) *Mensch und Tier in der Geschichte Europas* (Stuttgart: Alfred Krönau Verlag) pp. 404–568.

Meyer, T. 1999. *Natur, Technik und Wirtschaftswachstum im 18. Jahrhundert. Risikoperzeptionen und Sicherheitsversprechen* (Münster, New York, München, Berlin: Waxmann).

Moriceau, J.-M. 2011. *L'homme contre le loup. Une guerre de deux mille ans* (Paris: Fayard).

Musiani, M., L. Boitani and P.C. Paquet. 2009. 'Introduction – Newly Recovering Wolf Populations Produce New Trends in Human Attitudes and Policy', in M. Musiani, L. Boitani and P.C. Paquet (eds) *A New Era for Wolves and People. Wolf Recovery, Human Attitudes, and Policy* (Calgary: University of Calgary Press) pp. 1–12.

Nagel, T. 1974. 'What is it like to be a bat?' *Philosophical Review* **83**: 435–50.

Nash, R. 2001 [1967]. *Wilderness and the American Mind* (New Haven, London: Yale University Press).

Okarma, H. 1997. *Der Wolf. Ökologie, Verhalten, Schutz* (Berlin: Parey).

Ott, W. 2004. *Die besiegte Wildnis – Wie Bär, Wolf, Luchs und Steinadler aus unserer Heimat verschwanden* (Leinfelden-Echterdingen: DRW).

Pearson, S. and M. Weismantel. 2010. 'Gibt es das Tier? Sozialtheoretische Reflektionen', in D. Brantz and C. Mauch (eds) *Tierische Geschichte. Die Beziehung von Mensch und Tier in der Kultur der Moderne* (Paderborn: Schöningh) pp. 379–99.

Philo, C. and C. Wilbert 2000. 'Animal Spaces, Beastly Places – An Introduction', in C. Philo and C. Wilbert (eds) *Animal Spaces, Beastly Places. New Geographies of Human-Animal Relations* (London, New York: Routledge) pp. 1–34.

Ritvo, H. 2002. 'History and Animal Studies'. *Society & Animals* 10 (4): 403–6.

Robisch, S.K. 2009. *Wolves and the Wolf Myth in American Literature* (Reno, Las Vegas: University of Nevada Press).

Scarce, R. 2005. 'More than Mere Wolves at the Door: Reconstructing Community amidst a Wildlife Controversy', in A. Herda-Rapp and T.L. Goedeke (eds) *Mad About Wildlife: Looking at Social Conflict Over Wildlife* (Leiden, Boston: Brill) pp. 123–46.

Scherf, G. 2001. *Wolfsspuren in Bayern. Kulturgeschichte eines sagenhaften Tieres* (Amberg: Buch- und Kunstverlag Oberpfalz).

Schulz, O. 2011. *Wölfe. Ein Mythos kehrt zurück* (München: BLV).

Siemer, S. 2003. 'Wölfe in der Stadt. Wahrnehmungsmuster einer Tierkatastrophe am Beispiel des Journal d'un Bourgeois de Paris', in D. Groh, M. Kempe and F. Mauelshagen (eds) *Naturkatastrophen – Beiträge zu ihrer Deutung, Wahrnehmung und Darstellung in Text und Bild von der Antike bis ins 20. Jahrhundert* (Tübingen: Gunter Narr) pp. 347–65.

Skogen, K. 2001. 'Who's Afraid of the Big, Bad Wolf? Young People's Responses to the Conflicts Over Large Carnivores in Eastern Norway'. *Rural Sociology* 66 (2): 203–26.

Skogen, K., I. Mauzand and O. Krange. 2008. 'Cry Wolf! Narratives of Wolf Recovery in France and Norway'. *Rural Sociology* 37 (1): 105–33.

Skogen, K. and C. Thrane. 2008. 'Wolves in Context: Using Survey Data to Situate Attitudes Within a Wider Cultural Framework'. *Society & Natural Resources* 21 (1): 17–33.

Sprenger, J. 2011. *'Die Landplage des Raupenfraßes'. Wahrnehmung, Schaden und Bekämpfung von Insekten in der Forst- und Agrarwirtschaft des preußischen Brandenburgs (1700-1850)* (Quedlinburg: Julius-Kühn-Institut).

Walker, B.L. 2005. *The Lost Wolves of Japan* (Seattle, London: University of Washington Press).

Williams, C., G. Ericsson and T. Heberlein. 2002. 'A Quantitative Summary of Attitudes toward Wolves and their Reintroduction'. *Wildlife Society Bulletin* 30 (2): 575–84.

Zimen, E. 1990. *Der Wolf. Verhalten, Ökologie und Mythos* (München: von dem Knesebeck).

Zimmerman, B., P. Wabakken and M. Dötterer. 2001. 'Human-Carnivore Interactions in Norway: How Does the Re-appearance of Large Carnivores Affect People's Attitudes and Levels of Fear?' *Forest Snow and Landscape Research* 76 (1/2): 137–53.

1

War-Time, Wolf-Time. Material–Semiotic Knots in the Chronicles of the Thirty Years' War

Alexander Kling

Axe-time, sword-time,
shields are sundered,
Wind-time, Wolf-time,
ere the world falls.[1]

> The Prophecy of the Seeress, *The Poetic Edda* (Thirteenth Century)

INTRODUCTION

Observed historically, wolves are animals of crisis; they become visible in crisis situations, and it is during crisis situations that they are spoken of and written about. Located in a crisis situation – in England, the Civil War is beginning; on the Continent, it has been raging for a quarter-century already – Thomas Hobbes, in *De Cive* (1642), coins one of the most famous sentences in the history of political theory: 'Man is a Wolf to Man'.[2] Formed by the experience of crisis and war, for Hobbes the human being is no longer an Aristotelian *physei politikon zoon*, but a belligerent and anti-social creature, which can be pacified and induced to live as part of a community only by the deterring power of the artificially produced Leviathan. Hobbes' wolf metaphor therefore leads to an uncertainty as to the competence of humans to organise themselves in civil bodies. Yet Hobbes is not the first to formulate the sentence *Homo homini lupus*. In various contexts and complexes of meaning, it may be found from Antiquity to the Early Modern Period, in Plautus, Erasmus of Rotterdam, Francisco di Vitoria, Michel de Montaigne or Francis Bacon. The metaphorisation of humans by way of the wolf, therefore, has known a long tradition, and yet the metaphor only attains general – and controversially debated – fame in the context of Hobbes' political theory. It would be possible to conclude that, in thematising the warlike and anti-social human beings of the state of Nature, Hobbes has placed the wolf imagery in a context which, as such,

---

1. *The Poetic Edda* 1936, p. 20.
2. Hobbes 2002, p. 1.

corresponds to the nature or the essence of the wolf. This, therefore, would mean that, in Hobbes, the wolf metaphor is coming into its own.

However, a number of considerations may be juxtaposed against such an understanding of a use of metaphor suited to the nature of the wolf. Max Black, in the context of his theory of metaphor, and having recourse to the *Man is a wolf* statement, argues that there is an interactive relationship between the sub-components, and that therefore the image of the wolf used in a specific constellation becomes consequential for the image generator: 'The wolf-metaphor suppresses some details, emphasises others'; a 'wolf-system of related commonplaces' emerges which makes the wolf a vehicle for pejorative traits.[3] The interrelation, then, works as follows: as metaphor, the wolf structures the contexts of political theory into which it is placed; yet, vice-versa, these argumentative contexts – Black uses the term 'filter' – also inform the conceptual meaning of the wolf. This interrelation, as I aim to show in the following, not only applies to wolf metaphors and their (textual) contexts, but to the wolf and its environments as a whole.

About the generalising of the interaction approach of Black's theory of metaphor, one might, following Jacques Derrida, say that the perception of the wolf – or 'the totality of "experience"' – may not be separated from the 'field of the mark' organised by texts of various provenance (fables, fairy tales, zoological treatises, etc.) in a cultural-history situation.[4] This directs the focus to a differentiation that Derrida makes elsewhere:

> Without asking permission, real wolves cross humankind's national and institutional frontiers, and his sovereign nation-states; wolves out in nature [*dans la nature*] as we say, real wolves, are the same on this side or the other side of the Pyrenees or the Alps; but the figures of the wolf belong to cultures, nations, languages, myths, fables, fantasies, histories.[5]

Derrida distinguishes between the wolf as a natural living being and the wolf as a cultural construct. The first is an entity that remains identical with itself, ahistorical; the second is a figure that is rhetorical and formed by rhetoric. Derrida designates the relation existing between the two with the ambiguous term '*pas de loup*' (step of the wolf/no wolf), as one of abstinence: '*Pas de loup* signifies the absence, the literal non-presentation of the wolf itself in response to its name, and so an evocation that is only figural, tropic, fabulous, phantasmic, connotative: there is no wolf, there is *pas de loup*'.[6] Derrida's sharp separation of the materiality and the semioticity of the wolf is due to his interest in the rhetorical *energeia* of the wolf:

> The wolf is all the stronger, the meaning of its power is all the more terrorizing, armed,

---

3. Black 1954/55, p. 288.
4. Derrida 2000, p. 10.
5. Derrida 2009, p. 4–5.
6. Ibid., p. 6.

threatening, virtually predatory, for the fact that in these appellations, these turns of phrase, these sayings, the wolf does not yet appear in person but only in the theatrical *persona* of a mask, a simulacrum or a piece of language, i.e. a fable or a fantasy.[7]

At the end of this paper, Derrida's argumentation will have to be taken up again. At this point, initially, one aspect of his argument must be problematised: in focusing on the separation of the material and the semiotic wolf, Derrida may be able to thematise the metaphoric potentials of a 'genelycology'[8] – the *what* of metaphorical speaking; however, the process of metaphorisation – the *how* of metaphor formation – is hardly considered. In Derrida's conception, the wolves cannot be conceded an active role; after all, they are identical on both sides 'of the Pyrenees or the Alps'. On the one hand, therefore, metaphor formation must completely be attributed to humans, and their 'cultures', 'languages', etc. On the other hand, only the semiotic, but not the material, animals are subjected to cultural/historical variability: 'These *figures* of the wolf, these *fables* or *fantasies* vary from one place and one historical moment to another'.[9]

With the fixation of the material wolves on one side, and the variability of the semiotic wolves on the other side, a monism of Nature and a pluralism of Culture stand directly opposed. It is precisely this asymmetrical constellation that has been called into question by the research approaches of the *actor–network theory*.[10] Against the dichotomous distinction between Nature and Culture, between material and semiotic animals, Donna Haraway, for instance, introduces the term 'situated naturecultures'.[11] The term refers to a network in which the status of human and non-human agents – their affiliation with Culture and Nature, their ability to be acting subject or handled object – is permanently negotiated through interactions: 'The partners do not precede the meeting; species of all kinds, living and not, are consequent on a subject- and object dance of encounters'.[12] The imagery of the dance illustrates the mutual relatedness of human and non-human agents, which Haraway views equally as 'meaning-making figures'.[13] The actors, according to Haraway, are interwoven in 'material-semiotic nodes or knots in which diverse bodies and meanings coshape one another'.[14] Haraway's metaphors of the dance and the knot merit analysis in their own right, but that would lead too far from our focus on the wolves. As a starting point for this investigation, it must therefore suffice to concentrate on the theoretical conceptions of the reciprocal relatedness

---

7.   Ibid.
8.   Ibid., p. 81.
9.   Ibid., p. 4. My emphasis.
10. See Latour 2004, pp. 209–217; Descola, 2005, 251–258.
11. Haraway 2008, p. 25.
12. Ibid., p. 4.
13. Ibid., p. 5.
14. Ibid., p. 4.

of human and non-human agents and the interrelation between the material and the semiotic made visible by the metaphors.

The approach proposed here considers itself as a contribution and a necessary complement to what Bruno Latour has called 'collective experimentation'. Since 'no power has been given by nature the right to decide on the relative importance and respective hierarchy of the entities that compose, at any given moment, the common world', the 'compatibility' of the agents – for example, 'sheep, farmers, wolves' – must be tested experimentally, and the organisation of the networks must be structured on this basis.[15] In this context, a historical analysis can show how, in a given concrete situation, hegemonial order structures collapse, how this provokes conflicts between the heterogeneous agents and how this eventually leads to specific modes of perception and action. The subject of my investigation is the increase in the wolf population in the German-speaking territories during the Thirty Years' War (1618–1648). My materials are chronicles and eye-witness accounts from the time of the war, which describe the growth of the wolf population and report encounters between wolf and human. In a first step, the investigation is directed towards the network that establishes itself in wartime, which, proceeding from the figuration of the agents, is to be shown as a state of crisis.[16] This contribution therefore prefers a synchronic over a diachronic perspective, less asking about the cultural-history relationship of humans and wolves,[17] than aiming at situating this relationship itself within a network that, apart from humans and wolves, comprises further agents.[18] A second step is to thematise the contemporary perception of multiplying wolves. The central question will be how the wolves' becoming visible leads to the formation of a material–semiotic knot. A third step, will investigate how this material–semiotic knot is made rhetorically effective in the time after the Thirty Years' War. Here, it will become apparent that the texts construct horror scenarios affectively charged with wolf metaphors and wolf narratives, while simultaneously calling for an overcoming of these same scenarios. The activation and utilisation of wolf metaphors and wolf narratives thus serves – and this is the thesis put forward in this paper – as a rhetorical device for the re-institution of order.[19]

---

15. Latour 2004, pp. 196 ff.
16. On the concept of figuration, see Haraway 2008, p 4.
17. As a recent contribution to the cultural history of the man–wolf relationship, see Marvin 2012.
18. In this, the investigation pursues an objective formulated by Susan J. Pearson and Mary Weismantel, following Virginia Anderson: instead of asking 'whether animals have agency, we should be asking who the social actors are in any given situation' (2010, p. 27). For a classic model analysis, cf. Callon 1986, pp. 196–233. For an analysis of this kind especially with regard to wolves, cf. Marvin 2010, pp. 59–78.
19. For a similar research approach, see. Siemer 2003, pp. 347–365. Based on eye-witness accounts Siemer describes in his paper how, in the first half of the fifteenth century, wolf packs intruded into the city of Paris, how they attacked the Parisian inhabitants and how they thus became metaphors for a situation of social and natural disorder.

CRISIS OF THE SOCIAL – CRISIS OF NATURE

First, some remarks on the nature of the materials and the analytical method to be pursued are necessary. My investigation deals with the wartime chronicles of Maurus Friesenegger,[20] vicar and eventual Abbot of the monastery at Andechs; of Father Johannes Bozenhart of Elchingen;[21] of Hans Heberle,[22] shoemaker at Ulm; and of peasant Caspar Preis of Stausebach.[23] The chronicles selected are exemplary; their analysis is undertaken to show an internal perspective on times of war and crisis. Consequently, my remarks will concentrate on the commonalities of the accounts; the social differences of the respective authors will have to be neglected in the same way as the formal differences of the individual chronicles.

In the historical sciences, the chronicles to be analysed are regarded as varieties of 'ego-documents'.[24] From the very beginning of the emergence of research interest in such sources, there arises the problem of authentic perception on the one hand, and of the discursive shaping of perception and its textualisation on the other. War chronicles, for instance, employ different strategies to recover the experience of the crisis state discursively. Matter-of-fact descriptions can be found as well as recourses to cultural texts (e.g. the biblical texts about the Four Horsemen of the Apocalypse or the Plagues of Egypt) and to rhetorical *topoi* (e.g. the *topos* of the topsy-turvy/upside-down world or the ineffability *topos*).[25] Such devices point out that the chronicles cannot be read as objective textualisations of an authentic experience, but that perception and textualisation have been discursively (pre-) formed.[26] From cultural- and literary-studies perspectives, it appears imperative, consequently, to interrogate these chronicles in reference to the representation codes of the horror scenarios they depict. In the following, this query is to be linked with investigation of the web of relationships at the time of crisis and war, meaning the network of heterogeneous agents who articulate themselves and are articulated in the war chronicles.

All the chronicles agree in their verdict that wartime is characterised by a massive loss of order. This derives from two crisis constellations: firstly, a crisis of the Social in the relational web of different human agent-groups; secondly, a crisis of Nature in the relational web between human and non-human agents. In the following, both crisis situations are to be questioned in terms of how the loss of order associated with them affects the self- and the external perception of the chroniclers.

---

20. Friesenegger 1974.
21. Brunner [Bozenhart] 1876, pp. 157–282.
22. Heberle 1975, pp. 95–273.
23. Preis 1998, pp. 35–103. The quotes from the chronicles were translated for this paper by Uwe Hausmann, whom I thank for this support.
24. See Schulze 1992, pp. 417–450.
25. See Curtius 1965, pp. 104–108, 168–171.
26. See Meumann and Niefanger 1997, pp. 7–23.

Alexander Kling

A. Crises of the Social.

Despite all the battles of the Thirty Years' War, the actual horrors of the times resulted most of all from the violence relationship between two agent-groups: the civilian population and the representatives of the military.[27] In 1628, Hans Heberle's chronicle reports on the disarming of the populace, the authorities having commanded them to hand in all their guns at the Magistracy, on pain of 'harsh punishment'.[28] On the part of the authorities, this decree reveals the fear of an internal potential for violence. For the peasants, however, disarmament gives rise to feelings of defencelessness and helplessness. In the very same year, Heberle describes the violent deeds of the soldiers, who harrow and mistreat the civilians to such an extent that they no longer dare 'to travel afield even for half an hour' (p. 122). Accounts of soldiers robbing, gorging themselves on food and drink and slaughtering livestock and people alike, appear again and again for the following years (p. 132). The experience is at its most distressing when one's supposed allies – in the case of Protestant Heberle, the Swedish army – prove to be enemies, which intensifies the sense of being defenceless, helpless and unprotected (p. 148). In such a situation, all that remains is to articulate the impossibility of articulating the afflictions and the misery one is experiencing: 'One cannot tell and describe their vices enough, it is still greater and more, what they have done' (p. 132).

Similar accounts may be found in the chronicle of Maurus Friesenegger. For him, the allies – in the case of Catholic Friesenegger, the Imperial Army – turn out to be the real enemy as well. In December 1633, Imperial troops move into their winter camp in the environs of Andechs Monastery. With the arrival of the soldiers, the villagers immediately flee into the monastery, where, according to the chronicler, more than 1,000 people find sanctuary (p. 133).[29] From there, the civilian population is forced to witness the atrocities the soldiers commit in the villages: 'They took chairs and benches from out of the houses and unroofed them, and they filled all lanes with dreadful watchfires, and all the village they filled with screaming and howling, as elsewise only hunger and desperation are wont to do'.[30] The principle of justification of the soldiers is the assertion of shared ownership: 'For the goods and chattel of the peasants, they said, belonged to the soldiers as well as to the peasants themselves' (p. 63). In turn, the illegitimacy of these actions is reflected in the chroniclers' choice of linguistic forms for their accounts. Thus, Friesenegger calls the soldiers 'brutes' and 'beasts' (pp. 57, 145); Caspar Preis

---

27. For a differentiating view on the enmity between soldiers and the civilian population, see Kaiser 2000, pp. 79–120.
28. Heberle 1975, p. 118.
29. Friesenegger 1974, p. 61, also emphasises the impossibility of articulating his experience of the general misery of his situation: 'Our suffering these days truly cannot be described'.
30. Friesenegger 1974, p. 57.

speaks of 'wild boars',[31] Johannes Bozenhart of 'mad dogs'.[32] The enmity between the agent-groups makes one group perceive the other as animalised, respectively de-humanised.

These few examples illustrate that, with the conflict between soldiers and civilian population, abstract concepts of political theory manifest themselves in a concrete situation: the felt state of emergency, the demand for the sharing of property, the indistinguishability of friend and foe and the endangerment projections are elements of the self-location in a war situation which, as such, dominates everyday perceptions and interactions. With the collapse of order structures, the social bond dissolves, to be replaced by 'the law of the stronger'. Peace and security give way to a permanent endangerment situation, a state of nature and war as Hobbes conceptualises it contemporaneously.

B. Crises of Nature.

Next to these threat constellations in the social sphere, the chroniclers describe a number of other 'plagues' not primarily related to human agent-groups, but expanding the field of agents to include non-human beings. One instance would be the destruction of the harvest, which Friesenegger ascribes to the soldiers on the one hand, but also to a 'multitude of birds and mice' on the other.[33] This brings up a first animal plague, to be followed by others during the years of the war. Mice in particular figure prominently and repeatedly. In 1635, Friesenegger comments: 'A tremendous number of mice … did all the greater damage, the smaller the crops were' (p. 97). A short time later, Friesenegger again reports on the murine infestation: 'Even after the snow had come, there were still mice in incredible numbers … Therefore, it was forbidden, by order of the highest authorities, to catch a fox, for foxes had to do the duty of the cats, which had been devoured by the Spanish and the Italians.' (p. 100) In these remarks, the interconnectedness of heterogeneous agents becomes apparent: soldiers, peasants, instances of political power, mice, cats, foxes. Hunger leads to the eating of cats, which are animals not designated for food. As a consequence, they are no longer available as a means of regulating the mouse population. With the proliferation of mice comes the destruction of the crops, which then results in an aggravation of the hunger problem. The ban on killing foxes, decreed by the 'highest authorities', is intended to provide a means of coping with the problem of mice proliferation. Altogether, this creates the image of a deeply disturbed order, which in turn affects the self-perception of humans: the multiplication *phantasma* and the damage done by the mice evoke the fear of a Nature that is out of kilter, whose agents – as Heberle also reports with respect to

---

31.   Preis 1998, p. 36.

32.   Brunner [Bozenhart] 1876, p. 172.

33.   Friesenegger 1974, p. 78.

the increase of the mice[34] – invade and destroy the institutions of human culture. The mice therefore act as deconstructors of the anthropocentric design, questioning the human right to rule over Nature and the animals founded on the biblical *Dominium terrae* (*Gen.* 1,26 ff.).[35]

The breakdown of the anthropocentric design also becomes visible in the context of another plague: pestilence. The greatest problem (apart from the dying itself) is that the pestilence victims can no longer be buried and that their bodies are eaten by dogs.[36] In a twofold sense, this creates the constellation of an upside-down world: on the one hand, by eating dogs, cats, mice and carrion, the people consume food not meant for human consumption, praising it, as Heberle puts it, as 'delicious',[37] due to their hunger. On the other hand, by eating human corpses, the animals feed on those beings for whose purposes they have actually been created, according to the biblical right to rule.

The lowest point of these abject eating practices, as well as the interconnection of the crisis of Nature with the crisis of the Social, is reached when no more animals are available. Friesenegger, for instance, reporting on beleaguered Augsburg in his chronicle, mentions rumours that the besieged – after 'horses, dogs, cats, and mice had all been used up' – ate 'the flesh of children and men'.[38] The climax of the disturbance in the food chain transitions into the practice of cannibalism. The war, as one could interpret the fundamental *phantasma* here, not only destroys all order structures – it also leads to the extermination of all animal and human life.

Any number of other examples might be given here of the disturbed relational structure of Humans and Nature and of the uncertainty of humans in their self-perception. At least two instances should still be mentioned: firstly, Heberle reports that, due to the events of the war, people can no longer carry on farming and that, because of this, an 'entire field' is changing back into a wild forest.[39] Secondly, the ally/enemy's raids make the peasants flee into the woods, where they are then hunted like 'wild animals'.[40] The examples of the countryside and of people running wild therefore point to a civilisational topography in dissolution. If one adds the plagues of mice and pestilence, the eating of dead bodies by dogs, the eating of dogs, cats and carrion by humans, and the cases of anthropophagy, a comprehensive process becomes visible: domesticated spaces revert to the wilder-

34. See Heberle 1975, p. 159. On the mouse plague, see also Preis 1998, p. 48.
35. The animal plagues are consequently also viewed as a divine punishment. See Friesenegger 1974, p. 212.
36. Ibid., pp. 86–7. Similar accounts can also be found in Brunner [Bozenhart], p. 226. Preis 1998, p. 46, reports on massive numbers of deaths among the population due to diseases as well.
37. Heberle 1975, p. 161.
38. Friesenegger 1974, p. 92. Cases of cannibalism are also discussed by Heberle 1975, pp. 176–7. For a differentiated analysis of cannibalism cases during wartime, see Fulda 1997, pp. 240–69.
39. Heberle 1975, p. 167.
40. Ibid., p. 154.

ness, civilised human beings are forced to eke out an animal existence – in short, the de-cultivation of Nature and the de-civilising of humans go hand in hand. Into this constellation of a double loss of order, now enter the wolves.

WOLF REPORTS – WOLF ENCOUNTERS

Friesenegger's first report of the advent of the wolves is from 1638. His account of the previous year closed in gratitude that the monastery and its environs were spared the ravages of war.[41] Yet his mood remains pessimistic. A series of natural disasters in particular – fiery conflagrations, floods and storms – is troubling him, even in the absence of the actual tribulations of the war (p. 107). In this context of natural catastrophes, which are taken as apocalyptic portents, Friesenegger situates the arrival of the wolves: 'Like fire, water, air, the Earth did not lack for other plagues to make us feel them. It provided wolves in unusual numbers, which did much harm to ... men and cattle alike' (pp. 107–8). Next to the fires, the flooding, and the storms, the wolves are part of an ensemble of catastrophes, all pointing at a disturbed order of things.

In the following years, Friesenegger again and again reports the appearance of wolves. Mostly, his accounts date from the immediate beginning of the year in question, as with 1640:

> The first evil to arrive was once again the wolves, which in years past had already been doing much harm to men, and to animals local or wild. On the 10th day of February, the huntsman of Traubing caught 2 huge beasts with our nets and our people, which he sent to us to be viewed, and which looked horrific (p. 113).

It is not improbable that the wolves sent to the monastery 'to be viewed' are the first that Friesenegger has ever seen in his life. Before the Thirty Years' War the wolf population was so small that encounters with them were highly unlikely. Although a complete extinction of the wolves could not be achieved in the years and centuries before the war due to insufficient weapon technology, constant hunting nevertheless kept the wolf population within narrow limits. Wartime changed that situation: from about 1635 chroniclers report more and more on the proliferation of the wolves – the reasons for such a development will be thematised below. Only after the Thirty Years' War did institutionalised wolf hunting intensify again, leading to an almost complete extinction of native wolf packs in the eighteenth century. Finally, at the beginning of the nineteenth century, many German territories celebrated the killing of their 'last wolves'.[42]

---

41. Friesenegger 1974, p. 106.
42. For the history of the extinction politics before and after the Thirty Years' War, see Ott 2004, pp. 111–76.

The conditions of war – de-civilising and de-cultivation – under which the wolves become visible, lead Friesenegger to his verdict of the wolf being a horrific beast. One might argue that such a judgment (especially for a Christian minister) is hardly surprising; after all, the cultural history of the human–wolf relationship is characterised by a long tradition of human hatred for the wolf.[43] Yet it is decisive here that Friesenegger does not formulate his verdict by recourse to the available book learning, but face-to-face with the wolves. In this, textually-transmitted hate of the wolf – as it is found in biblical zoology and in bestiaries, in Renaissance zoology and in household literature – reactivates and updates itself in a concrete situation which, in turn, shapes a specific perception. The wolves appear as agents of de-civilising and de-cultivation. Another passage in Friesenegger's chronicle for 1642 attests to this:

> One must marvel at how the wolves are multiplying and turning rampant. Eight lambs from the monastery's flock they have … torn apart. Of small game, nothing at all can be found, one knows not, have they frightened it away, or devoured it entirely.[44]

The elements of this passage are already familiar: as in the case of the mouse plague, Friesenegger addresses the inexplicable proliferation and prevalence of the wolf population, wolves' incursion into the cultural spaces of humans, their devastation and their consumption of food resources which humans claim for themselves. The wolves, too, call into question the anthropocentric design. The main reason for the increasing wolf population is that during wartime the cultural technique of hunting can hardly be practiced, much as the suspension of agriculture leads to an accelerated regrowing of forests.[45] The wolves' becoming visible and their encroaching on humans are therefore induced by the interconnection of the agents during wartime and thus lead to a semiotic charging.

Friesenegger's comments are marked by the detached observer-perspective of the head of a monastery who receives his information about goings-on in his environs from third parties. When, as in the case of the visitation of the wolves sent in by the hunters, it comes to an actual encounter between chronicler and wolves, these encounters are not indexed as a concrete danger. In the following, I will now reflect the differentiation of distance and proximity between human and wolf using the terms of wolf *report* and wolf *encounter*. A wolf report is to be found in Hans Heberle's chronicle for 1640 as well:

> Early this year, as the war has left us in peace and quiet for a little while, nearly our greatest labour is the hunting of the wolves. For in this state of war, there are many wolves come to our lands. For God is sending evil beasts into the land, as a

---

43. See Marvin 2012, pp. 35–80.
44. Friesenegger 1974, p. 122.
45. This reason for the proliferation of wolves in wartime was already recognised in the seventeenth century: see Täntzer 1734, p. 38. Cf. Rheinheimer 1994, pp. 399–422.

punishment, for them to devour our sheep and cattle. Whereas, before the war, it was a marvel to see but one wolf, yet now during these recent years, it has not been strange for us to see a great many of them together … They run among the livestock … and take goats and sheep from the flock … Then we come upon them with all our might. Yea, they even come into the villages and houses, taking cats and dogs, so that all this while one cannot have any dog in the villages any more.[46]

The individual elements of this account agree with those in Friesenegger to a large degree. The appearance of the wolves comes at a time when the actual events of the war have slightly receded into the distance; yet the wolves prevent a sense of security from setting in. Another conspicuous aspect is the transgression of the boundary between Nature and Culture through the snatching of the sheep, the intrusion into villages and houses and the killing of the dogs. The most interesting feature of Heberle's report, however, is the temporality inscribed into it: if before the war wolf sightings were 'a marvel', they now routinely occur in wartime. By this, the coming-into-visibility of the wolves is inseparably bound to the time of war, so that a referential context between war and wolves is established. In addition, the attacks of the wolves evolve into a direct analogy to the raids of the soldiers, who also invade the living environment of the rural population, robbing livestock and threatening the lives of the peasants. Yet, while defensive measures against the soldiers as a rule lead to even more massive counterviolence, the violence potential of the civilians – pent-up due to their disarming, their sense of being threatened and defenceless – can act itself out against the wolves. Heberle's reference to the violence brought to bear on the wolves already marks this. And in the chronicle of Caspar Preis, we now find the narrative of a wolf encounter in which such an eruption of violence is unfolded in meticulous detail.

In the morning of 16 May 1643, as Preis reports, he and his wife hear a scream. Looking out of their bedroom window, they realise that their farmhand and their farmgirl are being attacked by a wolf.[47] Preis describes how the farmhand defends himself using a 'pole', and how 'two strong dogs' aid him in this: 'They fell on the wolf and snapped at him, so that it ran out of the yard' (p. 52) With the driving away of the wolf, the episode seems to be over already, but Preis sees the wolf fleeing into the churchyard. He orders his man and the girl to prevent the wolf from escaping from there. In all the 'hue and cry', Preis hardly manages to dress, running out of the house 'barenaked'. His wife – 'barefoot' as well, but at least clad in a skirt – follows him. Preis, who describes himself as 'frightened out of my wits', arms himself with a 'pole' and shouts for help in the village: 'Yet there was no one willing to leave his house, no one willing to come to our aid'. Left to his own devices by the village community, Preis suddenly notices that the wolf is getting ready to attack his wife:

---

46. Heberle 1975, p. 182.
47. Preis 1998, p. 51.

> And as I was looking around, there the wolf was near my wife. She struck out with her muck fork with all her strength, and as many blows as she struck, so many screams did she give as well. I did not think long … I jumped to the side of my wife and said, 'O wife, strike bravely, there's nothing for it', and I hit the wolf between the ears with my pole on the head, so that it almost dropped to the ground, yet it rallied again and made for my wife. Then I hit it another blow across its right eye, so that it hung down from its head. Then it dropped to the ground, and we struck it such a blow that it had to die.

Without any help, Preis and his wife defend themselves against their wolfish assailant with all their might. After the wolf is slain, Preis has it skinned and sells the pelt to the town clerk: 'Thus it happened with the wolf' (p. 53).

Comparing Preis' wolf battle with the accounts in Friesenegger and Heberle, it becomes noticeable that he is not trying to interpret the incident. Preis may mention various natural catastrophes[48] prior to his wolf encounter, in the same way that Friesenegger does, yet he does not connect them with the appearance of the wolves to form a sign ensemble indicating an insurrection of Nature against humans. Metaphysical models of explanation are not applicable here. One might explain this with the notion that complex cosmological explanatory models are not available to the simple peasant, and that he only writes down what he sees. But this is not enough to explicate the difference in the mode of representation. Preis' account differs from Friesenegger's and Heberle's reports not only because of the absence of an interpretation of the experience. Instead – proceeding from an actual encounter with the wolf – the sequential description of the action, the inclusion of the communication between the participants and the depiction of internal states form a micro-narrative that clearly transcends the wolf reports of Friesenegger and Heberle in its precise rendering of the incident. Asking what motivates such an elaborate textualisation of the wolf encounter, one is first referred back to the war syndrome – the hardships and anxieties, the defencelessness and helplessness against the soldiers, the distress of the peasants that Preis evokes time and again. In this context, the successful defence of house and wife against the wolfish assailant proves to be an acting-out of a potential for violence that reiterates itself in the detailed textualisation of endangerment and the repeated blows in one's own defence. The killing of the wolf and the narrative unfolding thereof turn into acts of an existential self-assertion.

The connection between wolf encounter and self-assertion also emerges in my last example. Johannes Bozenhart's chronicle gives several reports on wolves. There are passages on wolf sightings,[49] on measures to prevent the incursion of a wolf into an abandoned farmhouse (p. 259), on wolf hunts in which more than 200 people participate (pp. 261, 280–1), and on wolf attacks on livestock (p. 269)

48. See ibid., p. 51.
49. See Brunner [Bozenhart], p. 242.

and humans (p. 277). Here, I will restrict myself to the first and most extensive passage. In 1636, Bozenhart records rumours about the coming of wolves (p. 237). Before the year is out, these circulating rumours will become an experienced reality for him – he finds himself in direct confrontation with a wolf:

> We are looking at one another. It is not all that startled because of me, it is more that I am startled by him. I don't know what to do, don't know whether to run for … the forest, or whether I should stand still, as my very flight might stir the wolf into leaping for me. Had anyone been there, they would have seen my hair standing on end, and I don't know whether I could have given blood … Whereas I keep look-ing at the dreadful animal and turn towards our garden. The wolf, then, sits back on its hindquarters, watching closely where I am going. If it had followed me just one step, I don't know whether I could have walked on, for sheer terror. Yet when I was out of its sight a little, then you could have seen me leap away. Never would I have thought myself that a fifty-year-old man would be able to make such leaps and bounds. Truth to tell, all the while this wolf has been here, I desired to see it, but now I no longer wish to do so (pp. 238–9).

Alone and unarmed, a man is facing a wolf on a narrow path, the two of them separated by only a few paces. 'We are looking at one another'. A greater proximity between human and wolf can hardly be imagined. Nothing else but the mutual gaze happens; acts of violence do not occur, so that Bozenhart's depictions seems highly unspectacular when compared with those of Caspar Preis: man meets wolf, they look at each other, man goes away. Yet what is decisive here is not the external action, but the moment of giving pause, the stretching of narrative time through the descriptions of internal processes and projections, the sense of dread that the chronicler also experiences as physical reactions – his hair standing on end, his blood curdling, his physical abilities heightened. In this instance, one can again speak of a micro-narrative of self-assertion, yet one that gives particular importance to enacting the affections evoked by the wolf. In addition, Bozenhart articulates a desire for the wolf: his wish to see the animal expressly derives from circulating reports about wolf sightings. The direct confrontation, in which no secure borderline separates the observer from his object, may abruptly end this desire, but it still manifests itself in the micro-narrative of the encounter and in his subsequent accounts – starting with this first encounter, Bozenhart regularly includes wolf reports in his chronicle. Thus, the following surprising statement may be found in 1638: 'The wolves are still seen every day, both on this and the far side of the Danube, but they are hardly feared by the people, as they assail no one, nor do they do any other harm' (p. 242). A statement of this kind suggests that, with the knowledge of the ethology of the wolf, there comes a disempower-ment of the threat it poses. Yet why does this not lead to a general change of the attitude towards wolves, and why is the perception of wolves as 'terrorising, armed, threatening' instead reinforced during and after the war? An answer to this question might be provided by the relation of the presence and the absence of the wolf, as thematised by Derrida, since focusing on this relation brings into view something that is hardly considered by the research approaches of the *actor–network theory*: the efficacy of 'zoomorphic visions'[50] in the field of the political imaginary. While repeated encounters with material wolves lead to a diminution of the affections of fear and hate, inversely – as will be shown in the following – the texts of the post-war period make rhetorically useable the very same affections which arose in the first encounters. The material presence of the wolves in wartime, one might summarise, leads to a semiotic charging; this charging, however, is not reproduced and codified by further encounters with material wolves, but through texts. In this way, the wolf is turned into an affectively efficient metaphor which, as such, literally strikes back at the material animals.

WOLF METAPHORS – WOLF NARRATIVES

Wolf reports and wolf encounters from the times of war, as they have been discussed exemplarily in this paper, are compiled and archived in various texts after 1650.[51] Due to their textualisation and preservation, they enter into the cultural memory, so that they can still be found in the most important German-language encyclopaedia of the eighteenth century, the *Zedler-Lexikon*.[52] The cultural function of this manner of passing them on is founded on the *Memoria* of the time of war. Two examples illustrate this as a conclusion. The first is taken from the *Dedicatio* of the sixth volume of the *Theatrum Europaeum* (1663):

> People in their thousands were cut down, butchered, run through, shot to death, drowned, burned … or were made to part with life and limb in other cruel and barbaric fashions. Many hundreds of towns … were devastated, laid waste and razed, so that not even a dog, let alone a man, would have been able to sojourn or hide in them. The wolves, however, resided there, and in the cellars of the ruined houses especially, in entire packs. The land was no longer cultivated. Where fields of corn, fruit, or other crops had been, thorns and stinging nettles were growing. Lovely pleasure gardens were made into hideous charnel pits. Instead of flowers, one saw dead horses everywhere … instead of sweet and useful herbs, thistles … and stinging nettles; instead of mellifluous larks and canaries, black vultures and ravens, perched on the carrion and pecking at it; instead of good and healthy times, cruel pestilence reigned … instead of times of plenty, hunger held sway, which was so exceedingly great that the people, like unto the beast of the fields, were eating grass … and some even deemed it a treat when they could obtain a piece of a dead horse or of rotten carrion.[53]

---

50. Derrida 2009, p. 81.
51. See Lehmann 1699, pp. 569–75.
52. See Zedler 1748, col. 510–3.
53. *Theatrum Europaeum* 1748. Translated by Uwe Hausmann for this paper.

In this passage, it may clearly be recognised that individual aspects of the de-civilising and de-cultivation of wartime are arranged in a densely packed image, and that the wolf merely constitutes one compositional element among others. My interest here lies not in what is being said, but in the saying of it, i.e. the rhetorical devices and purposes. The passage is characterised by the opposition of a *locus amoenus* and a *locus terribilis*.[54] Juxtaposed are two images of Nature, as subdued, useful and pleasant on the one side, and as wild, harmful and ugly on the other: the once-populated villages are opposed by ruins and corpses; health by diseases; food-rich times by hunger; the cultivated fields and the flowers and herbs of the 'pleasure garden' by the thorns and nettles of the wilderness; the warbling larks and canaries by the carrion-feeding vultures and ravens; and finally, the dogs by the wolves. The juxtaposition of the *topoi* of the place of pleasure and the place of horror is affectively charged; the rhetorical purpose of this charging derives especially from the temporalisation of the *topoi*: with the 'before/after' contrast, the passage formulates an appeal for the restoration of the lost pleasure garden through measures of re-civilising and re-cultivation. In all its consequences, this means that the figures of the place of horror – including the wolves – must be exterminated.

A more extensive analysis could show how these measures of re-civilising and re-cultivation are implemented after the war and how imaginings – e.g. the notion of a restoration of the biblical Paradise – act as crucial driving forces in this. Instead, one further example will be discussed here, to illustrate the civilising and cultivating efficacy of rhetorically-charged horror images. It is an episode from the novel *Der seltzame Springinsfeld* (1670) by Hans Jakob Christoffel von Grimmelshausen. In brief, the novel's plot runs as follows: a few years after the end of the Thirty Years' War, the eponymous protagonist (an English-language equivalent for the character's telling name would be 'Madcap') meets his comrade Simplicius, with whom he used to rob peasants during the war. As opposed to Simplicius, who has morally improved after his wartime activities, Springinsfeld remains an anti-social character even now, which becomes clear not least because of some specific markers: Springinsfeld displays a number of wolf attributes – he pricks up his ears like a wolf, he imitates the howling of the wolves, he preys upon the peasants like a wolf. Springinsfeld, consequently, may be regarded as a type of wolf-man in the sense of Hobbes' *Homo homini lupus*.[55] The crucial constellation of the text now is constituted by Simplicius making an effort to re-civilise Springinsfeld. In order to achieve this goal, he makes Springinsfeld tell his life story, so that he will gain an insight into his own sins. Springinsfeld complies with this request, giving an account of his initiation into war society, of his crimes against the civilian populace and of his very personal encounter with a pack of wolves.

---

54.   See Curtius 1965, pp. 202–6.
55.   See Gaede 1983, pp. 240–58.

Springinsfeld's misadventure takes place in 1641 – at a time when wolf reports and wolf encounters also abound in the war chronicles. He narrates how he is wandering around a devastated part of the country deserted by all living beings and how he runs into a wolf: 'And as I was passing through a village in which not even mice, let alone cats, dogs, and other livestock, much less humans, were to be found, I saw a great wolf ... come towards me, its jaws open wide'. Springinsfeld tries to find safety in a house, but, since the doors and windows are broken and can no longer be closed, the wolf follows him. 'I had not thought that the wolf would follow me inside the house, but he was so bold that he did not *respect* the place that is dedicated to being the abode of Man'. His last refuge is the roof, from which Springsinsfeld notices that the wolf now has company: 'As I was looking down then, lo, it had more of its comrades with it, which were all looking at me'. 'Besieged' by the wolves, Springinsfeld on the roof is exposed to the 'sharp, cutting winds'; the stillness of the 'pitch-black' November night is only broken by the howling of the wolves – 'a terrible music'.[56] On ending the description of his external circumstances, Springinsfeld's internal reflections set in:

> In sum, it is impossible to believe what a terrible night I had of it then; and exactly because of this, my utmost extremity ... I began to think about what wretched state the desolate damned in Hell must be in, whose sufferings are everlasting; who are tortured not only by some wolves, but by the dreadful devils themselves; not only on a roof, but even in Hell; not only in the wicked cold, but in fire eternally burning; not only for one night, with the hope of deliverance, but forever and ever. This night was as long to me as any other four (p. 248).

Without 'hope of deliverance', Springinsfeld spends the night and the following day in his miserable situation. He doesn't allow himself to sleep, since then he would either freeze to death or fall off the roof. Only 'towards evening' does a band of soldiers arrive at the destroyed village. The officer in charge orders 'ten riders to dismount with their rifles, and to enter the house or surround it ... Then, as some of them stormed into the house, the eight wolves were shot, or put to death in another manner.' After the rescue operation, the men stumble onto a horrible tableau: in the cellar of the house, they discover 'five human cadavers'; moreover, they also find 'the carrion of other animals, so that this cellar looked like unto an old slaughtering pit' (pp. 250–1).

The wolf episode in Grimmelshausen's novel certainly belongs to the most impressive images of wartime. The fact that Grimmelshausen is able to design such a horror scenario derives from the semiotic charging of the wolves during the time of the war. As in the war chronicles, so in Gimmelshausen: the proliferation of the wolves and their intrusion into the human living space also run parallel to the processes of de-civilising and de-cultivation. The minutely detailed narration

---

56. Grimmelshausen 2000, pp. 247–8. Translated by Uwe Hausmann for this paper.

of the wolf episode shows marked similarities to the wolf encounters in Preis and Bozenhart: in each case, the texts give a meticulous account of the threat situation in which the narrating subjects have to assert themselves in the face of the wolves; in each case, both external actions and internal states are communicated. Yet despite these parallels, there is a massive difference between the wolf encounters of the chronicles and the wolf episode in Grimmelshausen's novel: the war chronicles showed – e.g. in Bozenhart's statement that, after a certain time, the wolves are no longer feared – a disempowerment of the material wolves. In the wolf episode of the novel, the exact opposite happens – here, the rhetoric of the horror scenario leads to a maximum potentiation of the semiotic wolves: from the roof of the destroyed farmhouse, Springinsfeld – standing in exemplarily for the wartime figure of *homo homini lupus* – observes the scenario of a creation in ruins. Human beings and animals are present only as corpses, the wolves alone remain. The novel marks the wolves, unlike the *Dedicatio* of the *Theatrum Europaeum*, as more than just one compositional element among others; they are the crucial vehicles of the horrific image. This goes so far as to make the metaphorised and the metaphorising indistinguishable: Who is responsible for the civilisational and cultural loss of order – the wolf-men or the wolves?

As the wolf episode concludes, the officer appreciates the run-in with the wolves as a 'good omen' for 'coming across still more unexpected spoils'. Springinsfeld, taking part in a raid on another village immediately after his rescue, thus following in the track of the wolves as laid out by the officer, clarifies that he has not managed to establish a connection between the horror scenario of a wolf-world and his own status as a wolf-man. Instead of following the moral impulse of the wolf encounter, as sparked during his reflections on damnation, Springinsfeld recognises 'no importance' to the episode (p. 246). Due to this, he does not understand that the hardships that descend upon him in the following years – among other calamities, he loses a leg – are a direct consequence of his refusal to re-civilise. Yet the civilising power of the wolf episode – i.e. of the meeting of wolf-man and wolves – also brings to bear its aesthetic effects on another addressee, and this is what ultimately matters to Grimmelshausen: in the wolf episode, the reader of the novel recognises the 'zoomorphic vision' of a creation destroyed; the indistinguishability of man-wolves and wolves demonstrates the necessity of overcoming one's own wolf-nature. The agenda resulting from this may be prognosticated easily: the re-civilising of humans will be followed by the re-cultivation of Nature – driven by an affectively charged semiotics, the extermination of the material wolves is set in motion.

SUMMARY

My approach in this paper was to reconstruct the human perception of the wolves in the seventeenth century in connection with the situation of the Thirty Years'

War. The argumentation was based on three steps: the first step aimed at analysing the war chronicles of Maurus Friesenegger, Hans Heberle, Caspar Preis and Johannes Bozenhart in regard to two scenarios of crisis – a crisis of the social and a crisis of nature. In a second step I have correlated the wolf reports and wolf encounters described in the chronicles with these crisis situations. It was necessary, on the one hand, to ask why all the chroniclers relate in their texts to wolf reports and wolf encounters – two main arguments for this were the illustration of the dreads of wartime and the self-assertion of man in a threatening situation. On the other hand the aim was to demonstrate how the war situation as a framework of the man–wolf relationship leads to a semiotic charging of the wolves – the wolves become representative figures for the state of violence and disorder. In a third step my investigation focused on texts written in the post-war period: the *Theatrum Europaeum* (1663) and Grimmelshausen's *Der seltzame Springinsfeld* (1670). In these texts it is remarkable that the semiotic charging of the wolves is utilised for a discursive strategy: wolf metaphors and wolf narratives serve as rhetorical means for the construction of horror scenarios with which the miseries of the wartime were visualised and memorised. Such a rhetorical configuration brings along a double effect: on the one hand the design of the horror scenarios aims to stabilise order – the images of wartime promote the yearning for security and peace. On the other hand the instrumentalisation of wolf metaphors and wolf narratives recoil on the material animals: the restarting of wolf hunting after the Thirty Years' War is empowered through the imagination of a coming pleasure garden – a garden that presents the exact opposite of the horror scenarios of wartime; a garden from which wolves are excluded.[57]

BIBLIOGRAPHY

Black, M. 1954/1955. 'Metaphor'. *Proceedings of the Aristotelian Society. New Series* 55: 273–94.

Brunner, P.L. (ed.) 1876. 'Schicksale des Klosters Elchingen und seiner Umgebung in der Zeit des dreissigjährigen Krieges (1629–1645). Aus dem Tagebuche des P. Johannes Bozenhart'. *Zeitschrift des Historischen Vereins für Schwaben und Neuburg* 3: 157–282.

Callon, M. 1986. 'Some Elements of a Sociology of Translation: Domestication of the Scallops and the Fishermen of St. Brieuc Bay', in J. Law (ed.) *Power, Action and Belief. A new Sociology of Knowledge?* (London: Routledge & Kegan Paul) pp. 196–233.

Curtius, E.R. 1965. *Europäische Literatur und lateinisches Mittelalter* (Bern, München: Francke Verlag).

Derrida, J. 2000. 'Signature Event Context', in J. Derrida (ed.) *Limited Inc* (Evanston: Northwestern University Press).

---

57. This paper comprises central aspects of my dissertation, currently in progress under the working title of *Die Zivilisation der Wölfe. Figurationen des Zoopolitischen in der Frühen Neuzeit*. Publication of the thesis is planned for early 2015.

— 2009. *The Beast and the Sovereign*, Vol. 1 (Chicago, London: The University of Chicago Press).

Descola, Ph. 2005. *Par-delà nature et culture* (Paris: Gallimard).

Friesenegger, M. 1974. *Tagebuch aus dem 30jährigen Krieg*. Nach einer Handschrift im Kloster Andechs mit Vorwort, Anmerkungen und Register herausgegeben von P. Willibald Mathäser (München: Alitera Verlag).

Fulda, D. 1997. 'Gewalt gegen Gott und die Natur. Ästhetik und Metaphorizität von Anthropophagieberichten aus dem Dreißigjährigen Krieg', in M. Meumann and D. Niefanger (eds) *Ein Schauplatz herber Angst. Wahrnehmung und Darstellung von Gewalt im 17. Jahrhundert* (Göttingen: Wallstein Verlag) pp. 240–69.

Gaede, F. 1983. 'Homo homini lupus et ludius est. Zu Grimmelshausens *Der Seltzsame Springinsfeld*. *Deutsche Vierteljahrsschrift für Literaturwissenschaft und Geistesgeschichte* 57 (2): 240–58.

Grimmelshausen, H.J.C. von. 2000 [1670]. 'Springinsfeld', in H.J.C. von Grimmelshausen (ed.) *Courasche. Springinsfeld. Wunderbarliches Vogelnest I und II. Rathstübel Plutonis.* Ed. by Dieter Breuer (Frankfurt a. M.: Deutscher Klassiker Verlag) pp. 153–295.

Haraway, D. 2008. *When Species Meet* (Minneapolis: University of Minnesota Press).

Heberle, H. 1975. 'Zeytregister', in G. Zillhardt (ed.) *Der Dreißigjährige Krieg in zeitgenössischer Darstellung. Hans Heberles 'Zeytregister' (1618–1672). Aufzeichnungen aus dem Ulmer Territorium. Ein Beitrag zu Geschichtsschreibung und Geschichtsverständnis der Unterschichten* (Ulm: Kohlhammer) pp. 95–273.

Hobbes, T. 2002 [1642]. *De Cive. The English Version Entitled in the First Edition Philosophical Rudiments Concerning Government and Society*. Ed. by Howard Warrender (Oxford: Clarendon).

Kaiser, M. 2000. 'Die Söldner und die Bevölkerung. Überlegungen zu Konstituierung und Überwindung eines lebensweltlichen Antagonismus', in S. Kroll amd K. Krüger (eds) *Militär und ländliche Gesellschaft in der frühen Neuzeit* (Münster: LIT) pp. 79–120.

Latour, B. 2004. *Politics of Nature. How to Bring the Sciences into Democracy* (Cambridge, London: Harvard University Press).

Lehmann, C. 1699. *Historischer Schauplatz derer natürlichen Merckwürdigkeiten in dem Meißnischen Ober-Erzgebirge* … (Leipzig).

Marvin, G. 2010. 'Wolves in Sheep's (and Others') Clothing', in D. Brantz (ed.) *Beastly Natures. Animals, Humans, and the Study of History* (Charlottesville, London: University of Virginia Press) pp. 59–78.

— 2012. *Wolf* (London: Reaktion Books).

Meumann, M. and D. Niefanger. 1997. 'Für eine interdisziplinäre Betrachtung von Gewaltdarstellungen des 17. Jahrhunderts. Einführende Überlegungen', in M. Meumann and D. Niefanger (eds) *Ein Schauplatz herber Angst. Wahrnehmung und Darstellung von Gewalt im 17. Jahrhundert* (Göttingen: Wallstein Verlag) pp. 7–23.

Ott, W. 2004. *Die besiegte Wildnis. Wie Bär, Wolf, Luchs und Steinadler aus unserer Heimat verschwanden* (Leinfelden-Echterdingen: DRW-Verlag).

Pearson, S.J. and M. Weismantel. 2010. 'Does "the Animal" Exist? Toward a Theory of Social Life with Animals', in D. Brantz (ed.) *Beastly Natures. Animals, Humans, and the Study of History* (Charlottesville, London: University of Virginia Press) pp. 17–37.

The Poetic Edda. [13th c.] 1936. Ed. by Henry Adam Bellows (Princeton: Princeton University Press).

Preis, C. 1998. 'Stausebacher Chronik', in W.A. Eckhardt and H. Klingelhöfer (eds) *Bauernleben im Zeitalter des Dreißigjährigen Krieges. Die Stausebacher Chronik des Caspar Preis 1636–1667*. Mit einer Einführung von Gerhard Menk (Marburg an der Lahn: Trautvetter & Fischer) pp. 35–103.

Rheinheimer, M. 1994. 'Wolf und Werwolfglaube. Die Ausrottung der Wölfe in Schlewig-Holstein'. *Historische Anthropologie* 2: 399–422.

Schulze, W. 1992. 'Ego-Dokumente: Annäherung an den Menschen in der Geschichte?' in B. Lundt and H. Reimöller (eds) *Von Aufbruch und Utopie. Perspektiven einer neuen Gesellschaftsgeschichte des Mittelalters* (Köln, Weimar, Wien: Böhlau Verlag) pp. 417–50.

Siemer, S. 2003. 'Wölfe in der Stadt. Wahrnehmungsmuster einer Tierkatastrophe am Beispiel des *Journal d'un Bourgeois de Paris*', in D. Groh, M. Kempe and F. Mauelshagen (eds) *Naturkatastrophen. Beiträge zu ihrer Deutung, Wahrnehmung und Darstellung in Text und Bild von der Antike bis ins 20. Jahrhundert* (Tübingen: Gunter Narr Verlag) pp. 347–65.

Täntzer, J. 1734 [1682]. *Der Dianen hohe und niedere Jagd-Geheimnisse, darinnen die gantze Jagd-Wissenschaft ausführlich zu befinden …* (Leipzig).

Theatrum Europaeum. 1748. *Theatri Evropaei Sechster vnd letzter Theil … biß auf das jahr 1649. Dasselbst gepflogen / auch geschlossen / endlich aber durch Göttliche Verleyung in des H. Reichs statt Nürnberg Anno 1650 vollzogenen General Friedens Tractaten / vom Jahr Christi 1647. biß 1651. Allerseits begeben vnd zugetragen … zusammen getragen vnd beschrieben / Durch Johannem Georgium Schlederum; Ratispona. Bavarum…* (Frankfurt a. M.: Merian).

Zedler, J.H. 1748. *Grosses vollständiges Universal-Lexikon*. Bd. 58 (Halle, Leipzig).

The Belief in Werewolves and the Extermination of Real Wolves in Schleswig-Holstein[1]

Martin Rheinheimer

1.

As the dangerous nature of wolves in general is questionable according to modern scientific knowledge,[2] new and up to date explanations are demanded for the extreme rigidity and brutality with which wolves were pursued and finally extirpated in the course of the seventeenth and eighteenth centuries. The hanging of wolves on gallows leads to the assumption that there was obviously more at stake than the simple killing of a destructive animal.

Until well into the eighteenth century, people in Schleswig-Holstein hanged wolves on so-called *wolf gallows*.[3] The Polish nobleman Jan Chryzostom Pasek, who spent the winter of 1658/59 with the Polish army in Haderslev, commented on the region in his memoirs:

> Because there is a law that everybody to the last man must set out if a wolf has been seen, be it in a village or in a town, they chase and hunt this wolf until they have either finished it off or drowned it or caught it alive. Then they hang it just as it is without skinning it to high gallows or a gibbet using strong chains; and there they leave it hanging until only the bones remain.[4]

A man born in 1735 told his granddaughter that, in his youth, he had seen no less than fourteen wolves hanged on such gallows after a battue in Dravit forest (borough of Løgumkloster).[5] In the borough of Hütten, too, old people at the beginning of the nineteenth century remembered having seen three wolves hanged on an oak tree

---

1. This chapter was originally published in *The Scandinavian Journal of History* 20(4): 281–94. It appears here with small editorial changes by permission of Taylor and Francis.
2. Weismann 1931, pp. 495–500; Zimen 1978, pp. 296–8; Bernard 1983, pp. 46–51. The archives are abbreviated to: LAS = Landesarchiv Schleswig-Holstein, Schleswig (State Archives Schleswig-Holstein). For the topic in question, also refer to Rheinheimer 1994, pp. 399–422; Rheinheimer 1995, pp. 25–78.
3. There is evidence for wolf gallows between Scandinavia and Switzerland: Christmann 1943, pp. 69–73; Brøndegaard 1986, pp. 133–4.
4. Wytrzens [Pasek] 1967, pp. 31–2.
5. Kristensen 1891–93, p. 102, no. 391.

after the latest chase.[6] The names of some villages such as 'Wolfsgalgen' in Holstein or 'Ulvegalge' in Denmark (both: wolf gallows) are derived from this practice.

As early as the beginning of the nineteenth century, however, the significance of the wolf gallows was a mystery to the peasants.[7] Interpretations of the inner meaning of the wolf gallows that escape our modern understanding are evoked by the 'belief in werewolves', a belief that, in early modern times, was connected with that in witches and witchcraft and that demonstrates the magical conceptions in which wolves play an important role. Using the example of Schleswig-Holstein, I now turn to the question of how fears that earlier were sublimated into magical ideas were later channelled into the extermination of wolves.

2.

Since the end of the Thirty Years' War, people had been complaining more and more about the increasing number of wolves and the damage they were inflicting on cattle. Finally, on 20 August 1650, the provincial diet of Schleswig-Holstein discussed the plaguing wolves and decided on a great wolf chase throughout the entire state.[8] However, the chase cannot have met with great success because after the event the complaints continued. In 1656, for example, the subjects of the parish of Kaltenkirchen (borough of Segeberg) complained before the king 'that the subjects experience great damage to their cattle by the growing number of wolves'.[9] A list drawn up in c. 1680 contains detailed statements about the number of cattle killed by wolves in the borough of Hütten over a very few years. There are precise indications about how many animals each farmer lost. 'Over a few years', a total of 1,275 horses and 255 'beasts' (i.e. cattle) are reported killed. 'As to the calves and pigs that the wolf has bitten dead, the people could not give any numbers; and people have thus also suffered great damage'.[10]

People, too, were reported to have been attacked. In 1648, the Havetoft cotter Thomas Hansen, who had to live off 'charcoal-burning in Stendorp forest', complained: 'I was, in the last winter, in great danger because of three wolves that wanted to get at me in the night and I had to flee into a tree'.[11] Such attacks by wolves have become deeply etched into popular tradition. Finally, in c. 1735 wolves apparently killed some children near Hamweddel (borough of Rendsburg)

---

6. Niemann 1820, pp. 526–7.
7. Rheinheimer 1994, pp. 399–400; Rheinheimer 1995, pp. 32–4.
8. LAS Abt. 400.5 No. 45.
9. LAS Abt. 65.1 No. 1826.
10. LAS Abt. 7 No. 1735. Vgl. Kock 1931, pp. 159–63, 186–9.
11. LAS Abt. 7 No. 3494.

and Norderjarup (borough of Åbenrå).[12] But as far as I know these are the only cases of death in Schleswig-Holstein ascribed to wolves. Furthermore, both cases are only known from verbal reports so that it is difficult to assess their degree of authenticity. All other cases in which people were reported to have been attacked by wolves always ended well for the person.

When interpreting the evidence, one has to take into consideration that the natural habitat of the wolves was changing dramatically. First, in the seventeenth century, the forested area of Schleswig-Holstein was permanently reduced by its conversion to arable land or by the need for wood; then, in the eighteenth century, the cultivation of the Schleswig-Holstein marshlands and heaths was started. Along with moor and heath, the numbers of hare, deer, and wild boar, i.e. the natural prey of wolves, decreased too.[13] Thus the wolf not only lost its last areas of retreat, but also, the more its natural habitat was reduced, thus forcing it to prey on cattle, the greater became its conflict with man. This vicious circle resulted in the wolves being deprived of their natural basis of existence.

It is a remarkable fact that most of the complaints about damage done by wolves were submitted together with pleas for a reduction of taxes or services. If one reads between the lines of the sources containing complaints about damage perpetrated by wolves one will always discover certain interests: the peasants wanted to reduce taxes and services; their sovereign, on the other hand, was interested in increasing them (and with it his superior power). In his decrees he therefore stressed the fact that 'great damage is done to the cattle of my subjects in many ways'.[14] For both sides wolves were a good pretext for supporting their own interests.

This interconnection between tax reductions and cattle apparently killed by wolves becomes particularly obvious in the borough of Hütten.[15] Here the immensely large numbers (1,275 horses, 255 cattle killed within a few years) correspond remarkably well to the accrued tax liabilities. The whole list therefore consistently ends with a plea to the duke: 'Would that your lordship have the grace to abate your poor but true subjects of the borough of Hütten the old remaining taxes due, and if not entirely but then give them such kind remission that they may suffer to carry the burden'. So in Hütten too the real reason behind the complaints was tax relief, and the wolves were a good excuse.

It has often been assumed that the wolves rapidly increased in number because of the confusion of war. The belief was widespread among the population that the wolves had come into the country 'because of the dead', or that the Polish

12. Piening 1797, p. 232; Kristensen 1991–93, Tillægsbind 1 (Århus 1900), nr. 1301. Cf. Rheinheimer 1995, pp. 62–3.
13. Wood: Hase 1983, pp. 83–94; Moor: Clausen 1981; Animals: Jessen 1988, pp. 278–328. For the reasons for the extermination of wolves, see Zimen 1978, p. 279.
14. Corpus Constitutionum Regio-Holsaticarum 1749, vol. 1, p. 1277.
15. LAS Abt. 7 No. 1735.

had brought them with them in 1660 'to use them against the Swedish'. Johann Täntzer, the royal wolf hunter, on the other hand, saw the reason for the increasing number of wolves as being that, because of the war, they were 'not pursued as strictly and that they can therefore peacefully multiply'.[16] Furthermore, the wolf was a symbol of war and death so that the ancient symbolic meaning was carried into the complaints. As they were based upon rationally comprehensible damage, these complaints resulted in the desired tax relief. At the same time, however, the princes engaged in the complete extermination of the wolves which, according to the complaints, were held responsible for the drop in tax returns.

3.

So much for the diverging financial interests of peasants and duke. This does not explain, however, why the conflict between the two parties should take the shape of a wolf. Obviously the wolf was not just a competitor for food, a beast of prey endangering the life and property of man and personifying the general threat posed by the environment. More than that: in the wolf, man rediscovered disturbing characteristics of his own inner nature. This is why inner and outer nature could merge into one another such that the wolf could symbolise certain characteristics of man and that the human individual who displayed wolf-like traits to a particular degree could be identified with a wolf or even identify himself with that animal. In the imagination of the people of those times, this human could then be turned into a wolf.[17] This process mainly orientated itself towards the death symbolism represented by the wolf. Every threat that issued forth from an all-powerful nature could now be given a name: the name of wolf.

The wolf was the harbinger of death and the conveyor of death in its function as the carrier of souls and the escort of death, as a hellhound and master of the underworld, as the devouring animal. The wolf represents 'the dark powers threatening life'.[18] Since the remotest past, the wolf has been seen in connection with certain gods. The Greek god Apollo, for example, was given the epithet of Lykeios, derived from *lykos* = wolf. The wolf was also seen as the companion of the Roman god of war, Mars and it is not for nothing that it was, according to the myth, a female *wolf* that nurtured Romulus and Remus: the city of Rome ascribed its origins to Mars, the father of the children. The Germanic god of war Wodan, too, was escorted by wolves. According to Nordic mythology, two wolves are

---

16. Täntzer 1682/89, vol. 1, cap. 44; cf. Meiborg 1896, p. 155.
17. On the meaning of transformations into wolves: Erler 1938/40, pp. 303–17; Koschorreck 1952, pp. 11–24; Unruh 1957, pp. 22–3; Hasenfratz 1982, pp. 51–4.
18. Lurker 1969, pp. 199–216. The wolf takes on another meaning in the fables, where it often appears as the deceived deceiver: see Bernard 1983, pp. 118–9.

chasing sun and moon in order to devour them when the world ends (Ragnarök). That is, when the Fenriswolf frees himself of his chains and devours Odin himself.

In the Middle Ages, Christian and ancient ideas combined with Germanic mythology and produced the image of the *werewolf*, which has become firmly entrenched in popular belief. Since the tenth century, the Germanic word *vargr* designating the outlawed criminal has been transferred to the wolf so that the Swedish word for 'wolf' is *varg*, even today.[19] In early times and for certain criminal acts which underlined the wolf-like character of the delinquent, the man was hanged along with a wolf that symbolised this demonic side.[20] But the animal, too, was treated as an evil-doer and therefore taken to the gallows.

The degree to which the personalities of man and wolf, the boundaries between inner and outer nature, originally blended into each other becomes obvious as late as in the year 1685 when, near Ansbach in Franken, a wolf attacked and killed several people. Not only was the animal hanged dressed up in human clothes and wearing a wig and a human mask, it was also identified with a man who had died not long before, the mayor of Ansbach Michael Leicht. People explained the unnatural viciousness with which the wolf had attacked its victims by the fact that the dead mayor, after obviously having haunted his house because of some unexpiated delicts and after having been exorcised by a chimney sweep, had got into the wolf.[21] If the attacks of the wolf could be the cause for discovering the deeds of a demon, then this was a slightly rationalised example of the survival of the ancient belief that the wolf was an emanation from the land of the dead and indeed a death demon.

Only slowly did the wolf change into a *demonstrative* symbol that points at the devouring forces – at Death, at Evil – but which is not Evil itself. The wolf gallows were a late and, in the eighteenth century, probably incomprehensible, reminiscence of the concept that the symbol was originally *identical*[22] with the symbolised object: for the humans of that time, the wolf itself was Evil, Death and devouring. It was a *death demon* and it was treated as such because hanging was originally a magical act, protective magic directed at banning the demon and rendering it harmless to humans. Hanging had to be carried out in accordance with certain rites. The demon was not allowed to have any contact with the ground in order to prevent it from gathering new strength from the earth; the corpse of the hanged demon was not allowed to be buried but was given to the ravens, the birds of the death god Odin, to be taken back to where it belonged: the land of

---

19. Koschorreck 1952, pp. 62–8; Unruh 1957, pp. 1–40; Jacoby 1974; Hasenfratz 1982, pp. 51–3.
20. Koschorreck 1952, pp. 5, 94, 125, 141–2.
21. Schemmel 1973, p. 185.
22. For a differentiation between symbol of identification and demonstrative symbol, see Nitschke 1982, p. 122.

the dead.[23] If the people of the borough of Hütten chose an *oak tree* for hanging the wolves, then this was an echo of another piece of old protective magic; the tree had to be withered and without leaves.

The Ordinance on Forestry and Hunt of the year 1737 tried to strip the hanging of its magical connotations. Although 'hanging the wolf' was still decreed, the animal was to be skinned first. Hanging was also only to 'be organised' after the animal had been delivered to the authorities. The person 'delivering the wolf dead or alive' was to 'deliver the skin separately' (§ 62).[24] According to this paragraph, after a wolf hunt in the borough of Løgumkloster on 25 October 1754, during which six wolves had been killed, the bailiff decreed that 'skinning and hanging of these wolves be done in accordance with the letter of the ordinance'.[25]

4.

The old idea of people turning into animals found its way into the belief in witchcraft in early modern times. Along with black magic, riding through the air to the Witches' Sabbath, pacts and illicit relations with the devil, witches were also ascribed the ability to change into wolves. Thus the belief in werewolves became part of the belief in witches. The Inquisitors Jakob Sprenger and Heinrich Institoris included the warning in their 'Witches' Hammer' (1487) 'that witches today are often turned into wolves and other beasts by the power of demons'.[26]

The *Malleus Maleficarum* – or Witches' Hammer – in the juxtaposition of literal transformation into wolves, the effect of demons and a possible imagination 'which often occurs' displayed a great incongruence[27] that derived from the fact that although the old magical belief in the notion of a real turning into a wolf was still alive, it had already been exposed to the effects of rationalisation. For the Inquisitors, the transformation into wolves no longer manifested the wolf-like nature of the demon but the demon was only a means of explanation. The transformation 'which often occurs' and only 'in imagination' at that, even prepared the ground for a psychological explanation. The *Malleus* obviously already contained the fundaments of discussion on the basis of which the following two centuries saw the replacement of the old magical imagery. Literature on witches and witchcraft, especially from Protestant areas, slowly repressed the omnipotence of devil and demons to the advantage of the omnipotence of God until the opponents of the witch craze

---

23. Koschorreck 1952, pp. 89–98.
24. Corpus Constitutionum Regio-Holsaticarum 1749, vol. 1, p. 1279.
25. Colmorgen 1955, p. 40. For the hanging of a killed female wolf in the year 1753, cf. Witt 1935, p. 258.
26. Sprenger and Institoris 1982, part 1, p. 14.
27. Later and up into modern werewolf literature, there is a differentiation between so-called lycanthropes based on pure imagination and real werewolves, e.g. in Summers 1966, pp. 1–132; and Woodward 1979.

could finally disqualify the belief in magic and sorcery as delusive imagination.[28] While the *Malleus* on the one hand still recognised a real turning into wolves, it also recognised a simply imagined one on the other. It explained the latter as being obsessed by demons. The demons were made redundant, however, when the view became prevalent that these transformations were due to an *illness*, or to some kind of melancholia to be more precise.[29] The magical explanation (real transformation, witchcraft, demons) was replaced by a medico-psychological one.

In the sixteenth and seventeenth centuries, entire books were written about this phenomenon[30] and almost every book that was written in support or in rejection of the witch hunt also contained a chapter on witches' possible transformation into wolves. In Schleswig-Holstein, too, this phenomenon was discussed broadly, with the individual authors always referring to Olaus Magnus.[31]

While the opinion prevailed in learned literature that *lycanthropy* was a delusive imagination,[32] the belief in human transformation into wolves persisted among the ordinary people and there were those who believed that they themselves had been turned into a wolf. As late as the beginning of the eighteenth century, Sterup priest Peter Goldschmidt,[33] who had written two documents about witches ('Höllischer Morpheus' (1698) and 'Verworffener Hexen und Zauberer Advocat' (1705)), brushed aside arguments against the reality of wolf transformations by saying 'one eyewitness account in that matter is worth more than all the fanciful talk of such people'.[34] His examples were very reminiscent of the legends about werewolves collected in the nineteenth and twentieth centuries and it is very likely that they had their source in such traditions. It remains an interesting fact, however, that Goldschmidt obviously believed stories to be true that we would clearly classify as legends today, stories which hardly claim any realistic historicity. Around the year 1700, scientific views were still being opposed by a popular belief that took wolf transformations seriously and which was shared by learned circles. Just as elements of popular tradition (the reality of the transformation) and science (rational, materialistic explanation) cross-linked with each other in priest Goldschmidt's view, traditional popular belief was subject to an increasing degree of rationalisation which, starting from learned circles, permeated only slowly to the lower classes.

---

28. Schwerhoff 1986, pp. 45–82.
29. 'Melancholia' is a medieval collective term for delusions. Cf. Schipperges 1967, pp. 723–36.
30. Bibliography in Hertz 1862, p. 5.
31. Rheinheimer 1994, pp. 408–10; Rheinheimer 1995, pp. 39–46.
32. Eisler 1969, pp. 160–5.
33. Peter Goldschmidt (1660–1713), born in Husum, was priest in Sterup (Anglia) between 1691 and 1707; cf. Diederichsen 1948, pp. 10–25; Terpstra 1965, pp. 361–83; Schleswig-Holsteinisches Biographisches Lexikon 1974, vol. 3, pp. 128–9.
34. Goldschmidt 1705, p. 507.

5.

In 1686, in a witch trial on the east Holstein estate of Schmoel, Mette Schlans accused, among others, her father Hans Lütke of being a sorcerer. He denied this when interrogated amicably; when tortured, however, he admitted to the accusations. When asked what his sorcery consisted of he answered on 21 April 1686: 'That he had wound a strap around his body which had made him a wolf. And that he as a wolf had killed one of his cows and a lamb. Satan had taken the strap away from him again.' While it is quite obvious that this confession extorted from the accused by torture is no proof at all of Lütke's actual ability to turn himself into a wolf or even of the assumption that he himself believed that he had this ability, he must, however, have assumed that he could escape torture by admitting to it because the *judges* would believe his story. He was quite right because, two days later, Count Christoph von Rantzau, lord of Schmoel, Hohenfelde and Övelgönne sentenced Lütke and his co-defendants 'to be brought from life to death and to be burned with fire because of the sorcery exercised by them, their denial of God, murder and other major criminal offences'.[35]

Hans Lütke's was no isolated case. From time to time in sixteenth century France there was a real werewolf epidemic. People were repeatedly accused of being werewolves, were tortured and burnt. Some of them had committed dreadful deeds really believing, like Giles Garnier in the year 1573, that they were wolves. And Peter Stump, too, who was executed on 31 October 1589, in Bedburg near Cologne had killed thirteen children, two women and one man.[36] Today we would regard all the individuals as being mentally deranged. As sexual motivation played a role in many of these cases, modern literature on the subject has stressed the connection between lycanthropic murders and sadism or cannibalism.[37] The confessions extorted by torture, on the other hand, again nourished popular belief and supported the legends already in circulation.

The witch trial of Schmoel was prompted by cattle deaths and inexplicable cases of death. It seemed only natural therefore to believe in black magic, and the sentence for sorcery was death. It is significant in this context that the accused confessed to being able to turn himself into a *wolf*. Even in the werewolf legends of the nineteenth century, *evil* humans turned into wolves.[38] Ideas that occurred in the 1686 trial have survived up to our own time.

---

35. LAS Abt. 11 No. 164. Another copy of the process protocol is in LAS Abt. 65.1 No. 112a. For the trial of Schmoel, see in particular Jacobsen 1994, pp. 99–118; also see Heberling 1915, pp. 194–7, and Prange 1965, pp. 76–94.

36. Leubuscher 1850, pp. 13–29; Hertz 1862, pp. 97–105; Summers 1966, pp. 225–8, 253–9; Woodward 1979, pp. 96–112.

37. Leubuscher 1850, pp. 46–65; Eisler 1969; Masters 1968, pp. 128–9, 195–6; Russell and Russell 1978, pp. 164–7.

38. Rheinheimer 1995, pp. 64–8.

Today it seems unimaginable that a human being could turn into a wolf
(which is the reason for the attempts of the positivistic nineteenth century simply
to ascribe the origins of belief in werewolves to mental illness).[39] But these people
lived in another time. We have to bear in mind how much man was exposed to the
forces of nature in earlier times. Extreme weather conditions, illness and war were
all immediate challenges to his life so that he was driven by a deep, existential fear.[40]
People tried various practices to assuage evil natural forces or even to harness them
for their own practical purposes. In the agrarian culture, man was still so much
embedded in the context of nature that he saw himself as part of this nature and
allowed the inner and outer worlds to merge. The *Magic*[41] which man tried to use
to master the threatening outer world worked to a corresponding analogy principle: internal processes within the individual were projected on external processes
in nature and vice versa. If outer nature, i.e. the environment, could be seen as a
representation of, or at least as being of the same structure as, the inner nature of
man, then it must be possible to influence the external world by changing one's inner
self, or changes in the external world would have an influence on the human soul.
Thus there were many possible practices, again working according to the analogy
principle, by which to influence one's own or somebody else's fate. In this context,
the belief in werewolves gave an image to certain fears and helped to channel them.

If the viciousness of a person exceeded the normal, in terms of the occurrence
of inexplicable damage or brutal crimes, the ideas of early times prescribed that the
evil-doer must have a 'wolfish' character and he was consequently regarded as an
evil demon who caused damage to the world of the living. That is why he had to
be banished to his accustomed realm of the demons, the land of the dead, where he
could cause no further harm. In early times, exorcism was effected by shouting and
throwing stones.[42] There was no place for a demon within the society of the living.
The werewolf died a *social death*.[43] Later, when the magical connection had already
been forgotten, the evil character of a person was exposed by calling this person
a 'werewolf'. This insult still reveals the old meaning of unmasking someone as a
demon, as a non-human, who belongs to the land of the dead and the peaceless.
The insult is therefore reminiscent of an ancient apotopaeic meaning. These ideas
of the early Middle Ages are reflected in the great number of defamation suits in

39. Leubuscher 1850, pp. 46–65.
40. Cf. Muchembled 1984, pp. 19–36; Delumeau 1989, pp. 49–107.
41. For magic and superstition in early modern times, see Muchembled 1984, pp. 63–94; van Dülmen
     1987; Labouvie 1991; Behringer 1993. For Schleswig-Holstein in particular: S. Anger 1947, pp.
     78–88; Kramer 1983, pp. 222–39; Kramer 1987, pp. 276–98; Sander 1991. For the interrelation
     between learned and popular magic: Daxelmüller 1985, pp. 837–63.
42. Koschorreck 1952, pp. 34–6, 98–103.
43. For the social death, see Hasenfratz 1982.

which somebody defended himself against being called a 'wolf' or 'werewolf'.[44] During the seventeenth and eighteenth centuries, the records of fines and court protocols of the Schleswig-Holstein lower judicial courts included a large number of such cases.[45]

In a defamation suit, the libellant had to prove to the court that the libellee really was a werewolf. Judging from the outcome of all the cases that have come to my knowledge, it would seem that in seventeenth century Schleswig-Holstein the libellant no longer met with success. As a rule these suits ended in the accuser being condemned for insult, because the judges demanded concrete proof that could be perceived with the senses.[46] Somebody must have seen the defamed person turn into a wolf. The 'wolf-like' character of certain types of people might have inspired numerous stories about werewolves – but the courts no longer accepted this as sufficient proof (at least provided that the case was *conducted correctly*). Even at that time, however, there were some who did not believe that the Schmoel witch trial, for example, had proceeded correctly. The king himself brought a court case against count Christoph von Rantzau who had had the 'werewolf' Hans Lütke burned. The reason was mistakes in the legal procedure and the count was heavily fined. This, of course, could not revive Hans Lütke and his co-defendants. But it is generally agreed that the condemnation of Christoph Rantzau was a gesture to the ending of all witch burning in Schleswig-Holstein.[47]

It is a reflection of the learned discussion which was in the process of understanding human transformations into wolves as pure imagination that legal practice had an increasingly critical attitude towards torture and witch burning. It is very interesting to follow the path that a transformation takes through legal confrontation: at first, everybody is convinced of the reality of the transformation; but exposure to rational criteria in court soon turns conviction itself into mere rumour. First, the character of the accused person had nourished the belief; then somebody had, apparently, seen the transformation happen before his own eyes. But on closer investigation nobody *had* actually seen it. Everybody maintained that he had heard it from somebody else who had witnessed the transformation. This happened in a case that occurred in Meinstorf in 1651 and that was brought to the court of Eutin.[48] Learned literature had originally intended to create a theoretical basis for human transformations into wolves by integrating the idea with the belief in witches. But it was this theoretical rationalisation which, in the long run, led

44. Kramer 1984, p. 83; Sander 1991, p. 72. A lot of evidence can be found in the source cardfile of the Seminar für Volkskunde of Kiel University, to which I was kindly permitted access. But there is such evidence not just for Schleswig-Holstein; see, for example, for Hesse: Höck 1985, pp. 73–4.
45. Rheinheimer 1994, p. 413; Rheinheimer 1995, pp. 36.
46. Concrete proof, perceivable with the senses, was also part of the tradition of magical thought: see Koschorreck 1952, pp. 81–2.
47. Jacobsen 1994, p. 99; vgl. Hoffmann 1979, p. 153.
48. LAS Abt. 275 No. 457, p. 77.

to an expelling of magical popular belief from legal and public practice so that it could and did only survive in legends.[49]

6.

The old merging of inner and outer reality which had manifested itself in belief in werewolves in particular did, however, continue to exist. Even if human transformations could no longer be proved, and even if rational reasoning and thinking had spread further afield, the wolf still remained an evil noxious animal for cattle and game. The authorities therefore readily found rational reasons for justifying wolf chases. The great battues in woods and moors – i.e. in eerie areas that had been identified with the land of the dead before – also had something to do with a (rationalised) expulsion of death and particularly so in a time when wars and epidemics were devastating the country. While it was impossible to defend oneself against wars and epidemics, it was quite possible to defend oneself against wolves. The entire fear of death was thus put into the wolf hunt. The seemingly irrational witch-hunting hysteria reached a climax in Schleswig-Holstein around the year 1640[50] – at the same time that the seemingly rational extermination of the wolves began. At about the same time a systematic extermination of birds of prey and of ravens was also begun;[51] that is, the extermination of birds which carried, like the wolf, a handicap from mythology. These different chases all served to channel the general feeling of fear that had spread after the Thirty Years' War with its aftermath of epidemics and social confusion. An additional factor was a global deterioration of the climate that began in the seventeenth century.[52] Society could no longer handle these fears in a traditional way, partly because of the Reformation and the spreading of a rational thinking in cause and effect chains, which repressed magical popular belief and its particular possibilities for channelling social fear. Therefore new and more 'rational' ways of dealing with fear became necessary.[53] Sorcery, magic and witchcraft, which had caused such a feeling of menace in those uncertain times, were done away with, but with them went the demons who made them possible. Evil itself was challenged. The dangerousness of wolves and the damage they caused, which was listed again and again, helped to rationalise this smouldering fear. New techniques[54] were constantly being devised for putting an end to the old enemy.

---

49. Rheinheimer 1995, p. 64–8.

50. Hoffmann 1979, p. 112.

51. Jessen 1958, pp. 273–4; cf. e.g. Corpus Constitutionum Regio-Holsaticarum 1749, vol. 1, pp. 1280–1.

52. Lehmann 1988, pp. 110–1.

53. For general information about the forming of new institutions for dealing with fear, see Schoene 1967, pp. 128–33.

54. Cf. the hunting practices of the wolf hunter general of Jutland and Schleswig. Also see Bernard 1983, pp. 53–87; Jessen 1958, pp. 173, 177.

Martin Rheinheimer

On the one hand, the internal and external 'infestation' was exterminated; on the other, however, the extermination of the wolves was also used as a means of *social disciplining* applied by the prince to extend and deepen his absolutist regime. A wolf hunt was particularly well-suited for this because it made it easy to explain to the subjects that the chase was really in *their* interests. It was, after all, their cattle to which the wolves did 'great damage in many a way', as it says in the Ordinance on Forestry and Hunt from 1737 (§ 56). In this way the wolf hunt could be used to extend corvée and power (the peasants had to do service as drivers and carters, etc.) making the subjects internalise the notion that the superiority of the prince was entirely in their interests. In some cases, up to 4,000 drivers were summoned.[55] Official wolf hunting was therefore not very popular and many people who had been summoned as drivers or carters did not even bother to come. In 1734 in the parish of Barlt alone, 124 drivers stayed away from the chase.[56]

Among other things, King Christian VI, in his 'Ordinance on Forestry and Hunt for the Duchies of Schleswig and Holstein' of the year 1737, decreed regulations about wolf hunting.[57] Outwardly, the king stressed the wish to protect the interests of the peasants who had to do service by decreeing that the organisation of a wolf hunt 'be not done at a time of year when the farmer is busy with sowing or harvesting so that he be not hindered in doing his house and farmer's duties' (§ 56). The core of the matter, i.e. the fact that peasants had to do service during the chase, was of course not touched by this. The ordinance contains detailed orders about how the officers had to summon the crew and how the chase was to be organised. It was also decreed that 'those subjects who ... remain absent for no considerable cause and justification ... must pay a penalty of half a Reichsthaler for each time' (§ 58). The gamekeeper complied with this order by reporting 'according to oath and duty' thirteen persons of the village of Rödenis alone who had stayed absent from a chase on 29 and 30 August 1747, for which 'all subjects' of the entire borough of Husum 'as well as the bailiwick of Schwabstedt' had been summoned.[58]

At the beginning of the corresponding paragraphs, the ordinance states the wish and the desire to completely exterminate the wolves. Therefore a reward was put up for each wolf killed.[59] Six taler were awarded to anyone who brought in an old wolf and two taler for a young one. This sum was an extraordinary amount of money compared to the average income of the time and it acted as an incentive to the lower ranks of the forest authorities, i.e. the stewards and the gamekeepers, to

---

55. Weismann 1931, p. 486.
56. Hansen 1969, p. 74; also see, Meiborg 1896, p. 156, note 1. More current literature often understands such behaviour as a sign of resistance: see Hiller 1992, pp. 59–60.
57. Corpus Constitutionum Regio-Holsaticarum 1749, vol. 1, pp. 1277–80.
58. LAS Abt. 163 S.-Goesh. No. 102.
59. Such attempts had been made before: see Rheinheimer 1994, p. 418; Rheinheimer 1995, p. 55.

increase their income by delivering as many wolves as possible.[60] The official ac-counts contain receipts for each wolf delivered, thus making a step-by-step account of the extermination of the wolves possible. The rewards indicate that wolves were more numerous in the north of the duchy of Schleswig (boroughs of Haderslev and Løgumkloster) while they decreased in number towards the south. Between 1737 and 1780, the considerable number of 443 wolves killed was reported from the borough of Haderslev, while the borough of Flensburg could only report 82 wolves killed and the borough of Rendsburg a total of twelve. Finally, from the borough of Segeberg the report was of no wolves killed at all in that period, although in the seventeenth century there was a number of complaints about the increase in number of the wolves from the parish of Kaltenkirchen.[61]

Wolves had already disappeared from the borough of Rendsburg by the 1740s, and the last rewards paid for a killed wolf were reported in 1771 for the borough of Flensburg and on 11 April 1780 for the borough of Haderslev. Although wolves were regarded as 'entirely extinct' in Schleswig-Holstein in 1797, individual specimens reappeared at that time.[62] In 1809, August Niemann wrote: 'Now they have nearly entirely disappeared. In this country, too, as in the south of Germany, people noticed them again as a rarity in the years 1797 and 1798'.[63] The last wolf of Schleswig-Holstein was apparently killed near Neumünster in 1820.[64] But wolves had already been exterminated as sedentary game by 1780.[65]

7.

In conclusion: the extermination of the wolves became a determined intention in Schleswig-Holstein at a time when unnatural death held the country in its grasp. An additional deep-rooted, irrational element was the symbolic meaning of the wolf, its connection with death. Extending the service of the statute to the apparent 'rational' benefit of the subjects and the extermination of magical popular belief gave the elite a means of socially disciplining and subduing the lower classes and

---

60. Cf. Hiller 1992, pp. 87–9.
61. The numbers for Hadersleben according to Colmorgen 1955, pp. 38–41 (here the sum total does not correspond to the individual data, however). Borough of Flensburg: LAS Abt. 167 AR (years 1760/61 are missing), for 1762 and 1765: LAS Abt. 167.1 No. 123. The borough of Rendsburg according to Reimer 1956, p. 199 (his numbers could not always be verified by LAS Abt. 104 AR, however). Borough of Segeberg: LAS Abt. 110 AR (checked for the years 1736–1750).
62. Piening, p. 232.
63. Niemann 1809, p. 232.
64. Jessen 1958, p. 121; see also Jessen 1988, p. 305. In Denmark, the last wolf was shot in 1813. Weismann 1931, pp. 492–4; Brøndegaard 1986, p. 140.
65. As the wolves had ceased to be a concrete threat for the prince or for the subjects, there was no longer any need either for detailed orders. The 'General new Ordinance on Forestry and Hunting' from the year 1784 therefore only comparatively briefly deals with the wolf hunt: Chronologische Sammlung 1794, pp. 88–9.

of filling their souls with the superior power of the upper class. Natural feelings were increasingly repressed during this process. The existential fear of death was channelled into new and rational forms by exterminating the wolves.

But the wolf is a tough species. Those features of the inner nature of man symbolised by the wolf could not be repressed completely and began seeking new ways of expression. The wolf thus survived in legends and fairytales and even today it re-emerges night after night in ominous nightmares. The character of the symbol has changed long since. The wolf is no longer identical with death or Death but is identified only as a sign pointing to death. A separation has taken place between the real wolf (the external world) and the things that it symbolised for man (the internal world). Now that the oral tradition of legends of wolves and werewolves is beginning to fade because of the extermination of the wolves and because it is increasingly being replaced by other motifs,[66] the wolf has still managed to maintain its presence in trivial literature, the gutter press and films, in media which are less interested in transporting up-to-date symbols than in using antiquated ones (i.e. clichés) to channel the unmastered fears of man. In doing so, however, they also keep man at an antiquated level of awareness because the symbolism they rely on is culturally outdated. It is a well-known fact that this is used as an instrument for maintaining and stabilising equally outdated power structures.[67] In this way the wolf creeps, on culturally determined paths, into our dreams even today, and it does not take much to reactivate all of these fears if only one wolf appears again so that the repressed fears crystallise around it. This indeed happened when, on 27 September 1963, four wolves escaped from Neumünster zoo.

There was considerable excitement because only two of the animals were caught. The third was run over by a car. The fourth one, however, remained missing. The State Hunters' Association of Schleswig-Holstein called on all hunters 'to use all means available to kill the runaway wolf as quickly as possible as it is a threat to the population'. After the wolf had been sighted several times near Neu-Duvenstedt it was finally trapped on 25 November. No less than forty drivers and hunters went out to bring the injured animal to bay in the forest into which it had retreated.[68] There was a similar reaction when, in 1976, seven wolves ran away in the Bayerischer Wald: they were chased by 300 policemen.[69]

So while, on the one hand, a regression is produced by modern legends, fairytales and films that lead us from rational thought back to symbolism, thus helping to cope with existential fear, on the other the wolves that ran away from the zoo became a signal for a second regression, which made the seemingly-mastered fears break through again as an uncontrollable force sweeping aside all rational

66. See Odstedt 1943, p. 228; Roeck 1973, pp. 146–7.
67. Gerhardt 1977, pp. 41–54; cf. Schulte 1978, pp. 879–920.
68. Jacobs 1964, pp. 155–9.
69. Gerhardt 1977, p. 41.

thought. The people who, up until then, were familiar with wolves only from stories and films now saw themselves immediately and suddenly confronted with an existential threat, with Death and Evil themselves. They experienced the wolf not as a demonstrative symbol, as would befit modern people, but as a symbol of identification, being identical with the symbolised object.

BIBLIOGRAPHY

Archival Sources

State Archives Schleswig-Holstein (LAS)

LAS Abt. 7 No. 1735.

LAS Abt. 7 No. 3494.

LAS Abt. 11 No. 164.

LAS Abt. 65.1 No. 112a.

LAS Abt. 65.1 No. 1826.

LAS Abt. 104 AR

LAS Abt. 110 AR.

LAS Abt. 163 S.-Goesh. No. 102.

LAS Abt. 167 AR

LAS Abt. 167.1 No. 123.

LAS Abt. 275 No. 457, p. 77.

LAS Abt. 400.5 No. 45.

Research Literature

Anger, S. 1947. *Das Recht in den Sagen, Legenden und Märchen Schleswig-Holsteins* (Diss.: Kiel).

Behringer, W. 1993 [1988]. *Hexen und Hexenprozesse in Deutschland* (München: dtv).

Bernard, D. 1983. *Wolf und Mensch* (Saarbrücken: SDV-Verlag).

Brøndegaard, V.J. 1986, *Folk og fauna. Dansk etnozoologi*, 3 (Kopenhagen: Rosenkilde og Bagger).

Christmann, E. 1943. 'Von Wolfsgalgen und Wolfsbalgträgern'. *Oberdeutsche Zeitschrift für Volkskunde* 17: 69–73.

Chronologische Sammlung der im Jahre 1784 ergangenen Verordnungen und Verfügungen für die Herzogthümer Schleswig und Holstein, die Herrschaft Pinneberg, Grafschaft Ranzau und Stadt Altona (Kiel 1794).

Clausen, O. 1981. *Chronik der Heide- und Moorkolonisation im Herzogtum Schleswig, 1760–1765* (Husum).

Colmorgen, H. 1955. 'Vorkommen des Wolfes im Amte Hadersleben v. 1739–1780'. *Die Heimat* 62: 37–41.

Corpus Constitutionum Regio-Holsaticarum, 1 (Altona 1749).

Daxelmüller, C. 1985. 'Das literarische Magieangebot. Zur Vermittlung von hochgeschichtlicher Magiediskussion und magischer Volkskultur im 17. Jahrhundert', in W. Brückner, P. Blickle and D. Breuer (eds) *Literatur und Volk im 17. Jahrhundert* (Wiesbaden: Otto Harrasowitz) pp. 837–63.

Delumeau, J. 1989. *Angst im Abendland. Die Geschichte kollektiver Ängste im Europa des 14.–18. Jahrhunderts* (Reinbek: Rowohlt).

Diederichsen, J. 1948. 'Pastor Peter Goldschmidt'. *Jahrbuch des Angler Heimatvereins* 12: 10–25.

Dülmen, R. van. (ed.) 1987. *Hexenwelten. Magie und Imagination vom 16.–20. Jahrhundert* (Frankfurt a. M.: Fischer).

Eisler, R. 1969 [1951]. *Man into Wolf. An Anthropological Interpretation of Sadism, Masochism, and Lycanthropy* (New York: Greenwood Press).

Erler, A. 1938/40. 'Friedlosigkeit und Werwolfglaube'. *Paideuma* 1: 303–17

Gerhardt T. 1977. 'Der Werwolf im Groschenroman'. *Kieler Blätter zur Volkskunde* 9: 41–54;

Goldschmidt, P. 1705. *Verworffener Hexen- und Zauberer-Advocat* (Hamburg).

Hansen, K. 1969. 'Besetz- und Wolfsjagden, welche in den Jahren 1729 bis 1741 in der Landschaft veranstaltet worden'. *Dithmarschen* 3: 73–5.

Hase, W. 1983. 'Abriß der Wald- und Forstgeschichte Schleswig-Holsteins im letzten Jahrtausend'. *Schriften des Naturwissenschaftlichen Vereins für Schleswig-Holstein* 33: 83–94.

Hasenfratz, H.-P. 1982. *Die toten Lebenden. Eine religionsphänomenologische Studie zum sozialen Tod in archaischen Gesellschaften* (Leiden: E.J. Brill).

Heberling, R. 1915. 'Zauberei und Hexenprozesse in Schleswig-Holstein-Lauenburg'. *Zeitschrift der Gesellschaft für Schleswig-Holsteinische Geschichte* 45: 116–247.

Hertz, W. 1862. *Der Werwolf. Ein Beitrag zur Sagengeschichte* (Stuttgart: A. Kröner).

Hiller, H. 1992. *Untertanen und obrigkeitliche Jagd. Zu einem konfliktträchtigen Verhältnis in Schleswig-Holstein zwischen 1600 und 1848* (Neumünster: Wachholtz).

Höck, A. 1985. 'Bemerkungen zum "Werwolf" nach hessischen Archivalien'. *Hessische Blätter für Volks- und Kulturforschung* 18: 71–5.

Hoffmann, B. 1979. 'Die Hexenverfolgung in Schleswig-Holstein zwischen Reformation und Aufklärung'. *Schriften des Vereins für Schleswig-Holsteinische Kirchengeschichte* 34/35: 110–172.

Jacobs W. 1964. 'Eine Wolfsjagd im 20. Jahrhundert. Das Schicksal des Neumünsteraner Wolfes'. *Jahrbuch der Heimatgemeinschaft des Kreises Eckernförde* 22: 155–9.

Jacobsen, M. 1994. 'Ein Hexenprozeß auf Gut Schmoel im Jahre 1686'. *Jahrbuch für Heimatkunde im Kreis Plön* 24: 99–118.

Jacoby, M. 1974. *Wargus, vargr 'Verbrecher' 'Wolf' – eine sprach- und rechtsgeschichtliche Untersuchung* (Uppsala: Almqvist & Wiksell).

Jessen, H. 1958. *Jagdgeschichte Schleswig-Holsteins* (Rendsburg: Heinrich Möller Söhne).

— 1988. *Wild und Jagd in Schleswig-Holstein* (Rendsburg: Heinrich Möller Söhne).

Kock, C. 1931. 'Wolfsplage im Amte Hütten vor 250 Jahren'. *Die Heimat* 41: 159–63.

Koschorreck, W. 1952. *Der Wolf. Eine Untersuchung über die Vorstellungen vom Verbrecher und seiner Tat sowie vom Wesen der Strafe in der Frühzeit* (Diss. Jena).

Kramer, K.-S. 1983. Schaden- und Gegenzauber im Alltagsleben des 16.–18. Jahrhunderts nach archivalischen Quellen aus Holstein', in C. Degn, H. Lehmann and D. Unverhau (eds) *Hexenprozesse. Deutsche und Skandinavische Beiträge* (Neumünster: Wachholtz) pp. 222–39.

— 1984. 'Hohnsprake, Wrakworte, Nachschnack und Ungebühr. Ehrenhändel in holstein-ischen Quellen'. *Kieler Blätter zur Volkskunde* 16: 49-85.

— 1987. *Volksleben in Holstein, 1550–1800* (Kiel: Mühlau).

Kristensen, E.T. (1891–93). *Gamle folks fortællinger om det jyske almueliv* (Kolding).

Labouvie, E. 1991. *Zauberei und Hexenwerk. Ländlicher Hexenglaube in der frühen Neuzeit* (Frankfurt a. M.: Fischer).

Lehmann, H. 1988. 'The Persecution of Witches as Restoration of Order: The Case of Germany, 1590s–1650s'. *Central European History* 21: 107–121.

Leubuscher, R. 1850. *Über die Wehrwölfe und Thierverwandlungen im Mittelalter* (Berlin).

Lurker, M. 1969. 'Hund und Wolf in ihrer Beziehung zum Tode'. *Antaios* 10: 199–216.

Masters, R.E.L. 1968. *Die teuflische Wollust* (München: Lichtenberg).

Meiborg, R. 1896. *Das Bauernhaus im Herzogtum Schleswig und das Leben des schleswigschen Bauernstandes im 16., 17. und 18. Jahrhundert* (Schleswig).

Muchembled, R. 1984 [1982]. *Kultur des Volks – Kultur der Eliten. Die Geschichte einer erfolgreichen Verdrängung* (Stuttgart: Klett-Cotta).

Niemann, A. 1809. *Forststatistik der dänischen Staaten* (Altona).

— 1820. *Vaterländische Waldberichte nebst Blikken in allgemeine Wälderkunde und in die Geschichte und Litteratur der Forstwirthschaft*, vol. 1 (Altona).

Nitschke, A. 1982. 'Symbolforschung und Märchenforschung', in M. Lurker (ed.) *Beiträge zu Symbol, Symbolbegriff und Symbolforschung* (Baden-Baden) pp. 121-138.

Odstedt, E. 1943. *Varulven i svensk folktradition* (Uppsala, Kopenhagen: Malört).

Piening. 1797. 'Etwas über die Wölfe im Amte Rendsburg'. *Schleswig-Holsteinische Provinzialberichte* II: 232–4.

Prange, W. 1965. *Christoph Rantzau auf Schmoel und die Schmoeler Leibeigenschaftsprozesse* (Neumünster: Wachholtz) pp. 76–94.

Reimer, G. 1956. Wölfe und Raubvögel im Amte Rendsburg, 1737–1820'. *Die Heimat* 63: 198–99.

Rheinheimer, M. 1994. 'Wolf und Werwolfglaube. Die Ausrottung der Wölfe in Schleswig-Holstein'. *Historische Anthropologie*, 2: 399–422.

— 1995. 'Die Angst vor dem Wolf. Werwolfglauben, Ausrottung der Wölfe und Wolfssagen in Schleswig-Holstein'. *Fabula* 36: 25–78.

Roeck, A. 1973. 'Der Werwolf als dämonisches Wesen im Zusammenhang mit den Plagegeistern', in L. Röhrich (ed.) *Probleme der Sagenforschung*. (Freiburg: Forschungsstelle Sage) pp. 139–48.

Russell, W.M.S. and C. Russell. 1978. 'The Social Biology of Werewolves', in J.R. Porter and W.M.S. Russell (eds) *Animals in Folklore* (Ipswich, Cambridge, Totowa: D.S. Brewer) pp. 143–82.

Sander, K. 1991. *Aberglauben im Spiegel schleswig-holsteinischer Quellen des 16. bis 18. Jahrhunderts* (Neumünster: Wachholtz).

Schemmel, B. 1973. 'Der "Werwolf" von Ansbach (1685)'. *Jahrbuch für fränkische Landesforschung* **33**: 167–200.

Schipperges, H. 1967. 'Melancolia als ein mittelalterlicher Sammelbegriff für Wahnvorstellungen'. *Studium Generale* **20**: 723–36.

Schleswig-Holsteinisches Biographisches Lexikon. 1974. Vol. 3 (Neumünster) pp. 128–9.

Schoene, W. 1967. 'Zur Frühgeschichte der Angst. Angst und Politik in nichtdurchrationalisierten Gesellschaften', in H. Wiesbrock (ed.) *Die politische und gesellschaftliche Rolle der Angst* (Frankfurt a. M.: Europäische Verl.-Anst.) pp. 113–34.

Schulte R. 1978. 'Dienstmädchen im herrschaftlichen Haushalt. Zur Genese ihrer Sozialpsychologie'. *Zeitschrift für bayerische Landesgeschichte* **41**: 879–920.

Schwerhoff, G. 1986. 'Rationalität im Wahn. Zum gelehrten Diskurs über die Hexen in der frühen Neuzeit'. *Saeculum* **37**: 45–82.

Sprenger, J. and H. Institoris. 1982 [1487]. *Der Hexenhammer (Malleus maleficarum),* aus dem Lateinischen übertragen und eingeleitet von J.W.R. Schmidt (München).

Summers, M. 1966 [1933]. *The Werewolf* (New York: University Books).

Täntzer, J. 1682/89. *Der Dianen Hohe und Niedere Jagt-Geheimnüß* (Kopenhagen).

Terpstra, J.U. 1965. 'Petrus Goldschmidt aus Husum. Ein nordfriesischer Gegner Balthasar Bekkers und Thomasius'. *Euphorion* **59**: 361–83.

Unruh, G.C. von. 1957. 'Wargus. Friedlosigkeit und magisch-kultische Vorstellungen bei den Germanen'. *Zeitschrift der Savigny-Stiftung für Rechtsgeschichte, Germ. Abt.* **74**: 1–40.

Weismann, C. 1931. *Vildtets og Jagtens Historie i Danmark* (Kopenhagen: Reitzel).

Witt, K. 1935. 'Nachrichten von Wölfen, Adlern, Klunckraben und anderem Getier in den Gottorfer Amtsrechnungen des Jahres 1753'. *Die Heimat* **45**: 257–58.

Woodward, I. 1979. *The Werewolf Delusion* (New York, London: Paddington Press).

Wytrzens, G (ed.) 1967. *Die goldene Freiheit der Polen. Aus den Denkwürdigkeiten Sr. Wohlgeboren des Herrn Jan Chryzostom Pasek (17. Jahrhundert)* (Graz, Wien, Köln: Styria).

Zimen, E. 1978. *Der Wolf. Mythos und Verhalten* (Wien, München: Meyster).

— 3 —

The Wolf War in Sweden during the Eighteenth Century
– Strategies, Measures and Leaders

Roger Bergström, Karin Dirke and Kjell Danell

Wolves in Sweden have been hunted from time immemorial. Ten medieval regional laws, which were among the first hand-written documents in Sweden, contained various regulations concerning wolves.[1] The laws stated that peasants were obliged to pay bounties to a hunter who killed wolves and that all citizens had to participate in wolf battues as well as in the building of traps.[2] The regional laws were primarily intended to exterminate wolves locally. A more complex system of eradicating large carnivores evolved during the seventeenth and eighteenth centuries.

In this chapter, we focus on the wolf and regard 1647, when the first national hunting law was created, as the starting point of the Swedish 'wolf war'.[3] It was a proclamation to exterminate the wolf and other large predators from the Swedish territories. We mainly focus on the process throughout the eighteenth century. During this time, many innovations were developed concerning regulations, organisation models and methods to trap and kill wolves. The killing of wolves was no longer only a concern for hunters and trappers – the whole society, including academics, was mobilised. We argue that the system constructed for exterminating the wolf was increasingly inspired by, and came to resemble, the system of warfare. Similarities can be recognised in the general expression of arguments, the organisation, the spreading of information, the punishments imposed and the equipment used. During the period under discussion, Finland was a part of Sweden. However, we focus on the area that is now Sweden.

THE WOLF WAR

Wolves played a role in the development of the Swedish nation. The war on wolves, fought during the eighteenth and nineteenth centuries, was partly about protecting Swedes from alien elements, and partly an attempt to define what it meant to

1. Grey (Gray) wolf: *Canis lupus.*
2. Holmbäck and Wessén 1940–1979.
3. Kongl. Maj:ts til Swerige, ordning och stadga huru alle rijkzens inbyggare sigh forhalla skole medh jachter, diurefang och fugleskiutande. 23 Martii 1647.

58

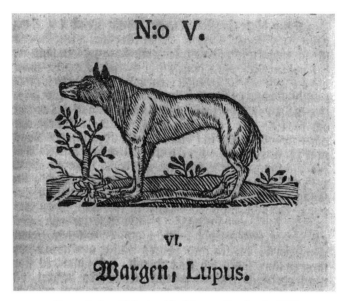

Figure 1. A wolf depicted by Magnus Orrelius in 1750.

be Swedish. An example is the rhetoric used for wolf hunting. The importance of exterminating the predators in all parts of the country was stressed. Wolves appeared to invade from other countries.[4] Eliminating them completely was described as futile, as there were constantly new ones coming from Norway, Finland and Russia over the Swedish borders.[5] In this way, the wolf was portrayed as the proverbial 'other' and as such had a role in the perception of what it meant to be Swedish. Being Swedish was viewed as *not* being 'wolfish' – that is, greedy, gluttonous or, for that matter, foreign.

The idea of wolves flooding in from the east was further reinforced during the nineteenth century and was confirmed in the discourse of natural history, where the wolves' origin was commonly mentioned. They were mainly thought to be immigrants from Finland and Russia.[6] Wolves were used in constructing what Benedict Anderson would call an 'imagined community' – the idea of a nation and who belongs to it. By emphasising the wolves as 'alien' elements and the importance of driving them across the Swedish borders, these borders could be stressed and the unity of the nation reinforced.[7]

4. von Liewen 1753, p. 1.
5. Berch 1750, p. 38.
6. Nilsson 1847, p. 223.
7. Anderson 1991, pp. 1–8.

The war on wolves had its roots in a Sweden marked by war and mobilisation. During the first half of the seventeenth century, Sweden was involved in uninterrupted aggressive conflicts.[8] Warfare was an important part of building the propaganda machine as well as the state. With reference to a constant threat of war, the king could establish his power. The rhetoric drew on the belief that the king was obliged to protect the people against threats from abroad, an idea stated in the royal oath where he promised to protect the peasantry from violence and threats.[9] Seventeenth-century Sweden consisted of 95 per cent peasantry, while the nobility owned sixty per cent of the area under cultivation. Sweden differed from other countries by having so much of its economy based on agriculture and by the peasants' relatively influential position through representation in the parliament. Therefore, the voice of the peasants was valued.[10] The constant wars demanded resources in the form of men as well as money. Such a controversial operation required skilled propaganda, which aimed at inducing people to participate with manpower, taxes and concrete contributions such as driving soldiers. The same tactics were also used in the war on wolves.

War was, in other words, a legitimisation for Swedish royalty as well as a point of departure for the propaganda machine. It is not surprising that this established organisation also worked well for a war on 'the strife' as the large predators were commonly called.[11] The hunt was seen as a form of military exercise, especially for young noblemen. War and hunting were 'symbolically interchangeable'.[12] The warfare organisation was, however, used not only symbolically but also materially in the war on wolves. Furthermore, many state officials had military training and experience. The building of the state, as it developed in Sweden, was a prerequisite for an organised war on wolves. It demanded a strong royalty with territorial claims as well as an effective national administration. This process continued in sixteenth- and seventeenth-century Sweden.[13] For all this, a formal juridical base in the legislation was also needed.

1647 – THE STARTING POINT

The beginning of nationwide striving to exterminate wolves can be pinpointed to 1647 and the regime of Queen Christina. In a proposition to parliament, the Queen asked for more stringent legislation on hunting. Her goal was to protect the livestock of the peasantry as well as wild game. The proposition included three

---

8.   Forssberg 2005, p. 19.
9.   Hildebrand 1891, p. 276–7.
10.   Forssberg 2005, pp. 2, 14, 18.
11.   Fridell and Svanberg 2007, p. 76.
12.   Nyrén 2012, p. 20.
13.   Forssberg 2005, p. 17.

Figure 2. Front page of the 1647 law (Kongl. Maj:ts til Swerige, ordning och stadga huru alle rijkzens inbyggare sigh forhalla skole medh jachter, diurefang och fugleskiutande. 23 Martii 1647 (1647). Scanning by Jens Östman, National Library of Sweden, Stockholm.

important points: 1) to protect peasants' livestock, 2) to protect moose, deer and roe deer from predators and 3) to prevent peasants from poaching.[14] The rhetoric of the proposition was similar to previous war propaganda. It began with a reassurance that the peasantry and their livestock should be protected (as is royalty's duty), but also attempts to hinder them from hunting game. The peasants are viewed both as victims and perpetrators.

The proposition was easily passed in parliament and resulted in the first coherent hunting law in Sweden.[15] It satisfied the nobility by strengthening their privileges. The nobility furthermore wanted to strengthen the duty of peasants to participate in wolf hunting, by increasing the fines.[16] The proposition followed directly on a proposition requesting more resources for warfare. Warfare and hunting were thus implicitly closely knit in Swedish legislation.

In 1664, a new hunting law, very similar to that of 1647, was launched which resulted in all commoners in central and southern Sweden losing their right to hunt 'useful' game. However, when it came to combatting large carnivores, all people, irrespective of social class (except for priests and single women), were expected to participate.[17]

POWER AND DISPUTES

Killing wolves was thus the norm in legislation and practice from the middle ages. The rationalisation and practice, however, changed over time. Hunting was practiced by peasants as well as nobility and royalty. Interest varied with class and residence location. Wolf hunting had several functions of which extermination was just one. Equally important was the hunt as a ritual and manifestation of power. Royal hunts were led by royal forest officers who were exclusively former military officers. The hunts were organised as military operations engaging large numbers of people. They functioned as a demonstration of power in which the peasants were forced to provide manpower, weapons and other equipment for several days. The purpose was to discipline the peasants as well as to educate the royalty and nobility in killing.

In 1734, hunting became the focus of a dispute between the nobility and the other estates of the Swedish parliament. The argument was a consequence of an attempt to revise legislation in order to produce a better and more unified law. The revision almost failed because of the difficulties in agreeing on the laws concern-

14. Ridderskapets och Adelns protokoll 1645–1649, Vol. 4, appendix c 'Kongl: Maij:tz proposition', pp. 100–1; moose: *Alces alces*, deer: *Cervus* spp., roe deer: *Capreolus capreolus*.

15. Kongl. Maj:ts til Swerige, ordning och stadga huru alle rijkzens inbyggare sigh forhalla skole medh jachter, diurefang och fugleskiutande. 23 Martii 1647 (1647).

16. Ridderskapets och Adelns protokoll 1645–1649, Vol. 4, report of the proceedings, pp. 47–8.

17. Kongl. May.tz ordning och stadga, om jachter, diurefang och fogelskiutande. Giord och forbattrat pa rijkzdagen som holtz i Stockholm ahr 1664. 29 Augusti 1664.

ing hunting.[18] The dispute involved hunting rights in relation to landownership and was partly about the interpretation of the hunt: was it a legitimate source of income, or merely a pleasure for the upper classes? The peasants were not allowed to hunt 'valuable' game on their own land and the aristocrats were afraid of losing their privileges, if hunting rights were made connected with landownership. Thus, views varied across estates but also between different parts of the country. The only hunting regulations that eventually became part of the law in 1734 concerned how to reduce pest animals, including wolves.

The parliamentary dispute is interesting in several ways. It points to the perceived importance and symbolic value of the hunt and access to wild meat. Hunting wild game was a sign of power, a business only for the upper classes. Meat-eating was a symbol of power and dominance. In the parliamentary debate, the link between power and meat-eating is obvious.[19] This power gave the human, the man, the nobleman or even just the royal man the sole right to wild meat. The power of male meat-eating is a strong undercurrent in the history of wolves in Sweden. It manifests itself as a general aversion to carnivores and in the nobility's claim to wild meat. The wolves, through their meat-eating diet, seemed to question the power of man over nature. The hunt could, however, also be conceptualised as a duty, pursued with less glamorous methods, with the aim of extermination. Taking part in this, it was thought, was an important duty of the peasants.

ORGANISATION OF THE WOLF WAR

From medieval times, documents indicate that the king had personnel involved in royal hunts, surveillance of royal deer parks and delivery of game meat to the court. These loosely organised staffs were called *Hovjägeristaten*. This organisation, however, never had the capacity to take the lead in a national battle against wolves. An additional, more formal national organisation, *Riksjägmästarämbetet*, with the division *Riksjägeristaten*, was formed in 1635. The head of this office was selected from the aristocracy and expected to fulfil his task without 'injustice and friendship'. Subordinates were employed in the various provinces. The organisation's main duties were to care for the state forests and to oversee the killing of pest animals.[20]

Riksjägmästarämbetet was withdrawn in 1682 and a reorganisation took place. Thereafter, the organisation structurally changed several times until a more modern authority superseded it in mid-nineteenth century. During some periods *Hovjägeristaten* and *Riksjägeristaten* were merged, during others they were independent and competed. We call them *Jägeristaten* below. The battle against wolves became more effectively organised at an official level. The system was inspired by

---

18.   Nyrén 2012; Östergren 1896, pp. 2–3.
19.   Nyrén 2012; Östergren 1896, pp. 2–3.
20.   Samzelius 1915, pp. 170–1.

experiences of organisation and propaganda from the Thirty Years' War, as well as by international influences.

Jägeristaten safeguarded the supply of important tree species, mainly oak for ship construction, and oversaw the hunting and extermination of pest animals. Most counties had a chief forest officer who served under the county governor. Additionally, lower ranked foresters were employed, but the number differed greatly between counties.[21] *Jägeristaten* closely resembled a police force, which scrutinised the peasantry in search of illegal activities.[22] The staffs of *Jägeristaten* therefore were not especially popular among commoners.[23]

At this time, there was no formal education for foresters. The higher-ranked foresters in the counties were often recruited from the aristocracy and trained in the army. Sometimes they had a university background, which also was a part of their military training. The king was advised by the estates of parliament to offer superannuated or unemployed military officers positions in *Jägeristaten*.[24] Military officers' involvement in *Jägeristaten* was probably popular, as hunting would bestow status and give training for military activities.[25]

The staffs of *Jägeristaten* had been used in the army at least since the beginning of the seventeenth century and they participated in several wars. Their capability in handling horses and weapons, as well as leadership skills, could be very useful in the army. According to the instruction for *Riksjägmästaren* given in 1638, it was not permitted to send employees of *Jägeristaten* to ordinary wars, but these rules were constantly violated. Ulf Nyrén calls *Jägeristaten* 'a military institution in civil disguise' and concludes that it was a tool for exercising power and control, both in military and civil contexts.[26]

ON THE BATTLEFIELD

Military wars stimulate rapid development of new techniques as well as improvement of old ones, in order to defeat the enemy. This was also the case in the wolf war. Old methods were improved during the eighteenth century and the use of baits and poisoned baits was developed. Furthermore, printed materials on the matter began to appear, and methods were described in detail. A few men took the lead and developed, described and advocated new techniques. Many factors prompted this advancement: new royal decrees and the progress of technology and pharmacology. Equally important, however, was the perceived inefficiency of the

---

21. Brummer 2010, p. 65 (80 in original document).
22. Nyrén 2008, p. 5.
23. Lönnaeus 2011.
24. Samzelius 1915, p. 178.
25. Nyrén 2008, p. 6.
26. Nyrén 2008, pp. 6–8; Samzelius 1915, pp. 170–1; Nyrén 2012, pp. 10–1.

Roger Bergström, Karin Dirke and Kjell Danell

older methods: these methods involved low catch per unit effort, as well as laborious routines conflicting with peasants' day-to-day activities.

In the first hunters' magazine in Sweden, an anonymous author listed the different methods of wolf hunting in use. In the winter, different forms of battues were mainly deployed, with or without bait, nets or traps. A hunter could also pursue the wolf on skis. In summertime, wolves were preferably caught in various forms of traps or by being attracted to bait. The wolves could also be decimated by locating their dens and killing the cubs.[27]

Some of these methods were used in combination. There were also regional differences in how the various methods were used. The northern two-thirds of Sweden were scarcely populated and had a tough climate in terms of snow and cold. For example, temperatures of minus twenty degrees Celsius and one metre of snow made battues very difficult but could be ideal for a hunter on skis tracking down a wolf. Well suited for such tasks were more or less professional hunters and the Saami people living in remote areas. Thus, in these northern regions the governors did not arrange large groups of people for wolf hunting.

ENGAGING THE PEOPLE

The first large battles with wolves required a considerable number of men, often hundreds, but sometimes thousands. Great efforts were spent in developing techniques to make the war more effective. This meant killing more wolves with less manpower. Below we give some examples of key elements of eighteenth century methods for combatting wolves. These methods were from time to time also recommended by the state.

One of the influential actors in the war on wolves was the nobleman Anders (Andreas) Schönberg (1689–1759) who mainly advocated and developed various forms of battues. He was born in Stockholm. After studying in Uppsala and Greifswald he became a forester and thereafter joined the army. He ended his career by receiving the honourable title of forest officer at court. Schönberg was also interested in bird breeding and communicated with Carl Linnaeus on the matter.[28] Schönberg was most renowned for leading 41 royal hunting parties during his time as a forest officer. Most of these were performed as battues, sometimes with an impressive number of people involved. Although some wolves were killed in these battues, the hunts focused mainly on more prestigious game such as moose and brown bear.[29]

Battues were used not only in the royal hunts, but were recurrent events, especially in central and southern Sweden. Someone within *Jägeristaten* most often initiated the activities, even if the country people sometimes organised battues

---

27. Anonymous 1833, pp. 498–9.
28. Sigurd Lindman, 'Schönberg, Anders', in *Svenskt biografiskt lexikon*.
29. Anonymous 1832, p. 184 (continues in several volumes); brown bear: *Ursus arctos*.

The Wolf War in Sweden

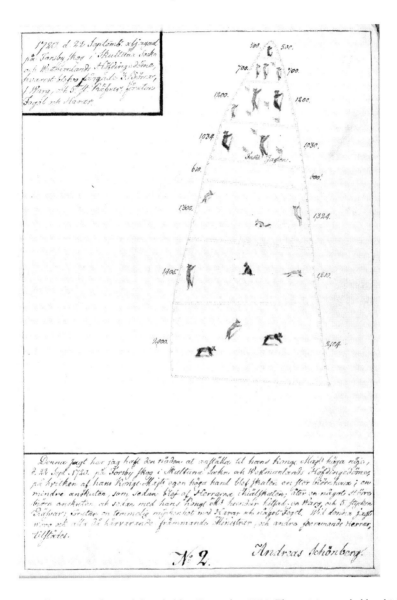

Figure 3. Illustration of a royal drive held in September 1720. The activity was led by chief forester Anders Schönberg, who also created the painting. Animals were driven towards the narrow end where gunners were standing. Flags were put out along the outer border. Three brown bears, one wolf, five foxes and a number of birds and hares were killed during this hunt (Robsahm 1813).

Roger Bergström, Karin Dirke and Kjell Danell

independently. The decision to carry out such an operation was often based on observations of wolves, wolf tracks or predated livestock in the area. Commonly at short notice, peasants and crofters were called to join the hunting party. People were ordered to gather at a specific time, bringing the right equipment – otherwise they would be punished. When all were gathered, a certain section of a forest was walked over according to patterns decided in advance. The people tried to drive the wolves towards armed men standing behind a shelter. To steer the wolves in the right direction, the search area was sometimes bordered with nets or flags, the latter being pieces of cloth painted with scary figures.

These battues were frequently criticised because the catch per unit effort was low and the participants thought they had more important things to do. An example from just after our study period shows that one battue with flags, involving 3,600 man days of work, in the county of Östergötland resulted in not a single wolf killed. However, several battues in the same county during the period of 1802–1822, gave on average one killed wolf per 286 man days of work.[30] A compilation of the number of battues, involving bait and managed hunting places, in the county of Stockholm (roughly 7,000 km^2 in size) during the period February 1821 to December 1828 shows that 35 battues were organised. A total of 154 wolves were killed (ranging from one to nine per battue), not counting fifty cubs, found in pregnant females.[31] As a measure of exterminating wolves, the success of the battues was thus variable. Nonetheless, they were useful as a way of controlling, and subordinating peasants. It was certainly a method of exercising power over people.

POISON – THE FINAL SOLUTION?

During the eighteenth century, the sciences of chemistry and pharmacy developed rapidly in Sweden. This led to an increased interest in poisoning wolves, mainly because the use of poisons could reduce the manpower needed in the wolf war.

Poisoning was based on the idea of wolves being greedy. In popular accounts as well as in zoological literature up into the twentieth century, the reckless gluttony and greed of the carnivores were emphasised. They were described as being hungrier and thirstier than other animals. One of the perceived objectionable behaviours of the large predators was their unbridled appetites. This notion often referred to their diet, but also implied a connection with sexuality. This was obvious in the association of the wolf or bear with masculinity but also manifests itself in the language used to describe the extermination of wolves. A striking example is the ambiguous use of the word *luder,* which in Swedish means a whore or trollop as well as an animal's corpse used as bait. This ambiguity illustrates the connection between food and sexuality. The luring of animals to the bait was based on the idea

30. Kugelberg 1998, p. 19.
31. Anonymous 1833, pp. 498–9.

of the moral recklessness of wolves and their inability to exercise self-control. This also made the killing of wolves a morally justified action. They were simply paying with their skin for their criminal behaviour. Yet, eighteenth century treatises on the poisoning of carnivores give evidence to the difficulties in luring wolves to the bait. The wolf was perceived as cunning, cowardly and suspicious. Complicated measures were required so as not to reveal the trap.[32]

In 1722, the Swedish government issued an official letter on how to best rid Stockholm of wolves. The letter stated that anyone who had a useless horse to spare must sell it to hunters at the official place of baiting, where it would be killed, skinned and put out as bait for wolves and other beasts. Animals that had died a natural death within the city had to be reported to the city executioner who would take them to the place where the bait was put. Special hunters had the duty of killing wolves at the lure and it was strictly forbidden for anyone else to kill wolves at the bait.[33] The above-mentioned Anders Schönberg probably invented the method described by the government.[34]

By the middle of the century, the use of poisoned bait as a method to kill wolves had become popular. One of the earliest letters on the method was a small pamphlet from 1728 by an unknown author, with the title *Information on how to, with small effort and expense, kill and exterminate wolves and other carnivores.* The text begins quite unsentimentally 'One strangles a dog, in which – when it has become cold – one sticks a hole with a knife …'[35] The use of poisoned bait was implemented in various ways – from just poisoning a single piece of bait and then waiting for a hungry wolf to show up, to combinations of bait with nets, flags and battues. Anders Schönberg was the person most engaged in the development of these methods, which were generally accepted and used, mainly in southern Sweden.

What types of poison were used? Berries from a native deciduous shrub, mezereon, *Daphne mezerum*, containing the poisons *daphnetoxin* and *mezerein*, were often mentioned and used. One strong proponent of this method was Berndt Wilhelm von Liewen (1685–1771), who was born in Estonia and enrolled in Karl XII's army at the age of fifteen. In 1759, von Liewen received his highest military rank, lieutenant general. He was a very skilful and caring agriculturalist.[36] Linnaeus visited von Liewen's estate in southernmost Sweden during his travel to Scania in 1749, and was impressed by his host. Linnaeus described von Liewen as an 'unparalleled genius'. According to Linnaeus, von Liewen claimed to be a master of wolf extermination. This assertion probably rested on his invention of the 'death

---

32. von Liewen 1753, p. 2.

33. Publication angående Wargar och andre Odiurs utdödande gifwen Stockholms Rådhus den 16 November 1722 unpaged, pp. 2–3.

34. Berch 1750, p. 43; Berch describes the method, dates it to 1722 and names Schönberg as its inventor.

35. Anonymous 1728, p. 1.

36. Gillingstam 1979, p. 753.

Roger Bergström, Karin Dirke and Kjell Danell

TIBAST, DAPHNE MEZEREUM L.

Figure 4. The berries from the deciduous shrub, mezereon, *Daphne mezereum*, were used to poison wolves (Lindmann 1922).

pill', a type of dough with berries from *D. mezerum*. The dough was surrounded by a thin coating, which would not break until the pill was in the wolf's guts, from where it could not be vomited. Many of these pills were to be distributed in the forests and a special scent was used to attract and lead the wolves to the poison. Any peasant who wanted to use this method on his land was required to pay 2 *daler silvermynt*, a sum today corresponding to about €25. Confident of the success of his method, von Liewen argued that this pill would solve the wolf plague in the whole country within a year.[37]

37.   Linnaeus 1977, pp. 398–9; von Liewen 1753.

The Wolf War in Sweden

During the eighteenth century, attempts to exterminate wolves also attracted pharmacologists. Frans Mikael von Aken (1698–1760) and his son Frans Joakim von Aken (1738–1798) were both involved in this work. Frans Mikael von Aken was a pharmacist, first in Germany, where he was born, and later in Sweden, where he bought a pharmacy. He subsequently extended his business and was appointed pharmacist at court. According to his son, Frans Mikael von Aken's book on how to best kill wolves was rewarded and approved by the estates of the parliament. It was distributed throughout the country by being sent to every church.[38] In the book one could read details on how to prepare and use *rävkakor* ('fox-cookies') to poison wolves and other unwanted beasts.[39] *Rävkakor* are the seeds of the deciduous strychnine tree *Strychnos nux-vomica*, native to India and East Asia. The active substance is the highly toxic alkaloid *strychnine*. Frans Mikael von Aken also mixed *arsenic* with *rävkakor*. Pharmacist von Aken was, however, not the first to recommend these methods. A short paper, probably written by Anders Schönberg, presented these ideas twenty years earlier.[40]

The younger von Aken was born in Sweden and educated in Uppsala and England. He was an all-round scientist with interests in, among other things, fireworks and means to extinguish fires. He continued his father's profession and published a couple of papers on the art of killing wolves.

Poisons for wolves were put in specially prepared sausages or alike, which were stuffed into dead animals. These in turn were laid in special places, 'bait places', which were – as we have seen – first recommended by Anders Schönberg in 1722.[41] An anonymous author, probably Schönberg as well, gave advice on 'how one with little effort and at low cost' can kill and exterminate wolves by using dead dogs prepared with arsenic. In 1714, one such bait animal apparently killed thirteen wolves, one lynx, two foxes and many ravens and hawks.[42]

In spite of this, the promises made by von Liewen and Frans Michael von Aken concerning the effects of large-scale extermination campaigns never came true. Frans Joakim von Aken was tasked with evaluating why this was the case. He defended the method and argued that it was the implementation that was faulty. A similar assurance that he could effectively rid the country of wolves was also given by a chief forester, Melchior Birckholtz. If each peasant paid an annual sum for three years, he promised to undertake the nation-wide eradication of pest animals.

38. von Aken 1793, p. 271; von Aken 1747.
39. von Aken 1754, pp. 1–4 (unpaginated).
40. Anonymous 1728.
41. Berch 1750, p. 45.
42. Anonymous 1728, pp. 1–2 (unpaginated); lynx = *Lynx lynx*, fox = *Vulpes vulpes*, raven = *Corvus corax*, hawk = probably mostly *Accipiter* spp.

Roger Bergström, Karin Dirke and Kjell Danell

The attempt was, however, a failure. Instead the 'beasts' increased in number, and the peasantry wanted their money back.[43]

CONSTANT IMPROVEMENTS

The use of poison was to some extent a disappointment and the method was abandoned for the most part. Those who had the required skills and could devote enough time, however, continued to use poison. There were nevertheless many old methods of extermination, which could be improved.

The grandest construction for trapping wolves was the enclosure trap built with a wooden fence at the periphery. The Swedish peasants had plenty of wood on their land and were experienced in building long stretches of wooden fences to keep cattle off arable land. The idea of this trap was to lure the wolves into an enclosure with bait or to drive the animals into it. Thereafter, the wolf or wolves were killed by armed men or caught in a pitfall trap. In 1750, Sweden's first professor of national economy, Anders Berch, argued that a wolf trap enclosure ought to be built in most parishes.[44]

The 'fence method' was particularly associated with the nobleman Johan Ludwig von Greiff (1757–1828). He was sent to Uppsala for studies at the age of twelve and was trained in subjects appropriate for a future military officer.[45] The nobleman subsequently reached the rank of captain and, in 1814, received the honourable title of colonel. Because of his 'astonishing properties as a hunter', he was also appointed forester at the court, but seems never to have worked as such.[46] Von Greiff worked for better game management and was a keen cynologist. At the beginning of the nineteenth century, he published small books about trapping wolves as well as hunting and trapping in Sweden.[47] He also argued in parliament for improving the methods of hunting in Sweden.

In his 1821 book, von Greiff described wolf enclosures in detail, in text and in two illustrations. The width of the enclosure was to be 360 metres. A cut-line was made and along this line an inward-leaning two and a half metre-high fence would be erected. The wolf could climb in but not out. A gate was constructed for transportation of bait, for example dead horses, into the enclosure. To escape its predicament, the wolf had to walk in a narrow 'tunnel' whence it fell into a three-metre-deep pit. In 1833, it was argued that von Greiff's technique was the most efficient way of killing wolves.[48]

---

43. Samzelius 1915, p. 177.
44. Berch 1750, p. 51.
45. Gillingstam 1967–1969.
46. Samzelius 1900, p. 96.
47. von Greiff 1804, pp. 23–32; von Greiff 1821, p. 35.
48. von Greiff 1821, p. 35; Anonymous 1833, p. 489.

PITFALL TRAPS

Pitfall traps are among the oldest methods for trapping and have been used for various Swedish game species. Extensive systems of pitfall traps were constructed for moose and wild reindeer, often in remote areas. A rough indication of the number of pitfall traps in Sweden is revealed by a search of a list of archaeological sites. There were altogether about 25,000 hits for 'pitfall traps' and about 1,800 if 'wolf' was included.[49]

Figure 5. A pitfall trap for wolves in southern Sweden. The pits sometimes had stone walls and were usually located close to villages (Photograph: Jan Falck).

Pitfall traps for wolves were preferably constructed close to villages. The pit was often dug three metres deep and wide and was lined with planks or stones. A supporting log was laid across the pit and thin rods and a layer of straw were used to conceal the opening. A duck or some other living bait was placed on top of this cover. Once a wolf had fallen into the pit, it would not be killed there. Instead, it would be hoisted up and killed some distance away from the pit.[50] Interestingly, when discussing the killing of wolves, euphemisms were often used. They were

---

49. Swedish National Heritage Board. www.raa.se (Accessed 8 Dec. 2013); search names in Swedish: pitfall trap = *fångstgrop* and wolf = *varg*.

50. Anonymous 1728, p. 40.

said to 'pay with their lives or their skins', they 'bit the grass' or 'were sent on their way as unwanted guests'. Notably, the vagueness of the descriptions of how to kill the captured wolf is in striking contrast to the elaborate and explicit descriptions of how to catch them.

Æskil Nordholm, who wrote a detailed thesis about hunting in the county of *Jämtland*, recommended the pitfall trap. He claimed that eight or nine wolves could be trapped in the same pit during a year. Nordholm and others argued that there should be two or three pitfall traps in every parish.[51] The success of this method seems to have varied considerably.

THE SWEDISH SYSTEM

One of the early Swedish dictionaries on forestry and hunting was written by Magnus Hendric Brummer (1735–1790). He was born into an aristocratic family, educated at university and enrolled in the army. After an injury, he got a position as chief forester. He reported on different methods of killing wolves and described what he thought was the best way. The idea was to go out and search for a den in April when the female wolf had just given birth. Fifty to sixty men should participate in this search, Brummer suggested. When a den was found, both the mother and the whole litter could be killed.[52] Others developed this method by suggesting that, if only the cubs were in or around the den, one cub could temporarily be spared and hung in a tree to scream. The mother or other adults in the pack would then be attracted to the den and could also be killed. In North America, this method was called the 'Swedish system'.[53]

INFORMATION TO CITIZENS

Because wolves can be highly mobile, the Swedish authorities considered it important to encourage wolf hunting in all parts of the country. In this way, the wolf war was also a propaganda war. The importance of killing wolves had to be conveyed to the people. Extermination would never be efficient if the wolves could merely escape to another region. Therefore, it became necessary to distribute information on how to kill wolves and the importance of doing so. This was not an easy task in a large and sparsely populated country like Sweden, with poor transport and communication.

New means of communication developed in Sweden during the seventeenth and eighteenth centuries in contrast to the older method of spreading news at markets and places where justice was administered.[54] The Swedish state in the

51. Nordholm 1953, p. 30.
52. Brummer 2010, p. 126.
53. Lönnberg 1934, p. 2.
54. Forssberg 2005, pp. 282–3 .

seventeenth century had an obvious advantage in relation to its population when it came to the power of information and its distribution. Active dissemination of information to all the populace on how best to kill wolves was a link in the campaign against large predators launched in eighteenth century Sweden. Almost everything written about the wolf war was therefore in Swedish and not in Latin, which would otherwise be the language of choice.

In a clerical law of 1686, it was stated that messages from the state should be announced from the church pulpit during the Sunday services, brought up at parish meetings or advertised outside the church.[55] This system was also used for issues related to the wolf war. As there was a duty for everyone to visit church on Sundays, the decrees were meant to reach all. During the second half of the eighteenth century, several texts on the matter of exterminating wolves were circulated in this way, as well as being published in newspapers.

In 1752, it was, for example, decided that a document, *The Knowledge of Killing Wolves*, should be read aloud in every church across the whole country. The document consisted of advice on how best to free the area of wolves.[56] The text was written by Berndt Wilhelm von Liewen. In his advice, von Liewen focused on the importance of understanding the wolf. The wolf was described as sly and cunning. The poisoning of wolves, as noted a preferred method of von Liewen, was recommended.

In domestic newspapers, skilful hunters were often mentioned and praised, in order to encourage people to hunt wolves. Statistics on the number of animals killed – both livestock and predators – were frequently published in newspapers. The statistics and the discussions on skilled hunters were meant to assert local wolf hunting as a matter of national interest (see Dirke, this volume).

THE CARROT AND STICK APPROACH

To attain the goal of exterminating wolves, there were a number of coercive measures, especially directed towards the peasantry. There was, as we have seen, an obligation to participate in battues, to keep nets and flags used for battues and to assist in the construction of pitfall traps and wolf enclosures. If anyone failed to fulfil these requirements, fines, jail sentences and flogging could be imposed. One could also be punished for disturbing behaviour during the hunt. There was, of course, opposition to many of these activities. Complaints from peasants were frequent in parliament and eventually resulted in battues being banned during farmers' busiest times in the summer. In 1756, the peasantry was fully freed from the time-consuming battues, if they worked together on the baiting method.[57]

55. Villstrand 2006, p. 51.
56. von Liewen 1753.
57. Eklundh 1930, p. 30.

Roger Bergström, Karin Dirke and Kjell Danell

Figure 6. At the beginning of the nineteenth century, wolves became accepted as a species belonging to the Swedish fauna. The pictures of wolves became more naturalistic from that time. Painting by Magnus Körner (Nilsson 1832–40).

The peasantry had several reasons for killing wolves, even without coercive measures. Apart from the obvious protection of livestock, there was a market for pelts, which were – at least periodically – profitable. Perhaps the most evident system of encouraging wolf extermination was the paying of bounties. Bounties were in general 'justified for direct and indirect economic, religious and ethical reasons'.[58] The bounty system started as a simple practice during the middle ages but became increasingly complicated. Rewards were paid by authorities, local municipalities, societies and even individual people. At a local level, the process of getting the bounty could be so troublesome and time-consuming that a hunter sometimes did not care to collect the monetary reward. Some counties in the north even argued that the skins of the killed predators were so valuable that bounties were not necessary.[59]

Bounties for wolves were regulated in the first coherent hunting law, of 1647.[60] Killing a wolf was awarded half the sum given for a brown bear. In comparison,

58. Pohja-Mykrä et al. 2005, pp. 284–91.
59. Hollgren 1909, p. 217.
60. Kongl. Maj:ts til Swerige, ordning och stadga huru alle rijkzens inbyggare sigh forhalla skole medh jachter, diurefang och fugleskiutande. 23 Martii 1647.

killing a pup was half the amount of an adult. These bounties remained the same from 1734 to 1808, the bounty for an adult wolf was half that of a bear and twice that of a wolverine. The hunter got a fifty per cent higher bounty for killing a lynx than for killing a wolf.[61] With time, some counties and parishes regarded the state-regulated bounties as being too low and allocated extra bounties.[62]

CONCLUSIONS

During the seventeenth and especially the eighteenth century, the monarchy and state authorities demonstrated a concerted effort to wage a wolf war. The struggle against wolves and other large carnivores came to resemble a military campaign. The wolf would be fought with all means and the goal was to exterminate or drive the 'alien' species from the country. The power of information was understood and the arguments for fighting wolves were similar to arguments for warfare. Controlling information was part of a strategy for building a nation and the idea of who belonged to it. The wolf was used in this plan to play the part of the proverbial 'other'.

An organisation, *Jägeristaten*, was formed; its leaders had backgrounds as noblemen and military officers. This organisation would not only oversee the use of forests and game, but also participate in the many wars Sweden was involved in before 1720.

The campaign fostered the development of new and improved methods and techniques to eliminate wolves. New poisons, with instructions for their use, were marketed and there was optimism about the possibility of eradicating the wolf. Nevertheless, several large-scale attempts failed. The battues developed into complex operations involving hundreds or even thousands of men. They represented not only a means of combatting wolves, but also a method for the authorities to exercise power and control.

In spite of all efforts to decrease or exterminate wolves, reports indicate that the wolf population increased from the early eighteenth century up to the beginning of the following century.

EPILOGUE

The objective of reducing the wolf population in Sweden, or preferably exterminating the species continued with almost unbroken strength into the twentieth century. The wolf war, however, no longer showed strong similarities to military campaigns.

In early nineteenth century, the collection began of data on the number of killed wolves, as well as the number of killed livestock and their value. The system was based on the payment of bounties and was reported in the county governors' report

61. Kongl. Maj:ts nådiga stadga angående jakt och diurfång 13 April 1808, 9; wolverine: *Gulo gulo*.
62. Hollgren 1909, p. 217.

Roger Bergström, Karin Dirke and Kjell Danell

from 1827 onwards. The money spent on bounties was compared with the losses through livestock predation, and the figures were often published in newspapers.

The animal rights and nature conservation movements which appeared in Sweden around 1900, had little effect to begin with on efforts to exterminate wolves. In 1965, the bounty on wolves was lifted and, some time thereafter, a new management system was launched, the aim being to obtain a sustainable wolf population.

Recent estimates claim that the Swedish wolf population at the beginning of the nineteenth century consisted of somewhere between 1,000 and 2,000 individuals.[63] Thereafter, there was a rapid population decline, most likely due to strong hunting pressure, intensified land use and weak populations of their main prey – moose, deer and roe deer.[64] The number of wolves at the end of the nineteenth century has been estimated at only a few hundred, and the population declined further until the species was functionally extinct around the 1970s. Since then, the Swedish wolf population has increased and has now reached about 350 individuals, of which some are shared with Norway.[65]

ACKNOWLEDGEMENT

We thank the Swedish Environmental Protection Agency for funding our projects on historical management of large predators.

BIBLIOGRAPHY

Aken, F.J. von. 1793. 'untitled'. *Ny Journal uti Hushållningen*. November och December: 271–5.

Aken, F.M. von. 1747. *Hus- och land-apotheque*. H. Arnold Moeller, Kongl. Gymnasii privil. (Skara: Boktryckare).

— 1754. *Tankar och rön, huru väl praeparerade Räfkakor och Wargpulfwer, som blifwit upfundne sedan år 1747, skola rätteligen brukas och nyttjas till små och stora Odiurs utdödande, å höga wederbörandes anmodan korteligen i ljuset framgifne, år 1754.*

Anderson, B. 1991. *Imagined Communities. Reflections on the Origin and Spread of Nationalism* (London, New York: Verso).

Anonymous. 1728. 'Underrättelse huru man med ringa möda och omkostnad kan döda och utdöda Wargar och andre Rof-diur'. *Stockholms-Calender*, 1729, (probably written by Anders Schönberg), unpaginated.

Anonymous. 1832. 'Andreas Schönberg och Konung Fredriks jagter'. *Svenska Jägareförbundets Tidskrift för Jägare och Naturforskare* 1 (5–6): 184–91 (contains i.a. Schönberg's own reports; continues in several volumes).

---

63. Aronson and Sand 2004, pp. 47–53.
64. Bergström and Danell 2011, p. 460.
65. www.viltskadecenter.se (Accessed 24 Dec. 2013).

Anonymous. 1833. 'Vargjakt'. *Svenska Jägareförbundets Tidskrift för Jägare och Naturforskare* **4/5**: 481–544.

Aronsson, Å. and H. Sand. 2004. 'Om vargens utveckling i Skandinavien under de senaste 30 åren', in G. Jansson, C. Seiler and H. Andrén (eds) *Skogsvilt III: vilt och landskap i förändring*. (Riddarhyttan: Grimsö Wildlife Research Station) pp. 47–53.

Berch, A. 1750. *Westmanlands Biörn- och Warg-Fänge* (Uppsala).

Bergström, R. and K. Danell. 2011. 'Game Management: A Period of Organization and Conservation', in H. Antonsson and U. Jansson (eds) *Agriculture and Forestry in Sweden since 1900*. The Royal Swedish Academy of Agriculture and Forestry, *Skogs- och Lantbrukshistoriska Meddelanden* **54**: 458–74.

Brummer, M.H. 2010 [1789]. *Försök til et Swenskt Skogs- och Jagt-Lexicon. Göteborg.* SOL-MED 49 (Stockholm: Kungl. Skogs- och Lantbruksakademien).

Eklundh, A. 1930. *Svensk Jakt. En överblick till hugfästande av Svenska Jägareförbundets etthundraåriga tillvaro* (Stockholm: Åhlén & Åkerlund).

Forssberg, A.M. 2005. *Att hålla folket på gott humör; Informationsspridning, krigspropaganda och mobilisering i Sverige 1655–1680* Ph.D. dissertation, Depatment of History, Stockholm University.

Fridell, S. and I. Svanberg. 2007. *Däggdjur i svensk folklig tradition* (Stockholm: Dialogos).

Gillingstam, H. 1967–1969. 'von Greiff'. *Svenskt Biografiskt Lexikon*, Vol. 17 (Stockholm) p. 256. http://sok.riksarkivet.se/sbl/artikel/13174.

— 1979. 'von Liewen'. *Svenskt Biografiskt Lexikon*, Vol. 22 (Stockholm) p. 753.

Greiff, J.L. von. 1804. 'Beskrifning på warg-gårdares anläggning och skötsel'. *Ny Journal uti Hushållningen* **23–32**.

— 1821. *Anteckningar angående Jagt och Diurfångst uti Swerige* (Stockholm).

Hildebrand, E. 1891. *Sveriges regeringsformer 1634–1809* (Stockholm: Norstedts).

Hollgren, C.A. 1909. 'Skottpremier'. *Svenska Jägareförbundets Tidskrift*: 215–24.

Holmbäck, Å. and E. Wessén. 1940–1979. *Svenska landskapslagar. Tolkade och förklarade för nutidens svenskar* (Stockholm: Hugo Gebers/AWE Gebers).

Kongl. Maj:ts til Swerige, ordning och stadga huru alle rijkzens inbyggare sigh forhalla skole medh jachter, diurefang och fugleskiutande. 23 Martii 1647 (1647) (Stockholm: Henrich Keyser).

Kongl. May.tz ordning och stadga, om jachter, diurefang och fogelskiutande. Giord och forbattrat pa rijkzdagen som holtz i Stockholm ahr 1664. 29 Augusti 1664 (Stockholm: Ignatio Meurer).

Kongl. Maj:ts nådiga stadga angående jakt och diurfång. 13 April 1808 (Stockholm: Kongl. Tryckeriet).

Kugelberg, V.. 1998. 'Det vildas förekomst och avjagning', in Östergötlands Jaktvårdsförbund (ed.) *Om villebråd och jakt i Östergötland under gångna tider*, pp. 13–46.

Liewen, B.W. von. 1753. *Wetenskap at döda Wargar. Kan ock dödas andra Rofdjur och Rof-foglar* (Stockholm).

Lindman, S. 1949. 'Schönberg, Anders'. *Svenskt Biografiskt Lexikon* (Stockholm).

Lindman, C.A.M. 1922. *Bilder ur Nordens flora* (Stockholm: Wahlström & Widstrand).

Linnaeus, C. 1977 [1749]. *Carl Linnaeus Skånska resa 1749* (Stockholm: Wahlström & Widstrand).

Lönnaeus, A. 2011. *Tjugo års vandranden i skogarna här. Den halländska jägeristaten vid Faurås häradsrätt 1761–1805*. Master's thesis, Department of History, Lund University (Lund).

Lönnberg, E. 1934. *Bidrag till vargens historia i Sverige*. Kungliga Svenska Vetenskapsakademiens Skrifter i Naturskyddsärenden No. 26.

Nilsson, S. 1832–1840. *Illuminerade figurer till Skandinaviens fauna*. (Lund: Academieboktryckeriet, C.F. Berling).

— 1847. *Skandinavisk fauna. Däggdjuren* (Lund: Gleerup).

Nordholm, Æ. 1953 [1749]. *Jämtelands djur-fänge* (Uppsala).

Nyrén, U. 2008. *Jägeristaten – militär institution i civil förklädnad.* http://www.hist.lu.se

— 2012. *Rätt till jakt. En studie av den svenska jakträtten ca 1600–1789*. Ph.D. Dissertation at Department of Historical Studies, University of Gothenburg (Gothenburg).

Orrelius, M. 1750. *Historia animalium eller Beskrifning öfwer diurriket* (Stockholm).

Östergren, P.A. 1896. *Tvisten om ägande- och nyttjanderätten till skattejord vid pröfningen af Lagkommissionens förslag till Sveriges Rikes Lag hos 1731 och 1734 års ständer* (Lund).

Pohja-Mykrä, M., T. Vuorisalo and S. Mykrä. 2005. 'Hunting Bounties as a Key Measure of Historical Wildlife Management and Game Conservation: Finnish Bounty Schemes 1647–1975'. *Oryx* **39** (3): 284–91.

Publication angående Wargar och andre Odiurs utdödande gifwen Stockholms Rådhus den 16 November 1722 (1722) (Stockholm).

Ridderskapets och Adelns protokoll 1645–1649. Vol. 4, appendix c 'Kongl: Maij:tz proposition'.

Ridderskapets och Adelns protokoll 1645–1649, Vol. 4, report of the proceedings, 8 February 1647.

Robsahm, C.M. 1813. *Copior af TjuguFyra JagtRitningar Med Derå Antecknade Berättelser.* Uppsala University Library, Westinska handskriftssamlingen No. 42.

Samzelius, H. 1900. 'J.L.B. von Greiff. Porträtt jämte biografi', in *Jägaren – Nordisk Årsbok för jakt- och naturvänner* (Stockholm).

— 1915. *Jägeristaten. Anteckningar om svenska väldets skogs- och jaktväsen* (Stockholm).

Villstrand, N.E. 2006. 'Nyheter från predikstolen', in J. Christensson (ed.) *Frihetstiden* (Lund: Signum) pp. 51–67.

— 4 —

The Story of a Man-Eating Beast in Dauphiné, France
(1746–1756)

Julien Alleau and John D.C. Linnell

1. INTRODUCTION

There can be few species on Earth that have a more complicated relationship with humans than the wolf. Admired, feared, loved and hated, the wolf exposes the entire human repertoire of emotions. The way that people react towards wolves is not a question of purely academic or poetic interest. The recent recovery of wolf populations across Europe, including their return to parts of the continent like the Alps from which they have been absent for more than a century, is currently triggering very heated debates between different stakeholder groups.[1] These debates focus on a diversity of conflicts that range from economic concerns over wolf depredation on livestock to more symbolic issues related to wider, and deeper, conflicts between rurality and urban life, between modernity and traditionalism.[2] However, one repeated component of modern wolf debates is the issue of fear for human safety. Debates variously cite myths such as 'Little Red Riding Hood' and a random collection of historical references that have greater or lesser support. Because contemporary accounts are rare,[3] a considerable part of the present wolf debate is actually a debate over historical knowledge with various factions trying to use 'facts' to give legitimacy to their position on wolf conservation. Until the last few decades there had been little systematic historical research into wolf–human relationships. This has changed dramatically in recent years, and there is now a far better material to use when exploring the historical relationships between wolves and people. The goal of this chapter is to summarise some of the latest results from systematic historical investigations in south-eastern France where the extensive public records have allowed the development of a very detailed insight into the changing nature of the way that wolves and humans have interacted over the course of four centuries.

1. Lopez 1978, Kaczensky et al. 2013, Skogen et al. 2006.
2. Skogen et al. 2006; Lescureux and Linnell 2010.
3. Rajpurohit 1999.

Julien Alleau and John D.C. Linnell

Figure 1. Location map. South-eastern France.
Data: IGN, Communes database and Carthage database; Earth Explorer, Digital Elevation database.

2. DATA

When considering a topic as controversial as wolf attacks on humans it is important to place considerable focus on the reliability of the data. Many studies of historical human demography in Europe and North America have utilised parish registers as a source of data, especially after the methodology developed by Fleury and Henry (1956) and the first applied research led by Goubert (1960). Orthodox, Protestant (Anglican church records seem to be the most commonly studied) and Catholic registers have been studied, mainly in rural areas, avoiding crowded places where studies are hard to conduct.[4] Issues like demographic trends, marriage mobility and the social and economic dynamics of families have been analysed in various studies. In France, both Protestant and Catholics registers exist. One of the main advantages of these types of archive is their availability. Every parish was required to have a register of baptisms, marriages, and burials. Thus, the available documentation in France concerns more than 36,000 churches, although there is variation in the completeness of the records between parishes and periods, dependent on the individual qualities of the priests and administrators.

Back to the Archives: State Politics and the Development of Law

In the Alps, burial registration rarely occured before the seventeenth century. Even if the Ordinance of Villers-Cotterêts (1539) and the Ordinance of Blois (May 1579) required priests to record baptisms and burials, the level of recording was low in practice. With the official ritual works 'Roman ritual' (published by Pope Paul V in 1614) and the *Code Louis* (Ordinance of Saint-Germain-en-Laye, April 1667), priests are obliged to record burials and to write two separate registers (one on official stamped paper to document legal authenticity). Later this the practice spread, and was reinforced by guidelines with the Declaration of the King on 9 April 1736 (Articles X–XIII). This last step is the first official text solely dedicated to birth, marriage and death registers.[5]

Because of the constant development of the system, we must recognise the limits of the data source. Firstly, the older the period, the less numerous the registers. According to Pierre Goubert's research in the Beauvaisis, the complete recording of burials only started between the two ordinances of 1667 and 1736 in the parishes of the Alps. The two separate records offer a guarantee to avoid loss due to fire, humidity, theft etc. The possibility of sanctions for priests who did not keep records forced the last recalcitrants to comply. Thus it is only after 1738 that almost all the documentation is available. A survey of 69 parishes of the Bas-Dauphiné demonstrates that between 1630 and 1640, only thirteen per cent of the documentation is available. This rate is around 52 per cent in the period 1670–1675, 77 per cent

---

4. Avdeev et al. 2004.
5. Goubert 1976; Cabourdin and Dupâquier 1988, p. 12; Moriceau 2007; Alleau 2011.

in 1691–1697, eighty per cent in 1708–1713, 94 per cent in 1737–1741 and a hundred per cent in 1746–1756.[6] The appearance of widespread documentation occurs in the same period as the *Révocation de l'Édit de Nantes* of October 1685, which erases all the rights of Protestants inside the kingdom of France. Thus, even if a few Protestants are excluded from the Catholic parish registers, a huge majority of the parishioners are registered in these archives.

Secondly, the framework of the law required that precise information be given. This impacts on the quality of the records and the critical work of analysing them. Before the two main ordinances, burials records are freely written. Therefore, although Catholic registers from the Early Modern Era can be very descriptive, the information depends on the whims of the writers. With time, quality was improved, driven by both legal power and spiritual authority. The registration of births and marriages became an important source of information to control respect of religious laws by parishioners (no marriage was permitted if the couple were linked at the seventh degree of heredity; children born outside marriage were stigmatised, etc.). The rule of registration was also enforced by the central powers, as priests were also state agents and their mission to record every birth, marriage and death was important to help maintain public administration procedures.

Registration of the Dead

Gaining insight into the procedures surround the registration of causes of death is central to our study of the extent of wolf attacks. There are two levels of information inside these parish registers. The first one establishes the civil identity of every subject: name, identity of parents, godfather and godmother, date, identify of husband or wife. For burials, the main information concerns the identity of the dead man, the date of death and the name of witnesses.

In the case of an undetermined cause of death, another procedure guided by the justice administration was used (mainly collected in the B series of the Archives départementales, but also in the G and H series).[7] An examination of the body was made through the '*levée du cadavre*', an old practice already used at the beginning of the sixteenth century.[8] These procedures were led by the local justice every time a murder or a rebellion against temporal or spiritual authorities was suspected ('*crime de lèse-majesté divine ou humaine*'). These cases concerned duels, suicide and rebellion against the authorities.[9]

Once a body was discovered, the judge was informed and had to attend the crime scene with the clerk, sometimes a sergeant or a bailiff, and, during the late

---

6. Alleau 2005, p. 26.
7. A series is a group of archives which groups archives on related themes.
8. Porret 2010.
9 Criminal Ordinance of Saint-Germain-en-Laye, August 1670, Title XXII.

Early Modern Era, as the science of medicine arose, he could also require a surgeon to attend as an expert.[10] Firstly, the direct environment in which the body had been found was described and then goods and clothes were mentioned. A description of the body was made and could be followed by an autopsy in order to reveal the cause of death. The dead body could only be buried once the full procedure was complete and the judge had given his agreement. Furthermore, the final verdict was supposed to be mentioned in the burial register.[11]

The second level of information concerns respect for religious laws. In this procedure, an important aspect concerns signs of catholicity. Rosaries or other religious objects were the keys to determining the faith of an unknown person accidentally dead. If this condition was not fulfilled it was forbidden to be buried in Christian ground.[12] Unknown persons without signs of catholicity or people who had taken their own lives were supposed to be buried outside Catholic burial grounds.

Accidental deaths allowed the priest to bury the deceased. But because of the formal procedures associated with the registers, he was supposed to state the cause of death.[13] Therefore, both temporal and spiritual authority gave the opportunity, and provided strong motivation, for the priest to write some descriptions and details of events.

Death Records and Comments

In addition to respecting the rules, priests often felt the need to describe the circumstances surrounding the death in cases where last rites were not given, for example following a violent or sudden death. Thus, priests justify their actions in dealing with accidental deaths. For example, in Revonnas (department of Ain), in 1709, a young boy named Noël Carbon had been eaten by 'a wolf' but, surprisingly, his death was not included in the parish register. His name only appears at the end of the yearly register, where the priests wrote a summary of the year's events, in between the weather reporting indices and the harvest evaluation. To end his description of a difficult year, he reveals the story of the wolf attack. Around noon the young child was taken by 'the wolf' and eaten in a stone quarry. The priest mentions that a part of the child's intestines were all that remained to bury:

> The wolf took, at noon, in Senissiac, forty steps from the little road going to Rignat, in the main road, place called en la Musine, a child called Noël Carbon, son of Joseph, his father, from Sinissiat, and aged 6 years, and eaten in the depression of

---

10. Alleau 2010, 2011; Porret 2010; Bayard 1989.
11. Déclaration du Roi Louis XV du 9 avril 1736, Article 12.
12. Bayard 1989.
13. Moriceau 2007.

the first perrière,[14] side of the wind and at night. We buried his intestines inside the cemetery.[15]

Thus, persons attacked, taken and moved are not always registered, even if a witness testifies. These kind of external comments at the end of the year register are rare but give precious local information. Among other details, weather phenomena of the year, cereal and wine price trends, the quality of the harvest, food problems, diseases, military movements and parish events are explained. Some priests were exceptionally likely to record information in this way, especially in Bas-Dauphiné, in the parishes of Pact, Saint-Barthélémy-de-Beaurepaire, Revel-Tourdan or Primarette, for instance.

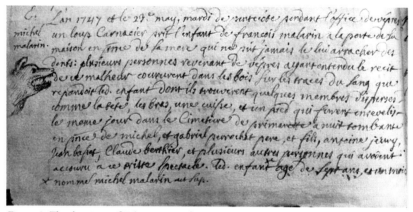

Figure 2. The drawings of Fabre, priest of Primarette (Arch. Dép. Isère 5Mi129 and 130).

The Revonnas example is important. It reveals that not all priests systematically recorded deaths that did not respect Catholic last rites. In this case, the historian is lucky to find the chronicle at the end of the register, and the rarity of such accounts indicates that such deaths may be under-recorded in the archives. The fact that this case was recorded at all is probably linked to the catastrophic year of 1709, a particular context driving the writing. Indeed, during catastrophic periods, the holy text guided priests in their interpretation. Thus, a certain vision of the apocalypse appears. The priest of Revonnas used a metaphoric perspective for his narrative text. He explains the bad harvest and the deaths through the action of divine justice against the lack of faith of his parishioners ('impenitent

---

14 Perrière could be translated as a stone quarry.

15 Arch. dép. Ain, parish of Revonnas, parish register digitised and available on the internet. Original text: 'Le loup a pris, sur l'heure de midy, à Senissiac, à quarante pas de la petite chemine en allant à Rignat sur le grand chemin, lieu-dit en la Musine, un enfant appellé Noël Carbon, fils de Joseph, son père, de Sinissiat, et âgé de six ans et le mange dans le creux de la première perrière du côté de vent et soir. On a enterré une partie de ses boyaux dans le cimetière.'

sinners'). In that sense, the wolf is 'the beast' and only 'Holy benediction' can save the parish from starvation.

The double record of the notices contributes to a better transmission of data, but it also provided flexibility in the way of writing. Thus, two approaches can be used in the parish registers. The first had to respect the wishes of the external administration. The second one, maintained inside the parish, could be more personal. When possible we consulted both sources of information.

The Wolf: A Special Case in Administration Archives and an Ideal Object for Storytelling

Information related to the human–wolf relationship can be found through the parish registers and the '*levées de cadavre*' procedures. These administrative records are not the only ones covering wolf attacks. Once the attack had been taken into account through the local administrative procedure, information often spread out, especially in the cases of periods with multiple attacks. Thus, communities could request the help of central administration in conducting a *battue* hunt or for economic support for the victims' families. Among others, reports were sometimes written to inform about the situation. In cases of rabies, the province offered special bounties to hunters, but could also dispatch a doctor for treatments, which appear in the ledgers. The registers of hospitals, letters from one administration to another, gazettes, journals, pictures, local literature and private notices are just some of the diverse historical documentation about wolves and their relationship with humans.

Since the book *The Wolves of North America*,[16] many works have been published about wolf attacks all over the world. These studies have been mainly based on historical sources. Thus, several types of archives have been used to collect data. In Western Europe, burial registers have formed the basis of several analyses.[17]

In France, a collective work directed by J.-M. Moriceau led to the creation of a national statistical database. The data relating to south-eastern France were collected during the first author's Ph.D. studies. Since 2014, archive quotes and references related to wolf attacks on humans have been integrated into a database available on a website.[18] Thus, all the archives mentioned in this paper are available there.

A cross-referencing of all documentation is necessary to underline the specificity of the historical human–wolf relationship. Using both quantitative and qualitative methods we will now go back to the eighteenth century and construct a narrative surrounding the specific situation in Dauphiné, in order to explore the human–wolf relationship in the Early Modern Era.

---

16. Young and Goldman 1944.
17. Beaufort 1987; Cagnolaro et al. 1992; etc.
18. www.unicaen.fr/homme_et_loup.

3. A MAN-EATING BEAST IN BAS-DAUPHINÉ (1746–1756)

57 People were Eaten

After the winter of 1709 and the resulting great famine, the presence of several 'beasts'[19] was recorded. Attacks on humans occurred sporadically in the neighborhood of Valence, in 1717, and in the small towns settled around the forest of Bonnevaux in the 1730s. On 31 March 1746, a four-year-old boy called Michel Morel was found 'pulled to pieces by a carnivorous wolf' (*mis en pièce par un loup carnassier*). This burial, registered by the priest of Semons, is the first in a long and substantial episode of attacks on humans in Bas-Dauphiné. Ten days later, Isabeau Courdier, a ten year-old girl from Bossieu was 'devoured by wolves in the woods' (*dévorée par des loups dans les bois*). The year remains quiet after this episode. But on 17 May 1747, attacks resume in the parish of Buis. This case looks like a major event. The behaviour of the beast had changed. Attacks continued, occurring, for example, on 23 May in Primarette, 1 June in Arzay and 6 June in Primarette. A total of nine victims can be found in the Archives for the year 1747 and seven in 1748. With an average of one victim per year from 1749 to 1752, the cycle of predation is less active. From 1746 to 1752, the area in question covers about 200 to 300 km^2 around the Bonnevaux forest, where several parish borders meet.

On 19 March 1752, the last victim of the first period is registered in Primarette. From this day to 30 April 1753, everything was quiet. But suddenly attacks resume. Benoitte Roussilon, an eight-year-old girl was killed in the parish of Saint-Just-Chaleyssin. Before the priest buried her body, a *levee de cadavre* was conducted. The investigation revealed that she was eaten and concluded that 'the enquirer and the witnesses all said that it was a wolf which devoured this child with more certitude that near the body, he saw foot marks of wolf printed in the ground'.[20] The rest of the year was peaceful but, from January 1754, a new episode starts ten kilometres to the north, in the northern part of the Terres Froides. The pattern of attacks is a bit different, with attacks occurring regularly. Fifteen victims in 1754, eight in 1755 and ten in 1756 can be found in the Archives.

Although the size of the area influenced is similar to the previous episode, the centre of gravity changes suddenly and attacks go from one area to another. Victims are located in small areas and a short time-frame of only a few years. The example of Dauphiné is not unique. On the contrary, similar situations have been recorded throughout French history. A simple overview of the whole kingdom in the same decades supports this idea. In the period 1742–1755, the beasts of Touraine and Vendômois revealed a similar pattern, as well as the famous Beast of Gevaudan between 1764 and 1767 or the beasts of Beaujolais and Lyonnais between 1754

---

19. 'Beast' is the term frequently used to describe wolves that killed people.
20. Arch. dép. Isère, 16 B supp, non-classified archives, Justice of Saint-Just.

and 1756.[21] Outside France, several historical studies relate a similar pattern. Thus, in Estonia, in the northern part of Tartumaa county, 45 victims were recorded in 1809–1810 in an area of about 35–40 km in diameter.[22] Moreover, checking the French database, most of the attacks on humans are very concentrated in space and time. The timing of these attacks and their geographic distribution are good indications to determine their motivation. If the archives are the only evidence, a clear pattern appears: cases are found all over a defined area during a period of a few years. In fact most records of wolf attacks in the database can be linked to these clusters associated with beasts. Single and isolated attacks are rare.

From the Wolf to the Beast

The burial records written by priests give different names for the aggressor. The 'wolf' is mentioned in twenty cases. The three other quotes use the name 'beast', associated with an adjective: carnivorous, ferocious or wild. In the construction of the sentences, the associated verbs evoke the lexical field of the devourer (64 per cent – the wolf eats, devours, etc.) as well as the lexical fields of movement (24 per cent). In this case, the wolf 'has taken' or 'snatched' (*pris, emporté, enlevé*). Checking the information in parish registers, other names appear. The priest of Primarette regularly wrote summaries of the remarkable events every year. At the end of the page, he mentions the 'loups cerviers' (literally 'deer-wolf'):

> Carnivorous wolves have devoured three children in Primarette. We think they are certainly deer-wolves; and the rabble maintains that they are werewolves authorised by the priests to give their prey to the glass factories.[23] Nothing can erase this stupidity.[24]

This example demonstrates the distance between men of letters and the local population. Firstly, the priest talks about a 'deer-wolf', a wolf that is not literally a common wolf. This name is related to a category mentioned in books of the sixteenth to seventeenth century. The dictionaries of *Trévoux* and *Furetière* distinguish three types of wolves: the *lupus molossus* ('mâtin'), the *lupus vertagus* (sighthound) and the *lupus cervarius*. The two first categories are behaviourally and bodily different. While the *molossus* eats carrion and is shaped like a 'mâtin' dog, the *vertagus* is shaped like a sighthound and is used to hunt big game species, and lives in forests.

---

21. Alleau 2011; Moriceau 2007.
22. Rootsi 2001.
23. The glass factory appears in Dauphiné in the 14th century. The places of production are located in the forests because of nearby firewood. Moyroud 2002, p. 126. The belief was that human fat was being used in the glass production process.
24. 'Les loups carnassiers ont dévoré trois enfants dans Primarette. On croit plus probablement que c'étaient des loups cerviers, et le vulgaire soutient que ce sont des loups garous à qui les curés donnent permission de faire semblable chasse pour fournir aux verreries. Rien n'est capable de leur tuer cette sotte crédulité.'

Julien Alleau and John D.C. Linnell

The identity of *cervarius* was a real problem for natural history during the Early Modern Era. Until the eighteenth century and the report of an autopsy published by Peraut in the *Mémoire de l'Académie royale des Sciences*, its identity was unclear.[25] It was described by the ancients as a mythic animal whose urine was able to turn itself to precious stone called *Lapis lyncurius* and whose vision was so penetrating that it was able to see through opaque elements. In the middle of the eighteenth century, the Eurasian lynx (*Lynx lynx*) was only present in the Pyrenees and the Alps.[26] In these areas, the *loup cervier* used to be the name of the lynx and was well known and hunted as a pest with a bounty system. Anywhere else, when a *loup cervier* is mentioned, it refers to the wolf able to catch a red deer or a wolf smarter and greedier than the common indigenous wolf.

The priests adopted two strategies to explain away circumstances that were difficult to explain and outside their normal experience. On one hand, the priest tries to refer to a beast which seems to have specific aptitudes. On the other hands, the parishioners directly accuse Fabre, the priest, of allowing the werewolves to provide human fat to glass factories. Are these werewolves humans transformed into wolves? Are these werewolves identified as wolves that everyone should avoid? In French, the werewolf is the *loup-garou*, which literally means the wolf anyone should keep away from. The werewolf can also be identified as a human transformed into a wolf. Beyond these semantic problems, the werewolf has to be observed as an argument of contestation.[27] The glass factories are located in forests. Firstly, their presence restricted rights of use by the inhabitants. Secondly, the glass factory owners were nobles.[28] Thirdly, these factories were located in the areas where wolves dwelt. The combination of these factors led wolves and werewolves becoming interwoven into the wider struggle between the wealthy and the poor that was symbolised by these factories

During the second period (1753–1756), the identity of the predator was portrayed in a different manner. While the wolf was mainly accused by name in the period 1746–1752, the priests mention carnivorous beasts, ferocious beasts, wild beasts in 71 per cent of the cases. The wolf is only mentioned five times, the *lupus cervarius* twice and the werewolf only once.[29] Facing a behaviour that nobody understands, the perpetrator cannot be understood as a normal predator.

Beyond the mythic images, it seems certain that some form of Canid was seen to be the perpetrator. This leads to the question of the identity of these Canids. Were they wolves, or dogs, or hybrids? Unfortunately history cannot answer these taxonomic questions with certainty. These Canids were recorded as eating their

25. *Mémoire de l'Académie Royale des Sciences*, 1733, tome 3, pp. 127–35.
26. Buffon, 1761, t. IX, pp. 231-259.
27. Abry and Joisten 2002.
28. Moyroud 2002.
29. Arch. Dép. Rhône, registre paroissial de Communay, 18 juillet 1756.

victims rather than simply biting, which would have been normal in the case of rabid animals. Rabies had been known since the Greco-Roman period at least.[30] In the early modern era, symptoms seem to be well known by most people, even if the disease mechanism was still unknown. A lot of explicit references to rabies attacks are made in the archives but the presence or absence of this term in the archives alone cannot be used to distinguish between rabid and man-eating attacks. The behaviour of the animal suffering this viral infection is more relevant. Once the clinical phase happens, Canids can develop the furious type of the disease. This period is quite short: from two to five days, rarely more. During the peak of hyper-excitability, the animal can bite several times and range widely in the countryside. Victims are numerous. Some die directly from wounds sustained during the attack, even though the animal cannot eat since its throat is paralysed. Some other victims die days or weeks after, because of the disease. This type of attack is quite easy to identify, as victims are numerous in a short time period within an area related to the movement of the rabid animal. The chronological pattern of the 1746–1756 attacks as well as their geographic distribution argues against rabies as an explanation of the deaths registered here.

Little Red Riding Hood was a Young Shepherd

The archival record permits an analysis of the characteristics of the victims and the circumstances of the attacks. Firstly, there was no obvious gender selection of victims. They were equally males and females: eleven boys and twelve girls were killed during the period 1746–1752 and eighteen males and fifteen females during the period 1753–1756. Comparatively, the relationship between male and female victims in the overall French database is about 57 per cent females and 43 per cent males. Similar observations have been made about the Hazaribagh area, in India.[31]

The average ages were different between periods. The median age of victims was about six years old from 1746 to 1752 and ten from 1753 to 1756. While only children were attacked during the first period, two adults were buried during the second (two boys about eighteen and nineteen years old and one woman about 45 years old). Once again, the fact that children are mainly concerned is relatively similar to other observations.[32] But the difference between our two periods probably hides something interesting. Children aged about one to thirteen years old were attacked in the first period, without real distinction, but about eighty per cent of the victims of the second period were between six and twelve years old. Several explanations can be mentioned. Firstly, in the area of the first period, infants were attacked as much as other categories. In the second area, infants were not attacked

30. Theodoridès 1986.
31. Rajpurohit 1999.
32. Linnell 2002; Moriceau 2007.

Julien Alleau and John D.C. Linnell

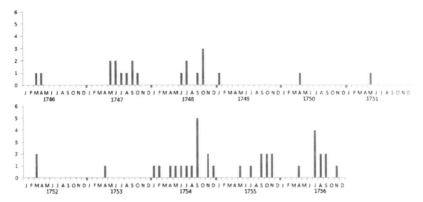

Figure 3. Chronology of attacks in the study area (1746–1756).

Table 1. Age of the victims

	1746–1752		1753–1756	
	m	f	m	F
1 y/o	1	1	1	0
2 y/o	0	2	1	0
3 y/o			0	1
4 y/o	1	1		
5 y/o	3	0		
6 y/o	0	1	1	3
7 y/o	1	2	3	0
8 y/o			5	2
9 y/o			3	2
10 y/o	0	1	0	3
11 y/o	1	0	0	2
12 y/o	2	1	1	1
13 y/o	1	1		
14 y/o			1	0
15 y/o				
16 y/o				
17 y/o				
18 y/o			1	0
18 y/o and more			1	1
'Children'	1	2		
TOTAL	11	12	18	15

which tends to attest to better protection of them. Secondly, the victims were older in the second area, which could be related to local differences in practices or adaptations of the practices to the dangerous context, with a better protection of the youngest. It could also be related to the behavioural evolution of the predator, progressively losing its fear of humans and trying to get older prey. To dig deeper, the landscape factor has to be considered (see also part 4 for more details).

In both periods, the priests gave little information about the jobs of the children. The few quotes indicate that shepherds seem to be highly represented. In Arzay, the son of Etienne Marmonier was taken and devoured by 'a wolf in the common wood'. In these areas of dispersed settlement, where every household had livestock, children from six to fourteen years of age took care of the cattle and the sheep. They were particularly vulnerable. Moreover crop fields occupied a huge place in the two areas. In this aspect, the landscape is divided in two with one category of parishes where the crop fields averaged about 75 per cent of the area, leaving just a few small and dispersed patches of heath and forest; and the other category containing a more even mix of crop fields and forest (average about 45 per cent for both). The forests were used for livestock grazing. Going there, shepherds came closer to the wolf and put themselves in a more dangerous situation than in the open fields.

Surprisingly, some attacks took place near houses. There, the surveillance of children by parents was probably lower. Thus, the child of François Malarin was taken by a carnivorous wolf 'at the door of his house' during the vespers.

Regarding the seasonality of the attacks, summer and autumn are particularly represented. The second period seems to have a less clear pattern, with a more equal distribution of attacks over the calendar. The movements of livestock and their shepherds are logically linked to vegetation growth in crop fields where grazing is only allowed once the harvest has been gathered. During other periods, livestock move from meadows to forests, raising the probability of contact with wolves.

4. SEARCHING FOR THE BEAST, KILLING THE WOLF

All Against the Wolf? The Battue Hunt of 1754

Once the first episode of attacks ended, the administration worried about the revival of the beast up in the north of the district. Facing the situation, with at least five new victims attacked and buried since the end of 1753, the lieutenant general[33] received a letter from the president of the Audit Office (Cours des Comptes) on 29 July 1754: 'in two years, they (the wolves) have devoured ten to twelve shepherds

---

33. From the upper aristocracy, the lieutenant general supported the governor who represented the king in a province. Maintaining order in the province was among his prerogatives.

and during the last month, they devoured again a woman and a young child'. The goal is clear. The president demands a battue hunt.

On 10 September 1754, about 2,000 people from 26 parishes were placed under the control of the army. The official hour to start the battue was 4 a.m.; however, by 8 o'clock, the troops were still not in position. The trackers did not keep their lines in the forest. Sixteen wolves crossed the lines, at least, but only one young she-wolf was killed. In the evening the men left, although they were supposed to camp in the forest. The next day, nothing changed. The battue was a failure.[34]

Grouping people for a battue is not an easy task. The efficiency of this method mainly depends on the landscape structures. In fact, few examples of battues can be found in the archives of Dauphiné. More important are the royal authorisations of battues. In Dauphiné and Provence, as elsewhere in the Kingdom of France, Henri IV had recognised the rise of the wolf population and the associated depredations. His political position was first to give a lot of authorisations for battues in 1599, but in 1600 his general edict gave the lords the right to group people to 'hunt in-side their lands, woods and heaths with dogs, guns and other weapons' four times a year and more if necessary.[35]

The battue ordinances we can find seem to be closely related to the increase in attacks on livestock or humans. Thus, a battue was organised in La Drosse (Isère) in 1697 and another in Beaurepaire (Isère) in 1710, while attacks on humans were ongoing. The particularity of the battue of 1754 is its importance. Only a few examples like this one can be observed in French history. This episode prefigures the battues for the Beast of Gevaudan a decade later. As the 1754 example testifies, battues of the Early Modern Era were often inefficient.

Such Uncommon Methods

Few effective responses emerged to fight the wolf in the Dauphiné. The forestry and water commission administrations didn't appear especially active on this topic. It seems that the intendants[36] and governors were more involved in crisis situations. Moreover, another corps of professional wolf-hunters arose: the *louveterie*. The exist-ence of several administrations with similar prerogatives was a source of conflict.

The French law of the time stipulated that the foresters had the right to hunt wolves in their district as well as the wolf-hunters. This situation created an overlap, which often led to administrative conflict between these two corps in many parts of the kingdom.[37] Once again, the situation was different in Dauphiné. While the institution had been created during the reign of Charlemagne, in 812, under the

---

34. Marcieu 1924.
35. Moriceau 2007.
36. The intendants occupied a central position in the administration. They had powers of justice and police. They were central in economic and tax systems.
37. Moriceau 2011, p. 292–3.

name of *luparii*, few wolf-hunters were active in the south-east of France. In the list of wolf-hunters from 1768, only one name is mentioned in Dauphiné. Indeed, on 5 October 1751, Jean Ferrier was the designated *louvetier* in the District of Vienne. Bourgeois rather than noble, this choice was probably made in the context of conflict between social groups. His name is not often mentioned in the archives and he doesn't seem to have taken part in the battue of 1754, even though he kept his status until the end of the 1770s at least. Overall, the administration was not particularly active in wolf control in Dauphiné. In the south-eastern part of the kingdom, the individual hunt was the most important control method.

Individual Rather than Collective Actions?

In the Alps, wolf hunting had been stimulated by bounties since the Middle Ages. The communities of Provence as well as of Dauphiné had their own bounty systems. In Lorgues (Var), archives can be found for the beginning of the seventeenth century. In the communities of Oisans (Isère), bounties were given for wolves and lynx at least from the sixteenth century. A similar situation can be observed in the Briançonnais (Hautes-Alpes). The proximity to Italy is probably important in this context. The communities of Northern Italy had established bounty systems from the end of the Middle Ages.[38] While the practices cannot be followed in detail from century to century, it seems that Dauphiné kept some of the benefits of its independent status before annexation to the kingdom in the fourteenth century. From the sixteenth to the eighteenth centuries, bounties were used for limited areas in France. In Provence, a *Pays d'État*,[39] the *Vigueries* (sub districts) decided to create a special bounty system whose practical application concerned the whole province. In 1632, in the city of Brignoles (Var), the 23 vigueries of Provence took the following measure: 'For every wolf – little or big – which is killed, 8 livres will be paid by the viguerie where it has been killed'.[40] This first general system created close to Dauphiné persisted until the 1789. In Dauphiné, an Élection[41] province since 1628, a similar system was created in 1732. An official statement renews it in 1734. The bounty was 6 *livres* per wolf pup and 12 *livres* per adult. This system was created fifteen years before the wolf attacks in Bas-Dauphiné, which means that the results of this policy were not as efficient in exterminating wolves as expected. Even if the bounty archives are not available from 1732 to 1749, an interesting trend appears for the next period. Wolf attacks on humans generated an increase in the number of bounties paid in the concerned Élection. The trend seems to

---

38. Comincini 2002.
39. Administrative district with a representative assembly (clergy, nobility, and the third state) and some liberties in the way they divide taxes.
40. Arch. Dép. Bouches-du-Rhône, C20, folio 255.
41. Administrative district divided by sub-structures where an official representative of the king divides the taxes locally.

Julien Alleau and John D.C. Linnell

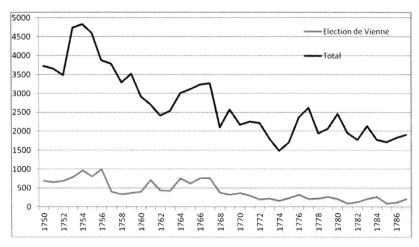

Figure 4. Bounty development: a comparison of the total amount of money distributed for wolf kills in the election of Vienne and the province of Dauphiné (Arch. dép. Isère IIC409 to 447).

follow the development of events: decreasing during the quiet years 1750–1752 and increasing again from 1753 to 1756, which was the peak of conflict. Another peak appears in the 1760s, related to the last attacks in the district of Vienne in 1766, in the parishes of Romagnieu and La Tour-du-Pin. These are the last attacks by non-rabid wolves on humans in this part of the kingdom.

The eighteenth century is the century associated with most wolf control. While the *Louveterie* was subject to reform in the 1770s, administrative correspondence sheds light on the previous decades and the results of these policies. Answering the request of the central powers, the Intendant of Dauphiné, Christophe Pajot de Marcheval, explains that efforts made to exterminate the wolf were successful.

> Monsieur,
>
> I received the letter you honored me by writing on April 10th, where you indicate that our Majesty judged it relevant to renew the long lasting rights of the *Grand Louvetier* with respect to wolf hunting in several provinces of the Kingdom with a judgment for his Council on February 28th.
>
> Monsieur, the Dauphiné is one of the Provinces where this species is abundant. However, it doesn't cause considerable damage because the peasants are used to destroying it using traps or shooting by hunting from a hide. Independently of the interest of people from the countryside in wolf destruction to preserve their livestock, they are also motivated by the bounties we give to them: 12 *livres* per wolf and 6 *livres* per wolf-pup. For more than forty years, these bounties have been established and they produce a good effect as a lot of these animals are destroyed every year.

This make me think that, Monsieur, it would be relevant not to change the actual policy that is observed in Dauphiné except if we realise that these methods are not sufficient and so to use the methods promoted by the *Louveterie's* judgment. But this won't prevent us from conforming ourselves with what you honored me to write about the rights attributed to *Monsieur le Grand Louvetier*. And I will look after the delivery of a payment of 890 *livres*, the amount corresponding to the rights payment of my circumscription, every year from this year.

    I am with respect,

Monsieur,

Your humble and obedient servant,

[Signature :] Pajot.[42]

5. THE DEPREDATION AND ITS CONTEXT

Why There and Not Elsewhere?

The fact that attacks were clustered in space and time begs the question as to why they occurred when and where they did? Some periods of high activity can be attached to the separate or combined effects of military conflicts (European wars of religion, Thirty Years' War), famine (especially in the 1690s and 1709) and the Black Death (1580s, 1630s, 1650s). The period from 1746–1756 doesn't represent a particularly bad political or social context. Thus other factors have to be analysed to understand why.

    Firstly, a comparison with the other cases registered in our database shows that some parts of the kingdom are more associated with attacks than others. An overview shows that mountain regions are not particularly associated with records of man-eating wolves. Attacks are frequently mentioned in low elevation mountains,

---

42.   A Paris le 11 mai 1773/ Monsieur, J'ai reçu la lettre que vous m'avez fait l'honneur de m'écrire le 10 avril, par laquelle vous me marquez que sa Majesté a jugé à propos de renouveler par arrêt de son conseil du 28 février 1773 les droits attribués anciennement au Grand Louvetier de faire faire la chasse des loups dans les différentes provinces du Royaume. Le Dauphiné, Monsieur, est une des Provinces qui abonde le plus dans cette espèce d'animaux ; néanmoins ils n'y font pas des ravages bien considérables, parce que les paysans sont habitués à les détruire, soit en leur tendant des pièges, soit en les tirant à l'affut. Indépendamment de l'intérêt que les gens de la campagne ont à la destruction des loups pour s'en préserver eux et leurs bestiaux, ils y sont encore excités par les gratifications que l'on donne à raison de 12 lt. par tête de loup que l'on apporte et 6 lt. par chaque louveteau. Il y a plus de 40 ans que ces gratifications sont établies et elles produisent un très bon effet, se détruisant chaque année un assez grand nombre de ces animaux ; ce qui me fait penser, monsieur, qu'il convient de ne rien changer à la police actuelle qui s'observe en Dauphiné sur cet objet, sauf à user des moyens prescrits par les règlements de la Louveterie dans le cas où l'on verrait que ceux que l'on emploie à présent seraient insuffisants ; mais cela n'empêchera pas, Monsieur, que je ne me conforme à ce que vous me faites l'honneur de me marquer concernant les droits attribués à M(onsieur) le Grand Louvetier et j'aurai soin de lui délivrer chaque année à commencer par la présente une ordonnance de 890 lt. formant la somme pour laquelle mon département doit contribuer à l'acquittement de ces droits, Je suis avec respect, Monsieur, Votre très humble et très obéissant serviteur Signé Pajot (pièce 176, AN H14XX).

Julien Alleau and John D.C. Linnell

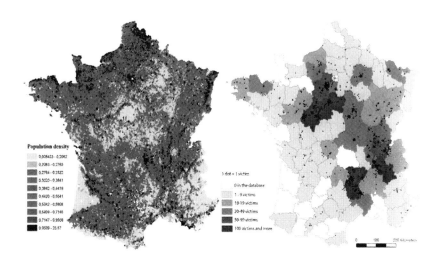

Figure 5. Human densities and wolf attacks on humans in France.
Data: Database of wolf attacks on humans (fifteenth to nineteenth century) available on the CRHQ website: www.unicaen.fr/homme_et_loup; population records of 1806 available on the Cassini website: www.cassini.ehess.fr.

on plateaus and the plains. There appears to be a pattern where attacks occur in areas that have regions of both locally high human density (e.g. agricultural areas) and low human density (e.g. forests that can serve as refuges for wolves) in close proximity.

Thus, an exploration of the landscape structure provides some insights into what might have been happening. From a survey of Napoleonic cadasters[43] based on community data from seven departments, we managed to define eleven types of landscape. When combining landscape properties (forests, heaths, gardens, crop fields, vineyards, fruit gardens, meadows) and human densities, some clear patterns emerge. The situation of Terres Froides could be presented as an archetype. There, forests covered ten to forty per cent of the surface. They were small, isolated and heavily used by people. The human density was high (average about fifty to sixty inhabitants per km^2). Heaths were not common, implying a sharp border between forests and fields. Crop fields clearly dominated the landscape. Pastures were isolated and not sufficient, which implies an important use of the forests as foraging areas

---

43. The Napoleonic cadaster was a document summarising all the ground properties of a commune. For every field, the owner, the quality of the ground (from 1 to 5) and the land-use are explained. From 1807 to the 1840s, every french commune got its Napoleonic cadaster.

for livestock, mainly cattle. Historical records show that wild ungulate populations had progressively decreased since the beginning of the Early Modern Era. For example, red deer, as well as roe deer, were generally absent in the south-east of France at the beginning of the nineteenth century. Only wild boar were still present. Human settlements were dispersed in different hamlets. Few wild prey, patchwork landscapes, small hamlets and mobile livestock grazing in the few areas of forest does not create a situation where wolves can live without coming into frequent proximity to humans. Livestock would have constituted the main potential food source for wolves, and the only thing between the wolf and its food was child shepherds. The only alternative food source would have been carrion, which would be located near barns and farmyards, again bringing wolves into proximity to young and vulnerable humans. Combined, these factors can explain why such areas were predisposed to attacks, but not the temporal clustering of attacks.

Interactivity of Human–Wolf Relationships

The records indicate that attacks were highly clustered in time in this region, with episodes occurring in 1670, and 1710, in addition to the cases mentioned in detail above. Typically a number of attacks occurred in close succession, before ceasing after a year or two.

This pattern can be explained by several hypotheses. The first one is a change in human behavioural practices, fostering a higher security for vulnerable children. Children could start guarding livestock in groups, although this was not usually the case, in order to avoid them playing together and thus becoming distracted from their tasks. Also, they could have sometimes been given weapons, most often wooden sticks or iron bars. The second hypothesis is the elimination or displacement of the individual problematic wolf (or wolf pack) through hunting. This was the case in 1752, when the hunts probably made the attacks stop in the area of Primarette before they started soon afterwards in the northern area. Moreover, ensuring public safety was a political issue in the context of the eighteenth century. Bounties were given by regional institutions in order to hunt wolves. Twenty years after the regional law for bounties was enacted, the wolf population had become greatly reduced. It was only a hundred years before their regional extinction.

Another remarkable feature of the data is that attacks tend to reoccur in the same areas after irregular intervals. The same area surrounding Primarette was associated with wolf attacks in several different periods. In 1670–1672, thirteen victims were recorded. In 1709–1713, tens of victims were recorded in the neighbourhood of Chambaran and Terres Froides forests. If we give a look to the periodicity of the attacks, forty years separate the first main episode recorded through the archives of burials from the second, and the same time elapses between the second and the period 1746–1756 that we describe above in detail. The same pattern can be observed in the Valromey (Ain) with series of attacks recorded in 1587–1596,

Julien Alleau and John D.C. Linnell

1631–1640, 1671–1680, 1710, 1739–1741.[44] This kind of observation can also be made for other locuses of attacks in France or abroad. Attacks happened in Tartumaa (Estonia) in 1809–1810 and then in 1846, which reveals a similar pattern in the relationship.[45] The temporal repetition of cycles like these, after about two human generations, is curious. It is possible to speculate that following the cessation of attacks people began to change their practices (which had become adapted to the presence of potentially dangerous wolves), which led to a new situation where they became increasingly vulnerable to a renewal of attacks.

6. CONCLUSION

Since the end of the sixteenth century, many records of wolf attacks can be found in the administrative and clerical archives of south-eastern France. The case study of Bas-Dauphiné, in 1746–1756, is the last episode of multiple predatory attacks in the province of Dauphiné, and is also the most documented. In comparison with other areas in the kingdom of France as well as some in other countries, a special pattern relative to man-eater behaviour seems to appear. Attacks took place in peculiar landscape contexts related to a practice of livestock production that used children to guard stock in grazing areas far from habitation. This pattern has to be distinguished from other cases of attacks on humans such as those caused by wolves with rabies. This example shows that rabies and man-eater cases occurred in the same landscape at the same time, which requires caution on the part of the historian when interpreting patterns.

Wolf hunting appears to have been a major tool in managing the human relationship with wild predators during history. The rise of hunting pressure in the 1750s led to an end of cases of man-eating wolves. After this, only rabid wolf attacks still occurred. When looking at the period from the fifteenth to the nineteenth centuries for all France a total of 3,500 victims were found for whom there is a name and location. This implies that being killed by a wolf was a relatively unusual event when viewed from any specific place and time in history. This may explain why the episodic events of multiple man-eating often led to the development of stories about mythical beasts and why, after wolf populations began to decline, there was a loss of the more nuanced understanding of the context of wolf attacks.

Our historical studies show a tendency for rural people to lose their adaptation to wolf presence during long periods of peaceful relations, until attacks occurred and they had to readapt to the new situation. We are currently seeing a parallel as wolves return to landscapes from which they have been absent for centuries. Rural people in France have lost practical and psychological adaptation to wolf presence, and these will take time to regain. On the surface, the fact that wolves

---

44.   Alleau 2011.
45.   Rootsi 2001.

appear to have killed people throughout history could be grounds for concern for present-day human safety. However, the social and ecological context has changed so much that it is impossible to compare with the past. Now, there are more wild game and forest than there have been for centuries. Child shepherds are no longer the only barrier between wolves and their main source of food. Rabies is no longer present in western Europe. From the study of history we have learnt a lot about the context of wolf attacks and, while it does not offer us a crystal ball to see the future, it does tell us that none of the historical predisposing factors associated with wolf attacks are currently present. The past can therefore only provide limited insight into the future of the constantly evolving relationship between humans and wolves.

BIBLIOGRAPHY

Abry, C. and A. Joisten. 2002. 'Trois notes sur les fondements du *complexe de Primarette*. Loups-garous, cauchemars, prédations et graisses', in V. Campion-Vincent, J.-C. Douclos and C. Abry (eds) *Le Fait du loup. De la peur à la passion : le renversement d'une image* (Grenoble: Centre Alpin et Rhodanien d'Ethnologie) pp. 135–59.

Avdeev, A., A. Blum, I. Troitskaiaand H. Juby. 2004. 'Peasant Marriage in Nineteenth-Century Russia'. *Population* **59** (6): 721–64.

Alleau, J. 2005. *Quand les loups attaquaient l'homme… Attaques de loups et mortalité accidentelle de la Bresse au Dauphiné sous l'Ancien Régime* (UFR Histoire. Caen, Université de Caen – Basse-Normandie).

— 2010. 'Une histoire du loup à l'époque moderne: méthode, sources et perspectives', in J.-M. Moriceau and P. Madeline (eds) *Repenser le sauvage grâce au retour du loup: les sciences humaines réinterrogées*. Bibliothèque du Pôle Rural, 2 (Caen: Presses Universitaires de Caen) pp. 23–39.

— 2011. *Garder ses distances. Une histoire des relations homme-loup dans les Alpes occidentales (XVIe – XVIIIe siècle)* (Dissertation: Université de Caen).

Bayard. 1989. 'Au cœur de l'intime: les poches des cadavres. Lyon, Lyonnais, Beaujolais, XVIIᵉ-XVIIIᵉ siècle'. *Bulletin du Centre Pierre Léon* **2**: 5–41.

Beaufort, F.G. de. 1987. *Ecologie historique du loup en France: Canis lupus linnaeus 1758* (Dissertation: Université de Rennes).

Buffon, G.-L. L. 1761. *Histoire naturelle, générale et particulière avec la description du cabinet du roi.* (Paris, Imprimerie royale) t. IX, 1761.

Cabourdin, G. and J. Dupâquier. 1988. 'Les sources et les institutions', in J. Dupâquier (ed.) *Histoire de la population française: 2 – Dela Renaissance à 1789.* (Paris: Presses Universitaires de France) pp. 9–50.

Cagnolaro, L., M. Comincini and A. Oriani. 1992. 'Dati storici sulla presenza e su casi di antropofagia del lupo nella Padania centrale', in Atti & Studi del WWF Italia (ed.) *Atti del Convegno Nazionale: Dalla parte del lupo* (Parma) pp. 83–99.

Comincini, M. 2002. *L'Uomo e la 'bestia antropofaga'* (Milan: Unicopli).

100

Julien Alleau and John D.C. Linnell

Fleury, M. and L. Henry. 1956. *Des registresparoissiaux à l'histoire de la population. Manuel de dépouillement et d'exploitation de l'état civil ancient.* (Paris: INED).

Goubert, P. 1960. *Beauvais et le Beauvaisis de 1600 à 1730: contribution à l'histoire sociale de la France du XVIIᵉ siècle* (Paris: EHESS).

— 1976. *Clio parmi les hommes* (Paris/La Haye: EHESS/Mouton).

Kaczensky P., G. Chapron, M. Von Arx, D. Huber, H. Andrén and J. Linnell. 2013. *Status, Management and Distribution of Large Carnivores – Bear, Lynx, Wolf and Wolverine – in Europe.* (Rome: Instituto di Ecologia Applicata).

Lescureux, N. and J.D.C. Linnell. 2010. 'Les montagnes sont-elles les derniers refuges des grands prédateurs?' *Histoire des Alpes* 15: 195–210.

Linnell, J.D.C., R. Andersen, Z. Andersone, L. Balciauskas, J.C. Blanco, L. Boitani, S. Brainerd, U. Breitenmoser, I. Kojola, O. Liberg, J. Løe, H. Okarma, H. Pedersen, C. Promberger, H. Sand, E.J. Solberg, H. Valdmannand P. Wabakken. 2002. *The Fear of Wolves: A Review of Wolf Attacks on Humans* (NINA Norsk institutt for naturforskning).

Lopez B.H. 1978. *Of Wolves and Men.* (New York: Charles Scribner's Sons).

Marcieu, le Marquis de. 1924. 'Une battue aux loups au pays des brûleurs de loups en 1754'. *Bulletin de l'Académie Delphinale* t15: 89–96.

Moriceau, J.-M. 2007. *Histoire du méchant loup: 3000 attaques sur l'homme en France (XV–XXᵉ siècle)* (Paris: Fayard).

— 2011. *L'Homme contre le loup: une guerre de deux mille ans* (Paris, Fayard).

Moyroud, R. 2002. 'Loups et loups-garous autour des verreries en Bas-Dauphiné sous l'Ancien Régime', in V. Campion-Vincent, J.-C. Douclos and C. Abry (eds) *Le Fait du loup: de la peur à la passion, le renversement d'une image* (Grenoble: Centre Alpin et Rhodanien d'Ethnologie) pp. 125–34.

Porret, M. 2010. 'La médecine légale entre doctrines et pratiques'. *Revue d'Histoire des Sciences Humaines* 22 (1): 3–15.

Rajpurohit, K.S. 1999. 'Child Lifting: Wolves in Hazaribagh, India'. *Ambio* 28 (2): 162–6.

Rootsi, I. 2001. 'Man-eater wolves in 19th century Estonia'. *Proceedings of the Baltic Large Carnivore Initiative Symposium 'Human dimensions of large carnivores in Baltic Countries'*, pp. 77–89.

Skogen K., I. Mauz and O. Krange. 2006. 'Wolves and Eco-power. A French-Norwegian Analysis of the Narratives of the Return of Large Carnivores'. *Journal of Alpine Research* 94: 78–87.

Theodoridès, J. 1986. *Histoire de la rage. Cave canem* (Paris: Masson).

Young, S.P. and E.A. Goldman. 1944. *The Wolves of North America: Part 1* (New York: Dover Publications Inc.).

Where is the Big Bad Wolf?
Notes and Narratives on Wolves in Swedish Newspapers during the Eighteenth and Nineteenth Centuries

Karin Dirke

INTRODUCTION

This chapter investigates reports and representations of the wolf in Swedish media from the eighteenth and nineteenth centuries. The time span is equivalent to the period when the wolf was being exterminated in Sweden. At the same time as the wolf disappeared from the wild, the discourse on the wolf in the newspapers changed. During the period notes on the movements and actions of wolves, as well as statistics on the number of animals killed, were published in the papers. The chapter will discuss how the wolves were described, what actions of the wolves prompted mentions in the papers and how the publication of numbers of killed wolves was related to the national project of exterminating the wolf.

From 1645 periodic newspapers were published in Sweden. The early papers mainly consisted of a collection of short paragraphs and news items. They were predominantly collected from foreign sources. The dominant newspaper in Sweden during the eighteenth century was *Posttidningen*. It mainly consisted of foreign news items and was therefore in 1760 supplemented by the domestic publication *Inrikes Tidningar*. Both periodicals were official, authorised by the State, a status reinforced when publication was taken over by the Swedish academy in 1791.[1] The Swedish press was censored from 1684–1766 a fact both hindering the freedom of speech and also providing source material for later research. The Swedish publishers were from 1661 obliged to send a copy of all printed material to the Royal Library, making the press archive a unique collection of source material for press history.[2]

The sources used in this chapter consist of a collection of newspaper articles in the Royal Library digital archive. The digitised publications have been chosen by the Royal Library to provide a representative selection of both provincial and

---

1. Gustafsson et al. (eds) 2000, pp. 119, 129.
2. Ibid., pp. 54, 97.

national newspapers. The archive contains more than 200,000 pages of text and covers titles from the eighteenth to the twentieth centuries.[3] The source material was found through a search in the digital archive of newspapers in the Royal Swedish library. The search word 'varg/warg' (wolf) gave 2,086 hits from the eighteenth and nineteenth centuries, of which about 22 per cent were found to be more or less relevant. The relevant articles range from stories about encounters with wolves to advertisements for wolf skins. Any article containing the word wolf was checked but many were dismissed because, for example, they dealt with people or places of the name 'varg'.

The geographical coverage of provincial newspapers in the collection is mainly the southern part of Sweden. Wolves were most often mentioned in papers from the south-east of Sweden and from the county of Dalarna. The provincial newspapers where wolves were mentioned reflect their geographical prevalence at the beginning of the period. Later the newspapers rather seem to respond to perceived interest from the general public in reading about strong feelings associated with wolves. During the eighteenth century, the wolf was mainly mentioned in the newspaper for three reasons: it was to be exterminated, it was rabid or it was unusual in some other way. As the press developed, the focus changed towards the entertainment value of the story. In this process, as we shall see, the stories about wolves became more elaborate, emotional and narrative.

EXTERMINATION: METHODS AND STATISTICS

Discussing extermination of wolves was certainly a method of motivating the general public to kill wolves (compare Bergström et al. in this volume). The newspaper, at the beginning of the period studied here, often functioned as the voice of the authorities. The aim was to instruct and guide the general public so as to act in the nation's interest.[4] One of the important goals was to exterminate large carnivores or at least drive them to the borders of the nation. This was explicitly stated in an article in the domestic paper *Inrikes tidningar*. The Swedish parliament decided to have an extract from the minutes published in the paper because it discussed the reward that should be bestowed on a zealous gamekeeper who had killed lots of carnivores during his years of service. The man was put forward as a real model hunter and it was hoped that his example would be followed by others.[5] Such examples of skilled hunters were quite frequent.

During the period 1830–1850, articles on the extermination of wolves or giving information about the bounty system were especially abundant. In the period 31 such articles were published, all in the state-authorised *Post-och inrikes*

---

3. magasin.kb.se/searchinterface/about.html
4. Gustafsson et al. (eds), p. 129.
5. *Inrikes tidningar*, 23. Dec. 1771, p. 1.

tidningar. The extermination of wolves was obviously thought of as an issue of national interest.

Search parties as a hunting method were often mentioned in the newspapers, although they seemed less efficient in relation to the number of people involved.[6] Since the Middle Ages, the Swedish peasantry had been obliged to participate in the hunting of large carnivores. The duty of having, at any time, to leave home and participate in tedious and quite dangerous hunts was difficult and unpopular. Ordinary people's weariness, distaste and fear of new duties in relation to the large hunts organised by the forest officers were, for example, conveyed in parliament in 1723. The peasantry, according to the minutes, complained of being forced to participate in large search parties, often for several days. They protested against having their horses destroyed by travelling forest officers, and they objected at having to spend days marching through the cold forest, often without enough food, since they were not given sufficient time to prepare. All this, the peasantry asked parliament to spare them.[7]

Complaints about the efforts spent in hunting wolves were recurrent in parliament during the first half of the nineteenth century, although the hunting was never called into question from other perspectives than the economic or organisational. Everyone wanted to get rid of wolves but the degree of urgency seemed to vary with class. The upper classes, being the only ones allowed to hunt game and thus the ones benefiting from access to wild meat, were more insistent about relieving the country from wolves. The peasants had only their own cattle to protect and therefore were reluctant to spend efforts on fruitless wolf hunting. Complaints about tiresome and time-consuming search parties were, however, never mentioned in the newspaper. Instead the peasantry was praised for its temperance and orderliness in the search parties.[8] The state-authorised newspapers evidently did not convey the voice of the peasantry but were eager to call attention to exemplary models.

The general public was encouraged in the newspapers by statistics noting how many animals had been killed as well as instructions on how to construct effective traps and killing devices. The peasantry was not allowed to bear firearms so the purpose was to disseminate other methods of killing carnivores. In the domestic newspaper *Inrikes tidningar* from 1772 it was, for example, discussed how to kill wolf, bear and lynx through a complicated 'spear-machine'.[9] Beside von Greiff's complicated contraptions (discussed in Bergström et al. in this volume) new inventions of killing devices were often noted, as in *Folkets röst* [Voice of the people] in

6. See for example *Post-och Inrikes tidningar,* 31. Mar. 1832, p. 1.; *Post-och inrikes tidningar,* 26. Mar. 1836, p. 1; *Post-och Inrikes tidningar,* 14. Apr. 1837, p. 1; *Post-och Inrikes tidningar,* 27. Dec. 1837, p. 1; *Post-och Inrikes tidningar,* 18. Jun. 1844, p. 2.

7. *Bondeståndets riksdagsprotokoll,* Vol 1, 1720–1727, p. 274.

8. *Post-och inrikes tidningar,* 31. Mar. 1832, p. 1.

9. *Inrikes tidningar,* 2. Jan. 1772, p. 4 (all translations from Swedish in citations from newspaper articles are by the author).

1853 where a trap consisting of four iron hooks designed to grab the wolf by the neck when it reached for the bait was described.[10]

Wolf hunting intensified in Sweden during the first half of the nineteenth century and was, as we have seen, encouraged by the authorities. From the beginning of the 1800s, Swedish agriculture changed dramatically and was streamlined, with larger land areas being brought together. At the same time there was a great increase in the population and an increase of the area under cultivation.[11] Possibly the raging of epidemic cattle disease in Sweden and Europe during the eighteenth century also influenced the war on wolves. In the middle of the century a disease, presumed to be cattle plague, reached its climax and tens of thousands of animals died.[12] This of course made people more keen to protect the remaining animals from predators.

During the 1830s and 1840s the newspaper articles were mainly about the abundance of wolves and how to kill them. The efficiency of different methods was discussed and statistics could sometimes include the killing methods used.[13] In this process it was important to convey an image of the wolf as a monster, a morally detestable creature. This view of the wolf was neither new nor alien to the Swedish people. No one, before the twentieth century, wanted to protect wolves and they were always seen as evil, yet interest in the question seems to have varied. The authorities had a goal to free the nation from large carnivores. The local people were, however, only interested if the wolves were a problem locally. In the parliamentary discussions of 1815 one can note a difference of opinion according to estate. The peasantry did not question the extermination of wolves but they doubted the use of so much effort without pay. The peasants' main interest was to be spared further duties. The nobility in their turn referred to their better knowledge about hunting and forestry.[14] The idea of the wolf as evil and deserving of extermination was confirmed in natural history where the wolves were known as 'cruel, plundering, hostile and quite greedy animals'.[15] An important measure in exterminating wolves was therefore at the level of information, presenting the wolf as a threat, an evil monster and a danger to humans.

---

10. *Folkets röst*, 9. Mar. 1853, p. 3.
11. Haraldsson 1987, p. 30.
12. Hallgren 1960, p. 16.
13. *Post-och Inrikes tidningar*, 7. Feb. 1838, p. 1.
14. *Protocoll, hållna hos Höglofige Ridderskapet och Adeln vid Urtima Riksdagen i Stockholm 1815*, vol. 5, p. 547 (where von Greiff refers to his knowledge of search parties and using animal corpses as bait), p. 550 (where von Greiff speaks of a new hunting method) and p. 554 (where it is complained that the royal forest officer Bunge is not present and able to share his great experience of hunting carnivores since he is off hunting bear instead of attending the parliament).
15. Berch 1750, p. 35.

Where is the Big Bad Wolf?

THE WOLF AS MONSTER

The monster of monsters, the notorious beast of Gévaudan, killing children and women in France 1764–1768 provided a model for how to narrate wolf attacks in the newspaper. The occurrences in Gévaudan prompted great fear and anxiety among the authorities and inhabitants of Gévaudan as well as the rest of southern France. Reports of the killings echoed in newspapers all over Europe. Over one hundred people were killed by presumably one or two wolves, reported to have been exceptionally large and of an unusual colour.[16] The beast was perceived as a monster of unknown origin.[17] It was widely speculated that the beast was a hyena, a large cat or some sort of hybrid, most commonly thought of as a werewolf.[18] The beast of Gévaudan was not directly mentioned in the Swedish newspapers examined here; however, it was certainly known to Swedish readers. The story about the Gévaudan-monster was told 1765 in a booklet by natural historian and moralist Magnus Orrelius.[19] The discussion of the beast of Gévaudan was, in Orrelius' writing, closely connected with morality.[20] The beast reflected all evil and, as Orrelius noted in his earlier work *Historia animalum* (1750), the wolf mirrors a human who insists on being malicious.[21] Aspects of the reports of the French wolf killings can be recognised in the Swedish newspapers. In particular, the tendency to describe the wolf as an unknown threat, as a creature behaving erratically, is common in eighteenth and nineteenth century newspapers.

The incidence of wolves which are described as unusual in some way – exceptionally large or of an unusual colour – is high in the newspapers. Individual wolves are almost always given the epithet 'large' or sometimes even 'unusually large'.[22] Whether the animals really were (or were perceived as) especially large or unusual is impossible to know. There is, however, reason to believe that the reporters displayed a journalist's sense of what is interesting in these accounts. Large, exceptional and dangerous events and items were of course more likely to appear in the paper. The events portrayed as unusual were in the earlier period often explained by some external factor such as rabies, or in some cases extremely cold weather, or the wolf being famished.

16. Linnell et al., 2002, p. 19.
17. Smith 2011, p. 11.
18. Smith 2011, pp. 20–21 and 38–45; Orrelius 1765, p. 3.
19. Ibid., pp. 3–40.
20. Ibid., p. 40.
21. Orrelius 1750, part IV, unpaginated, p. 8.
22. See, for example, *Jönköpingsbladet*, 14 Dec. 1850, p. 1; *Jönköpingsbladet*, 17 Jan. 1861, p. 2; *Dalpilen*, 13 Jan. 1866, *Kalmar*, 23 Jan.1871, p. 2 and *Faluposten*, 25 Jan. 1871; *Dalpilen*, 13 Mar.1875, p. 3; *Faluposten*, 26 Feb. 1876, p. 2; *Faluposten*, 16 Mar. 1878, p. 2; *Kalmar*, 8 Jan. 1890, p. 4, *Kalmar* 10 May 1890, p. 2.

Karin Dirke

RABID WOLVES

The most common factor explaining wolf attacks in the newspapers was rabies. Often the disease was portrayed as a larger threat than the wolf itself. Especially during the 1780s and 1790s, stories about 'rabid' or 'raging' wolves – both terms suggesting the animal was infected with rabies – were published in Swedish newspapers. These were usually reports from abroad, although rabies existed in Sweden until 1886.[23] Rabies, being a viral infection most commonly spread by the domestic dog, was probably more prevalent in wolves before the nineteenth century when rabies in dogs was subsequently eliminated.[24] Rabies as a factor leading to wolves attacking humans seems to have been well known. The disease develops, at a higher incidence in wolves than in other animals, into its short but very devastating furious stage of hyperactive and aggressive behaviour. This explains the often-extreme numbers of victims reported in rabid wolf attacks.[25]

Thus, a story was told in a Swedish newspaper about a French wolf rabidly attacking and biting fifteen people and an ox in 1771. Apparently the ox managed to kill the wolf but, because of fear of infection, it was then killed itself and buried together with the wolf.[26] Another story from France told of an unusually large wolf being killed by a soldier after it had harmed two people who were now being treated for rabies.[27] These news items were presented as accounts of extraordinary events and were often surprisingly detailed. In a tale from the border between France and Germany we are provided with complex information about the injuries caused by the wolf. Apparently it tore the face off one person, reported the newspaper with a vivid image, harmed another and bit a piece from the calf of a third. Because of this, a search party was organised and the wolf fled into the forest where it attacked a bird catcher. It then, according to the paper, continued and attacked a young farmhand, ripped the hair and skin from his scalp, harmed his eye and bit his thumb off. The farmhand tried to defend himself with a knife but it was unclear, the newspaper said, whether he would survive.[28] Stories such as this one were surprisingly detailed and equally dramatic. The specific mentioning of injuries added both drama and credibility to the story. Rabid wolves were also reported from Russia in 1780. A raging wolf attacked a dog and then its owner. The man apparently died three weeks later from 'great fear (Hydrophobia)', as the newspaper put it.[29]

The stories about rabid wolves attacking humans became, over time, even more elaborate and detailed. In the 1860s a story from Helsinki, Finland, about a

---

23. http://www.smittskyddsinstitutet.se/sjukdomar/rabies/
24. Linnell et al 2002, p. 14.
25. Ibid.
26. *Posttidningar*, 18 Jul. 1771, p. 2.
27. *Stockholms Post Tidningar*, 10 Feb. 1780, p. 1.
28. Ibid.
29. *Inrikes Tidningar*, 22 May 1780, p. 1.

wolf attacking horses and drivers as well as other people getting in its way, described both the actual event and the rumours about numbers of people and animals injured. Whether the wolf was rabid or not was not known to the reporter; however, he supposed that, *if* this were the case, there was no hope for the victims.[30] The tendency to speculate about the dire outcome of wolf attacks increased during the later part of the nineteenth century as newspapers became more developed and elaborate.

WOLF NARRATIVES

In the contemporary debate on the existence of wolves in Sweden, the notion that the fear of wolves increases as the real threat from wolves diminishes is often put forward. Supposedly people fear wolves because they are an unknown threat. The pro-wolf side of the Swedish controversy often refers to the relative acceptance of wolves where they are more common, as in southern and eastern Europe.

This idea seems partly to be supported by the development of wolf narratives in Swedish newspapers. During the course of the nineteenth century, narratives about wolves changed. The stories about wolves became more usual as well as elaborate and extended during the course of the century. This is, of course, partly due to the overall development of the newspapers. In the first half of the 1800s, wolves were hardly mentioned besides information on how to kill them or statistics on animals killed. However, from the 1860s, stories about wolves attacking humans became more frequent. Whether the attack was fatal, or without any harm coming to the human involved, it was mentioned in the paper.

During the second half of the nineteenth century, stories narrating a dramatic battle between man and wolf became popular. These narratives can be seen as a specific theme conveying a message about man's dominance over nature. The battles are, almost always, won by the human, and the prerequisite for the theme is the perceived dangerousness and threat of the wolf. Essential to the narrative is the wolf being a prominent opponent. Without this point of departure, the story would have no effect. Thus, under the caption 'Dangerous battle', the story was told of a Hungarian government official who was attacked by a wolf. The man finally managed to overcome the wolf but was badly injured on the hand in the process. The struggle was carefully commented upon in the paper and reported in great detail.[31] The provincial newspaper *Kalmar* related a story in 1887 of a man in Odessa who was attacked by a rabid wolf. The man, displaying great courage (which probably merited the story appearing in the newspaper), grabbed the wolf by its tongue and tried to strangle it with his other hand. After ten minutes of desperately fighting the wolf, the man was finally saved by the arrival of a couple of neighbours who killed the wolf. The man bragged to the paper that, in his younger

30. *Kalmar*, 22 Feb. 1865, p. 2.
31. *Kalmar*, 2 Mar. 1870, p. 3.

days, he would have had no trouble in overcoming the rabid wolf on his own.[32] The provincial newspaper *Blekingsposten* also reported an incident in 1860 when a farmer engaged in a battle with a wolf. The farmer had to throw his whole stock of wood at the wolf before it finally left. The story had a comical touch, ending in the statement that the farmer should claim right of way.[33]

The theme of man versus wolf is also applicable to the accounts about wolf hunting in the north. The Sami people were often said to hunt wolf or lynx by skiing after the animal until it tired and then killing it. Stories about such hunts often focused on the power of endurance of the skier. A recurrent story tells of a man, or a few men, following an animal at a strong pace and subsequently throwing off items of clothing, one after the other, to be able to keep up with the carnivore.[34] These stories convey a message about the exotic and mythical strength of the indigenous Sami people, a discourse quite common at the time.[35]

These related stories have a few things in common. The described encounters are man versus wolf struggles, which appear in the paper because the fight is expected to evoke interest. The struggle itself is the main focus of the story, not the fact that wolves are common, dangerous or threatening as was the case earlier. Rabies or any other reason for the wolf attack is no longer at the centre of attention of the articles. The main interest is the fight itself, the individual's battle with the wild wolf. The narratives have the harsh, laconic touch of the Icelandic saga and, of course, share the theme of human versus wild wolf with several folkloric tales, such as *Little Red Riding Hood* or *Peter and the Wolf*. The stories were mediated because they mirrored a larger statement about man conquering nature.

Many researchers have noted how the human relationship with animals is used as a manifestation of power, dominance and superiority in relation to animals but also as a symbol of power over other humans. The development of nineteenth century natural history and its popular and spectacular manifestation in zoos, dioramas and museums seems to mirror imperialism and colonialism.[36] Animals of all sorts have been arranged and exposed in a way that increases the power of the arranger. This is true of dioramas, trophy photography and hunting stories. They all function through objectifying the animal. The newspaper articles discussed here also place the reporter in a certain relationship with the 'object', in this case the wolf. The wolf narrative functions as an establishment of a power relation. The fictional character of the wolf narratives also increases with time.

32. *Kalmar*, 2 Jun. 1887, p. 2.
33. *Blekingsposten*, 30 Mar. 1860, p. 1.
34. *Kalmar*, 5 Feb. 1876, p. 3; *Norra Skåne*, 15 Mar. 1887, p. 2. The hunting method and the subsequent stripping of the hunter have been described in ethnological works such as in Kjellström 1995, pp. 147–149.
35. Broberg 1982, pp. 76–78; Lantto 2000, pp. 40–42.
36. Kalof 2007, p. 148; Åkerberg 2001, pp. 104–69.

The relation between news items (or perhaps rather unfounded rumours) and fictional folklore is closer than we perhaps imagine. The news items about wolves can occasionally be recognised as the source of anecdotes in literature. This is the case with the story in a provincial newspaper in 1887 about a woman falling into a wolf pit already containing a wolf. The woman was, according to the newspaper, the worst gossipmonger of the area. 'She, who without hesitation had eaten her neighbours' good name and reputation, now feared being mauled herself', noted the newspaper, not without satisfaction. The reporter ended the article by establishing the fact that 'wolves are no longer to be seen in the area, but foxes and gossipmongers are unfortunately abundant'.[37] The story seems likely to be the origin of the tale told in Swedish author Astrid Lindgren's book about the little mischievous boy Emil, where the boy digs a wolf pit and a greedy woman, superintendent of the paupers, falls into it. Lindgren's story has the same moralistic tone as the news item: 'Perhaps it was right that the superintendent should have stumbled into the trap. Perhaps one might tame her a bit, so that she would become gentler and not so ill-tempered. Yes, it would be a way of teaching her manners, because she was certainly in need of such a lesson.'[38] When discussing wolves, moral aspects were never far away. The wolf represented a sinful human in need of punishment.

ATTACKS ON HUMANS

More serious were the reports of a series of fatal attacks in Finland during the 1860s through the 1880s. Wolves attacking humans were of course dramatic events in the papers. An attack on humans was an incident of such gravity that it was discussed with great interest, whether the attacked human came to harm or not. Wolves assaulting humans or their property were considered newsworthy and notable. It was evidently seen as quite an extraordinary event. As we have seen, the attacks on humans were often depicted as being the result of the wolf being 'rabid' or 'raging'. In the latter part of the nineteenth century, however, rabies as an explanation for wolf-attacks on humans decreased in the newspapers. Attacking humans was instead put forward as something wolves do, as normal wolf behaviour. That is, the attacks were often perceived as predatory.

Most of the wolf attacks mentioned in Swedish newspapers were reports from Finland, where a series of assaults by wild animals on children attracted much attention. Between November 1876 and November 1881 no less than 24 articles were published in Sweden about wolf attacks on children.[39] In none of these arti-

---

37. *Norra Skåne*, 17 Nov. 1887, p. 3.
38. Lindgren 2001, p. 111 (trans. Ed Holmes).
39. See for example *Bollnäs tidning*, 25 Nov. 1876, p. 4; *Kalmar*, 1 Nov. 1877, p. 2, *Kalmar*, 8 Nov. 1877, p. 2; *Kalmar*, 8 Feb. 1879, p. 2; *Gotlands tidning*, 4 Feb. 1880, p. 1, *Kalmar*, 11 Aug. 1880; *Kalmar*, 16 Aug., p. 2; *Gotlands tidning*, 18 Aug. 1880, p. 2, *Kalmar*, 3 Nov. 1880, p. 2, *Kalmar*, 14 Nov. 1881, p. 2.

cles was rabies or any other remarkable cause of the animal's aggressive behaviour mentioned.[40] The stories about children being attacked by presumed wolves were detailed and explicit. Often the articles suggested the child had been eaten, the reason for the attack thus being predatory. The level of credibility of the stories is difficult to evaluate from the information given in the newspaper articles. Linnell et al. argue that some attacks were given such national importance and were so widely reported that there is reason to believe the reports were probably based on facts rather than fiction.[41] Furthermore, in 1882 two wolves were killed in the area, one of them being an old she wolf with worn down teeth. After the wolves were killed the attacks ceased.[42]

The stories in the newspapers were often detailed and specific but rarely had anyone actually seen the wolf killing the child. The child had most often disappeared and later been found to be killed by animals. Or, as described in *Bollnäs tidning* under the caption 'A child eaten by wolves':

> With the help of neighbours a search party was put together to look for the disap-
> peared child. Only its torn and bloodied clothes were found in the forest ... As wolf
> tracks had been noticed close by the cottage, it was presumed the child had been
> taken and eaten by wolves.[43]

In the local newspaper *Kalmar* a story was told in 1877 about the Finnish five-year old boy Carl Fredrik Avola who had been taken away and killed by a wolf. The fact that the newspaper mentioned the boy's name of course gave credibility to the story. It was true, noted the newspaper, that the wolf had not been seen taking the boy; however, a search party was organised when the disappearance was discovered 'which lead to the sad knowledge that the child had been torn to pieces by the beast'.[44] The year after, it was reported in the provincial newspaper *Faluposten* that an unusually large wolf had been caught in a wolf pit in Finland and the local people thought the wolf to be the same creature which 'last summer had eaten several children'.[45] The same year, reports were published about an eight-year old girl who had been bitten to death by a wolf.[46] A bounty had been put on wolves in the area, according to the newspapers, owing to the fact that 'several children in the parish of Wirmo have been eaten by wolves'.[47] The newspaper *Kalmar* reported

---

40. This is probably partly due to the fact that the incidence of rabies was reduced in Sweden towards the end of the century. The disease was considered eradicated by 1886.
41. Linnell et al. 2002, pp. 23–4. The attacks on humans are also thoroughly accounted for in Pousette 2000.
42. Linnell et al. 2002, p. 24, Pousette 2000, p. 147.
43. *Bollnäs tidning*, 25 Nov. 1876, p. 4.
44. *Kalmar*, 8 Nov. 1877, p. 2.
45. *Faluposten*, 16 Mar. 1878, p. 2.
46. *Kalmar*, 8 Feb. 1879, p. 2. The event was said to have occurred in December 1878.
47. *Gotlands tidning*, 18 Aug. 1880, p. 2.

information from a Finnish newspaper about children being killed by wolves. Again, wolf tracks had been seen in the area where the mangled bodies of the children had been found, but no one had actually seen the wolves attacking:

> In all probability it is one and the same beast which is responsible for all the newly occurred kidnappings, because it is well known, that when a wolf gets the taste of human flesh, it will not quench its hunger with anything else.[48]

The wolf was, in other words, seen as an obvious threat to children in these articles however the evidence pointing towards specific animals was rather sparse. The articles about wolves attacking humans were of course written in a shocked and excited tone. The terrible event of a child being taken by a beast from the wild was naturally revolting. The reports were, in spite of this, rather vague and unspecific.

Sometimes the species of the attacking animal remained somewhat unclear and, notably, not especially important or interesting for the reporter. The word *wolf* seemed to suggest any aggressive wild beast. The logic of the newspapers demanded this mystery creature, just as in the older stories about the Gévaudan-killings. This is the case in the story from Finland about an assault on two young shepherd boys, which was told under the caption 'A wolf attacking two boys'. The boys had, when shepherding their cattle, received a visit from a wolf, which according to its colour, reported the newspaper, was a lynx.[49] Under the headline 'Wolf hunt in Småland' the story is told about how an animal is driven towards a search party of 200 people. The animal was encircled and driven towards several people who, according to the newspaper, shot at it; however, no one was able either to determine the species of the animal, or kill it. From the description of the animal's size and colour, the reporter stated, the animal was commonly thought to be a large wolf.[50]

The concept *wolf* seems rather to have functioned in these reports as a description of a more unspecific threat from the wild. Whether the animal really was a wolf or not was of secondary importance. Therefore an article with the headline 'The wolves on Åland' could be about the doubt as to whether the animals were wolves or not. After an introduction about how the country is 'flooded' with carnivores, the article stated that the animals seen were large and black; however 'we are still not agreed on the race of the animals'.[51]

Occasionally reports about wolves attacking humans in other countries than Sweden and Finland were also published. A story about a girl who was attacked by a wolf in Italy was told in the provincial newspaper *Kalmar*, which also gladly reported the girl's ability to defend herself. The same newspaper also told of the woman and child attacked by a wolf in Serbia where the woman was killed but the

48. *Kalmar*, 3 Nov. 1880, p. 2.
49. *Kalmar*, 11 Aug. 1880, p. 2.
50. *Kalmar*, 10 May 1890, p. 2.
51. *Norra Skåne*, 7 Dec. 1883, p. 3.

Karin Dirke

child survived.[52] Very few stories have been recounted from Norway. The reason for this remains unclear, knowing the Scandinavian wolf population incorporates both Swedish and Norwegian wolves. The evidence of Norwegian encounters with wolves given in Linnell et al.'s investigation of wolf attacks on humans in history, is mainly folkloric since a systematic search of parish registers remains to be done.[53]

THE FEAR

Towards the later nineteenth century the reports on wolves changed in character. The articles increasingly focused on the feelings – mainly the fear – the encounters with wolves evoked. Wolves were rarely seen but their rare appearance evoked terror which was reported and discussed in the paper. It seemed important to portray the animals as a threat even though very few wolves were actually killed towards the end of the nineteenth century. The fear of wolves became the main focus of the story. In this process the stories also became increasingly elaborate and narrative. In a provincial newspaper a dramatic story was told about a man travelling by sleigh who was chased by wolves at night. The wolves tried to attack the traveller's dog, which jumped on to the sleigh. As soon as the basic premises of the story are given the reporter changes to the present tense and the story's intensity increases. The journalist interprets the traveller's feelings and dramatises the event:

> What is there to do for our traveler who neither carries a revolver nor other firearms? He whips his stallion which bolts at the speed of lightning. But the wolves keep following, not allowing themselves to be intimidated either by the man's desperate cries nor by the whiplashes he provided them with. A race between life and death![54]

The dramatic story was also published in another newspaper with the same wording.[55] Stories such as this one were often sensationalised in the papers. They were enacted on the border between fact and fiction and whether they belonged to one category or the other was never clarified. Under the caption 'A drama on the plains of Siberia', a couple of provincial newspapers reported a story read in Russian newspapers about a landlord, with wife and young child, whose sleigh got stuck in the snow. 'An enormous wolf approached and behind him a large group of grey figures dimly could be seen in the semi-darkness', the newspapers reported.[56] The wolves attacked and several were shot but as their blood thirst was awakened and they feared nothing, it did not stop them, explained the papers. The young wife and boy were dragged off and killed by the wolves, but the landlord was saved by

---

52. *Kalmar*, 27 Dec. 1890, p. 4 and *Kalmar*, 9 Feb. 1891, S. 4.
53. Linnell et al. 2002, S. 24.
54. *Kalmar*, 14 Apr. 1880, p. 2.
55. *Bollnäs tidning*, 24 Apr. 1880, p. 4.
56. *Kalmar*, 12 Dec. 1896, p. 6; *Dalpilen*, 18. Dec. 1896, p. 6.

passersby, who had heard the gunshots. The poor landlord, concluded the papers, 'sobbed while the wolves howled their death song over the ones that had been his dearest in life – his wife and little son'.[57] The emotional tone of the article is insistent. The story seems fictional, lacking all details such as exact place or time of the event, or the name of the original Russian newspaper referred to. Yet it is not presented as fiction. Another semi-fictional story was earlier published in two different versions. The first version was a short paragraph about a group of sleighs being attacked outside Moscow, Russia. Twenty-four people were killed by a large group of wolves, reported the paper, and only the horse's driver survived.[58] The same story was also related in another paper but now in a more vivid, exaggerated and fictionalised form. The article reported that 'the attack was horrible to witness' (though the reporter obviously was not there, since only the driver survived). The wolves came as a 'thick mass covering several acres of land, surrounding the sleighs and their unfortunate passengers'.[59]

Obviously stories such as these were published because of their sentimental, entertaining and dramatic value. At the same time, they contributed to a discourse on wolves, which was semi-fictional and became all the more narrative as real wolf populations diminished in the wild. The concept *wolf* came to mean hard winter and dire circumstances. In the newspaper the headline 'Hard winter' could be followed by the information that a wolf had been seen in Stockholm.[60] The sight of the wolf apparently signalled cold winter and harsh conditions.

The theme of the race between sleigh and wolves was recurrent during the nineteenth century and seemed to be confirmed in the natural history of the time.[61] It could also be found in the colourful hunting stories of the Englishman Llewellyn Lloyd, who wrote folkloristic accounts about his years spent in Sweden.[62] It was of course most of all a vivid and spectacular scene in Swedish author Selma Lagerlöf's novel *Gösta Berling's Saga* (1891).[63] It was evidently by way of the newspapers that the wicked wolf seriously entered imaginative literature in Sweden.[64]

---

57. *Dalpilen*, 18 Dec. 1896, p. 6.
58. *Dalpilen*, 19 Apr. 1876, p. 3.
59. *Wermlands Läns Tidning*, 19 Apr. 1876, p. 3.
60. *Dalpilen*, 29 Jan 1886, p. 3.
61. Nilsson 1847, p. 224; Thorell 1865, p. 106.
62. Lloyd 1855, p. 203.
63. Lagerlöf 1981, pp. 60–62, 100.
64. Coleman (2004) discusses how folklore as well as ritual fuelled a hatred of wolves in America. The cruel violence Coleman finds expressed in the American sources is however more or less absent in the Swedish material studied here. People wanted to get rid of the wolves but did not seem to take pleasure in torturing them.

Karin Dirke

THE CRITICS

The emotional turn in reports about wolves also evoked critical reaction. The discrepancy between the many dramatic and sensational stories in newspapers on encounters with wolves and the actual numbers of wolves in the wild caused some reporters to criticise the newspapers. The stories simply did not seem trustworthy. 'No wolf has actually been seen in Stockholm or its surroundings in the past twenty years', one reporter stated.[65] A short paragraph reporting that a wolf had been seen in Skåne was given the ironic headline 'Surely a canard?'[66]

Many articles mocked the inability to distinguish a wolf from just about anything else, as well as the tendency to imagine wolves all over the place. At the end of the nineteenth century the concept *wolf-story* referred to a good story with somewhat weak credibility. These stories were abundant in the newspapers. Appearing in several newspapers was a story about the so-called 'Kuggeboda-wolf' which was shot, bounty collected, and then found to be a dog. The question remained, stated the newspapers, whether the wolf's slayer should be allowed to keep the bounty or not.[67] Sometimes the reporters referred to the many imagined wolves when stating that this article, as opposed to all others, really was about a wolf. An example is the short paragraph in the provincial paper *Dalpilen* where a reporter noted that a wolf had been seen in Näs and that it was *not* one of the well-known imitated 'Näs-wolves' like the one dressed in a gauze hood.[68] The bantering tone is ubiquitous in these articles, the reporters making fun of an exaggerated fear of wolves. The stories about encounters with wolves were – as one newspaper expressed it – 'ordinary winter tales, transmitted by a vivid imagination'.[69] One such story, published in a couple of newspapers, told of a woman who thought she saw a wolf. When the hunters, a party of 23 men, went after the wolf, they first thought it was a bear but after shooting at it discovered it to be a large rock.[70] In one paper the reporter begged the newspapers not to scare people unnecessarily with wolf-stories. A wolf story was obviously understood as a story about humans' general fear of nature. Wolves represented a threat, uncontrolled and sometimes imaginary.

WHERE IS THE BIG BAD WOLF?

As we have seen, the narratives on wolves in Swedish newspapers developed during the eighteenth and nineteenth centuries. As wolves became less abundant in the wild,

---

65. *Kalmar*, 21 Feb. 1881, p. 2.
66. *Dalpilen*, 9 May 1899, p. 3.
67. *Kalmar*, 22 Apr. 1893, p. 2; *Norra Skåne*, 22 Apr. 1893, p. 2; *Tidning för Wenersborgs stad och län*, 28 Apr. 1893, p. 3.
68. *Dalpilen*, 21 Dec. 1894, p. 3.
69. Östergötlands veckoblad, 11 May 1888, p. 1.
70. *Kalmar*, 4 Apr. 1888, p. 2, *Norra Skåne*, 4 Apr. 1888, p. 2.

stories about them in the newspapers changed.[71] At the beginning of the period the articles were exclusively about three aspects: extermination of wolves, rabid wolves and unusual wolves. At the end of the period the main focus was the fear of wolves. The fictional character of the stories increased with time. Certain themes can be noted in the wolf narratives of Swedish newspapers. The extermination of wolves was central at the beginning of the period. The goal was to encourage the extermination of wolves and the stories were published as models besides providing the obviously useful information about wolves being present in the area. Encouraging wolf hunting also appears to have been the purpose of the publication of statistics, both about the amount of damage done by the wolves and the number of wolves killed. Killing wolves was presented as a duty of national interest.

The rabid wolf attack was quite a common story in the older newspapers. The stories were often detailed, vivid and rather credible; however, the wolf was more often than not described as unusual in some way, mainly as being larger than normal wolves. The rabid wolf attacks were often stories from abroad, the purpose obviously not being to warn about local wolves. The stories, however, warned about wolves in general, giving information about wolves becoming rabid. The narratives on rabid wolves therefore also seem to have been a part of a national goal to relieve the country of wolves.

The theme of the struggle between man and wolf had quite a different tone and function. It was, rather, a story about human dominance over nature. The story appeared in the paper, not because it conveyed necessary information about the whereabouts of dangerous wolves, but because it entertained with its focus on the dramatic battle. The man versus wolf battle was of course more entertaining than disastrous, as the incidence of rabies had been reduced.

By the end of the nineteenth century, when wolf populations in Sweden were strongly decimated, the stories about wolves in newspapers became emotional, sensationalised and often exaggerated. This evoked criticism from journalists, who were more critical of their sources. The concept *wolf* over time became loaded with different meaning. The word *wolf* in the newspapers meant any threat whatsoever from the wild. The connotations of the word were cold winter, disease and dire circumstances. Just like its precursor – the word *monster*, from the Latin word *monstrum* meaning the portent of disaster – it came to forebode misfortune of all kinds. The wolf-stories had now become more or less detached from facts and had a life of their own. And, as good stories, for a long time they outlived the real wolves of Sweden.

---

71. Wolves were never extinct in Sweden during the period but the number at the end of the nineteenth century was probably merely a few hundred individuals. During the twentieth century the decline continued and the wolf was considered functionally extinct by the 1970s (See Bergström et al. in this volume).

Karin Dirke

BIBLIOGRAPHY

Archival Sources

Bondeståndets riksdagsprotokoll, band 1, 1720-1727, bilaga nr 39 [The Records of the Peasantry of the Swedish parliament 1720-1727].

Protocoll, hållna hos Högloflige Ridderskapet och Adeln vid Urtima Riksdagen i Stockholm 1815, vol. 5 [The Records of the Nobility of the Swedish parliament 1815]

Research Literature

Åkerberg, S. 2001. *Knowledge and Pleasure at Regent's Park: the Gardens of the Zoological Society of London during the nineteenth century* (Diss. Umeå University).

Broberg, G. 1982. 'Lappkaravaner på villovägar: antropologin och synen på samerna fram mot sekelskiftet 1900'. *Lychnos* 1981/1982: 27–86.

Coleman, J.T. 2004. *Vicious: Wolves and Men in America* (New Haven: Yale University Press).

Gustafsson, K.E., P. Rydén, C.-G. Holmberg, I. Oscarsson and J. Torbacke (eds). 2000. *Den svenska pressens historia. 1, I begynnelsen (tiden före 1830).* (Stockholm: Ekerlid).

Hallgren, W. 1960. *Svensk veterinärhistoria i ord och bilder* (Malmö: Allhem).

Haraldsson, D. 1987. *Skydda vår natur! Svenska Naturskyddsföreningens framväxt och tidiga utveckling* (Lund: Lund University Press).

Berch, A. 1750. *Vestmanlands björn- och vargfänge, under Anders Berchs biträde, förestält af Anders Hillerström uti then större Carolinske lärosalen den [23] Maji år 1750.* Diss. Uppsala Univ. (Printed in Uppsala).

Kalof, L. 2007. *Looking at Animals in Human History* (London: Reaktion Books).

Lagerlöf, S. 1981 [1891]. *Gösta Berlings saga* (Stockholm: Albert Bonniers Förlag).

Lantto, P. 2000. *Tiden börjar på nytt: en analys av samernas etnopolitiska mobilisering i Sverige 1900–1950* (Diss. Umeå University).

Lindgren, A. 2001. *Emil's Pranks* (new edition, trans. by Ed Holmes) (Stockholm: Kvint).

Linnell, J.D.C. et al. 2002. 'The Fear of Wolves: A Review of Wolf Attacks on Humans'. *NINA oppdragsmelding* 731: 1–65.

Lloyd, L. 1855. *Anteckningar under ett tjuguårigt vistande i Skandinavien: innehållande jagtäfventyr, råd för jägare och fiskare, samt strödda bidrag till Nordens fauna* (Stockholm: Bonnier).

Kjellström, R. 1995. *Jakt och fångst i södra Lappland i äldre tid* (Stockholm: Nordiska museet).

Nilsson, S. 1847. *Skandinavisk fauna, första delen: däggdjuren* (second revised edition) (Lund: Gleerup).

Orrelius, M. 1750. *Historia animalum, eller Beskrifning öfver diur riket* (Stockholm).

1765. *Berättelse, om det Grymma Människo-frätande Wildjuret, som Öfver et års tid åstadkommit i Frankrikes södra Provincier mycken upmärksamhet, skada och olägenhet* (Stockholm: Nyström och Stolpe).

Pousette, E. 2000. *De människoätande vargarna* (Bjørkelangen: Bjørkelangen bok & papir).

Smith, J.M. 2011. *Monsters of the Gévaudan: the Making of a Beast* (Cambridge, Mass.: Harvard University Press).

Thorell, T. 1865. *Zoologiens grunder* (Stockholm: Axel Hellsten).

Internet sites

magasin.kb.se/searchinterface/about.html

http://www.smittskyddsinstitutet.se/sjukdomar/rabies/

Newspapers

Blekingsposten 30 Mar. 1860

Bollnäs tidning 25 Nov. 1876

Bollnäs tidning 24 Apr. 1880

Dalpilen 13 Jan.1866

Dalpilen 13 Mar. 1875

Dalpilen 19 Apr. 1876

Dalpilen 29 Jan. 1886

Dalpilen 21 Dec. 1894

Dalpilen 18 Dec. 1896

Dalpilen 9 May 1899

Faluposten 25 Jan. 1871

Faluposten 26 Feb. 1876

Faluposten 16 Mar. 1878

Folkets röst 9 Mar. 1853

Gotlands tidning 4 Feb. 1880

Gotlands tidning 18 Aug. 1880

Inrikes tidningar 23 Dec. 1771

Inrikes tidningar 2 Jan. 1772

Inrikes Tidningar 22 May 1780

Jönköpingsbladet 14 Dec. 1850

Jönköpingsbladet 17 Jan. 1861

Kalmar 22 Feb. 1865

Kalmar 23 Jan. 1871

Kalmar 2 Mar. 1870

Kalmar 5 Feb. 1876

Kalmar 1 Nov. 1877

Karin Dirke

Kalmar 8 Nov. 1877

Kalmar 8 Feb. 1879

Kalmar 14 Apr. 1880

Kalmar 11 Aug. 1880

Kalmar 16 Aug 1880

Kalmar 3 Nov. 1880

Kalmar 21 Feb. 1881

Kalmar 14 Nov 1881

Kalmar 2 Jun. 1887

Kalmar 4 Apr. 1888

Kalmar 8 Jan. 1890

Kalmar 10 May 1890

Kalmar 27 Dec. 1890

Kalmar 9 Feb. 1891

Kalmar 22 Apr. 1893

Norra Skåne 7 Dec. 1883

Norra Skåne 17 Nov. 1887

Norra Skåne 17 Nov. 1887

Norra Skåne 15 Mar. 1887

Norra Skåne 4 Apr. 1888

Norra Skåne 22 Apr. 1893

Post-och Inrikes tidningar 31 Mar. 1832

Post-och inrikes tidningar 26 Mar. 1836

Post-och Inrikes tidningar 14 Apr. 1837

Post-och Inrikes tidningar 27 Dec. 1837

Post-och Inrikes tidningar 7 Feb. 1838

Post-och Inrikes tidningar 18 Jun. 1844

Posttidningar 18 Jul. 1771

Stockholms Post-Tidningar 10 Feb. 1780

Tidning för Wenersborgs stad och län 28 Apr. 1893

Wermlands Läns Tidning 19 Apr. 1876

Östergötlands veckoblad 11 May 1888

6

Reconstructing the Extermination of Wolves in Germany. Case Studies from Brandenburg and Rhineland-Palatinate

Patrick Masius and Jana Sprenger

INTRODUCTION

Wolves only recently returned to Germany. The first known reproduction after more than a hundred years occurred at the turn of the twenty-first century. It marked the beginning of a thriving comeback. Numerous political and societal actors have made significant efforts to minimise conflicts and make coexistence possible. Fundamental changes in the perception of wolves during the twentieth century allowed for a change in policies. In Germany, as in many European countries, wolf persecution has an age-old tradition caused by resource conflicts between pastoral societies and the predators. By herding their livestock in forests and pastures humans unintentionally provided excellent food alternatives while at the same time extending agricultural cultivation into the wolves' habitats. The threat for domestic animals rendered the implementation of control measures a necessity. Furthermore, wolves were regarded as hunting competitors, challenging sovereign privileges.[1]

Numerous historic records document the often-extensive persecution effort. In the mid-eighteenth century, a common German encyclopaedia described wolves as 'ravenous, vicious, malicious, and the most dangerous enemy of wild and tame animals, in particular of sheep'.[2] They were even considered as the 'most harmful creature on earth'[3] and a serious threat not only to livestock and game but to humans as well. Even in daylight they would intrude into settlements and 'attack, maul, and devour' people.[4] A regional ordinance from the mid-seventeenth century refers to several recent attacks by wolves on children close to a village south of Koblenz.[5]

---

1. Ott 2004, pp. 115–6.
2. Zedler 1758, vol. 58, col. 496 (all quotations from German original texts translated by the authors).
3. Ibid., col. 497. Compare also Bechstein (1792), who categorised the wolf together with lynx, bark beetle and adder as the most harmful pests.
4. Zedler 1758, vol. 58, col. 497.
5. Main State Archive Koblenz (LHAK), Best. 700/110, No. 74, 27 Aug. 1658 (Zell). However, there are no further details of the incidents given.

Many sources portrayed wolves, as well as other large predators such as brown bears and lynxes, as ferocious and ill-natured creatures. Each behavioural pattern was interpreted unfavourably, following the common concept of the enemy. Their hunting was characterised as bloodthirsty, their howling as ghastly, their personality as depraved and untamed, their caution as cowardly and their approach of villages as insolent.[6] In 1815, the forest officer (*Oberforstmeister*) Hartig reported to the General Government (*Generalgouvernement*) of the Rhine provinces in Aachen that wolf numbers 'had gotten out of hand, and had become a plague' in the districts west of the river.[7] According to the account, each flock was now guarded by four shepherds, and rabid predators had caused many 'unfortunate incidents'. People were 'alarmed and terrified', and in many regions 'one only dared to travel in large company and armed'. The benefit of wolf extermination was undisputed; the animals were to be 'injured, caught or killed' by everyone.[8] However, the historic documentation furthermore illustrates the unreliability of accounts dealing with uncontrollable wolf numbers as well as wolf attacks. For example, a newspaper article from November 1835 reported an unusual increase in the local wolf population causing considerable damages and an attack on a horseman near Koblenz. These incidents proved to be false after further official investigation.[9] There appear to be only very few confirmed reports of cases where non-rabid wolves killed humans in modern German history though some sources remain to be explored.[10] However, to this day, folktales that characterise wolves as dangerous enemies, such as *Little Red Riding Hood* or *The Wolf and the Seven Young Goats*, belong to our cultural heritage.[11]

The article analyses the history of wolf persecution with a main focus on Brandenburg and the Rhineland throughout the eighteenth and nineteenth centuries (Figure 1).[12] We concentrate on common hunting methods and the underlying legislation as well as on the resulting consequences for the local wolf populations. A final perspective examines subsequent changes in wolf perception and the challenges that today's wolf management faces.

METHODS OF WOLF PERSECUTION

Evidence for systematically organised wolf hunting in the territory of today's Germany can be found as early as the Burgundian migration period and the Merovingian dynasty. During the reign of Charlemagne, in each countship, two specialised

6. Ott 2004, pp. 111, 113.
7. LHAK, Best. 363, No. 37, 17 Sept. 1815.
8. Krafft 1712, p. 559.
9. LHAK, Best. 403, No. 2371, 3 Feb. 1836.
10. Linnell 2002, p. 61.
11. Scherf 2001.
12. Compare also Masius and Sprenger 2012.

Reconstructing the Extermination of Wolves in Germany

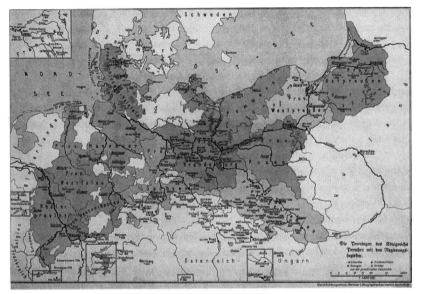

Figure 1. Prussian provinces around 1900 (Mück 1911, p. 11).

The eighteenth-century Prussian territory *Kurmark* Brandenburg is located west of the river Oder, the adjacent district to the east was called Neumark. Pomerania (*Pommern*) lies north-east of Brandenburg, East Prussia (*Ostpreußen*) is situated further east, and the Rhine Province is located in the south-west.

huntsmen were responsible for wolf hunting.[13] Due to advancing inland colonisation in the medieval warm period, wolves lost important retreat areas. Subsequently, conflicts between humans and the predators accumulated, resulting in increased hunting pressure. In the sixteenth century, further agricultural expansion as well as enhanced weaponry intensified tracking efforts into the last remote and densely forested areas.[14] In the seventeenth century, the Thirty Years' War (1618–1648) briefly interrupted the continuous wolf persecution in many German regions. Large agricultural areas and entire villages were abandoned. Hunting pressure decreased, and perished or straying livestock as well as war victims provided sufficient food.[15] Wolf populations rapidly recovered. During this period, chronicles often referred to extensive wolf plagues (see Kling, this volume). But that was just a short respite. In the post-war period, hunting pressure increased and wolves were again killed

13. Delort 1987, p. 262, 268; cf. also Kalb 2007, pp. 320–1.
14. See Ott 2004, p. 158.
15. See Ibid., pp. 128–9. Compare also Zimen 1990, pp. 410–2.

with a variety of methods. Administrative programmes for extermination were usually triggered by the loss of cattle or a perceived threat to human security. In hard winters, rumours of people being attacked on country roads by hungry wolves sometimes entered the political arena and led to intensified measures.[16]

The most important method to combat wolves was drive hunting (Figure 2). In the early modern period, these hunts were often conducted with the so-called '*Wolfszeug*', which consisted of nets and long lines with pieces of cloth. After the hideout of the wolves was enclosed, beaters moved in tight formation through the area driving the wolves in the direction of the barriers, where they were shot or slain.[17]

Participants in the wolf hunts were state foresters, hunters, stewards as well as the rural population who were summoned to serve as beaters. The drives lasted many hours, sometimes several days, and took place in the coldest season, since, in order to detect wolves, fresh snow was essential. Peasants and poor day labourers, who did not own sufficient clothing, often became sick or even froze to death.[18]

Innumerable reports from different regions of Germany prove the regular implementation of public drive hunts including the participation of local inhabitants. In the beginning of the eighteenth century, in the region of Oranienburg (Brandenburg) alone, ten to 25 wolf hunts were conducted each year.[19] It is not surprising that whole parishes and cities tried to free themselves from this obligation. In 1672, the city of Neu-Ruppin asked for an exemption, because war and fire had already brought great distress. The request was granted in return for a payment of several hundred taler (*Reichstaler*).[20]

Additionally, private citizens were often encouraged to pursue independent wolf hunts. Anyone 'entitled to hunt ought to shoot wolves'.[21] A few people successfully used leg-hold traps. In the district of Treves, forest steward (*Jagdhüter*) Johann Dorus was known to possess eighty such iron traps, and would check them every morning.[22] Others collected wolf pups directly from the den.[23] In order to increase the willingness to kill wolves, high rewards were established. According to a decree of 1693, the administration paid 6 taler for a full-grown wolf, 3 taler for a young wolf and 2 taler for each of the pups caught in a wolf den. Between 1817 and 1871, in Prussia, an adult female wolf was awarded with 12 taler, an adult male with 10 taler. The catcher received 8 taler for the submission of a juvenile and 4 taler for a whelp. This distribution shows a certain biological understanding, since adults

16.   LHAK, Best. 712, No. 2284, Dec. 1798.
17.   See Ott 2004, pp. 135–40; Sommer 1999, pp. 25–8.
18.   See Ott 2004, pp. 141–3; Sommer 1999, p. 27.
19.   Suter 2003, p. 52.
20.   Secret State Archives Prussian Cultural Heritage (GSTAPK), II. HA, Abt. 33 Kurmark, Tit. 65, No. 2.
21.   LHAK, Best. 640, No. 73, 4 Jan. 1806.
22.   LHAK, Best. 442, No. 154, 22 Feb. 1862.
23.   LHAK, Best. 655, 200, No. 1948.

Figure 2. Illustration of a wolf hunt in a hunting book from 1682 (Täntzer 1682, p. 105).

are of central importance for the reproductive success and the supply of the wolf pack.[24] To prevent multiple rewards for the same wolf, the administration would cut off the paws and ears of the submitted animal. The bounty system developed into a decisive instrument for the eradication of wolves in Germany. However, it was not without flaws. Hunters complained that these programmes would support poaching, because people would be able to shoot deer while pretending to hunt for wolves.[25] Sometimes administrative borders made it difficult to allocate the rewards properly. For example, in February 1868, Johann Redlinger, a tailor from Perl,[26] killed a wolf just over the French border while travelling in search of work. According to his statement, the already injured predator was slain with a pitchfork after a fifteen-minute chase. Redlinger refused the French reward in favour of a higher Prussian bounty. In Treves, his claim was processed but later denied due to the foreign location of the incident.[27] Furthermore, there were regular quarrels

---

24. Herrmann 2003, pp. 49–50.

25. LHAK, Best. 403, No. 2371.

26. Local district of Saarburg in the administrative district of Treves.

27. Subsequently, justifying it with his family's poverty, Redlinger submitted a supplication directly to the minister for agrarian affairs (*Minister für landwirthschaftliche Angelegenheiten*) in Berlin asking for the award or, at least, a reimbursement of his travel expenses. The minister rejected the petition due to non-existent funds. Referring to his indigence, the amount was finally paid as a financial

over the rightful recipient of a reward, in particular if it was unclear whose bullet killed a wolf on a drive hunt.[28]

In many regions, drive hunts and private initiatives were not sufficient to decimate wolf populations. In particular, when there was no snow, tracking and hunting were impossible. Therefore, poisoned baits were used.[29] Poisoning wolves had a long tradition. In 1712, a guidebook on pest control stated different recipes for the production of wolf baits. Poisons such as strychnine, arsenic and aconitum (*'Wolffs-Wurz'*) were mixed with flower, honey and bacon. This concoction was formed into pellet shaped baits (*'Wolfskugeln'*). Of the different poisons, *'Krähenaugen'* proved to be the deadliest.[30] These seeds from the strychnine tree (*Strychnos nux-vomica*) were imported from Southern Asia (Figure 3). In the Rhine Province, the French administration decided in 1809 that the poisoning of these harmful animals would be necessary. 'Il est nécessaire d'employer l'empoisonnent contre ces animaux destructeurs', said a circular of the department's headquarters (*Departmentskommandantur*).[31] The Prussian administration carried on this measure after 1815. The forest stewards would prepare dead cattle with strychnine from ground *'Krähenaugen'*. Yearly in the 1820s, the province government in Koblenz bought about thirty pounds of *'Krähenaugen'* for twenty taler.[32] The district forester reported about the success of the poisoning from Zell in July 1825:

> In order to poison three wolves, which were detected in this district, I have – since the forest steward is not reliable – taken matters into my own hands, … and poisoned a dead foal and a pig and transported them on a well known wolf path, with good effects. Soon after that, a peasant … found a heavily poisoned wolf not far off from the spot, where I had transported the bait, dead.[33]

The carcass of a second wolf was found some time later; the forester speculated that it had also died by poison. In rare cases, the wolf succumbed to the venom near the bait, making the allocation of a reward simple.[34] In other instances, when a dead wolf was detected far away from the bait or not found at all, it was difficult to determine whether a wolf was poisoned. Hence, a reward could not be handed out and the success of the measure remained unclear.[35] Rarely, whole packs were

support by the royal administration in Treves (LHAK, Best. 442, No. 154, correspondence from 28 Mar. 1868, 28 Jun. 1868, 8 Jul. 1868).

28. E.g. LHAK, Best. 655, 200, No. 1948, pp. 13–4, 26 May 1820.
29. LHAK, Best. 537, 057, No. 390.
30. Krafft 1712, Vol. II, p. 3–4.
31. LHAK, Best. 256, No. 872.
32. LHAK, Best. 441, No. 7976. In other districts poison was used as well, for example in Frankfurt (Oder) at least until 1842 (Butzeck et al. 1988, p. 413).
33. LHAK, Best. 441, No. 7976.
34. E.g. LHAK, Best. 441, No. 11370.
35. See LHAK, Best. 441, No. 7976; Best. 537,057, No. 390.

Reconstructing the Extermination of Wolves in Germany

Figure 3. Poison-nut (*Strychnos nux vomica*). Bottom left: the seeds known as
'*Krähenaugen*' ('Crow's eyes'). Source: Köhler 1887.

exterminated by poisoning, for example, in the local district of Blankenheim in
the winter of 1816/17.[36] In general, the proportion of wolves killed by poison
remained low. For instance, in the administrative district of Gumbinnen (East
Prussia) only 39 wolves (3.7 per cent) had been effectively poisoned between 1817
and 1825,[37] and in the district of Treves in the Rhine Province only seven (one per
cent) between 1821 and 1880.[38]

Since the Middle Ages, wolves had also been caught in 'wolfgardens' and
pit traps.[39] Many such capture systems were installed after the Thirty Years' War.
Until the end of the nineteenth century this method was part of the standard
repertoire of wolf eradication.[40] The wolves were lured in these traps by carcasses

36. LHAK, Best. 441, No. 7976.
37. Suter 2003, p. 33.
38. LHAK, Best. V 1000, Vol. 1822–1881.
39. Landau 1849, p. 223.
40. For instance, in the Rhine Province in the district of Treves, 109 wolves (12%) were caught with
     different trapping devices between 1821 and 1880. However, this number includes at least 30
     wolves caught in leg-hold traps. The sources only rarely distinguish between the different trapping
     devices (LHAK, Best. V 1000, Vol. 1822–1881).

or animal intestines and caught with bait – mostly a living duck. Ducks were appropriate because their loud chattering and flapping of wings attracts the wolf's attention effectively. Wolfgardens were relatively large fenced areas equipped with trap doors. Once the wolf seized the bait, the trap door shut automatically. The most effective pit traps included big wooden boxes with a trap door and bait on top tied to a pole in the middle. Otherwise the wolf would sometimes be able to dig his way out of the pit trap.[41] In 1815, models for a wolfgarden and an elaborate pit trap were distributed in the Rhine Province (Figure 4), and subsequently many such traps were installed.[42] They were to be placed on common land and situated in remote locations to avoid accidents with human travellers and livestock.[43] The province government would bear the expenses while the boroughs were supposed to deliver the requisite amount of wood for the construction.[44] However, in 1835, the central Prussian government in Berlin criticised such expensive trapping devices, and emphasised the advantages of ordinary pit traps.[45]

Throughout the eighteenth and nineteenth centuries, drive hunting remained the most important method for extirpating wolves. In Gumbinnen, between 1817 and 1825, 92 per cent of killed wolves were shot during hunts; in the district of Treves it was more than 75 per cent between 1821 and 1880.[46] The success of other methods such as poisoning and leg-hold traps strongly depended on the individual engagement of foresters and bounty hunters and thus differed regionally and temporarily. Forest steward Johann Dorus, who lived close to the French border in an area with many wolves, managed to catch about thirty wolves in leg-hold traps between 1852 and 1866.[47]

Combatting wolves created communication between state and citizens. Through wolf persecution governments appeared to guarantee the security of the citizens and thereby reinforced authority.[48] The Prussian system relied on the participation of a major part of the rural population, in contrast to the United States, where, in the nineteenth and twentieth centuries, a few professional hunt-

---

41. LHAK, Best. 441, No. 11370.
42. LHAK, Best. 363, No. 37.
43. See LHAK, Best. 655,158, No. 34, 17 Oct. 1815; LHAK, Best. 363, No. 37, 23 Sep. 1815.
44. LHAK, Best. 363, No. 37. It is unclear to what extent these ideas were implemented over time and how many older traps had already existed throughout the region (see for example, report from 19 Oct. 1815). For more plans to build trapping devices, see further documentation (e.g. 2 Nov. 1815; LHAK, Best. 441, No. 7976, May / Jun. 1817; LHAK, Best. 537,057, No. 390, 30 Jul. 1820).
45. LHAK, Best. 403, No. 2371, 8 Dec. 1835.
46. LHAK, Best. V 1000, Vol. 1822–1881. The historical statistics are not always clear as to whether a wolf was shot on a hunt or in a trap. Therefore, this number has to be treated carefully.
47. LHAK, Best. V 1000, Vol. 1823–1867. In 1861, he caught so many wolves that the authorities became suspicious and accused him of fraud. However, the charges turned out to be unjustified (LHAK, Best. 442, No. 154, 22 Feb. 1862).
48. Compare Meyer 1999, pp. 124–7.

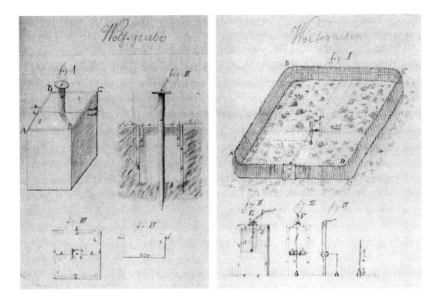

Figure 4. Models of a wolf pit trap and a 'wolfgarden', designed by forest officer (*Oberforstmeister*) Hartig in 1815 and subsequently distributed in the Prussian Rhine Province (LHAK, Best. 441, No. 11370.).

ers specialised in wolves.[49] The publication of killing statistics in newspapers and administrative journals proved the effectiveness of the measures and justified the often extensive public obligations. Against this background, it is not surprising that the extermination programmes, though costly and time-consuming, were never questioned.

WOLF EXTERMINATION

In many Prussian territories, wolf populations could not withstand the intensive hunting pressure for long and collapsed in many areas at the turn of the eighteenth century.[50] The predators survived mainly along the eastern and western borders, where spacious remote areas were shared with neighbouring territories. Immigration could originate from the vast forests of Eastern Europe as well as from the mountainous regions of the French Vosges and the Belgian Ardennes. Throughout

---

49. Marvin 2012, pp. 111–2.
50. Ott 2004, pp. 159–60.

the eighteenth and nineteenth centuries, today's Poland and France both supported larger wolf populations than Germany.[51]

Numerous Prussian decrees valid for the *Kurmark* Brandenburg were issued in the decades around 1700 – such as those of 1688, 1693, 1696 and 1708.[52] They recalled and complemented established instructions, remaining in force well into the eighteenth century. Further renewals or additional regulations were, for example, passed in 1724 (Neumark and Sternberg),[53] 1728[54] and 1734 (*Kurmark* Brandenburg, Neumark and Pomerania).[55] At the turn of the eighteenth century, wolf numbers in Brandenburg had dropped considerably, in contrast to the Prussian provinces further east. From 1723 to 1737, each year an average number of 230 wolves was killed in East Prussia. Throughout this period, wolf hunters culled only 57 wolves in the western territories, *Kurmark* Brandenburg, the adjacent Neumark east of the Oder, and Pomerania (Figure 1).[56] Whereas 241 wolves were killed in winter 1747/48 in East Prussia, only 24 were eliminated in the three western territories. Only one of these animals was caught in the *Kurmark*.[57] However, individual wanderers, presumably migrating over the river Oder, were still recorded regularly and sometimes established packs. For example, between 1735 and 1737, several wolves were tracked along the Oder, in the district of Lehnin south-west of Berlin, and in the forest district Gross-Schoenebeck, part of a large woodland north of Berlin.[58] In 1741, three adults and two juveniles were found in the forests around Lindow, north-west of Berlin. According to the documentation, two years later, a pack crossed the Oder and killed forty sheep and some game in a single night, causing an immediate public drive hunt.[59] Following the continuous appearance of individual wolves, in 1753, the government repealed an earlier regulation from 1734 that had restricted public hunts to the emergence of two or more wolves.[60] Likewise, in the second half of the century, hunters tracked wolves repeatedly throughout the province, in particular in the northern woodlands. For example, in 1764, ten wolves, an unusually high number, roaming the forests north-west of Berlin, startled the authorities and instantly caused increased tracking efforts. Soon, they were successfully caught.[61] Nine years later, two adults and

51. See Ott 2004, p. 160.
52. See Mylius, CCM, part 4, section 1, ch. 2.
53. GStAPK, II. HA, Abt. 33 Gen, Tit. XVII, No. 5.
54. Mylius, CCM, part 4, section 1, chapter 2, 20 Jan. 1734 (no regional specification).
55. Ibid., 22 Dec. 1728.
56. See Suter 2003, p. 82.
57. Ibid.
58. GStAPK, II. HA, Abt. 33 Kurmark, Tit. 65, No. 4.
59. Ibid., No. 8, Vol. 1.
60. Ibid.
61. Ibid.

three juveniles were killed after preying on several foals north of Berlin.[62] At the end of the century, wolf numbers had already been reduced so much that a wolf killed in the gardens of Oranienburg palace in 1796 was believed to be a captured animal that had escaped from a boat on the river Havel.[63] Less frequent renewals of official ordinances later in the century provide further evidence for a decline in Brandenburg's wolf population and a decreasing need for hunting.

In contrast, in the Prussian Rhine Province, wolves survived well into the nineteenth century, despite concerted extermination efforts. For instance, in January 1814, the government passed a decree regarding the necessary manpower in public wolf hunts.[64] Two years later, the official gazette of Treves (*Amtsblatt*) published a reminder of the continued importance of wolf persecution: 'Although all means have been applied for the extermination of these most harmful animals, … we have … seen that a large number of wolves still remain in the local district'.[65] Hunting of wolves was well documented in parts of the Rhineland. Over the period 1817 to 1885, a total of 881 adult and 135 juvenile wolves were culled in the administrative district of Treves (Figure 5a). The sex ratios of the adult wolves remained relatively stable over the analysed time period. Altogether, 52.3 per cent were male (Table 1).[66] Additionally, the authorities recorded 586 whelps as well as 32 unborn pups (Figure 5b).

Killings in the first half of the nineteenth century account for more than eighty per cent of the total number. Throughout this period, the wolf population in the Rhineland was still reproducing regularly. Almost every year, Treves' hunting statistics reported not only the killing of adults but also of younger wolves and whelps. In contrast, these entries became rare in the second half of the century, indicating the final collapse of the population. Whereas from the 1820s to the 1840s records documented on average 2.6–6.1 juveniles per year, in the 1850s only six younger wolves were killed throughout the entire ten-year period (Table 1). According to the available hunting statistics, the last juvenile was killed in 1868. Between 1850 and 1885, only six years provided records of whelps.[67] Until 1849, pups were killed every year except 1833 (Figure 5b). However, attempts at fraud might have affected the number of whelps being delivered to the authorities. In the 1830s, in the administrative district of Koblenz, Adam Lauxen frequently received

62. Ibid., Vol. 2.
63. GStAPK, II. HA, Abt. 33 Kurmark, Tit. 65, No. 8, Vol. 3.
64. See Weinand 2010.
65. LHAK, Best. V 1000, Vol. 1816.
66. In a study of similar historic data in northern Spain the male/female ratio in the wolf recordings increased significantly over time, indicating that food stress which often affects females more than males might have played a bigger role – alongside persecution – in the continued decrease of the analysed wolf population than previously thought (Fernández and Ruiz de Azua 2010). Our data indicate no increase in the male/female ratio.
67. 1853, 1859, 1865, 1871/72, 1876.

130

Patrick Masius and Jana Sprenger

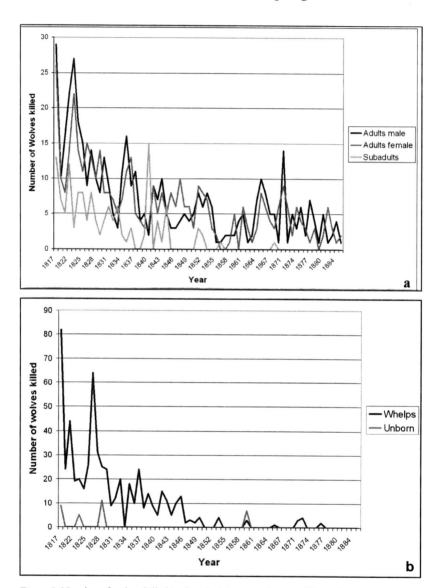

Figure 5. Number of wolves killed in the administrative district of Treves between 1817 and 1885: (a) Adults and juveniles, (b) Whelps and unborn pups.

In 1877, the underlying accounting year was changed. The 1877 statistic included wolf kills from January 1877 to March 1878. The following years contained kills from April to March. No data is available for 1818, 1819, 1869 and 1881. These years were excluded from the graphics (LHAK, Best. V 1000, Vol. 1817–1886; LHA Best. 442, No. 155).

Reconstructing the Extermination of Wolves in Germany

Table 1. Wolves killed in the administrative district of Treves in ten/five-year periods between 1820 and 1885 (1869, 1881 missing).

	Wolves killed per year (Ø ten/five-year period)			Total number of wolves killed					
Year	Total	Adult	Subadult	Male	Female	Subadult	Male %	Female %	Sex ratio (m/f)
1820-29	34,1	28	6,1	149	131	61	53,2	46,8	1,1
1830-39	18,5	15,7	2,8	86	71	28	54,8	45,2	1,2
1840-49	14,4	11,8	2,6	52	66	26	44,1	55,9	0,8
1850-59	8,5	7,9	0,6	41	38	6	51,9	48,1	1,1
1860-68	9,1	9	0,1	47	34	1	58,0	42,0	1,4
1870-79	8,4	8,4	0	44	40	0	52,4	47,6	1,1
1880-85	5,4	5,4	0	13	14	0	48,1	51,9	0,9
Total				432	394	122	52,3	47,7	1,1

The table shows the average yearly catches of adults and juveniles as well as the total number of male, female and juvenile wolves killed in each period. The sexes of juveniles were not documented in the files. Whelps and unborn cubs are excluded from the table (LHAK, Best. 441, No. 7975).

wolf bounties for fox pups. Not every official had the ability to distinguish between young whelps of the two species. Originally, the attentive administrator (*Landrat*) in the district office Cochem (*Landratsamt*) had refused to accept the animals but subsequently, Lauxen successfully passed them off as wolf pups in Koblenz. The documentation reports several cases of Lauxen avoiding the agency in Cochem and delivering whelps in Koblenz, Mayen and Zell.[68] Wolf hunting statistics in 1835 and 1836 demonstrate an especially high ratio of pups (Table 2). Interestingly, ten of the whelps recorded and compensated with four taler each were brought by Barbara Lauxen, the wife of Adam Lauxen, on 2 May 1836 to the district office in Koblenz.[69] After the administrator in Cochem had warned the province government in Koblenz against the possibility of fraud, the number and percentage of delivered wolf whelps decreased noticeably. Officials henceforth issued bounties more cautiously and occasionally even raised a pup to determine its species. Likewise, the high numbers of wolf whelps in the district of Treves – such as 82 in 1817 (51.6 per cent of wolves killed) and 64 (58.9 per cent) in 1826 (Figure 5b) – might have been increased by successful fraud. However, in combination with the frequently

68. LHAK, Best. 441, No. 11370.
69. LHAK, Best. 441, No. 7975.

caught juveniles, the data provide adequate evidence for the existence of reproducing wolf packs throughout the first half of the nineteenth century.

Table 2. Percentage of whelps in the administrative district of Koblenz between 1835 and 1838.[70]

	Wolves (total)	Adults / Subadults	Whelps	Whelps (%)
1835	59	15	44	75 %
1836	40	14	26	65 %
1837	33	16	17	51 %
1838	14	8	6	43 %

During wars, hunting pressure usually dropped and wolf populations often recovered or even expanded. Thus, the Napoleonic Wars provided ideal conditions for high wolf densities.[71] Hunting statistics confirm the trapping of large numbers of wolves in the post-war period.[72] In 1817, a total number of 1,080 wolves were killed throughout Prussia.[73] The director of Treves' forest department reported large numbers of wolves migrating into the area in 1815:

> by far the greatest number of wolves most likely originate from the mountainous woods of the Ardennes and Vosges ... This year's experience, having these large mountain areas disturbed by turmoil of war, and large numbers of wolves migrating into our local regions, provide strong evidence for this. At least, this year's great numbers of these robbers cannot be well explained differently.[74]

Although the letter emphasises disturbance as the cause for war-related migration, it was more likely improved living conditions.

In the Rhine Province and the adjacent French districts, a period of intensive wolf persecution followed the Napoleonic Wars, causing a significant decline in wolf numbers.[75] For example, the authorities of the Lorraine department Vosges paid rewards for a total number of 1,612 wolves between 1817 and 1842.[76] In Treves, statistics prove the death of 593 adult and juvenile wolves in the same period; additionally, 530 whelps and 25 unborn cubs were recorded.

In the district of Treves most wolves were killed in the Saar regions in the south (*Saarkreise*), indicating immigration over the French–German border

70. Compiled from LHAK, Best. 441, No. 11370 and Best. 537,057, No. 390.
71. See Ott 2004, p. 129.
72. Similarly, the Franco-Prussian War (1870–1871) caused an increased hunting result (Fig. 5).
73. Roth 1930.
74. LHAK, Best. 363, No. 37.
75. Similarly, about one hundred years later, intensive hunting almost exterminated the wolf population in the Polish Białowieża Forest in an even shorter time period (1950–1960) (Okarma 1997).
76. Pfeiffer 2011, p. 114.

Reconstructing the Extermination of Wolves in Germany

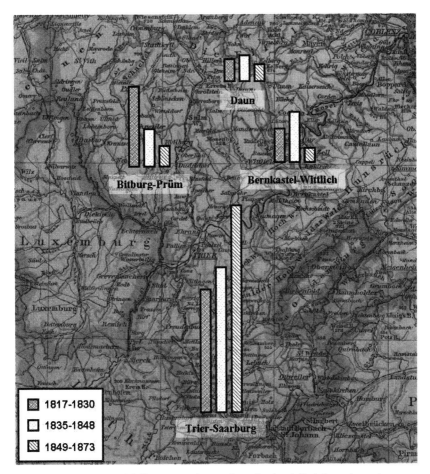

Figure 6. Regional differences in the number of wolves killed throughout the administrative district of Treves.

The graphic illustrates the percentage of recorded wolf kills for three time periods. Locations found in the records were assigned to today's four districts (*Landkreise*): 1817–1830: Bitburg-Pruem 31%, Trier-Saarburg 47.5%, Daun (today Vulkaneifel) 8.5%, Bernkastel-Wittlich 13%; 1835–1848: Bitburg-Pruem 14.5%, Trier-Saarburg 56%, Daun 10%, Bernkastel-Wittlich 19.5%; 1849–1873: Bitburg-Pruem 8%, Trier-Saarburg 80%, Daun 6.5%, Bernkastel-Wittlich 5.5%. The calculation for the first period is based on the exemplary data from 1817, 1820, 1825 and 1830; for the second period on 1835, 1840, 1845 and 1848; and for the third period all years were analysed (LHAK, Best. V 1000, Vol. 1817–1886; LHAK, Best. 442, No. 153–5; map source: Andree 1881).

(Figure 6). From the 1860s, wolf kills occurred exclusively in the southern districts of Saarburg, Saarlouis, Merzig and Saarbrücken (*Trier-Saarburg*).[77] In the second half of the nineteenth century, despite similar persecution efforts, wolf populations in France seem to have been more stable than in Germany.[78] It is well known from other regions that migration has the potential to stabilise an almost exterminated population.[79] After 1885, detailed statistics are no longer available for the district of Treves but records still prove the persistence of individual wolves in its southern regions until 1900.

Drawing conclusions about historic wolf populations from hunting reports causes difficulties, as the number of animals killed depended on numerous factors – such as hunting intensity and geography.[80] The examined sources do not suggest substantial changes in hunting effort that could have considerably altered the relation between wolf killings and the actual population sizes. In the absence of reliable information about hunting intensity, migration and the degree of fraud, the data provide rough estimates. According to ecologist François de Beaufort, recorded wolf killings in eighteenth-century France represent thirty to seventy per cent of the actual population.[81] In compliance with the hypothesis of Beaufort, the actual population density in 1816 could range from 2.3 up to 5.3 animals per 100 km^2.[82] In the following decades, hunting statistics indicate a population from 1.3 to 3 wolves per 100 km^2 in the 1820s, from 0.6 to 1.4 in the 1830s and from 0.2 to 0.4 in the 1860s.[83] The current population density of wolves in eastern Germany averages two to three animals per 100 km^2 (Lusatia 2000–2009).[84] In the case of nineteenth-century Treves, similar densities can only be detected shortly after the Napoleonic Wars.

CHANGING PERCEPTIONS

In many regions of Germany memorial stones from the eighteenth and nineteenth centuries witness the shooting of single wolves. Often constructed years after the

77. LHAK, Best. 442, No. 154.
78. See Moriceau 2011.
79. E.g. Okarma 1997, p. 78.
80. See Herrmann 2006.
81. Beaufort 1988, pp. 695–6.
82. In 1816, a total of 114 wolves were killed in the administrative district of Treves. The data do not allow a differentiation between whelps and juveniles and were therefore excluded from figure five. In the 1840s, the administrative district of Treves had a total land surface of 131.2 geographical square miles (Anonymous 1841; 7,200 km^2 (Eytelwein 1810)).
83. In the 1820s, the hunting results averaged 65 wolves per year, including all age groups. In the 1830s, the ten-year average of killings was reduced to 31 wolves; and, in the 1860s, only 9 culled wolves were recorded.
84. Wolfsregion Lausitz 2014, http://www.wolfsregion-lausitz.de/index.php/biologie-und-lebensweise/das-wolfsrudel (Accessed 10 May 2014).

event, these memorials remember the alleged last wolf in an area.[85] As long as wolves were frequent in a region, a wolf kill would not draw enough public attention to construct a specific memorial.[86] Some of these last wolves even gained colourful names, like 'Abd-el-Kader' (an Algerian freedom fighter), who was killed in 1847 in Württemberg,[87] or the famous 'tiger of Sabrodt', who was shot in Sachsen in 1904.[88] These 'last wolves' were usually migrating animals. By the end of the nineteenth century, reproductive wolf populations belonged to the past. With increasing rareness, the image of the wolf improved gradually. Slight changes can be detected in the late nineteenth century. In his guidebook for hunting in 1880, Oscar von Riesenthal, despite considering wolves as potential threats for humans in times of scarcity, regarded many stories of wolf attacks as overstated.[89]

Popular literature such as Kipling's *The Jungle Book* (1894) and London's *White Fang* (1906) contributed to a new perception (Jones, this volume). Wolves were seen as exemplars of wild liberty, intelligence and sociability rather than being associated with attributes like deceitfulness, grimness and deadliness. In the twentieth century, children knew the wolf only from exotic stories and not as a genuine threat for farmers. The rising environmental movement stabilised a positive image of the wolf.[90]

With advances in mechanisation and new technologies to control nature, a counter movement developed that was critical of modern civilisation. For instance, Wilhelm Heinrich Riehl (1823–1897) advocated for the right of wilderness and argued for the holiness of virgin nature, which was most visible in the German forest.[91] The ecological revolution around 1970[92] helped to establish such ideas in a wider social consciousness. Against this background, today's industrial and post-industrial societies see the reasons for wolf persecution as obsolete. Wolves are protected by the Berne Convention on the Conservation of European Wildlife and Natural Habitats (1979) and the Habitats Directive (1992). Apart from a few immigrants, no wolves inhabited German territory until the 1990s. Since then, they have migrated increasingly from Poland into eastern Germany, in particular into Saxony. The first litter of pups was born in 2000, and recognised by a new

---

85. In some cases the stones were referring to particular wolves with distinctive attitudes rather than the alleged last wolf.

86. E.g. Sprenger 2009, p. 183–4.

87. Ott 2004, pp. 171–2.

88. See Schulz 2011; Weinand 2010; Rausch 1967.

89. Riesenthal 1880, pp. 250–1. However, Riesenthal still described wolves as a serious danger to domestic animals 'Wolves can easily rob whole regions and even make any livestock breeding impossible. They can thus become a public menace and terrorise the regional police unlike any other criminal' (ibid, p. 253).

90. See Delort 1987, pp. 279–81.

91. Piechocki 2010, p. 168.

92. Radkau 2011.

memorial stone in the Muskau heath. This stone symbolises a reversal of the long tradition of wolf persecution.

As of summer 2014, at least seventy adult wolves inhabit north and north-eastern Germany; about one third of these occur in Saxony.[93] Wolf management includes scientific research as well as public information and consultation services. Farmers are supported by precautionary measures such as guarding dogs and wolf-secure fences. However, not all livestock losses can be prevented. Between 2002 and 2008, damages of around 35,000 Euros were registered in Saxony.[94] Farmers were compensated by the state government. The biggest losses occurred in areas where wolf populations had expanded recently and precautionary measures had not yet been implemented. In established wolf habitat, safety measures have produced significant results and damages have been considerably mitigated.[95] As analyses of faeces have shown, the diet of the Lusatia wolves consists mainly of roe deer (52 per cent), red deer (25 per cent) and wild boar (16 per cent); sheep and goats constitute only 0.4 per cent of the diet.[96]

Fear of the predators is along with livestock damages still one of the most relevant problems for wolf management as empirical data confirm. However, in 2014, only thirteen per cent of interviewed people stated that they were afraid of wild wolves. About eighty per cent of the population is not afraid of the predators.[97] A 2006 study concerning the acceptance of wolves revealed that, in general, the public perceived their return positively.[98] The support from particular interest groups such as hunters is much lower than in the general population: 63 per cent of the subjects from the 2006 study thought the wolf to be tolerable in today's cultural landscape, only ten per cent found it intolerable;[99] a different study from 2005 showed that only 48 per cent of hunters thought wolves to be tolerable while 43 per cent deemed them intolerable.[100] Many hunters expect that competition with wolves will lead to a population decline of game animals.[101]

---

93. NABU 2014, http://www.nabu.de/wolf/wolfspopulation.jpg (Accessed 10 May 2014).

94. Dankert 2010, p. 8.

95. Kluth and Reinhardt 2010, p. 62.

96. Ansorge et al. 2011, p. 168.

97. WWF, February 2014, http://www.wwf.de/themen-projekte/bedrohte-tier-und-pflanzenarten/ woelfe/wie-denken-die-menschen-in-deutschland-ueber-den-wolf/ (Accessed 10 December 2014).

98. Kaczensky 2006.

99. In the 2014 WWF survey 71% of the participants were in favour of the return of the predators while 15% did not support them (ibid.).

100. See Kaczensky 2006, p. 63.

101. Wotschikowsky 2006, p. 5.

CONCLUSION

There has been a long tradition of wolf persecution in Germany. From the seventeenth and eighteenth centuries, technological innovations and political unifications led to more effective extermination programmes. The predators were considered a serious threat to animal husbandry and public safety. Local administrations regularly organised public drive hunts, foresters poisoned cattle as bait and citizens were encouraged to trap wolves, slay them or catch their pups wherever possible. As a reconstruction of wolf densities shows, the populations could not withstand the severe hunting pressure and rapidly declined. They only recovered in times of war, when the attention of people and politics lay elsewhere, as seen in the Rhineland during the Napoleonic Wars.

Furthermore, the immigration of wolves from adjacent regions, in particular France and Eastern Europe, has helped occasionally to increase populations. In the second half of the nineteenth century, reproductive populations were nearly extinct, with migrants repopulating the former wolf territories in western parts of the country. The extermination of wolves is one of the few examples where the modern state achieved its goal of controlling nature to its full extent. This level of control was made possible by the cooperation between the state and its citizens. The reasons for wolf persecution remained unquestioned until wolves were finally exterminated at the turn of the twentieth century. With a rising environmental movement and popular literature that showed a positive image of the wolf, public perception slowly started to change. Politics followed and, from the 1970s, the wolf has been protected in West Germany as an endangered species. In light of this new ethic, killing a wolf is seen as a crime, and the perception of man-eating wolves is regarded as rooted in old fairytales rather than in rational experience.

Since their return from Poland to eastern Germany at the turn of the twenty-first century, wolf populations have gradually expanded. Several packs have repopulated areas in Brandenburg and juveniles are migrating westwards. It is only a matter of time until the opportunistic predators once again reach the former Rhine Province. Despite many anthropogenic changes in the cultural landscape, they will find suitable conditions[102] and a historically unique situation where they won't be hunted for the first time in centuries.

---

102. See Rheinhardt and Kluth 2007, pp. 39–40.

BIBLIOGRAPHY

Archival Sources

GStAPK (Secret State Archives Prussian Cultural Heritage), Berlin:

II. HA, Abt. 33 Kurmark, Tit. 65, No. 2

II. HA, Abt. 33 Kurmark, Tit. 65, No. 4

II. HA, Abt. 33 Kurmark, Tit. 65, No. 8, Vol. 1

II. HA, Abt. 33 Kurmark, Tit. 65, No. 8, Vol. 2

II. HA, Abt. 33 Kurmark, Tit. 65, No. 8, Vol. 3

LHAK (Main State Archive Koblenz):

Best. 256, Nr. 872	Best. 363, Nr. 37
Best. 403, No. 2371	Best. 441, Nr. 7975
Best. 441, Nr. 7976	Best. 441, Nr. 11370
Best. 442, Nr. 153	Best. 442, Nr. 154
Best. 442, Nr. 155	Best. 537,057, No. 390
Best. 640, No. 73	Best. 655,158, No. 34
Best. 655, 200, No.1948	Best. 700/110, No. 74
Best. 712, No. 2284	Best. V 1000, Vol. 1816–1886

Research Literature

Andree, R. 1881. *Allgemeiner Handatlas in sechsundachtzig Karten* (Bielefeld, Leipzig: Velhagen und Klasing).

Anonymous. 1841. *Statistisch-topographische Beschreibung des Regierungs-Bezirks Trier* (Trier: Lintz'sche Buchhandlung).

Ansorge, H., J. Endel, K. Hertweck, M. Holzapfel, G. Kluth, S. Körner, I. Reinhardt and C. Wagner. 2011. 'Sie sind wieder da! Seit 10 Jahren gibt es wieder Wölfe in Deutschland'. *Das Senckenberg-Wissenschaftsmagazin* **141**: 162–73.

Beaufort, F. de. 1988. *Écologie historique du loup, Canis lupus L. 1758, en France* (Université de Rennes).

Bechstein, J.M. 1792. *Kurze aber gründliche Musterung aller bisher mit Recht oder Unrecht von dem Jäger als schädlich geachteten und getödeten Thiere* (Gotha).

Butzeck, S., M. Stubbe and R. Piechocki. 1988. 'Beiträge zur Geschichte der Säugetierfauna der DDR Teil 3: Der Wolf Canis lupus L., 1758'. *Hercynia N. F.* **25** (3): 278–317.

Dankert, B. 2010. 'Entwicklung des sächsischen Wolfsmanagements', in NABU Landesverband Sachsen (ed.) *Wölfe in Sachsen. Chancen für eine bedrohte Tierart* (Leipzig: NABU) pp. 6–10.

Delort, R. 1987. *Der Elefant, die Biene und der heilige Wolf* (München, Wien: Hanser).

Eytelwein, J.A. 1810. *Vergleichungen der gegenwärtig und vormals in den königlich preußischen Staaten eingeführten Maaße und Gewichte, mit Rücksicht auf die vorzüglichsten Maaße und Gewichte in Europa* (Berlin).

Fernández, J.M. and N. Ruiz de Azua. 2010. 'Historical Dynamics of a Declining Wolf Population: Persecution vs. Prey Reduction'. *European Journal of Wildlife Research* 56: 169–79.

Herrmann, B. 2003. 'Die Entvölkerung der Landschaft – Der Kampf gegen "culturschädliche Thiere" in Brandenburg im 18. Jahrhundert', in G. Bayerl and T. Meyer (eds) *Die Veränderung der Kulturlandschaft. Nutzungen – Sichtweisen – Planungen* (Münster, New York, München, Berlin: Waxmann) pp. 33–59.

— 2006. '"Auf keinen Fall mehr als dreimal wöchentlich Krebse, Lachs oder Hasenbraten essen müssen!" Einige vernachlässigte Probleme der "historischen Biodiversität"', in H.-P. Baum, R. Leng and J. Schneider (eds) *Wirtschaft – Gesellschaft – Mentalitäten im Mittelalter. Festschrift zum 75. Geburtstag von Rolf Sprandel* (Stuttgart: Steiner) pp. 175–203.

Kaczensky, P. 2006. 'Medienpräsenz- und Akzeptanzstudie "Wölfe in Deutschland"'. Werkvertrag des Bundesministeriums für Umwelt, Naturschutz und Reaktorsicherheit und des Bundesamtes für Naturschutz', in http://www.kora.ch/malme/05_library/5_1_publications/K/Kaczensky_2006_Akzeptanzstudie_Woelfe_in_Deutschland.pdf [Accessed 28 March 2014].

Kalb, R. 2007. *Bär, Luchs, Wolf – Verfolgt, Ausgerottet, Zurückgekehrt* (Graz: Leopold Stocker).

Kluth, G. and I. Reinhardt. 2010. 'Wölfe in der Lausitz – Wölfe in Deutschland', in NABU Landesverband Sachsen (ed.) *Wölfe in Sachsen. Chancen für eine bedrohte Tierart* (Leipzig: NABU) pp. 58–67.

Köhler, H.A. 1887. *Köhler's Medizinal-Pflanzen in naturgetreuen Abbildungen mit kurz erläuterndem Texte* (Gera-Untermhaus: Köhler).

Krafft, A.F. 1712. *Der Sowohl Menschen und Viehe Grausamen Thiere/ schädlichen Ungeziefers Und Verderblichen Gewürmer Gäntzliche Ausrottung* (Nürnberg).

Landau, G. 1849. *Beiträge zur Geschichte der Jagd und der Falknerei in Deutschland. Die Geschichte der Jagd und der Falknerei in beiden Hessen* (Kassel: Theodor Fischer).

Linnell, J.D.C., R. Andersen, Z. Andersone, L. Balciauskas, J.C. Blanco, L. Boitani, S. Brainerd, U. Breitenmoser, I. Kojola, O. Liberg, J. Løe, H. Okarma, H.C. Pedersen, C. Promberger, H. Sand, E.J. Solberg, H. Valdmann and P. Wabakken. 2002. *The Fear of Wolves: A Review of Wolf Attacks on Humans* (Trondheim: NINA Norsk institutt for naturforskning).

Marvin, G. 2012. *Wolf* (London: Reaktion Books).

Masius, P. and J. Sprenger. 2012. 'Die Geschichte vom bösen Wolf – Verfolgung, Ausrottung und Wiederkehr'. *Natur und Landschaft* 1/2012: 11–6.

Meyer, T. 1999. *Natur, Technik und Wirtschaftswachstum im 18. Jahrhundert. Risikoperzeption und Sicherheitsversprechen* (Münster, New York, München, Berlin: Waxmann).

Moriceau, J.-M. 2011. *L'homme contre le loup. Une guerre de deux mille ans* (Paris: Fayard).

Mück, I. 1911. *Atlas zur territorialen Entwicklung Preußens mit geschichtlichen Erläuterungen und einer Abbildung des Königlich Preussischen großen Wappenschildes* (Berlin: Gea Verlag).

Mylius, C.O. 1737–1755. *Corpus Constitutionum Marchicarum* (CCM) […] (Berlin).

Okarma, H. 1997. *Der Wolf. Ökologie, Verhalten, Schutz* (Berlin: Parey).

Ott, W. 2004. *Die besiegte Wildnis – Wie Bär, Wolf, Luchs und Steinadler aus unserer Heimat verschwanden* (Leinfelden-Echterdingen: DRW-Verlag).

Pfeiffer, T. 2011. *Alsace. Le retour du loup* (Strasbourg: La Nuée Bleue).

Piechocki, R. 2010. *Landschaft, Heimat, Wildnis* (München: Beck).

Radkau, J. 2011. *Die Ära der Ökologie* (München: Beck).

Rausch, J. 1967. 'Von den letzten Wölfen in unserer Heimat', in *Heimatjahrbuch, Kreis Ahrweiler* (Ahrweiler) pp. 70–2.

Reinhard, I. and G. Kluth. 2007. *Leben mit Wölfen. Leitfaden für den Umgang mit einer konfliktträchtigen Tierart in Deutschland.* BfN-Skripten 201.

Riesenthal, O. von 1880. *Das Waidwerk. Handbuch der Naturgeschichte, Jagd und Hege aller in Mitteleuropa jagdbaren Thiere* (Berlin: Wiegandt, Hempel und Parey).

Roth, L. 1930. 'Wolfsjagden vergangener Tage'. *Naturschutz. Monatsschrift für alle Freunde der deutschen Heimat* 11 (4): 123.

Scherf, G. 2001. *Wolfsspuren in Bayern – Kulturgeschichte eines sagenhaften Tieres* (Amberg: Buch- und Kunstverlag Oberpfalz).

Schulz, O. 2011. *Wölfe. Ein Mythos kehrt zurück* (München: BLV).

Sommer, R. 1999. Der Wolf in Mecklenburg-Vorpommern. Vorkommen und Geschichte (Schwerin: Stock & Stein).

Sprenger, J. 2009. 'In der Muskauer Heide: Ein Denkmal für den Wolf', in *Schauplätze und Themen der Umweltgeschichte – Umwelthistorische Miszellen aus dem Graduiertenkolleg* (Göttingen: Universitätsverlag Göttingen) pp. 179–87.

Suter, H. 2003. *Einwanderer ohne Pass – Wölfe in Brandenburg* (Schorfheide Museum 10).

Täntzer, J. 1682. *Der Dianen Hohe und Niedere Jagtgeheimnüß / Darinnen Die gantze Jagt-Wissenschafft Außführlich zu befinden.* Vol. 1 (Kopenhagen: Neuhoff).

Weinand, H. 2010. *Homo lupo lupus est. Der Mensch ist dem Wolf ein Wolf. Die Ausrottung der Wölfe im 19. Jahrhundert und ihre Rückkehr in unsere Gegenwart* (Andernach-Miesenheim: Selbstverlag).

Wotschikowsky, U. 2006. *Wölfe, Jagd und Wald in der Oberlausitz.* (Görlitz: Staatliches Museum für Naturkunde Görlitz).

Zedler, J.H. 1758. *Grosses vollständiges Universal-Lexikon.* Bd. 58 (Halle, Leipzig).

Zimen, E. 1990. *Der Wolf. Verhalten, Ökologie und Mythos* (München: von dem Knesebeck).

7

Historical Decline (and Persistence) of the Grey Wolf in Spain

José María Fernández-García

Run, run, run, but even the devil cannot catch him.

Abel Chapman and Walter J. Buck, Wild Spain (1893)

The life of the beasts is only revealed to man in fragments, but a good knowledge may be achieved using the accumulated experience of many observers through time.

José Antonio Valverde and Salvador Teruelo, Los lobos de Morla (1992)

INTRODUCTION: THE IBERIAN SCENE

Spain is one of the largest countries in Europe (c. 500,000 km^2) and occupies most of the Iberian Peninsula, straddled between the Western Mediterranean and the Atlantic, and close to the northern African coast. The territory comprises a vast central plateau at a relatively high altitude (600–700 m on average); several mountain ranges east-west oriented (Pyrenees, Cantabrian, Iberian, Central, Betic and Sierra Nevada) reaching up to 3,500 m high; and two wide river valleys, namely the Guadalquivir and Ebro lowlands.

Since the beginning of the Holocene (10,000 years BP), temperate forests extended from their coastal glacial refuges, favoured by humid and mild climate conditions. The current bioclimatic and biogeographical zones were already recognisable in this period, showing Atlantic-influenced vegetation in the north, Mediterranean in the south and east, and the inland territory with a transitional gradient. Therefore, Iberian ecosystems were dominated by broad-leaved forests, basically with deciduous (*Fagus sylvatica*, *Quercus robur*), evergreen (*Q. ilex*, *Q. rotundifolia*) and semi-deciduous trees (*Q. faginea*, *Q. pyrenaica*). Coniferous (*Pinus* spp., *Juniperus thurifera*) forests, scrublands and smaller, relict steppes were confined to more specific locations.

The wolf has been an outstanding component of these ecosystems, as witnessed by paleozoological records. Bones of the species have been found in a regular fashion in many prehistoric deposits of this period, though its frequency is

José María Fernández-García

Figure 1. Free-ranging wolves in the Cantabrian Mountains of the province of León, Northern Spain (Photograph: Más que Pájaros).

low, which may indicate that wolves were rarely captured by humans.[1] Remains of morphologically modern wolves appear since the Würm glaciation, about 100,000 years BP.[2] They coexisted with another middle-sized, social canid, the Dhole *Cuon alpinus europaeus*, but this became extinct in Spain and Europe before the Holocene.[3]

The range of the wolf included much of Western Europe and Iberia during the late Pleistocene period, as judged by sub-fossil records. It has been hypothesised that the species' even distribution in the Holocene ecosystems was not the consequence of recolonisation from glacial refuges.[4] Phylogeographic studies evidence the existence of past gene flow between Iberian and Eastern European populations, supporting the view of a continuous distribution throughout ancient Europe. Reconstructing the ecology, demography and relationship with humans of these populations is truly difficult, but the dominant Pleistocene wolf ecomorph, specialised on megafaunal prey, was able to adapt to the changing availability and composition of mammal assemblages during the Pleistocene-Holocene transition.[5] Two Iberian subspecies

---

1   Altuna 1992. Álvarez 2003.
2   Castaños 1992.
3   Brugal and Boudadi-Maligne 2011.
4   Sommer and Benecke 2005.
5   Pilot et al. 2010.

of wolves were traditionally acknowledged by taxonomists, following Cabrera.[6] *Canis lupus deitanus*, a smaller wolf restricted to the semi-arid south-east, and *C. l. signatus*, the proper Spanish wolf, told by its whitish belly, white strip on the cheek and teeth features. Contemporary researchers do not recognise either subspecies, as *C. l. deitanus* is considered an invalid form, insufficiently described, and *C. l. signatus* is not distinct enough from *C. l. lupus* and should rather be lumped together with it.[7] However, mitochondrial DNA and microsatellite analysis have shown differences between contemporary Iberian wolves and the rest of European populations, supporting the view of a separate evolutionary potential.[8]

RISE AND FALL IN A TRANSFORMED LANDSCAPE

The earliest signs of human presence in Spain date back to 800,000 years BP. The capacity of the primitive hunter-gatherer groups to transform the landscape is thought to have been limited, because of their low growth rate and the lack of technology. Having said that, they could take higher responsibility for the extinction of several large-bodied prey species. The acquisition of fire, known since 40,000 years BP, probably helped to create open areas and clearings. Agriculture was introduced in Spain around 7,000 years BP, but its early impact on the landscape was not relevant, because only the lighter soils could be cultivated. Roman exploitation of the territory was based on agricultural *villae* and the proportion of farmland was then significantly increased, but quoting the Greek geographer Estrabón (first century), Spain was still covered at that time with a vast woodland (*saltus*). Agricultural expansion was constrained by political instability and warfare following the Gothic and Arab invasions, but around the tenth to thirteenth centuries the chronicles already mentioned intense deforestation as a response to human demographic increase and foundations of new settlements in previously unpopulated regions.[9]

The views of the wolf in the classical and medieval worlds are dominated by symbolic and religious expressions. Wolf remains are infrequently found at archaeological sites, preventing detailed knowledge about wolf–human relationship. The wolf was generally regarded as a perfidious animal, but the Catholic Church also promoted the vision of wolves' behaviour as a moral example.[10]

Wolves did not appear regularly in Spanish historic, written sources until the fifteenth century, when the problem of damage to livestock achieved a high political profile. This was probably a consequence of the increasing relevance of sheep husbandry in the Kingdom's economy. Thousands of herds and millions

---

6 Cabrera 1907.
7 Nowak 2003.
8 Vilà et al. 1999.
9 Blanco et al. 1997.
10 Macias 2012.

of *merina* breed sheeps (around 3.5 million at the beginning of the eighteenth century)[11] exploited vast pasturelands, migrating each year from the Northern mountain ranges to the central and Southern temperate lowlands, and back. The shepherds' union, *Honrado Concejo de la Mesta*, held privileges and concessions and became a powerful, influential organisation. In this context, the persecution of the so-called *fieras* or pest animals became a subject of political concern, and local governments were involved in issuing bounties to wolf hunters. Besides, medieval aristocratic privileges regarding game animals and limitations on hunting methods were gradually abolished. The eradication of wolves was then favoured by institutions, legislators and society as a means to defend property and improve economic conditions in rural communities.

It has been argued that bounties were also used as a tool to gain control over such societies, irrespective of their actual effectiveness in wolf extirpation.[12] However, they promoted expert trappers – *alimañeros* or, even more specifically, *loberos* – as regular characters in traditional rural Spain. These people were professionally devoted to wolf trapping, their services being hired by shepherds' associations or town councils, and earned their living on the basis of bounties and prizes. In the long term, these economic incentives became an unsustainable proportion of council budgets, and bounty schemes had to be interrupted or irregularly applied in some regions during the eighteenth and nineteenth centuries.[13] As long as the wolf's range was gradually shrinking, trappers focused their activity on the remaining medium to small-sized predators, namely the Red Fox (*Vulpes vulpes*), the Badger (*Meles meles*) and the Stone Marten (*Martes foina*).

The wolf was one of the game species most appreciated by Spanish kings and the aristocracy from the sixteenth to eighteenth centuries.[14] This type of noble hunting was practiced in game reserves with the aid of hundreds of armed people, horsemen and dogs (*monterías*). But gradually the persecution of pest animals became a social duty for rural community members and legislation was passed to drive and enforce collective efforts. The first particular mentions of popular, collective drive hunts (*corridas*) in Northern Spain date back to the fifteenth century,[15] in the framework of confrontation against feudal privileges over land and game ownerships. But the seventeenth and eighteenth centuries saw the peak of these collective hunts, which were subject to detailed legislation as to where, when, by whom and how they should be organised. The *Real Cédula de Su Magestad y Señores del Consejo* dated 1788 and signed by King Carlos III is the best known example of

11   Rodríguez 2001.
12   Mech and Boitani 2003.
13   Torrente 1999.
14   Valverde and Teruelo 2001.
15   Iranzo (c. 1475).

The Grey Wolf in Spain

Figure 2. The long historical relationship between humans and wolves has left its mark in toponymy. Here is the name of a village in the province of Palencia. 'Lobera' means 'wolf trap' or 'wolf den' (Photograph: José María Fernández-García).

this policy. Strict penalties were imposed on those people or villages who did not meet the agreed regulations, or whose contribution was not as expected.

Since the middle nineteenth century, a new alkaloid – strychnine – began to be used for killing wolves. Although several other plant-extracted poisons had been traditionally applied and the properties of the seeds of the Asian tree *Strychnos nux-vomica* were previously well known, the popularisation of strychnine was a milestone for wolf extirpation. The small doses needed and low cost were the main reasons for a quick expansion in its use. The first written quote in Spain dates back to 1861, but strychnine soon became a widely applied method, in spite of the danger to domestic animals and even children, which led some local councils to establish precautionary regulations. Although explicit literary references and archive reports are not very numerous,[16] strychnine was apparently responsible for a rapid decimation of wolf populations all over the country. The decline and regional extinctions of the Griffon Vulture (*Gyps fulvus*) and the Lammergeier (*Gypaetus barbatus*) acted as a reliable indicator of the impact of strychnine on wildlife, and these two scavenger birds became increasingly scarce and restricted to remote areas around the turn of the century.[17] Poisoning was enforced until the 1960s and 1970s, when

16   Chapman and Buck 1910.
17   Hiraldo et al 1979.

several ambitious and successful campaigns were undertaken in Northern Spain. Just before the definitive ban of poisoning in 1982, the Spanish wolf population was thought to be at its historical lowest.[18]

WOLF-TRAPS IN SPAIN, AN ETHNOGRAPHIC HERITAGE

The social endeavour to eradicate wolves was helped by a number of types of traps, specifically designed for the persecution of wolves. Hunting with nets was documented in the fifteenth century and was probably practiced in Galicia until the eighteenth. There is also written evidence about leg-hold traps as early as the twelfth century, but they were probably in use from Roman times, as suggested by one of these devices being found in an archaeological deposit from Huelva (Southern Spain). The most antique types were built in a solid piece of oak wood, about a metre long and weighing ten kilograms, and they were still operating in the early twentieth century in the Cantabrian and Pyrenean mountains in Northern Spain, although their effectiveness towards wolves is not proven and they were possibly intended for trapping ungulate species.

Iron-made leg-hold traps (*cepos loberos*) were the most common device for wolf hunting, as stated by medieval and modern chronicles, and their impact on wolf extirpation was possibly very significant. About 48 per cent of the recorded wolves captured in the Basque Country, Northern Spain, during the nineteenth century were leg-hold trapped.[19] The widest diffusion of these traps was probably around the sixteenth to nineteenth centuries, but they were in use until the mid-twentieth century, as a consequence of the rise in the price of fur just after the Spanish Civil War (1936–1939). Several eco-regional designs have been described, including the 'snow' type of European origin, the 'arab' of Northern African influence, the 'Mediterranean braó' and the genuine 'Iberian'.[20] The most robust iron traps were used by wolf hunters until the decline of this professional activity. Many such traps were also communally owned by local councils affected by the wolf remnant populations, until their ultimate disuse.

Other popular and easily operated wolf traps were the so-called *zarazas*, consisting of two sharp needles tied up inside a meat ball, able to drill the wolf's stomach once ingested by the animal. In contrast, the use of neck snares for wolf hunting is less frequently cited in Spanish literature, possibly because this device was less specific and less effective in the wild countryside. The effectiveness of neck snares is probably higher in densely fenced states, where animals are forced to move using particular passages; but this type of landscape was not common in Spain until the mid-twentieth century.

---

18   Valverde 1971.
19   Fernández and Ruiz de Azua 2003.
20   Valverde 1991.

The Grey Wolf in Spain

Figure 3. Showcase in the Shepherd's Museum of Piqueras, La Rioja. Wolf carcass and skulls, as well as iron-made leg-hold traps are shown (Photograph: José María Fernández-García).

José María Fernández-García

Figure 4. The *cortello* of Barjacoba (province of Zamora). Notice the uneven ground that helped the wolf to jump into the trap, but prevented his escape due to the high walls. The inner diameters of this elliptical *cortello* are 19 and 13 metres (Photograph: José María Fernández-García).

But the Iberian Peninsula is home to a number of elaborate built structures, specifically intended for wolf persecution. Three basic types have been described: pit-fall traps (*pozos* or *hoyos*); enclosures (*corrales, cousos, caleyos* and *cortellos*); and traps of converging walls (*callejos, chorcos, loberas*).[21] The baited pit-fall traps evolved from simple designs and included variations with sloping walls and slabs to prevent the trapped wolf from escaping, once it had fallen in. Most of these structures – which were probably widely distributed across Northern Spain, as witnessed by the frequent place names indicating ancient presence of *pozos loberos* – have now disappeared and only a few deteriorated remains are preserved in Asturias, Galicia and Zamora.[22]

Corrales and *cortellos* were baited traps surrounded by walls (up to three metres high) accessible from the outside, but impossible to jump out of from the inside. The *corrales* were modest traps built in wood, so that today written descriptions are the main source of information. The *cortellos* were relatively large, circular

21 Alvares et al. 2000.
22 Boza 2006.

Figure 5. Aerial view of a *callejo* (Barrón, province of Álava). The pit is located by a white arrow. The converging walls of this *callejo* currently measure 164 and 138 metres long. Notice the steep cliff to the top of the image (Image available from http://sigpac.mapa.es/fega/visor/).

or ellipsoidal structures (twenty to sixty metres wide, with an eighty to 200 metre perimeter) with stone walls, and some of them were still used in the 1950s. The wolf was attracted to the *cortello* by a captive goat, jumped in easily due to the steep topography of the site, but could not find a way out because the slabs placed on top of the wall prevented doing so. Sixty-nine *cortellos* have been recorded so far in Spain (and seven more in neighbouring Portugal).[23] Their area of occurrence is restricted to the north-western corner (Asturias, León and Zamora), although there are a few unconfirmed claims from other regions.[24]

But the most impressive traps were the *callejos*: a 'funnel' with two high permanent walls, progressively converging into a narrow space and ending in a pit. The longest walls remaining in one Spanish *callejo* reach 1,111 metres (Toyo, Burgos) and the longest individual wall is 894 metres (San Miguel, Burgos),

---

23   Alvares 2011.
24   García y Asensio 1995.

José María Fernández-García

Figure 6. The wolf's perspective inside a *callejo*, two high walls converging into a narrow space to escape. The walls of the most ancient *callejos* could have been built in wood, as in this case located in Valdeón, León (Photograph: José María Fernández-García).

although originally they were probably much longer.[25] These figures express the amazing effort and expertise needed to erect such structures, transporting about 4,000 tons of stones. The *callejos* were built on sites where local topography favoured their trapping efficiency, aided by cliffs or steep slopes that extended the area of influence of the walls. Wolves were harassed by dozens or even hundreds of people from nearby villages, who tried to push the animals into the wide mouth of the funnel. Once the wolf was in, its only option was to run towards the pit, where it was finally captured. Such hunting events were organised in detail, and in some cases local legislation arranging who should take part and when and how the hunting should take place, dating back to the sixteenth century, is still preserved (as in Valdeón, León).

There is written evidence about the building of a particular *callejo* in 1598–1605 in the province of Cantabria, although documents suggest that many of them must be of older origin, possibly medieval. The walls in such ancient *callejos* could have been built in wooden intertwined sticks forming a palisade, but obvi-

25   Murga 1978.

The Grey Wolf in Spain

Figure 7. The pit where the wolf finally fell down and was trapped. *Callejo* in Barrón, Álava (Photograph: José María Fernández-García).

ously there are no remains except the reconstructed *chorcos* of Valdeón and Prioro (León). Some references also suggest the use of nets to extend the length of the walls. Most of the traps ceased to be used around the end of the nineteenth century, when more efficient persecution methods became available and wolf densities decreased. In some cases, maybe because collective hunts were still successful, the use and communal maintenance of the *callejos* persisted more. The last recorded captures date back to the 1950s (Berberana, Burgos; Valdeón, León; and Barrón, Álava).[26]

Seventy-seven *callejos* have been confirmed in several mountain ranges in Northern Spain (Galicia, Asturias, León, Cantabria, Palencia, Burgos and Álava) and 34 more in Northern Portugal. Interestingly, this area largely corresponds to the Iberian strongholds for the species in the twentieth century, as well as to the main communally exploited pasturelands. The *callejos* could also have occurred in Southern Spain, but only vague references have survived.[27] But both *callejos* and *cortellos* seem to be genuine Iberian expressions of popular architecture, as similar

---

26 Murga 1988.
27 Gutiérrez 2005.

José María Fernández-García

structures are not known in other parts of Europe. Therefore, their ethnographic value as cultural heritage is remarkable, and the current abandonment and deterioration of many of these traps should be reversed.

TRENDS IN RANGE AND NUMBERS

Wolves undoubtedly ranged over the whole of Spain throughout history. But the global dynamics – possible reductions and expansions – of this range cannot be objectively tracked until the nineteenth century. A systematic assessment of the wolf's distribution is limited if based on the literary sources. That was not the case with other big mammals, notably the Brown bear (*Ursus arctos*), which was a greatly appreciated game species. Chronicles written on behalf of Kings Alfonso XI and Felipe II allow precise reconstruction of the bear's distribution in the fourteenth and sixteenth centuries respectively.[28]

It is generally admitted that wolves first disappeared from the Mediterranean coastal fringe, traditionally an area of dense human population. The extinction of the species in the cultivated lowlands of the regions of Murcia, Valencia and Cataluña probably took place around the mid-nineteenth century. As shown by bounties, the wolf was still abundant in Valencia during the seventeenth century[29] and in Cataluña during the first decades of the eighteenth century, but one hundred years later the density of captures was three times lower,[30] and the remnant individuals were possibly immigrants from neighbouring regions. In the remoter mountain ranges of Valencia and Murcia, wolves apparently persisted until the end of the nineteenth century.

Early declines are also documented for the area of Madrid, a province with the highest human population in Central Spain. Wolves were frequently killed during the eighteenth century in the Kingdom's hunting states, but became virtually absent from the beginning of the next century.[31] In another inland region, Aragón, wolves still wandered in the Ebro valley around the middle of the nineteenth century, as deduced from the valuable geographic dictionary by Pascual Madoz,[32] but the scarcity of occurrence locations suggests that the species was already rare. In Southern Spain, the decline of the wolf was first evident in the lowlands of Andalucía. Again the species disappeared from the most populated and cultivated areas – the coast and the Guadalquivir valley – around the mid-nineteenth century.

---

28 Nores and Naves 1993.
29 Rosas 2009.
30 Grau et al. 1990.
31 Alcántara and Cantos 1992.
32 Madoz 1845–50.

In fact, the national hunting statistics compiled by the Ministerio de Fomento in the years 1855–1859[33] showed that wolves were distributed all over the country, with the exceptions mentioned above. The number of individuals killed during that five-year period is estimated at 13,300–15,150, with an average annual density of 0.6 captures per 100 km². In six provinces, over 500 wolves were captured. The map of provincial densities does not show a defined distribution pattern, with the highest numbers from Southern and Northern provinces alike, and the lowest from Eastern Mediterranean.[34] In 1864 national statistics about wolves killed were again compiled and published, showing a total bag of 5,394 individuals.[35] These figures clearly evidence the abundance of the wolf in the middle of the nineteenth century.

But around the turn of the century the situation for the wolf worsened. Regional declines and local extinctions are documented. In Southern Spain, the wolf definitely disappeared from the lowlands and was relegated to the mountain ranges of Sierra Morena and few additional, small and isolated populations, doomed to extinction. In the North, a sharp decline in the number of wolves captured in the Basque Country was recorded after 1850, and three decades later the wolf was virtually eradicated. The last litters indicating breeding attempts were taken in the 1880s and 1890s.[36] The same was true for the Pyrenees, with some individuals still surviving in the western sector of this mountain range until the first decades of the twentieth century.[37]

This process of shrinking distribution continued without halt over the next decades. By the mid-twentieth century, the species was thought to be extinct from most of Eastern and Central Spain. In the mountain ranges of the Sistema Central and Sistema Ibérico some populations persisted, but in the 1950s and 1960s they were subjected to heavy persecution and by the end of these decades only dispersing wolves were recorded. Incomplete statistics compiled by the Spanish Ministerio de Agricultura between 1954–1961 assessed that annual density of captures were still high in some north-western provinces (0.2–0.7 wolves per 100 km²). For instance, the wolf's range in Galicia included the whole region at that time, as credited by independent studies.[38] But in the rest of the country the species was absent or too scarce to provide significant bags.[39] A Southern exception was Extremadura, which still boasted a population worthy of note, wandering across much of the region.

33   Ministerio de Fomento 1861.
34   Rico and Torrente 2000.
35   Junta General de Estadística 1865.
36   Garayo 2008.
37   Woutersen 2000.
38   Núñez et al. 2007.
39   Servicio Nacional de Pesca Fluvial y Caza 1962.

José María Fernández-García

Figure 8. Image from a panel showing wolves captured in the *callejo* of Berberana, Burgos, in 1921 (right) and 1955 (left). The ones from 1955 were the last wolves known to have been trapped in this particular *callejo* (Photograph: José María Fernández-García).

But in the 1960s the isolation of this progressively relict population from the main north-western range became inescapable.[40]

The first systematic assessment of the distribution and abundance of the wolf in Spain was performed in the 1980s. Previously, the species was thought to be at its historical lowest, and concern over its conservation rose among naturalists and researchers. Nearly 300 packs were estimated, which could tentatively represent 1,500–2,000 wolves and an average density of 1.5–2 wolves per 100 km². The main continuous population ranged in the north-west, covering about 100,000 km². In Southern Spain only four small and endangered populations survived.[41] It was also found that, in the previous decade, the species had been able to colonise the cultivated plateau of Castilla, where it had gone undetected by authors who had studied the wolf's distribution in the 1970s. This fact strongly suggested an expanding dynamic for the north-western population, the source for dispersers.

40   Gragera 1996.
41   Blanco et al. 1992.

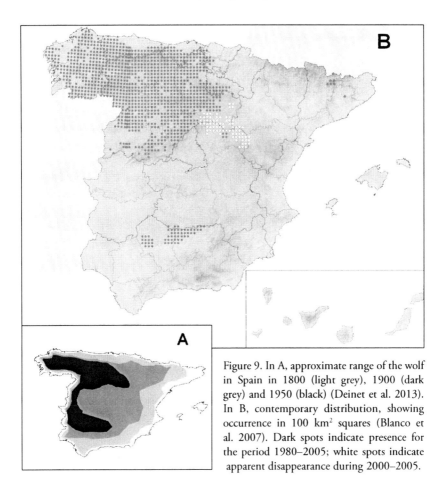

Figure 9. In A, approximate range of the wolf in Spain in 1800 (light grey), 1900 (dark grey) and 1950 (black) (Deinet et al. 2013). In B, contemporary distribution, showing occurrence in 100 km² squares (Blanco et al. 2007). Dark spots indicate presence for the period 1980–2005; white spots indicate apparent disappearance during 2000–2005.

Such an expansion southward was reversed by other unsuccessful colonising movements, towards the Atlantic coastline, the Basque Country and La Rioja. In these areas, with high numbers of cattle and sheep but a dense human population, the presence of dispersed wolves and even breeding packs was regular throughout the 1990s. But the damage to livestock in the absence of husbandry raised the latent conflict with farmers, and the resulting persecution has prevented the permanent colonisation of such regions to date.[42] Meanwhile, two of the four threatened populations in Southern Spain went extinct.

---

42   Echegaray and Vilá 2011.

José María Fernández-García

During the 2000s only partial distribution and abundance assessments have been performed. This has facilitated controversies among researchers over the real trend of the Spanish population of wolves.[43] In Castilla and León, the core regions for the wolf in Spain, the range increase towards the Southern fringe was still ongoing in this period, and breeding in new provinces of Central Spain has been recorded. The conservation implications of this expansion – a 35 per cent significant increase, referred to the wolf's distribution in Castilla and León in 1988[44] – has been debated on the basis of methodological concerns over the abundance indexes and the status of both the peripheral and central populations.

Finally, an unexpected colonisation event has occurred in the Eastern Pyrenees since the year 2000. Genetic assessments proved that the origin of the dispersing wolves was the French Alps, which in turn had been colonised by Italian wolves in the early 1990s. Up to thirteen different wolves have been identified so far, but still no breeding has been confirmed.[45] Anyway, this amazing movement across nearly 500 km of unsuitable habitat expresses the resilient and adaptive nature of the wolf.

DRIVERS, PROCESSES AND THE FUTURE

For conservation biologists, understanding the causes of decline of a particular population of animals is crucial. The diagnosis of an extinction process is key in so-called evidence-based conservation, which should prevail against 'expert' and dogmatic approaches. As for the wolf, the literature has attributed the long-term decline of most populations to the direct effect of persecution,[46] and Spain is by no means an exception. In fact, our knowledge about the wolf's demography and dynamics is greatly based on exploitation data, the only available to collect robust series. But deeper insights into the wolf's historical ecology may help to interpret past and present events.

The annual mortality that a wolf population can stand before going into a decline has been set around 35 per cent for several well-studied populations.[47] Unsustainable harvests have probably been responsible for declines in certain historical periods. In Spain in particular, the steep range reduction around the last decades of the nineteenth century could be associated with the popularisation of strychnine. Poisoning campaigns performed in the second half of the twentieth century led to documented regional extinctions. Poison is regarded as the most effective method for the eradication of wolf populations.

---

43   Naves 2010.
44   Llaneza and Blanco 2005.
45   Lampreave et al. 2011.
46   MacDonald and Sillero-Zubiri 2004.
47   Fuller et al. 2003.

But the temporal and spatial distributions of wolf extinctions suggest that persecution alone does not explain the whole picture. The role of ecological conditions (habitat and food resources) has often been neglected because the species is considered to be a flexible predator. The extinction of wild ungulates –Roe deer (*Capreolus capreolus*), Red deer (*Cervus elaphus*) and to a lesser extent Wild boar (*Sus scrofa*) – seemed to be a prerequisite for the decline of wolves in many regions. Deer and boar populations were unsustainably exploited by hunters in the nineteenth century and wolves shifting to anthropogenic food resources were persecuted in revenge. The process of depleted ungulate biomass driving the wolf's eradication has also been described in North America[48] and Eastern Europe,[49] and likely occurred in Spain. The correlative character of this analysis is not conclusive, but historical quantitative data series can help to test the hypothesis.

When exposed to intense persecution, wolf populations tend to increase their reproductive output as a means to compensate for losses. In the Basque Country, demographic indicators – sex and age ratios, litter size – suggested that the population suffered from increased food stress through the nineteenth century.[50] This situation also prevented immigration from neighbouring saturated areas, and in the long-term the population was not able to cope with a constant rate of extraction by hunting.

In the second half of the twentieth century, populations of wild ungulates recovered and expanded to a great extent over Northern and Central Spain. The Roe deer in particular has re-colonised many provinces where it had been absent for decades.[51] This is thought to be a consequence of socio-economic changes and land abandonment in rural Spain, which led to a relevant increase in woodland surface. Besides, the predominantly urban society has shown growing acceptance towards the wolf, as have certain rural sectors linked to tourism and recreational activities. In this context, the core north-western wolf population has been able to increase its range towards favourable areas, taking advantage of ecological opportunities. In the Castillian plateau, retained husbandry practices prevent the wolves from preying upon sheep, and the availability of alternative prey allows the area to hold dense but unnoticed wolf populations. Dispersing wolves have reached other ecologically favourable regions, but where livestock is not under surveillance while in communal or private pasturelands. Here, human intolerance determines a halt or even regression in the wolf's recovery.[52]

In recent years, wolves have been detected breeding in several mountain ranges of Central Spain. If such an expansion continues in the near future, colonisation

---

48   Phillips et al. 2004.
49   Sidorovich at al. 2003.
50   Fernández and Ruiz de Azua 2010.
51   Rossell 2001.
52   Blanco and Cortés 2002.

of vacant but suitable provinces could happen, eventually leading to the rescue of the critically endangered Southern populations. But the future of the Spanish wolf is not guaranteed yet, even from the genetic point of view.[53] The complex influence of ecological, cultural and socio-economic factors and the way they interact and develop in each historical period turns prediction into a highly risky exercise.

SUMMARY

Since the Holocene, the Grey Wolf *Canis lupus* has occurred in every natural ecosystem of the Iberian Peninsula, including mountain ranges, the extensive highlands of the central plateau and even lowlands on coastal fringes. As a top predator, its abundance was probably never high, but its flexible ecology and behaviour enabled the species to persist or even thrive in historically transformed ecosystems. The increasing economic and political relevance of sheep husbandry and the emergence of the associated influential organisations could have driven a shift in attitudes and social perceptions towards the wolf, which can be tracked in Spanish literature back to the Lower Middle Ages. Collective hunting techniques were developed, aided with the construction of specific wolf-traps. Several types of these are apparently unique to north-western Spain and are unknown in other parts of Europe. National and local institutions were involved in the eradication of wolf populations at least from the eighteenth century, and bounties issued to qualified hunters were the most common mechanism. These bounties remained in force, irregularly across regions and time, up to the middle of the twentieth century. The historical evolution of the wolf's range in Spain can only be estimated for the last two centuries, because bounty documents kept in archives are the only reliable source of data, along with a few socio-geographic dictionaries and statistical surveys compiled and published in the nineteenth century. It is believed that, as a consequence of persecution and exclusion from intensively transformed ecosystems, wolves disappeared early from Eastern Spain, and populations became progressively fragmented and eventually extinct in the Southern and Central parts of the country throughout the twentieth century. The broad use of poison possibly played a major role. But populations persisted in the north-western corner, despite such persecution. The long-term trend of the wolf and the persistence of populations were probably dependent on the availability of trophic resources and the staple prey, namely the Roe deer (*Capreolus capreolus*) and to a lesser extent the Wild boar (*Sus scrofa*), whose abundances had also been depleted in Eastern, Southern and Central regions. Since the 1980s, the range of this north-western core population has increased, but the rate of expansion seems to be lessened by potential conflicts with husbandry arising in those re-colonised areas.

---

53   Echegaray et al. 2008.

ACKNOWLEDGEMENTS

My father always remembered the time when, as a child shepherding cattle in his home village of León, he was able to see a wolf in the distance. Thanks to Nerea Ruiz de Azua for her valuable help in data searching. I appreciate comments by Jorge Echegaray, Manuel González and Álvaro Oleaga.

BIBLIOGRAPHY

Alcántara, M. and F.J. Cantos. 1992. 'Tendencias históricas de la comunidad de carnívoros del Monte de El Pardo (Madrid, España central)'. *Miscelània Zoologica* **16**: 171–8.

Altuna, J. 1992. 'El medio ambiente durante el Pleistoceno Superior en la región cantábrica con referencia especial a sus faunas de mamíferos'. *Munibe (Antropología-Arqueología)* **43**: 13–29.

Alvares, F. 2011. *Ecologia e conservaçao do lobo no noroeste de Portugal* (Lisboa: Universidade de Lisboa).

Alvares, F., P. Alonso, P. Sierra. and F. Petrucci-Fonseca. 2000. 'Os fojos dos lobos na Península Ibérica. Sua inventariaçao, caracterizaçao e conservaçao'. *Galemys* **12**: 57–77.

Álvarez, D. 2003. 'Macromamíferos fósiles del Pleistoceno de Asturias. Revisión bibliográfica y datos actuales'. *Naturalia Cantabricae* **2**: 11–23.

Blanco, E., M.Á. Casado, M. Costa, R. Escribano, M. García, M. Génova, Á. Gómez, F. Gómez, J.C. Moreno, C. Morla, P. Regato and H. Sáinz. 1997. *Los bosques ibéricos. Una interpretación geobotánica* (Barcelona: Planeta).

Blanco, J.C. and Y. Cortés. 2002. *Ecología, censos, percepción y evolución del lobo en España. Análisis de un conflicto* (Malaga: Sociedad Española para la Conservación y Estudio de los Mamíferos).

Blanco, J.C., S. Reig and L. Cuesta. 1992. 'Distribution, Status and Conservation Problems of the Wolf in Spain'. *Biological Conservation* **60**: 73–80.

Blanco, J.C., M. Sáenz de Buruaga and L. Llaneza. 2007. '*Canis lupus* Linnaeus, 1758', in L.J. Palomo, J. Gisbert and J.C. Blanco (eds) *Atlas y libro rojo de los mamíferos terrestres de España* (Madrid: Ministerio de Medio Ambiente) pp. 272–6.

Boza, M. 2006. *El trampeo y demás artes de caza tradicionales en la Península Ibérica* (Barcelona: Hispano Europea).

Brugal, J.-P. and M. Boudadi-Maligne. 2011. 'Quaternary Small to Large Canids in Europe: Taxonomic Status and Biochronological Contribution'. *Quaternary International* **243**: 171–82.

Cabrera, Á. 1907. 'Los lobos de España'. *Boletín de la Real Sociedad Española de Historia Natural* 7: 193–8.

Castaños, P. 1992. 'Los mamíferos del Cuaternario de Eurasia', in H. Astibia (ed.) *Paleontología de vertebrados. Faunas y filogenia, aplicación y sociedad* (Bilbao: Universidad del País Vasco) pp. 257–86.

Chapman, A and W.J. Buck. 1910. *Unexplored Spain* (London).

José María Fernández-García

Deinet, S., C. Leronymidou, L. McRae, I. Burfield, R. Foppen, B. Collen and M. Böhm. 2013. *Wildlife Comeback in Europe. The Recovery of Selected Mammal and Bird Species* (London: Rewilding Europe).

Echegaray, J. and C. Vilá. 2011. 'Noninvasive Monitoring of Wolves at the Edge of their Distribution and the Cost of their Conservation'. *Animal Conservation* 13: 157–61.

Echegaray, J., J. Leonard and C. Vilá. 2008. '¿Está asegurada la conservación del lobo ibérico a largo plazo?' *Quercus* 263: 14–23.

Fernández, J.M. and N. Ruiz de Azua. 2003. 'Notas históricas sobre algunas especies faunísticas', in J.M. Fernández (ed.) *Estudio faunístico del Parque Natural de Gorbeia. Fauna de vertebrados (excepto quirópteros)* (Vitoria: Diputación Foral de Álava) pp. 35–81.

— 2010. 'Historical Dynamics of a Declining Wolf Population: Persecution vs. Prey Reduction'. *European Journal of Wildlife Research* 56: 169–79.

Fuller, T., D. Mech and J. Cochrane. 2003. 'Wolf Population Dynamics', in D. Mech and L. Boitani (eds) *Wolves. Behaviour, Ecology and Conservation* (Chicago: University of Chicago Press) pp. 161–91.

Garayo, J.M. 2008. 'Datos sobre la rarificación, extinción e intentos de reasentamiento del lobo en el País Vasco (1814–1967)'. *Naturzale* 19: 5–38.

García y Asensio, J.M. 1995. *Historia de la fauna de Soria* (Soria: Asociación Soriana de Defensa de la Naturaleza).

Gragera, F. 1996. *El lobo ibérico en la Baja Extremadura* (Badajoz: Universitas).

Grande del Brío, R. 1984. *El lobo ibérico. Biología y mitología* (Madrid: Hermann Blume).

Grau, J., R. Puig and J. Ruiz-Olmo. 1990. 'Persecución del lobo en Girona (NE ibérico) durante los siglos XVIII y XIX. Ejemplo de utilización de datos de archivo'. *Miscelània Zoologica* 14: 217–23.

Gutiérrez, V. 2005. *El lobo ibérico en Andalucía* (Sevilla: Junta de Andalucía).

Hiraldo, F., M. Delibes and J. Calderón. 1979. *El quebrantahuesos* Gypaetus barbatus *(L.)* (Madrid: Ministerio de Agricultura).

Iranzo, F. c. 1475. *Tratado de montería.*

Junta General de Estadística. 1865. *Animales dañinos extinguidos en la Península é islas adyacentes, por los cuales se abonaron premios durante el año 1864* (Madrid: Imprenta Nacional).

Lampreave, G., J. Ruiz-Olmo, J. García-Petit, J. López-Martín, A. Bataille, O. Francino, N. Sastre and O. Ramírez. 2011. 'El lobo vuelve a Cataluña. Historia del regreso y medidas de conservación'. *Quercus* 302: 16–25.

Llaneza, L. and J.C. Blanco. 2005. 'Situación del lobo en Castilla y León. Evolución de sus poblaciones'. *Galemys* 17 (sp.): 15–28.

MacDonald, D. and C. Sillero-Zubiri (eds). 2004. *Biology and Conservation of Wild Canids* (Oxford: Oxford University Press).

Macías, F. 2012. 'El miedo al lobo en la España del siglo XVIII', in M.J. Pérez and L. Rubio (eds) *Campo y campesinos en la España moderna. Culturas políticas en el mundo hispano* (Madrid: Fundación Española de Historia Moderna) pp. 859–70.

Madoz, P. 1845–1850. *Diccionario geográfico-estadístico-histórico de España y sus posesiones de Ultramar*.

Mech, D. and L. Boitani (eds). 2003. *Wolves. Behavior, Ecology and Conservation* (Chicago: The University of Chicago).

Ministerio de Fomento. 1861. *Apuntes relativos a la aparición y extinción de animales dañinos en las provincias del Reino* (Madrid: Boletín Oficial).

Murga, F. 1978. 'Catálogo de las loberas de las provincias de Álava, Burgos y León'. *Kobie* 8: 159–89.

— 1988. 'La caza del lobo en Álava. La lobera de Barrón y ordenanza de corridas de lobos de Archua'. *Kobie Antropología Cultural* 3: 91–104.

Naves, J. 2010. 'Propuestas para el monitoreo de las poblaciones de lobos en la Península Ibérica', in A. Fernández, F. Alvares, C. Vilá and A. Ordiz (eds) *Los lobos de la Península Ibérica. Propuestas para el diagnóstico de sus poblaciones* (Palencia: Asociación para la Conservación y Estudio del Lobo Ibérico) pp. 175–99.

Nores, C. and J. Naves. 1993. 'Distribución histórica del oso pardo en la Península Ibérica', in J. Naves and G. Palomero (eds) *El oso pardo (*Ursus arctos*) en España* (Madrid: Ministerio de Agricultura) pp. 13–33.

Nowak, R. 2003. 'Wolf Evolution and Taxonomy', in D. Mech and L. Boitani (eds) *Wolves. Behaviour, Ecology and Conservation* (Chicago: The University of Chicago Press) pp. 239–58.

Núñez, P., R. García and L. Llaneza. 2007. 'Análisis de la distritribución histórica del lobo (*Canis lupus*) en Galicia: 1850, 1960 Y 2003'. *Ecología* 21: 195–206.

Philips, M., E. Bangs, D. Mech, B. Kelly and B. Fazio. 2004. 'Extermination and Recovery of Red Wolf and Grey Wolf in the Contiguous United States', in D. MacDonald and C. Sillero-Zubiri (eds) *Biology and Conservation of Wild Canids* (Oxford: Oxford University Press) pp. 297–309.

Pilot, M., W. Branicki, W. Jędrzejewski, J. Goszczyński, B. Jędrzejewska, I. Dykyy, M. Shkvyrya and E. Tsingarska. 2010. 'Phylogeographic History of Grey wolves in Europe'. *BMC Evolutionary Biology* 10: 104–15.

Rico, M. and J.P. Torrente. 2000. 'Caza y rarificación del lobo en España: investigación histórica y conclusiones biológicas'. *Galemys* 12 (sp.): 163–79.

Rodríguez, M. 2001. *La trashumancia. Cultura, cañadas y viajes* (Leon: Edilesa).

Rosas, M. 2009. 'Dinámica poblacional del lobo (*Canis lupus* Linnaeus, 1758) en la zona este de la provincia de Castelló de la Plana durante los siglos XVI–XVII (1566–1624)'. *Galemys* 21: 3–15.

Rossell, C. 2001. 'Los ungulados y los ecosistemas forestales: los ejemplos del jabalí y el corzo', in J. Camprodon and E. Plana (eds) *Conservación de la biodiversidad y gestión forestal. Su aplicación en la fauna vertebrada* (Barcelona: Universidad de Barcelona) pp. 377–96.

Servicio Nacional de Pesca Fluvial y Caza 1962. *Control de animales dañinos. Información estadística* (Madrid: Ministerio de Agricultura).

José María Fernández-García

Sidorovich, V., L. Tikhomirova and B. Jędrzejewska. 2003. 'Wolf *Canis lupus* Numbers, Diet and Damage to Livestock in Relation to Hunting and Ungulate Abundance in Northeastern Belarus during 1990–2000'. *Wildlife Biology* 9: 103–11.

Sommer, R. and N. Benecke. 2005. 'Late-Pleistocene and Early Holocene History of the Canid Fauna of Europe (Canidae)'. *Mammalian Biology* 70: 227–41.

Torrente, J.P. 1999. *Osos y otras fieras en el pasado de Asturias* (Oviedo: Fundación Oso de Asturias).

Valverde, J.A. 1971. 'El lobo español'. *Montes* 159: 229–42.

— 1991. 'Trampas y cepos en España', in A. Fuentes, L. Pajuelo and I. Sánchez (eds) *Manual de ordenación y gestión cinegética* (Badajoz: Institución Ferial de Badajoz) pp. 321–32.

Valverde, J.A. and S. Teruelo. 2001. *Los lobos de Morla* (Sevilla: Al Andalus Ediciones).

Vilà, C., I.R. Amorin, J. Leonard, D. Posada, J. Castroviejo, F. Petrucci-Fonseca, A. Crandall, S.H. Ellegren and R.K. Wayne. 1999. 'Mitochondrial DNA Phylogeography and Population History of the Grey Wolf *Canis lupus*'. *Molecular Ecology* 8: 2089–103.

Woutersen, K. 2000. *Fieras, rapiña y caza. Historia de la fauna de Aragón* (Huesca: Woutersen Publicaciones).

8

British Programmes for the Extermination of the Indian Wolf, c. 1870–1915

Steven Rodriguez

INTRODUCTION

In the 1870s, the British administration in India adopted a new policy for the extermination of noxious wildlife that would have a catastrophic impact on the future of the wolf. Although these programmes were initially designed to address depredations by tigers, leopards and snakes, government reports revealed that in the 1870s wolves in British India were responsible for the death of almost one thousand children a year, surpassing the death rate due to tigers – India's most notorious man-eaters. Subsequent extermination programmes implemented across British India rendered the Indian wolf nearly extinct by the middle of the twentieth century.[1] Employing documents from the India Office Records in the British Library and published writings by British colonial agents, this article will examine the conditions that resulted in the targeting of the wolf as a menace, the programmes for its destruction and why the wolf continued to be persecuted after it ceased to be a principal wildlife threat to humans in India. The purpose of this article is to draw attention to the massacre of the wolf outside Europe and North America, and to discover what insights the colonial documents on wolf extermination provide into the nagging problem of wolf predation on children in India.

The 'Cowardly Brute'

First identified by the British in 1831, the Indian wolf (*Canis lupus pallipes*) was commonly described by naturalists as a smaller (twenty kilogram) and slighter version of the European wolf, with reddish or brown hair and little or no underfur. In the nineteenth century, the Indian wolf existed across the subcontinent; however it was only rarely encountered in India's vast forest regions. British officers normally found the animal in flat and open country or hilly and rocky areas, ostensibly because in these habitats the wolf's view was unobstructed. The subspecies further distinguished itself by not howling and by hunting in small groups of two to four,

---

1. Rajpurohit 2001, p. 106.

rather than large packs. British hunters – and most officers in India were hunters – complained that the Indian wolf did not yield good sport. The animal was
considered impossible to ride down and spear; unlike the fox or the boar, which
could only run so far before being overtaken by dogs and horses, the wolf could
outrun and outdistance any attempt to catch it, seemingly without effort. The wolf
was also not much fun to shoot at. Unlike more approachable animals, sportsmen
criticised the Indian wolf for always remaining at a distance of one or two hundred
metres, never allowing hunters to approach any closer. At this distance the animal
was not an easy target to hit. Unlike the European wolf, the Indian wolf did not
acquire a reputation as a menacing and ferocious beast, but rather as a 'shy and
distant' creature. Indeed, the most common epithet for the animal was 'cowardly'.[2]

Indian wolves frequently became a subject for concern as a consequence
of their predilection for attacking and devouring Indian infants and children. In
some regions of northern India, the number of children killed by wolves could
be substantial – some districts reporting dozens of deaths every year.[3] Typically
referred to as 'child lifting', wolves did not attack wayward kids wandering in the
forest, but would, rather, seize children playing in front of their homes or when
they were sleeping outside at night – a common practice in the summer in India.
The wolves responsible for the attacks often lived around the villages or in the
villages themselves, sometimes under one of the peasants' homes.[4] Paradoxically,
Indian wolves also gained notoriety for supposedly raising Indian children. From
the 1840s, colonial military officers, administrators, and missionaries submitted
reports of discovering abandoned Indian children in the company of wolves. The
children were described as behaving like animals: they moved on all fours, could
not speak, resisted captivity and generally died soon after being discovered. There
was widespread speculation that these children had been raised by wolves. Although
most professionals dismissed the idea, the possibility continued to be a subject
debated by reputable scholars into the twentieth century.[5]

Generally, British agents did not evince as much interest in wolves as in India's
other magnificent fauna: tigers, leopards, elephants and rhinos among others. The
terror inspired by tigers could disrupt mail and transportation, inhibit cultivation

2. Hamilton 1892, pp. 18–24; Kinloch 1892, pp. 47–8; Lydekker 1907, pp. 356–9; Pollock 1894,
    pp. 221–2.
3. Newall 1866, pp. 431, 453; Johnson 1827, pp. 42–3; Jerdon 1874, p. 140–1.
4. Johnson 1827, pp. 42–3.
5. Tylor 1863, pp. 21–32; Benzaquén 2006, pp. 215–39. No child was ever actually observed living
    with wolves, while many of the cases in which children were claimed to have been found in the
    company of wolves were discovered to be fraudulent. The general scholarly consensus was that,
    on occasion, Indian children who were already developmentally handicapped wandered off and
    were in the company of wolves for only a day or two when discovered. The children's appearance
    and behaviour were then interpreted as 'animal-like'. The topic continues to inspire scholarship,
    but this current research generally focuses on the persistence of the myth of the wolf-child and
    what it reveals about Victorian culture.

and even clear out entire villages. Tigers and leopards regularly destroyed domestic cattle, resulting in substantial economic loss. The tiger was exciting to hunt, it was a magnificent trophy and there was glory in killing this 250 kilo man-eating monster. Wolves were a nuisance, but they were not a threat to the lives of the British or the imperial plans for the agricultural and economic progress of the colony. British officers themselves acknowledged the lack of attention to the Indian wolf, attributing the neglect to the abundance of other more prestigious game animals in India:

> We don't look upon wolves as much in the way of 'shikar', and so we don't hunt for them – perhaps, indeed, hardly observe them sometimes, when, if they were more in esteem as sport, we should note the circumstance ... It seems rather strange that wolves, and even hyaenas, should be usually considered as beneath an Indian sportsman's attention. No one ever thinks, somehow, of securing their skins ... there is so much game in this country yielding handsomer trophies, and of better fighting qualities[6]

TARGETING THE WOLF FOR EXTERMINATION

Prior to the 1870s, the control of dangerous wildlife in India was addressed in an ad hoc manner. Individual provinces enacted different control measures, generally through bounties for animals in areas where they had become a serious threat to the safety and economic development of the region.[7] However, in the 1870s, the damage caused by carnivores and noxious animals received more serious attention from imperial administrators in India and London. The larger debate was sparked when several high-ranking medical and military officers brought attention to statistics that suggested that approximately 20,000 people and 50,000 head of cattle were being killed every year by wild animals in British India.[8] For some, such as Lt. Colonel Romaine Wragge, the problem was economic – he contended that there was a drawback to the safe cultivation and transport of cotton, arising from the dread entertained by the natives of the attacks of wild beasts. According to Wragge, 'It may almost be a question if the fear of these wild beasts may not, in a minor way, operate against extending cotton cultivation in the neighbourhood of places infested by them'.[9] As proof, Wragge revealed that, between 1868 and 1870, the number of acres under cultivation of cotton had diminished in several districts where people had been killed by wild beasts.[10] Joseph Fayrer of the Indian Medical Service argued that wild animals attacked not only crops and domesticated animals but also villagers and their families, and should be considered alongside

---

6.   Newall 1866, pp. 431–2.
7.   Rangarajan 1998, pp. 271–2.
8.   Fayrer 1878, p. 187.
9.   Wragge 1871, p. 456.
10.   Wragge 1871, pp. 456–7.

Steven Rodriguez

other public health concerns such as the control of epidemic disease and improved sanitation. According to Fayrer,

> The death-rate from disease has been reduced to less than one-third of its former figure (69 to 18) by the scientific application of sanitary laws. Let the same enlightened attention be given to this death cause, and depend on it, equally good results would, in time, ensue. In a few years, it would no longer be the duty of the registrar to chronicle such figures of mortality as those I have given you.[11]

Reports on the depredations of wild animals in India excited considerable interest in the UK and resulted in a suggestion by the Foreign Department for a yearly review of the losses of life and property caused by tigers, leopards, wild elephants, snakes and other noxious animals in order to determine the best means that could be adopted for their destruction. Consequently, the Government of India was requested to prepare annual reports on the mortality from wild animals and the progress made towards the extermination of these dangerous beasts. From 1875, the collection of statistics and reports on 'noxious animals' remained a regular duty of all provincial administrations of British India.[12]

Early statistics of human casualties collected during the 1870s confirmed the projections of the proponents of wildlife control – wild animals in British India were reported to have annually killed approximately 20,000 people (16,000–17,000 due to snakes and 3,000–4,000 due to wild beasts). What was surprising about the statistics was that wolves were responsible for more human casualties than any other carnivore – in 1875, wolves were reported to have claimed 1,061 lives, while tigers, the most notorious man-eaters, killed 828 people (see Table 1). In several of the provinces wolves were depicted as being particularly destructive; in 1876, the North-West Provinces alone suffered the loss of 721 lives due to wolves.[13] By 1877, the annual reports depicted the wolf as a principal threat to human life, and the report for 1878 singled out wolves as being largely responsible for the rise in human casualties.[14] The 'bad preeminence' of the wolf during the decade when the promotion of extermination policies was most intense, and the animal's subsequent identification as a major threat to public health, would set in motion the species's widespread extermination over the next fifty years.

While all sides agreed that it was necessary to eradicate 'the evil' of wildlife predation that was considered 'totally preventable', there were different proposed methods for undertaking the extermination programme. In the past, bounties had been a conventional method for dealing with problem animals in India; however many critics complained that the rise of reported animal attacks proved that bounties

---

11. Fayrer 1878, p. 188.
12. India Office Records, British Library (hereafter IOR), L/PJ/3/1052, File 10, 27 Nov. 1874; IOR/L/E/7/1352, File 3178, 26 Jul. 1924 – 8 Jan. 1934.
13. Rangarajan 1998, p. 289.
14. IOR/L/PJ/6/2, File 66, 19 Dec. 1879.

Table 1. Number of persons killed by wolves and tigers in British India, 1875–1912.

Year	Wolves	Tigers
1875	1,061	828
1876	887	923
1877	564	819
1878	845	816
1879	492	698
1880	347	872
1881	256	889
1882	278	895
1883	287	985
1884	265	831
1885	248	838
1886	222	928
1887	177	1,063
1888	139	975
1889	207	985
1890	242	798
1891	218	979
1892	182	947
1893	175	969
1894	227	864
1895	340	909
1896	483	944
1897	596	1,071
1898	462	927
1899	338	899
1900	424	943
1901	403	1,171
1902	338	1,046
1903	463	866
1904	244	786
1905	153	786
1906	273	698
1907	277	793
1908	269	909
1909	256	896
1910	319	882
1911	190	762
1912	255	885

Source: Great Britain. India Office 1878, pp. 132–5; Great Britain. India Office 1887, pp. 240–7; Great Britain. India Office 1896, pp. 268–75; Great Britain. India Office 1905, pp. 238–9; Great Britain. India Office 1915, pp. 240–1.

were insufficient. There were calls for the establishment of an official extermination corps that would systematically destroy all dangerous wildlife in India, while some groups supported the widespread use of various experimental traps, poisons and 'asphyxiating devices'.[15] But experiments with these plans were not a success. A government extermination programme in the Madras Presidency resulted in 22 tigers killed at a cost of over 10,000 rupees – almost ten times the standard tiger bounty price of 50 rupees. There was also concern that the widespread deployment of traps and poisons could endanger humans and domestic cattle. Critics argued that the extermination corps exacerbated the depredations caused by wild animals – slaughtering all carnivores in an area allowed crop-destroying deer and pigs to proliferate, leaving the locality in a worse plight than before; moreover, competition from the temporary corps drove away the resident Indian hunters, the best long-term guards against both destructive carnivores and herbivores.[16]

Many colonial agents believed that the improved engagement of autonomous local hunters was the most effective defence against destructive wildlife. They advocated the expansion and normalisation of the bounty system, arguing that bounties had not succeeded in motivating native hunters because they had never been implemented in a consistent manner, the payment and amount of bounties being determined at the discretion of the local officer in charge. Collecting a bounty was time consuming, requiring the hunter to visit the village head, then see the *tahsildar* (the district revenue officer) and then travel the considerable distance to the office of the collector of the district.[17] Without assurance of being paid – or paid fairly – native hunters were unwilling to risk their time. However, the standardisation of bounties would encourage hunters to seek out and exterminate wild animals. By the 1880s, the government had put its support behind the regularisation of bounties and indicated to all administrations that 'Collectors should impress upon their subordinates that they are not allowed any discretion in the matter, and that the full scale of reward should be paid in all cases'.[18] The extermination of noxious animals in India became a regular responsibility of provincial administrations; the occasional and irregular efforts to destroy problem animals were replaced by a bounty programme designed for the total extermination of all noxious animals throughout British India.

The implementation of a regularised bounty system was especially disastrous for the wolf. While the tiger and leopard had routinely been hunted for sport, bounties or the value of their pelts, the revised bounty system created a new and steady demand for the wolf. The dependable payment of rewards motivated native hunters and trappers to take up killing wolves in earnest – once their attention was

---

15. IOR/L/PJ/6/55, File 1721, 24 Oct. 1881.

16. IOR/L/PJ/6/88, File 2151, 5 Dec. 1882.

17. Wragge 1871, p. 457.

18. IOR/L/PJ/6/166, File 2305, 24 Nov. 1885.

directed towards the wolves, these local professionals were well equipped to eradicate them. Unlike hunting the tiger or elephant, which generally required enormous expense and special equipment, killing wolves was relatively easy. For example, local hunters could seek out the wolves' dens, smoke the animals out and spear them as they emerged. The situation was exacerbated by the wolf's preeminence in the 1870s as a threat to humans, resulting in unusually high bounties for the animal. In areas that were particularly affected by wolf attacks, including the North-West Provinces, Oude and Bihar, the provincial administrations also employed a body of special hunters specifically charged with the task of destroying wolves.[19]

Wolves suffered from the principle of total extermination that underlay the war against dangerous beasts. Previous bounties had generally been instituted for animals that directly inhibited or destroyed agriculture, in particular elephants, tigers and leopards. The decision to implement a regular bounty system in all regions of British India, not just the boundaries of agriculture, gave an incentive to seek out and kill all wolves irrespective of whether they were predatory on humans or interfered with agriculture. The result for the wolf was almost complete annihilation – over 100,000 wolves were massacred for bounties in the British Indian territories from 1870 to 1920.[20]

EXPLANATIONS FOR THE RISE IN WOLF PREDATION

Colonial reports generally focused on the problem of increased damage by noxious animals and how to best exterminate them rather than devoting energy to investigating the causes of the attacks. Depredations by wild animals were attributed to the expansion of British administration in India, which brought British colonial agents into increased contact with wild animals and resulted in a rise in human–animal conflict. The opening up of the country to cultivation and the expansion of the railroads into remote regions also led to more clashes between humans and wild animals. The increase in reported attacks by wolves may have been a consequence of the expansion of British bureaucracy and statistical reporting on all facets of India that occurred after the establishment of the British Raj in 1858. In the early reports, the disarming of the natives after the rebellion of 1857 was often cited as a source of the rise in wildlife attacks.[21] However these reasons are less convincing as an explanation for the surge of attacks by wolves – shy, distant and cowardly animals that did not generally live in the forest. It is significant that the alarm over wolf attacks at the time came largely from London; the concern with Indian wolves in the 1870s may have been more metropolitan hysteria than an actual growing

---

19. IOR/L/PJ/6/88, File 2151, 5 Dec. 1882.
20. Rangarajan 1998, p. 292.
21. IOR/L/PJ/6/55, File 1721, 24 Oct. 1881.

problem, less a change in the number of attacks than an increase in the interest in the problem.

Colonial agents often attributed the rise of wolf attacks to the 'apathy and inaction' of the native Indians.[22] Several officers claimed that the villagers were afraid of killing wolves due to a superstitious dread that this would bring misfortune to their families or render their cultivated land barren, and these beliefs allowed child-killing wolves to survive and flourish.[23] Administrators also blamed infanticide, claiming that Indian children were being abandoned to be taken by wolves, citing as evidence the fact that more girls than boys were casualties.[24] However, in the debates that took place during this decade over increased depredations by noxious animals, the widespread famines that impacted on India were not emphasised as the cause for the rise in attacks by animals in general, or wolves in particular. In the later nineteenth century, a series of disastrous crop failures in India resulted in mass starvation and epidemics. The death toll was appalling. In British India, two million people starved to death in the North-West Provinces, Punjab, and Rajasthan in 1860–61; nearly a million in 1866–67; 4.3 million in 1876–78; and an additional 1.2 million in the North-West Provinces and Kashmir in 1877–78. Over five million perished in a famine in 1896–97 and in 1899–1900, over a million more starved to death. These were only the most catastrophic famines.[25] In the period from 1869 to 1878, severe famine was prevalent in those regions where wolf attacks were most common, and wolf predation surged again from 1896 to 1902 – another era of extreme famine. Some British officers did report that, as a result of famines, starving wolves were feeding on human corpses and subsequently turning to prey on the starving people, but insofar as famine was viewed as a cause, again it was often attributed to the failings of the Indian villagers who did not properly bury the corpses of famine victims (millions of them) and therefore were responsible themselves for creating the problem of wolf predation.[26]

There is also strong evidence that human casualties might have been inaccurately attributed to wolves instead of other animals. There was widespread criticism of the accuracy of the wildlife reports and, owing to the unreliability of the statistics, the Government of India several times considered discontinuing the submission of the returns. In the case of the wolf, provincial officers often discovered that bounties that had paid out for wolves were in fact given for jackals, hyenas and wild dogs.[27] Hunters, naturalists and colonial agents all frequently admitted that it was difficult to distinguish them, and that they often confused the separate

22. IOR/L/PJ/6/192, File 15, 14 Dec. 1886.
23. Forsyth 1889, pp. 72–5; Hamilton 1892, p. 24.
24. Baldwin 1876, p. 119; Fayrer 1878, pp. 205–6; Burton 1931, p. 223.
25. Fieldhouse 2006, pp. 132–4; Davis 2002, pp. 34–60.
26. Burton 1931, pp. 222–5.
27. IOR/L/E/7/1352, File 3178, 26 Jul. 1924 – 8 Jan. 1934; Fayrer 1878, p. 191.

species. The District Magistrate of Hamirpur, for example, felt that many casualties attributed to wolves in his region were actually a result of attacks by hyenas.[28] It is necessary to consider that the statistics for fatalities due to wolves may be more indicative of casualties due to Indian *canids* in general.

After the turn of the twentieth century, concerns over depredations by wild animals dissipated. In many regions dangerous beasts had become rare and there was a widespread belief that the expansion of agriculture and continued deforestation would soon render noxious wildlife extinct in India, as had previously occurred in Britain. In fact, in many quarters there was concern that too many tigers and leopards had been exterminated, allowing pigs and other herbivores to proliferate, causing even greater damage to agriculture.[29] Wildlife conservation in the British Empire was starting to attract more attention, signalled by the formation of the Society for the Preservation of the Fauna of the Empire (SPFE) in London in 1903. Bounties for tigers were discontinued in many parts of India after 1903, while the Asiatic lion became a protected species in 1907.

However, in the new century, the destruction of the Indian wolf continued unabated, and in some regions accelerated. Yet, statistically, after 1900 the number of people reportedly killed by wolves had declined to fewer than 300 a year.[30] Tigers, meanwhile, were receiving reprieves, yet continued annually to kill between 800 and 1,100 people. While in the twentieth century the tiger was able to find defenders who argued that the animal only took to man-eating as a consequence of sickness, injury or some factor that altered its natural behaviour, no such defences emerged for the wolf, even when the number of fatalities attributed to them had dramatically declined. Unlike tigers, there was no aesthetic or sporting significance attached to maintaining the wolf population. The recognition of the wolf as a problem, its lack of prestige and the creation of an organised bounty system for its total elimination provided the incentive for the Indian wolf's continued destruction; by the middle of the twentieth century, approximately one thousand specimens remained – fewer than the tiger.

CONCLUSION

Unlike the concurrent state-directed wolf-extermination programmes taking place in the US – motivated by the damage caused by wolves to agricultural and ranching interests – in India the principal motivation for the destruction of the wolf was its predation on children. If the history of human–wolf interaction in North America did not yield human casualties, in India wolves have a long documented record for killing children. This paper has been constructed from only one collection of

28. Rangarajan 1998, p. 291.
29. IOR/L/PJ/6/769, File 2067, 10 Jul. 1906; IOR/L/PJ/802, File 882, 27 Mar. 1907.
30. IOR/L/PJ/6/648, File 2106, 10 Sep. 1903.

Steven Rodriguez

reports on Indian wolves; however, accounts of their depredations are found in a wide variety of official documents, such as survey reports, general administration reports, applications for sanction to the offer of rewards, special reports of missionaries residing in the interior and a range of other sources located in India and Britain. A thorough examination of this material would contribute to our understanding of human–wolf interactions, the contexts for wolf attacks, the dynamics of wolf predation and the factors accounting for this aberrant behaviour.

Despite suffering the full brunt of British extermination programmes, the Indian wolf managed to endure the onslaught and survived the twentieth century. Unlike the tiger, the little wolf proved extremely adaptable – it could live in a variety of inhabited and uninhabited environments, it could travel by day or night and it could rapidly reproduce. From a low point of approximately one thousand specimens, in recent decades the wolf population has increased. So has the number of attacks on Indian villagers. In the state of Bihar, one of the world's poorest regions, predation by wolves in the 1980s and 1990s was reported to have caused the death of at least 200 people. Wolf attacks regrettably continue to pose problems for India's poorest, but the history of British wolf-extermination programmes suggests that the solution is to eliminate poverty, not the Indian wolf.

BIBLIOGRAPHY

Archival Sources

India Office Records, British Library, IOR/L/E/7/1352, File 3178. 'Annual Returns of Destruction of and Persons Killed by Wild Animals', 26 July 1924 – 8 January 1934.

India Office Records, British Library, IOR/L/PJ/3/1052, File 10. 'Relative to the Destruction of Wild Animals and Venomous Snakes', 27 November 1874.

India Office Records, British Library, IOR/L/PJ/6/2, File 66. 'Report on Destruction of Wild Animals and Venomous Snakes in India in 1878', 19 December 1879.

India Office Records, British Library, IOR/L/PJ/6/55, File 1721. 'Report of Mortality from and Destruction of Wild Animals and Venomous Snakes during 1880', 24 October 1881.

India Office Records, British Library, IOR/L/PJ/6/88, File 2151. 'Reports on Mortality from Wild Animals and Snakes', 5 December 1882.

India Office Records, British Library, IOR/L/PJ/6/166, File 2305. 'Report on Destruction of Life and Property by Wild Animals and Snakes', 24 November 1885.

India Office Records, British Library, IOR/L/PJ/6/192, File 15. 'Reports on Measures for Destruction of Wild Animals and Venomous Snakes', 14 December 1886.

India Office Records, British Library, IOR/L/PJ/6/459, File 2182. 'Reports on the Destruction of Wild Animals and Venomous Snakes during 1896', 14 October 1897.

India Office Records, British Library, IOR/L/PJ/6/648, File 2106. 'Destruction of Wild Animals and Venomous Snakes during 1902', 10 September 1903.

India Office Records, British Library, IOR/L/PJ/6/769, File 2067. 'Report on the House of Commons Question on the Indiscriminate Offer of Rewards for the Destruction of Tigers and Leopards', 10 July 1906.

India Office Records, British Library, IOR/L/PJ/6/802, File 882. 'House of Commons Question Regarding Damage to Crops in India by Wild Animals', 27 March 1907.

Research Literature

Baldwin, J.H. 1876. *The Large and Small Game of Bengal and the North-Western Provinces of India* (London: Henry S. King & Co.).

Benzaquén, A.S. 2006. *Encounters with Wild Children: Temptation and Disappointment in the Study of Human Nature* (Montreal: McGill-Queen's University Press).

Burton. R.G. 1931. *A Book of Man-Eaters* (London: Hutchinson & Co.).

Davis, M. 2002. *Late Victorian Holocausts: El Niño Famines and the Making of the Third World* (New York: Verso).

Fayrer, J. 1878. 'Destruction of Life by Wild Animals and Venomous Snakes in India'. *Journal of the Society of Arts* 26: 187–226.

Fieldhouse, D. 2006. 'For Richer, for Poorer?' In P.J. Marshall (ed.) *The Cambridge Illustrated History of the British Empire* (Cambridge: Cambridge University Press) pp. 108–46.

Forsyth, J. 1889. *The Highlands of Central India: Notes on their Forests and Wild Tribes, Natural History and Sports* (London: Chapman and Hall).

Great Britain. India Office. 1878. *Statistical Abstract relating to British India from 1867/8 to 1876/7* (London: Her Majesty's Stationery Office).

Great Britain. India Office. 1887. *Statistical Abstract relating to British India from 1876/7 to 1885/6* (London: Her Majesty's Stationery Office).

Great Britain. India Office. 1896. *Statistical Abstract relating to British India from 1885–86 to 1894–95* (London: Her Majesty's Stationery Office).

Great Britain. India Office. 1905. *Statistical Abstract relating to British India from 1894–95 to 1903–04* (London: Her Majesty's Stationery Office).

Great Britain. India Office. 1915. *Statistical Abstract relating to British India from 1903–04 to 1912–13* (London: His Majesty's Stationery Office).

Hamilton, D. 1892. *Records of Sport in Southern India* (London: R.H. Porter).

Jerdon, T. 1874. *The Mammals of India* (London: John Wheldon).

Johnson, D. 1827. *Sketches of Indian Field Sports* (London: Robert Jennings).

Kinloch, A.A.A. 1892. *Large Game Shooting in Thibet, the Himalayas, Northern and Central India* (Calcutta: Thacker, Spink & Co.).

Lydekker, R. 1907. *The Game Animals of India, Burma, Malaya and Tibet* (London: Rowland Ward).

Newall, J.T. 1866. *The Eastern Hunters* (London: Tinsley Brothers).

Pollock, A.J.O. 1894. *Sporting Days in Southern India* (London: Horace Cox).

Steven Rodriguez

Rajpurohit, K.S. 2001. 'Child Lifting Wolves in India: A Strategy for their Management and Control', in B.B. Hosetti and M. Venkateshwarlu (eds) *Trends in Wildlife Biodiversity Conservation and Management* (Delhi: Daya Publishing House) pp. 104–25.

Rangarajan, M. 1998. 'The Raj and the Natural World: The War against "Dangerous Beasts" in colonial India'. *Studies in History* 14: 265–99.

Tylor, E.B. 1863. 'Wild Men and Beast-Children'. *Anthropological Review* 1: 21–32.

Wragge, A.R. 1871. 'Wild Beasts in India'. *Journal of the Society of Arts* 19: 456–7.

9

Writing the Wolf:
Canine Tales and North American Environmental-Literary Tradition[1]

Karen Jones

Wild nature has served as an enduring foil for storytelling. From James Fenimore Cooper to Edward Abbey, a cadre of distinguished literary figures have placed wilderness at the forefront of their stories. The natural world has acted as a platform for tales of pioneer endurance, biotic splendour, national redemption, individual expression and moral certitude. The wilderness experience provides North American literary tradition with one of its most distinctive features. In American writings on wilderness, one animal has attained a remarkable resonance – *Canis lupus*, or the grey wolf. The literary wolf is a deeply symbolic creature. It has become a 'carrier animal' for deeply felt sentiments of identity, progress, ethnicity and gender. Traditionally used by Euro-American authors to invoke fear and anxiety, the hideous reputation of the wolf led eighteenth-century naturalist Mark Catesby to deride the species as 'destructive' animals with 'dismal, yelling cries'. However, others came to write differently of their lupine experiences. Nineteenth-century transcendentalist Henry David Thoreau celebrated the howl for giving 'voice' to the wilderness. Since the post-1945 environmental revolution, writers have used the wolf as a symbol of sacred ecological vitality. In 2009, the Internet bookstore Amazon.com listed over 127,587 titles concerning 'wolves' – a testament to the enduring appeal of *Canis lupus* in the North American eco-literary imagination.[2]

It is important to note that literary fascination with *Canis lupus* first emerged in Europe. Old World legends recounted how Romulus and Remus were suckled by a maternal she-wolf, while fables attributed to Greek slave Aesop branded lupine animals as wily. Medieval fairytales and fiery religious dogma defined wolves as demoniacal, lascivious and thoroughly brutal forms. Meanwhile, creation myths imparted by indigenous shamans attested to the wolf as a historic character in North American storytelling. The Tlingit of Alaska believed that they descended from

---

1. This chapter originally appeared in *Environment and History* 17 (2) (2011): 201–228.
2. Catesby 1985, p. 157; Thoreau 1864, p. 306.

two wolves that shed their skins to become human, while 'Big Wolf' of Blackfeet mythology imparted essential hunting skills to the tribe.[3]

In *Waterland* (1983), novelist Graham Swift posited that 'only animals live entirely in the Here and Now. Only nature knows neither memory nor history.' Biologists have since shown *Canis lupus* to be a highly intelligent species, capable of remembering detailed geographic information. Prominent North American writers have also refuted the notion of the wolf as an animal without memory or history, drawing on mythology, artistic license and environmental tenets to explore the nature of the beast. In the annals of North American nature writing, the wolf has often been configured as a faunal totem signifying untamed terrain and untamed spirit. Many works of fiction have situated *Canis lupus* as a dominant protagonist in a separate realm of nature, a verdant domain visited by humans solely for the purposes of conquest or recreation. Literary expositions on wilderness have featured wolves as criminals and luminaries, aggressors and victims, creatures of instinct and individual thinkers. Such variegated definitions of canine temperament attest to shifting cultural attitudes over the direction of modern society, the place of humans in nature and popular environmental thinking.[4]

This article explores the relationship between literature and environmental values by examining the portrayal of wolves in North American texts from the late nineteenth century onwards. Of particular interest are those figures that contributed to a positive canon of lupine storytelling. The writings of Ernest Thompson Seton and Jack London in the late 1800s; Farley Mowat and Roger Caras in the 1960s; and Whitley Strieber, Cormac McCarthy and Asta Bowen in the late twentieth century contain descriptions of intelligent canine protagonists that countered the images of bestial excess in traditional Euro-American wolf tales. The 'realistic animal story' genre of the Victorian era, coupled with environmentalist treatises of the 1960s and recovery narratives in the 1990s forwarded the rehabilitation of *Canis lupus* from despised varmint to American faunal hero. The historiography on wolves in North America has typically cited scientific erudition, empirical analysis and ecological models as catalysts for species re-evaluation. Thomas Dunlap, in *Saving America's Wildlife* (1988), situated the redemption of the 'big bad wolf' in the professionalisation of the wildlife community and emerging debates about biotic health and integrity in the interwar period. For Jon T. Coleman, 'scientific observation' countered the prejudice of past ideas founded on 'folklore and property', while evolutionary biology itself served to explain our ancestral hostility to the wolf as a competing apex predator. Instead, this article points to the value of storytelling, of emotion, visualisation and connection as rhetorical guides to action in framing our (positive) engagements with other species. Read in this fashion, the landmark return of the wolf to Yellowstone in 1995 signalled not the revolt of sci-

3. For an exhaustive survey of the wolf of folklore, see Lopez 1978.
4. Swift 1983, p. 53.

ence against the allied forces of folklore, ritual and prejudice but the emergence of a new story about *Canis lupus*. Meanwhile, as both scientists and writers redefined or 'retold' their paradigms of the wolf, they engaged in a competitive struggle for environmental authority, grappling for sway over the public mind based on the figurative polarities of 'science' versus 'sentiment.' This tension, often construed in binaries of the professional/amateur and the objective/subjective played out in debates surrounding the 'realistic animal story' and, as I argue here, proved a recurring feature of dialogues about animal authority through the twentieth century. The article concludes by making a further, more elemental, contention regarding the salience of the science–sentiment demarcation itself and the possibility of 'knowing' the wolf. Adolph Murie, in his pioneering ecological study *The Wolves of Mount McKinley* (1944), repeatedly referred to the 'friendliness' of the pack while many literary figures sported backgrounds in empirical natural history. Despite the assertion of wolf biologist L. David Mech that science espouses 'a clearer, more objective view of animals', the goal to present animals 'as they really are' represented a common aim for both scientist and storyteller. Significantly, however, authorial claims of detachment always fell short, whether written up as biological report or short story. Narratives about the wolf reflect changing cultural ideas, technical expertise, environmental values and ethical judgments. For all the lofty claims to 'get inside the skin' of the wolf – a practice literally adopted by Lakota hunters seeking to hunt bison on the American Plains – tales about *Canis lupus* often tell us a great deal more about *Homo sapiens*.[5]

'INTO THE PRIMITIVE': SETON, LONDON, AND THE CULT OF THE WILD

Nature stories proved immensely popular in late nineteenth-century American society. As well as engaging in pursuits of taxidermy, painting, ornithology and woodcraft, citizens displayed an avid interest in the natural world by eagerly digesting tales of the wild. Ralph Lutts classified this fervent curiosity in nature as 'a public environmental awakening equalled only by the great reawakening later in the twentieth century'. For an increasingly urbanised society with concerns over the debilitating smog of industrial progress, nature served as a wholesome Arcadian refuge. Thousands of urbanites escaped the city using the bookstore as well as the railroad, satiating their desires for spiritual renewal and nostalgic romanticism in

5. Contemporary works presenting the restoration of wolves to the American West as the triumph of ecological science over folklore and prejudice, and vaunting the primacy of the professional biologist as a species guide include: Phillips and Smith 1995; Fischer 1995; McIntyre 1996. See Dunlap 1988, 1984; Coleman 2004, pp. 1, 13. For debates surrounding 'the realistic animal story', see Lutts 1990, 1998; Mighetto 1985; Murie 1944, pp. 24–31; Mech 1970, p. xxi. This article builds on my own prior scholarship on wolf recovery (Jones 2002a); wolves and science (Jones 2002b); and the furore over Mowat's *Never Cry Wolf* (Jones 2003).

textual and material landscapes alike. Victorian fascination with nature also reflected a society wrestling with metaphysical questions regarding evolutionary theory and the place of *Homo sapiens* in the natural world. Biological theories promulgated by the likes of Herbert Spencer, Charles Darwin and August Weismann posited nature as an amoral realm where humans and other animals engaged in elemental struggles for existence.[6]

The rise of the 'realistic animal story' genre in the 1890s revealed an American populace eager to immerse themselves in matters of natural order, the survival of the fittest and questions of morality in nature. Readers sought to learn about the habits and lifestyles of their 'horizontal brothers'. *Canis lupus* emerged as a prominent character in these tales. The life of a predator afforded ideal literary terrain for writers to expound on 'nature red in tooth and claw', natural selection and the unending struggle for subsistence. The hunt also served as a vehicle for dramatic literary action, allowing authors to revel in the thrill of the chase and the choreography of faunal protagonists. Offering narratives told 'from the animal's point of view', writers combined biological observations with artistic prose to forge evocative depictions of non-human life. While scientists had raised fundamental questions regarding the connections between people and other animals, storytellers assumed the task of exploring how canine brethren lived and reasoned.[7]

Canadian naturalist Ernest Thompson Seton proved an instrumental figure in the establishment of the 'realistic animal story' genre. Seton published *Wild Animals I Have Known*, a collection of faunal life histories, in 1898. The first edition – with its suitably rough-hewn cover offering sketches of wolf heads, pawprints, a rabbit and raven – received copious acclaim for its sympathetic portrayal of non-human protagonists. The inaugural print run of 2,000 copies sold out in three weeks. The Canadian naturalist asserted the realistic nature of his depictions, positing drama, emotion and tragedy as essential features of the natural canvas. The first lines of *Wild Animals I Have Known* read, 'These stories are true ... the animals in this book were all real characters. They lived the lives I have depicted, and showed the stamp of heroism and personality more strongly by far than it has been in the power of my pen to tell.' The first story in the collection, 'Lobo: King of Currampaw', related the tale of a grand outlaw wolf and his 'reign of terror' as a cattle rustler in the American South-west. Seton based the yarn on his experiences as a trapper at the Fitz-Randolph ranch, New Mexico, where he spent four months in 1893–4 in pursuit of the Mexican wolf that locals had christened 'Lobo.' The sojourn in the desert proved a seminal experience, deepening Seton's his interest in wild canines and ushering in a personal commitment to their preservation. He later used the

6. Lutts 1990, pp. ix–x.
7. Mighetto 1985: 48.

nickname 'Wolf' and the mark of a pawprint as a signature, suggesting a sense of empathy and a symbolic transgression from human to animal identity.[8]

'Lobo: King of Currumpaw' conveyed the story of an extraordinary faunal protagonist. Seton crafted the character of Lobo as a suitably rugged and romantic western hero, a wily uber-masculine outlaw eking out an existence on the rangelands of New Mexico. Lobo was a charismatic beast, a 'king' who ruled the Currumpaw using 'despotic power.' He was, albeit in four-legged form, a testament to frontier lore as championed by Frederick Jackson Turner. Lupine peers respected Lobo for his cunning and strength. Cattlemen balked at his commanding howl. Seton's creation of Lobo highlighted a literary imperative to create an enigmatic lead character that readers would embrace. It also reflected a general tendency of pro-wolf stories to focus on the individual as a way to induce audience familiarity, identification and assist communication. Seton's outlaw wolf inspired readers to connect with his personality, particular actions and individualistic motivations. This stood in contrast to traditional frontier presentations of the wolf as part of a pack, an undifferentiated mob ruled by bloodlust. Where pioneer newspapers spoke of the lurking threat of wolf packs at the margins of frontier settlement – the *Edmonton Journal* carried an article in 1925 about a mob of dastardly wolves preventing residents of the town of Vilna, Alberta attending dances after dark – Seton focused on the singular animal as a definable, charismatic, knowable and far less dangerous entity.[9]

Moreover, the desire to emphasise Lobo's 'real personality ... and his view of life' reflected Seton's unease with contemporary scientific discourse that framed humans and animals solely in terms of species. While Lobo *appeared* a truly Darwinian hero, an animal whose physical strength and vigour assured his pre-eminence, Seton took pains to craft his leading lupine as a unique, noble creature, capable of outstanding acts of compassion. For Seton, the ability of animals to perform remarkable feats disavowed Darwinist visions of nature as a domain governed by obdurate natural forces where individuals mattered little.[10]

Seton employed the character of the wolf to elaborate on his rich definition of wilderness. In the writer's cult of the wild, untamed landscapes exhibited spiritual truths and communicated virtuous principles. Nature represented a beneficent realm governed by moral laws. Asked to expound on his theory of life, Seton reputedly advised, 'take two trips into the wilderness each year, and spend six months on each trip'. The wolf represented the central performer in Seton's romanticised wild, the canine soul embodying the freedom and vitality of pristine nature. In 'Lobo: King of Currumpaw', the drama of raw nature was elucidated by acts of predation. Seton's detailed descriptions of hunting activities and graphic illustrations showed the wolf as a masterful predator and the author as an empirical naturalist. While

---

8.   Seton 1987, p. 9.
9.   Ibid. p. 17; See *Calgary Herald*, 18 Mar. 1925.
10. Seton 1987, p. 9.

180

Karen Jones

contemporary nature writers such as John Muir and William Long ignored, even denied, the existence of pain in the natural world, Seton savoured the predatory prowess of *Canis lupus*. Many nineteenth-century humanitarians denigrated wild carnivores as contemptible killers, yet Seton perceived death at the fangs of a wolf or the talons of an owl as 'wholly kind'. The Canadian writer successfully wrested the contest between predator and prey from the jaws of modish scientific dogma, positing nature as competitive and cruel, and incorporated it within his moral conception of a cooperative, benevolent natural world. For Seton, that 'every animal that has some great strength or it could not live, and some great weakness or the others could not live' illuminated divine order rather than competition in nature.[11]

Seton situated the tale of Lobo within an elemental conflict between wolves and humans. In their quest to dominate the Currumpaw range, ranchers construed Lobo and his pack as a 'destructive band', viewing the lead wolf's guileful pursuit of cattle as the act of a 'grizzly devastator'. Lobo, meanwhile, gloried in routing his two-legged adversaries and engaged in sheep-killing sprees for sheer exhilaration. This was, put simply, the Turnerian struggle for the frontier – between savagery (the wolf) and civilisation (the cowboy). While Seton regarded the predatory nature of *Canis lupus* as natural, Lobo and his fellow canines were stigmatised for preying on domestic stock. The naturalist thus established rules of faunal conduct, positing Lobo as a 'bad' animal whose wanton behaviour signified a moral crime. The ensuing contest between the trapper and Lobo embodied a grand narrative of man against nature, civilised *Homo sapiens* pitted against the great wilderness hunter. The inevitable triumph of one predator at the expense of the other added pathos. The writer provided a clue as to the denouement of his canine melodrama at the start of *Wild Animals I Have Known*, noting that, 'the life of a wild animal *always has a tragic end*' – a phrase resonant with a sense of inevitability about the victory of two-legged over four-legged heroes. Lobo and his faunal guerillas seemed doomed to fall before sapient forces, as soon as humans learned woodcraft skills (in other words became adapted to the frontier). On finally capturing Lobo, Seton (assuming the role of the trapper) mused: 'Grand old outlaw, hero of a thousand lawless raids, in a few minutes you will be a great load of carrion. It cannot be otherwise.' Emblematic of an archaic order, the wolf was destined to pass into history.[12]

Although the fate of the outlaw wolf illuminated the enmity between *Homo sapiens* and *Canis lupus*, civilisation and the wild, the character of Lobo exuded distinctly human qualities. Seton's portrayal of Lobo as an individual thinker capable of hate and love demonstrated the author's belief in the similitude of humans and other species. He proclaimed, 'We and the beasts are kin. Man has nothing that the animals have not at least a vestige of, the animals have nothing that man does not in some degree share.' This desire for kinship embroiled the author in ethical

11. Ibid., pp. xii, 358, 206.
12. Ibid., pp. 21, 29, 12, 51.

questions. A deepening empathy with native carnivores, combined with regret at his actions towards Lobo, instilled in Seton a heartfelt concern for animal welfare. In the naturalist's conception of an ordered nature bound by inalienable laws, humans were obligated to act responsibly towards the environment. Moreover, Seton articulated a fervent belief in animal rights, asserting: 'Since, then, the animals are creatures with wants and feelings differing in degree only from our own, they surely have their rights'. Demonstrating a nascent biocentrism, he argued 'What right has a man to inflict such long and fearful agony on a fellow-creature, simply because that creature does not speak his language?'[13]

Seton received praise from contemporary critic Charles Koifoid for his sympathetic stories of 'animal friends'. The book fused skills in art, writing and amateur naturalism, and drew significant public acclaim. However, a group of literary notaries derided Seton as a 'nature faker' and criticised him for positing themes of lupine passion and reason. Amateurs and professionals involved in wildlife study locked horns over the relationship between scientific surveys (read as objective) and the vocation of the naturalist (read as a hobby, fed by emotion). President Theodore Roosevelt chastised Seton for his sentimental interpretation of canine social mechanics, while naturalist John Burroughs suggested an alternative title for Seton's bestseller, *Wild Animals I ALONE Have Known*. Defending the efficacy of his depictions, Seton railed: 'Those who do not know the animals well may think I have humanized them, but those who have lived so near them as to know somewhat of their ways and their minds will not think so.' This was a contest about the authority of the naturalist to impart credible zoological information. Crucially, it came at a time when scientific ideas about wolves themselves were in flux. Although Seton's portrayal of wild mustangs committing suicide and vixens poisoning their cubs to spare them from capture strained the limits of credulity, descriptions of lupine intelligence and pack bonding were verified by biologists in subsequent years. Biologists in Montana in the early 1980s even found evidence of wolves burying dead pups – a supposition that would certainly have been scoffed at by the professional wildlife community in the early 1900s. Judged in this light, Seton's struggle to accurately impart canine life represented a challenge of storytelling and of science – namely, how to extrapolate the non-human experience without recourse to anthropomorphism or sociological extrapolations.[14]

Published in 1903 and 1906 respectively, *The Call of the Wild* and *White Fang* communicated Jack London's attempts to explore canine consciousness. The companion novels, one dealing with a dog's attempts to adjust to life in the Alaskan wilds, the other considering the experiences of an Arctic wolf forced into a domestic sphere, offered a canine perspective on issues of evolution, species behaviour and environmental conditioning. Based on London's extended trip to the

13. Ibid., pp. 12, 13, 357.
14. Koiford 1901; Burroughs 1903; Seton 1987, p. 93; Boyd et al. 1993: 230—1.

Karen Jones

Klondike gold fields in 1897–8, the lively depictions of Northern life in *The Call of the Wild* and *White Fang* brought the author international renown. London's fascination with *Canis lupus* added to his enigma as a writer. In common with Seton, London indulged his obsession with the wolf by surrounding himself with lupine motifs. George Sterling knew the writer by the epithet 'Wolf' and London christened his retreat in Sonoma Valley, California 'Wolf House', suggesting, like Seton, an authorial affinity with the animal and a subconscious desire to take on a lupine metaphorical identity.[15]

London sought to narrate the stories of Buck and White Fang from a four-legged vantage point, extrapolating the responses of his central protagonists as they navigated between wilderness and civilisation. Far from animated machines, London configured his canine characters as inquisitive explorers. On witnessing snow for the first time, Buck 'sniffed it curiously, then licked some up on his tongue. It bit like fire, and the next instant was gone. This puzzled him.' Learning to survive in the harsh Alaskan snows, the hero of *The Call of the Wild* demonstrated a capacity not only to classify experiences as favourable and unfavourable but also to ponder his fate and make moral judgments regarding the behaviour of others. London strayed further into the territory of canine empathy in *White Fang* by describing the intimate thoughts of a newborn pup. White Fang's first cognitive sensations comprised elemental urges, desires to strain towards the light, to avoid pain, to satisfy hunger. Later, he learned the joys of hunting, describing his education in superlatives of 'unending happiness' and 'elation'. In his musings on the nature of lupine thought, London betrayed an interest in contemporary scientific debates concerning the ability of animals to reason. Through the mediums of Buck and White Fang, London characterised *Canis lupus* as a species 'not given to thinking – at least, to the kind of thinking customary of men', yet capable of reaching 'sharp and distinct' conclusions. Significantly, the astute senses and inveterate survival skills possessed by wild canines fostered a natural wariness of *Homo sapiens*. From the perspective of a wolf, the human world represented a hostile environment of strange smells, infernal noise and cranking electric vehicles that London inventively termed 'colossal screaming lynxes'. Through the yellow eyes of their leading protagonists, *The Call of the Wild* and *White Fang* thus offered readers a rare gaze at human culture as 'the other'.[16]

The American public applauded *The Call of the Wild* and *White Fang* for their innovative, 'insider' viewpoint on canine society. However, London's literary animalism betrayed significant flaws. Buck and White Fang represented idealised versions of canine protagonists, their mental musings an inevitable reflection of how London thought *he* would feel incarnated in lupine form. In describing how blood coursed through Buck's veins during his first hunt or the awe experienced by

15. London 1993.
16. Ibid., pp. 54, 244, 224, 399.

White Fang on witnessing the city of San Francisco, London articulated his own sentiments on wilderness and civilisation: offering an essentially sociological reading of animal behaviour, based around a Darwinian conception of man as a fighting animal. The writer configured his canine heroes as extraordinary individuals, great 'men' who displayed ideal masculine traits in keeping with the gender and scientific norms of the time. Master of his California estate, Buck was 'king over all creeping, crawling, flying things of Judge Miller's place, humans included'. The eponymous cub of *White Fang* appeared 'different from his brothers and sisters … bred true to the straight wolf stock.' Portrayed as canine supermen, what London scholar Alfred Kazin dubbed 'Nietzschean hounds', Buck and White Fang exhibited humanised qualities of loyalty, courage, strength and resourcefulness. When London noted how 'hunting and kindred outdoor delights had kept down the fat and hardened his [Buck's] muscles', he imparted the ecstasy and vigour of the chase as imagined by the late nineteenth-century sportsman rather than the lupine hunter.[17]

In London's cult of the wild, nature denoted a brutal proving ground for individual fortitude. *White Fang* commenced with a fervid pack preying on hapless travellers, with the icy landscape labelled as 'the Wild, the savage, frozen-hearted Northland Wild'. *The Call of the Wild* similarly identified the Alaskan tundra as a desolate, silent realm, given voice by the actions of strong-willed men and spirited wolves. This was the stage on which Herbert Spencer's scientific theory and Frederick Jackson Turner's frontier thesis converged to create an ultimate venue of competition, masculinity and action. Images of hostile nature exaggerated the heroism of London's characters in a manner akin to triumphal narratives about westward expansionism. In the author's striking prose, Buck and White Fang resembled rugged canine pioneers pitting their wits against unyielding environmental forces. For London, the wild represented a competitive domain of primal fear, mortal conflict and physicality. It also served as a spectacular setting for romantic adventurism. As London noted on Buck's arrival in Alaska, 'He had been suddenly jerked from the heart of civilization and flung into the heart of all things primordial. No lazy, sun-kissed life was this … All was confusion and action, and every moment life and limb were in peril.' For London, as with Seton, the western frontier was the place for dramatic change, both biological and historical.[18]

The experiences of Buck and White Fang as they struggled to assimilate the worlds of wildness and domesticity represented a moral parable on the role of instinct versus conditioning in determining individual character. The primordial impulses lurking in Buck and White Fang reflected on humanity's bestial nature. For London, the 'Call of the Wild' conjured a world of primitive desire, instinct and natural virtue. Wolfishness emerged as a potent signifier for the brutal simplicity of wilderness life. When White Fang engaged in his inaugural hunt, he realised the

17. London 1993, pp. 44, 221; Kazin 1942; London, 1993, p. 45.
18. London 1993, pp. 169, 55.

truth of his existence, 'that for which he was made – killing meat and battling to kill it'. London glorified the incipient carnality of the law of the wild, regurgitating survivalist maxims such as 'EAT OR BE EATEN'. His stories were predicated on the wolf as a carrier of carnivorous carnality and thus subscribed to notions of therophobia – the fear of wild beasts – common to traditional Euro-American wolf tales, albeit beneath a modish coating of 'survival of the fittest' dogma. In losing his civilised veneer, Buck became fully alive, discarding 'moral' nature as 'a vain thing and a handicap in the ruthless struggle for existence' in favour of 'sounding the deeps of his nature'. The savagery of the Alaskan wilds augmented Buck's physical prowess and steeped him in primordial wisdom. Significantly, London's rhapsody to atavism reflected the writings of Spencer and Darwin on science and romantic naturalism. The writer perceived Buck's metamorphosis into a wilderness creature fully present in the joy of living as genetically, naturally and historically self-fulfilling: 'He linked the past with the present, and the eternity behind him throbbed through him in a mighty rhythm to which he swayed as the tides and seasons swayed.'[19]

Despite his attention to wilderness iconography and obsession with canine heroics, Jack London articulated a belief in the benefits of moral, civilised life. In the writer's Darwinian vernacular, civilisation represented the pinnacle of evolutionary dynamics, humans asserting rightful control over the rest of nature by virtue of their unbridled power. Even Buck and White Fang endorsed the higher position of sapient protagonists in the natural hierarchy by deeming humans as 'gods', suggesting that even when afforded agency and voice, non-human narratives and experience remained dominated by *Homo sapiens*. Crucially, London judged that society should act as a benevolent steward towards its human and faunal charges – a principle that illuminated the author's socialistic leanings *and* his love of nature: political economy and ecology conjoined. Moreover, in describing White Fang's transition from embittered predator to a 'Blessed Wolf', eking out a lazy existence in sun-kissed California, London explored the impact of human compulsions on canine character. While the brutalising tutelage of dog-owner Beauty Smith bred cruelty and ferocity in White Fang, the compassionate attentions of subsequent master Weedon Scott brought a contentment that he had craved since the family den. As an upstanding and kind-hearted white American, Scott represented a model citizen in London's altruistic world. Scott identified his crusade to redeem 'mankind from the wrong it had done White Fang' as 'a matter of principle and conscience'. Thereby articulating a popular humanitarian precept, London insisted that human protagonists brutalised themselves and tainted the characters of their victims through acts of barbarity, a common motif in humanist/animal rights literature of the period and manifest in writings from Henry Bergh's 'Declaration of the Rights of Animals (1866) to Anna Sewell's *Black Beauty* (1877). *The Call of the Wild* and *White Fang* thus imparted powerful lessons in congeniality, urging

---

19. Ibid., pp. 234, 63, 77, 110–11.

a need for humans to behave with civility towards the animals with which they shared a common heritage.[20]

In an essay entitled 'The Other Animals', London addressed the reception to his tales amongst the natural history fraternity, thereby highlighting issues of truth and authority on animal matters. As he remonstrated 'Time and again, and many times, in my narratives, I wrote, speaking of my dog-heroes: "He did not think these things; he merely did them" etc. And I did this repeatedly, to the clogging of my narrative and in violation of my artistic canons; and I did it in order to hammer into the average human understanding that the dog-heroes of mine were not directed by abstract reasoning, but by instinct, sensation, and emotion, and by simple reasoning.' The author had subdued his storytelling impulses in favour of imparting the rubric of evolutionary thought to his readers. This was the science of natural selection, condensed and spat out for populist consumption (for instance, the rapid evolutionary dynamics that Buck encountered were in stark contrast to Herbert Spencer's assertions that no one individual would be aware of the subtleties of such a process). Meanwhile, London countered critics Theodore Roosevelt and John Burroughs by stressing his empirical (and thus scientific) approach to wolf behaviour, having assessed his dogs Rollo and Glen as canine subjects for evidence of reasoned thinking. His essay ended acerbically: 'You must not deny your relatives, the other animals. Their history is your history. What you repudiate in them you repudiate in yourself – a pretty spectacle, truly, of an exalted animal striving to disown the stuff of life out of which it is made ... That may be good egotism, but it is not good science.' Such debates pointed to the kudos attached to scientific method as a method of 'knowing' the animal and, more critically, elucidated the role of the wolf as a totemic carrier for discussions about society and its relationship to the natural world.[21]

Both Seton and London insisted their writings were about wolves and not men and consciously advertised their efforts in terms of animal advocacy. In this arena, they achieved much. However, Lobo, Buck and White Fang said as much about humans as they did about wolves. As Joan London remarked, her father was not aware until much later of 'the human allegory in the dog's life-and-death struggle to adapt himself to a hostile environment'. In the case of 'Lobo: King of Currampaw', *The Call of the Wild* and *White Fang*, Seton and London essentialised three key debates under review in American intellectual and popular culture. The reworking of the wolf from demonic savagery to iconic savagery highlighted contemporary fascinations with rugged landscapes and the great outdoors, as demonstrated in the formation of Yellowstone National Park (1872) and the Boone and Crockett Club (1887); spoke of the veneration of the American West as a crucible of action, freedom and abandon, as expounded in the historical analysis of Frederick

20. Ibid., p. 350.
21. 'The Other Animals', in London 1910, pp. 238–9.

Karen Jones

Jackson Turner, the writing of Theodore Roosevelt and Owen Wister and the lurid sensationalism of dime novel pulp fiction; and howled out scientific philosophies of natural selection, instinct and the survival of the fittest. As contemporary nature writer John Burroughs perceptively noted, 'True it is that all the animals whose lives are portrayed … are simply human beings disguised as animals'.[22]

'THE IDEALIZED STORY OF A WOLF FAMILY': MOWAT, CARAS AND THE NURTURING OF ECOLOGICAL CONSCIENCE

In portraying wolves as intelligent and gracious animals, Seton and London challenged traditional Euro-American perceptions of wild carnivores as wanton killers. Their books served an important conservationist purpose in highlighting the positive character traits of a much-maligned species. Yet, as Ralph Lutts pointed out, 'the nature lover and nature fakers had great difficulty linking their new vision of nature and wildlife with the real animals in a real, evolving ecological setting'. By configuring wolves as fantastic characters in tales of tragedy and adventure, both Seton and London failed to comment on preservation issues affecting wild predators in the material landscape. Their canine supermen reflected contemporary interests in the survival of the fittest, natural selection and competition – seen in scientific dogma, outdoors crazes, theories on national progress and, of course, race and eugenics. Focus remained on the individual masculine hero. From the 1920s and 1930s, the development of ecological science afforded new opportunities for writing the wolf in a functional, biotic context. Interestingly, pioneer ecologist Charles Elton saw a direct line of ascent from his emergent discipline and prior writings from the naturalist community: 'Ecology is a new name for a very old subject. It simply means scientific natural history'. In terms of *Canis lupus*, fresh discourses from wildlife biologists Paul Errington, Aldo Leopold and Adolph Murie situated the species as an important ecological agent in North American wild landscapes and a vital component to biotic health. The pack also earned redefinition as a social organisation rather than a random, slavering mass, consciously referencing not only developments in animal ecology but also sociological discussions in the 1950s about the dynamics of the nuclear family, systems theory, gender norms and rituals of stability and socialisation. Meanwhile, the environmental revolution of the 1960s contributed a sense of humans as eminently destructive forces and argued for a more respectful, ethical relationship with the natural world. These themes of ecological integrity, group dynamics and biocentric conscience provided the framework for a new genre of North American wolf literature in the 1960s. Employing scientific theory and artistic verve, a cadre of literary environmentalists imparted salient

---

22. London 1939, p. 252; John Burroughs on Charles D. Roberts' *Kindred of the Wild*, in Burroughs 1903, p. 299.

lessons on the state of modern, industrial civilisation and its predatory attitude towards nature through their writings on *Canis lupus*.[23]

A cardinal text of lupine environmental advocacy, *Never Cry Wolf* (1963) by Canadian nature writer Farley Mowat, has been hailed as the most 'influential book ever written about wolves'. Loosely based on the author's personal experiences working for the Dominion Wildlife Service in the Northwest Territories during the 1940s, *Never Cry Wolf* told the story of a greenhorn biologist dispatched to the Canadian wilds to document the interactions between wolves and caribou. In writing *Never Cry Wolf*, Mowat had originally intended to expose bureaucratic ineptitude in the Canadian government, yet soon became captivated by his lupine narrative. In a testament to the ability of wild canines to inspire literary passions, Mowat noted, 'Eventually the wolf took the book right out of my hands so that it became a plea for understanding, and preservation, of an extraordinarily highly evolved and attractive animal which was, and is, being harried into extinction by the murderous enmity and proclivities of man'. Mowat's environmental treatise proved immensely popular, winning many converts to the lupine cause.[24]

The allure of Mowat's canine fable lay in its consistency with a trope of American nature literature, the retreat into wilderness as a spiritual journey. In Mowat's wilderness sojourn, the wolf signified an erudite guide to nature, a totem animal that drew the biologist away from rationalist dictates and Euro-American prejudice and towards a more empathic, reverential, and indigenous perception of the land. In common with Seton and London, Mowat crafted the North American wilderness as character-building terrain. By learning the laws of the wild, the young biologist acquired woodcraft skills, questioned his metropolitan values and embraced a more nature-centred existence. Spiritual epiphany came through engagement with a local wolf pack, whose well-ordered social routines and affable personalities railed against the biologist's preconceptions of wolves as bloodthirsty killers. Alone in the wild, contemplating his intra-species communications over a glass of 'Wolf Juice' (a heady blend of preserving alcohol and beer), the scientist confessed, 'Inescapably, the realization was being borne in upon my preconditioned mind that the centuries-old and universally accepted human concept of wolf character was a palpable lie'. He duly resolved to 'go open-minded into the lupine world and learn to see and know the wolves, not for what they were supposed to be, but for what they actually were' – empiricism once more invoked as the best way to 'know' the non-human.[25]

---

23. Lutts 1990, p. 174; Elton 1927, p. 1. Canonical texts of wolf biology include Murie 1944; Errington 1967; Allen 1979; Leopold 1970; Mech 1970; Cowan 1947. On systems theory and the sociology of the family, see Parsons et al. 1955. Significantly, the pioneers of systems theory drew on discussions in the 1930s about processes of community interaction in biotic as well as human communities: see Von Bertalanffy, 1968.
24. Hampton 1997, p. 167; Mowat, 1979, p. v.
25. Mowat 1979, pp. 51, 52.

Karen Jones

Immersing himself in lupine social conventions, Mowat (as the biologist) engaged in scent marking, howling, and hunting, living life as a pseudo wolf in the Canadian North. Despite his paeans to 'knowing the wolf', the writer nonetheless relied on methods of humanisation to bring his lupine characters to life. Eager to dispel hackneyed images of *Canis lupus* as a savage and ferocious beast, Mowat conjured the wolf as an irrepressible, friendly predator. This narrative of fun, familiarity and frolic represented a frequent device in visual and textual communications about animals – witness Disney's natural history and animated productions of the 1950s, the Adams' Born Free feline soap opera saga of the 1960s and Jean Craighead George's work of juvenile fiction, *Julie of the Wolves* (1972). Such works humanised the beast for the purposes of entertainment, empathy and environmental rehabilitation, as well as creating a narrative structure in which to situate animal behaviour. Anthropomorphism offered a route towards cross-species identification and advocacy, even though the ability to 'cross' into the world of the wolf meant transforming that social terrain into a human one. Thus *Never Cry Wolf* presented the pack as a humanised band of endearing, anthropomorphic figures – a nuclear family that fitted the social mores of the 1950s more than the nature of lupine society. Mowat freely admitted the sentimentality of his portrayal but attributed it to the irrefutable appeal of his canine actors: 'As I grew completely attuned to their daily round of family life I found it increasingly difficult to maintain an impersonal attitude towards the wolves. No matter how hard I tried to regard them with scientific objectivity, I could not resist the impact of their individual personalities.' George, the alpha male, signified an 'eminently regal beast' while Angeline, the alpha female, was 'equally memorable … beautiful, ebullient, passionate'.[26]

The focus on family life in *Never Cry Wolf* conveyed a powerful ecological narrative that prioritised interaction and community over competition and struggle. Whereas London had concentrated on individual protagonists honing survival skills in the face of natural adversity, Farley Mowat looked to the pack for lessons in biotic community and social structure. Buck's sled team operated according to a coercive hierarchy where the strong dominated the weak, whereas the Canadian pack living in 'Wolf House Bay' worked as a cohesive unit. The wolves in *Call of the Wild* fought to the death, while the animals in *Never Cry Wolf* caroused, learned and hunted together. According to Mowat's vernacular, predation was not a ferocious contest but a mutual engagement that ensured natural balance. *Never Cry Wolf* thereby translated the mantras of ecological science – trophic levels, bioenergetics, mutualism and biocoenosis – into a popular framework, bringing Elton's 'scientific natural history' back into a cultural domain. Likewise, the book broadcast powerful sociological messages about the role of the family in socialisation, patterns of community harmony, and typical gender roles. The Canadian North thus represented a prelapsarian landscape of symmetry rather than strife.

---

26. George 1972; Singer 1983; Stone 1974; Mowat 1979, p. 61.

Writing the Wolf

A modern industrial society driven by a domineering attitude towards the environment represented the villain of *Never Cry Wolf*. Mowat configured the Northern wilderness, a harmonious world that 'belonged to the deer, the wolves, and the smaller beasts', as a landscape under threat from trigger-happy sportsmen and deluded government bureaucrats. In this eco-parable, wilderness and civilisation existed as literal oppositions, the wolf and the human destined to clash in the Arctic just as in the Currumpaw. However, Mowat refused to view the real-world demise of *Canis lupus* as acceptable or inevitable. Cognisant of the power of literary pathos to rouse sympathy for species preservation, Mowat deliberately crafted *Never Cry Wolf* to impart a tangible environmental message: ensuring that his work offered a blend of traditional romantic naturalism and modern environmental protest. As he noted in the preface, 'it may be that there is still time to prevent mankind from committing yet another in the long list of his crimes against nature'. The author elucidated his literary–environmental supplication in a curt epilogue, explaining how government control agents placed cyanide guns outside the den at 'Wolf House Bay' in May 1959. In its succinct and sanitised prose, the epilogue offered a distinct change of style from the jocular sentimentalism of previous chapters. Designed to shock readers into environmental activism, the last line of *Never Cry Wolf* read: 'it is not known what results were obtained'.[27]

Never Cry Wolf became an instant bestseller and went on to sell more than a million copies. The Toronto *Globe & Mail* noted that wolves 'owed Mowat a debt of gratitude for rescuing their reputation'. Readers warmed to its entertaining pace, populist romanticism, intuitive engagement with nature and accessible, ecologically-informed narrative. Mowat's intimacy with the pack fostered empathy and concern, while his stylistic allusions to scientific credibility – a first-hand vantage on the 'real' wolf via field study of a pack at Nueltin Lake in 1948–9 – garnered him authority to speak for the wolf in the estimation of mainstream society. Growing public criticism of modernity, the power of the state and social conformity in the 1960s fomented interest in Mowat's discourse of the lone whistleblower standing up against a misguided bureaucratic apparatus. In fact, the book prompted a keen letter-writing campaign to the Canadian Wildlife Service in defence of the wolf that continued through the 1960s and 1970s. Many respondents credited the book with changing their opinions on *Canis lupus* and highlighted its educational value. Readers consistently praised Mowat for speaking truth to power and situated the fate of the wolf in a broader environmental malaise threatening the entire planet. Others articulated an animal rights narrative that emphasised the barbaric nature of humanity and put forward a radical liberationist agenda along the lines of contemporaneous works by Christopher Stone and Peter Singer. As one letter

---

27. Mowat 1979, pp. 126, vii, 164.

asserted, 'wolves are not the vicious killers that some authors pictured them as. We are! Yes us … Man. Preacher of peace. User of violence.'[28]

A signal of its popular currency, *Never Cry Wolf* made it to the big screen courtesy of Disney Pictures in 1983. Directed by Carroll Ballard, the feature contained all the hallmarks of the Disney brand: a sweeping moralistic meta-narrative, comedic asides and anthropomorphised animals playing family. *Never Cry Wolf* stayed relatively true to its original source in focusing on the encroachment of civilisation–capitalism on the mystical–intuitive North, the fallacy of the 'wolf threat' to the caribou and the adventures of the biologist hero. Notably, it made a few adjustments. The hunt was relatively bloodless, with the pack gently picking off a weak and sickened animal (German Shepherds with hairspray 'stood in' as wolves) and the movie rejected the negativity of the novel's epilogue and its insinuations of canine pogrom. *Never Cry Wolf* the movie readily subscribed to the contemporary formula of Disney's 'True Life Adventure' nature pseudo-documentary series (the best comparison being *White Wilderness*, 1958) in its emphasis on the observation of the scientist, the detailed beauty of the landscape, dramatic storytelling, and conservation message and stress on faunal personalities. Intimate photography and characterisations lent the movie a realist cachet that duped the audience into feeling they were 'seeing the real wolf' rather than anthropomorphised humanoids. As the *New York Times* extrapolated 'the three animals Tyler comes to call George, Angeline and Uncle Albert emerge as real characters who watch Tyler when he doesn't realize it, but only allow him to watch them when they choose. Their habits structure Tyler's days, and in the end they propel the film's dramatic climax'. The film offered a visual broadcast of nature lore from the days of Seton, of a moral fable about animal celebrities writ large for an urban audience looking for celluloid escapism. This fusion of education and entertainment, saccharine coating and social instruction, exemplified 'Disneyfication' at work: talking animals dispensing moral lessons to America's youth and serving as 'mirror' for social commentary. Meanwhile, prime 'Mickey Mouse' moments included montages of the biologist dining on mice stew to the cutesy squeals of watching rodents. *Variety* magazine paid heed to the movie's placement in the American naturalist tradition and to its fresh injection of Disney whimsy: 'No biologist is that dumb, to begin with, on an expedition in the wilds of the North-west. And, if he was, he should have taken Jack London's *Call of the Wild* along with him to read in his spare time.'[29]

In contrast, the scientific community reacted to *Never Cry Wolf* with unbridled vitriol, replaying the terse debates that had raged over the so-called 'nature fakers' of the late 1800s. Biologist A.W. Banfield noted the popular appeal of the book in asserting that 'not since Little Red Riding Hood has a story been written

28. *Toronto Globe & Mail*, 9 Nov. 1963; See correspondence in the archives of the Canadian Wildlife Service, RG109, vol.384, WLU200 & RG109, vol.30, WLT200, National Archives Canada, Ottawa.

29. 'Filming "Never Cry Wolf"', 16 Oct. 1983, *New York Times Magazine*; *Variety*, 1 Sept. 1983.

that will influence the attitude of so many toward these animals' but added a sharp disclaimer: 'both stories have about the same factual content.' Mowat earned criticism for passing himself off as an expert when he had logged only ninety hours in the field. In the words of biologist C.H.D. Clarke, he was 'a raconteur posing as a scientist.' Douglas Pimlott called *Never Cry Wolf* 'a satire' and Wildlife Service employees took to calling Mowat 'Hardly Knowit'. But why such enmity? Surely Mowat was aiding the cause of wolf conservation? Herein lay the problem. The scientific community viewed the replacement of the 'big bad wolf' of traditional tales with Mowat's much-maligned 'good wolf' as a problematic transformation that did the species a disservice. Mowat was a novelist, guided by sentiment and anthropocentrism more than rational objectivity, they argued. The natural resource community balked at letters of complaint that described 'married' wolves, 'old maids' and 'bachelors' under threat, seeing little of merit in creating an anthropomorphic world of persecuted personalities in wolf clothing. More critically, in his diatribe against the Wildlife Service, Mowat questioned the hallowed role of the scientist as ultimate authority on animal behaviour. Put simply, the controversy over *Never Cry Wolf* highlighted a contest for authenticity in wildlife matters between the scientist and the storyteller: who did speak for the wolf?[30]

Roger Caras published *The Custer Wolf* three years after Mowat's ecological expose. Subtitled *Biography of an American Renegade*, the book told the life story of a historic lupine outlaw renowned for preying on stock in South Dakota during the 1910s. In common with Buck, White Fang and Lobo, the Custer Wolf represented a charismatic trickster with a penchant for extraordinary behaviour. Caras aggrandised the eponymous lupine as a four-legged Western hero. As a pup, the Custer Wolf appeared 'somewhat different' from his siblings, reflecting his reputation later in life as an American renegade. Caras revelled in the myth surrounding the white wolf, exclaiming: 'Before his story reached its end his name was known to people on the shores of both oceans and on the floor of Congress … So well known did he become, in fact, that his footprint was immediately recognizable to ranchers and hunters.' With its leading character mythologised as a wily bandit, a lone, mysterious figure roaming the prairie, *The Custer Wolf* drew on classic frontier iconography, trading in images of the troubled, rugged individualist usually reserved for two-legged Western heroes.[31]

In writing a biography of the Custer Wolf, Caras endeavoured to capture the spirit of the animal. The book commenced with a genealogy, recalling the meeting of the Custer Wolf's parents, their courtship, pairing and raising of young. Passages

30. A.W. Banfield, 'Never Cry Wolf', Dec. 1963 draft review; C.H.D. Clarke, 'Review Never Cry Wolf: 6 December 1963'; Douglas Pimlott, 'What will a man give in exchange for his soul?' unpublished review. All held in RG109, vol.30, file 7 & RG109, vol.384, WLU200, National Archives Canada, Ottawa; 'Hardly Knowit' quip related in Steinhart 1995, p. 60.

31. Caras 1966, pp. 14, 120.

relating the pup's early sensations, the 'joy of movement', the aching desire for food and the 'hot light' at the den entrance, recalled London's attempts at empathy half a century earlier. The world operated according to simple laws of survival, with its characters plagued by neither emotional nor psychological dilemmas. As Caras asseverated, 'Wolves are not human beings who must run around reassuring each other, thumping each other on the back; these great wild predators do exactly what they have to do, or they die'.[32]

While Caras exalted the Custer Wolf as a traditional Western hero, his narrative offered a critique of westward expansionism. The author lamented the eradication of resident carnivores and situated the range economy as a landscape not of progress but of loss. Like *Never Cry Wolf*, *The Custer Wolf* subscribed to an environmental mythology that idealised *Canis lupus* as a symbol of pristine, ecologically vibrant North America and deplored modern society for its arrogant, rapacious attitude towards nature: in this respect his narrative was very much a product of the 1960s and its questioning of the values of the modern industrial state. Whereas cattle were described as 'huge, dumb beasts ... their brains bred out of them to make room for filets and ground round', Caras crafted wolves as vital, quick-witted creatures, intricately connected to the landscape and psycho-spiritually alive. The delicate senses of the Custer Wolf even allowed him to *feel* the night. Farley Mowat based his environmental treatise on biological observations. Roger Caras' cult of the wild instead relied on a mystical appreciation of the primordial wolf and the 'genius of nature's secret knowledge'. Imparting a literary romanticism reminiscent of nineteenth-century naturalist John Muir, Caras framed nature as a harmonious place where 'nothing cruel, nothing savage, harmful or tragic' occurred.[33]

Homo sapiens represented the villain of *The Custer Wolf* just as in *Never Cry Wolf*. Whereas Mowat drew on personal experience to narrate his critique of modern technocratic society, Caras looked to historical precedent and the vitriolic war waged on wolves by Euro-American pioneers. Adopting a misanthropic tone, Caras evaluated the human race as 'eternally guilty of crimes beyond counting – man the killer, the slayer, the luster-for-blood has always sought to expurgate himself of his sin and guilt by condemning the predatory animals'. In the writer's vernacular, humans were to blame for creating the aberrant behaviour of the Custer Wolf, instilling in the animal a burning desire to 'even a very lopsided score with the men and cattle who had taken over his range and declared him an outlaw in his own ancestral hunting grounds'. Apprehending the Custer Wolf from a sympathetic, eco-centric perspective, Roger Caras performed an important task of historical, environmental, and literary revisionism.[34]

---

32. Ibid., pp. 15, 48.
33. Ibid., pp. 101, 30.
34. Ibid., pp. 59, 137.

Caras, like Mowat, won the admiration of his audience via a fecund blend of science, history and sentiment. Foremost in the mix was the role of the storyteller, the environmental advocate, stoking empathy and fury among his readers for the fate of the wolf. As Caras noted in the epilogue, this work was a 'fictionalised biography, a fact that is acknowledged without apology'. On the charge of sentimentality, he appeared candid, viewing a connection with the animal as an essential part of 'knowing': 'Somehow, across the years since the blood dried and the hurt ceased to matter, I feel as if I have some slight understanding of this strange, tormented animal. One has to be sentimental about a thing like that.' That said, Caras' tale also gained converts courtesy of its historical and scientific credentials. The Custer wolf did exist, lending authenticity to the account. Moreover, as the book asserted, Caras based his depictions on close readings of works by wildlife biologists including Adolph Murie and Douglas Pimlott. The storyteller segued into pseudo-scientist on the jacket cover for all readers for apprehend: 'From close observation of a pack of full-blooded timber wolves and films of the birth and rearing of a litter of cubs, and after years of travel and study, the author has been able to knowledgably and compassionately reconstruct the idealized life of the Custer wolf'. This blend of empiricism and literary panache won plaudits, not least from the *Times Literary Supplement*, which deemed *The Custer Wolf* a 'powerful, moving and beautifully written tale, fit to stand comparison with White Fang or even Tarka, to the factual historical report. The telling is utterly devoid of sentimentality, forthright yet never crude, and the feelings and instincts of the animals are explicit in their actions.' Once more, the storyteller served as critical intermediary between the worlds of science and popular culture, translating the mediums of ecology and history into a narrative framework with considerable popular impact.[35]

THE RETURN OF THE NATIVE: TALES OF WOLF RECOVERY AND RESTOR(Y)ATION

In the preface to his 1993 book, *Out Among the Wolves*, naturalist John Murray noted his 'good fortune to have lived in what posterity may well call "The Decade of the Wolf"'. A series of successful restoration programmes in the West, notably the high profile reintroduction of wolves to Yellowstone National Park in 1995, suggested that Americans had acquired a more tolerant attitude towards wild carnivores. *Canis lupus* gained cachet as a victim of frontier progress and a hallowed icon of the North American wild. Lupine images adorned T-shirts and mugs, compact discs offered haunting vocalisations of wild canines as wilderness symphony. The saliency of conservation issues resulted in an extraordinary proliferation of wolf literature. Even EarthFirst!-er Dave Foreman got in on the action by writing a wolf novel, *The Lobo Outback Funeral Home* (2000), an irreverent eco-thriller/romance

---

35. Ibid., pp. 172, 175, cover.

Karen Jones

about a ex-Sierra clubber and a wildlife biologist in the South-west who teamed up to protect wild lands from corporate industrialism and protect the itinerant Mexican wolves who had stolen into the area to reclaim ancestral territory. The story of how wolves lost, and regained, parts of the United States offered a powerful narrative of tragedy and rebirth and provided an ideal forum for authors to craft environmentalist narratives preaching human responsibilities towards nature. And yet, in common with prior years, the wolf also emerged as a carrier to discuss sociological issues pertaining to the human zoo. In the late nineteenth century, it was natural selection and the survival of the fittest; in the 1960s, popular readings of ecology, community organisation and family dynamics; and, in the 1980s and 1990s, holocaust (both human and animal), multiculturalism, immigration and the border.[36]

Set in a post-apocalyptic United States ravaged by nuclear war, Whitley Strieber's novel *Wolf of Shadows* (1985) related the trials of a human survivor and her daughter as they sought to escape the atomic holocaust. Central in the story stood the eponymous 'Wolf of Shadows', who leads his pack, as well as the bedraggled humans, from their homes in contaminated Minnesota to seek safe stomping grounds in the South. In talking about her work, Strieber described the responsibility of the storyteller as that of public consciousness raiser, in this case using the written word as a tool of environmental advocacy in order to generate interest in 'the plight of helpless life which, after the terrible war, also includes humanity'. No longer a symbol of a remnant western frontier or an idyllic, pristine North, *Canis lupus* now served as a totemic functionary, highlighting the deadly chasm separating modern industrial society from nature. The contemporary context of the second Cold War and the potential for global ecocide courtesy of multiple nuclear explosions, radiation poisoning and nuclear winter set the frame for the narrative, again forwarding the character of wolf as a rhetorical device for communicating social, environmental and political issues. In Strieber's tale, atomic Armageddon levelled the gap between wolves and humans as fellow travellers faced extinction and, in somewhat macabre tone, illuminated a pressing need to re-connect with other species. As the author pointed out, 'the bond that develops between the wolves and humans beings in the story is meant to suggest that we can find new ways of thinking about, and relating to, animals'.[37]

We meet Wolf of Shadows at birth, 'a giant of his kind' he conformed to the super-canine stereotype as established in the stories of London and Seton. From the start, Strieber centred attention on wolves and their world, making a conscious effort to present the story from a lupine vantage in a process of imaginative shapeshifting in keeping with the broader environmental-literary tradition. We witness humanity as the 'other', two-leggeds carrying 'death-sticks', inhabiting 'dens' and

36. Murray 1993, p. 11; Foreman 2000.
37. Strieber 1985, pp. 125, 126.

visiting places that 'blazed with light and stank of burned meat, and men went into them'. Wolf of Shadows appeared bemused by human footwear, puzzling over how 'paws … understand the ground if they couldn't touch it'. Lupine society, in contrast, apprehended the world directly and gleefully, glorying in the rush of the hunt, the taste of blood and the comfort of the pack. Theirs was a storied landscape defined by finely tuned cognition: 'Wolves bear as remembered smells the history of the lives, the kills, the hot summer nights, the odour of their winter coats, the drowsy, exciting mustiness of sex.' [38]

As 'seen' from the perspective of the wolf, the A-bomb appeared alien, hostile and malevolent, a perturbing intrusion into the realms of nature. The *realpolitik* deception of nuclear deterrence and 'winnable war' was exposed by the earth knowledge of the wolf: 'His sensitive footpads knew the language of the ground, and it was beginning to speak in an unaccustomed way'. Accordingly, when Wolf of Shadows experienced the sounds, sights and vibrations of nuclear war, his hackles were raised and he began to whine. Like a surrogate miner's canary, *Canis lupus* howled out to humanity at its destructive course. [39]

Seized by an abiding need to rescue his brethren from the impending nuclear threat, Wolf of Shadows mobilised the pack for the exodus south (a process which involved usurping the dominant alpha male in a show of canine strength reminiscent of the antics of Buck). Moving through the forest, Wolf of Shadows also encountered the humans with whom he travelled for the rest of the novel. The human mother who was 'regurgitated' from the 'bird-thing' that crashed in the lake turned out to be an animal biologist who had spent the prior summer observing the pack. She had already 'shared his gaze'. The choice of female lead reflected an authorial desire for authenticity: this human had to have a 'past' with the wolves that marked her out as a one of the good 'two-leggeds' as well as arming her with sufficient knowledge to navigate the contours of pack society. Tellingly, Strieber cast a wildlife biologist as the most suitable ambassador for inter-species communication, an expert witness and paragon of understanding. [40]

Significantly, the remainder of the novel construed the engagement between the bedraggled human and canine survivors in emotive, intuitive terms. Wolf of Shadows experienced empathy as he watched the woman struggle with her dying 'cub' and, as bonds developed, wolves and humans shared food (from scavenged kills and food cans), huddled together for warmth, and relished one another's touch. Species boundaries were seemingly transcended. The humans steered clear of their kin and felt 'safer with wolves' – a judgement not only on humanity's post-apocalyptic regression to mob rule but also a misanthropic nod to the environmental crimes of *Homo sapiens*. *Wolf of Shadows* tendered a powerful environmental fable

---

38. Ibid. pp. 9, 14, 15, 104, 50.
39. Ibid., p. 17.
40. Ibid., p. 27.

of reckoning and redemption, conjoining the kinship narratives common to Seton and London's work with Mowat's eco-parable approach to create a sense of humans and wolves as co-dependents in a world facing biotic breakdown. The rag-tag band of survivors stumbled through a broken, silent and decayed landscape that harkened back to the opening chapter of Rachel Carson's *Silent Spring*: 'The land, though, was quiet. Where beaver had once cut the underbrush there were no living things … South of the great ruin some birds still lived. In all their many languages: only two things were being spoken: "We are cold; we are lost."'[41]

The Crossing (1994) by Cormac McCarthy typified wolf literature in the 1990s in dealing with themes of dispossession, stewardship and species restoration. In this manner it combined debates about animal recovery and belonging with pertinent social issues surrounding immigration, mobility and the US–Mexican border. The second book in a South-western trilogy, *The Crossing* considered three journeys undertaken by sixteen-year-old Billy Parham from his home in Hidalgo County, New Mexico across the international boundary in the 1930s. During the first of his 'crossings', Billy facilitated the repatriation of a she-wolf to her homeland in the Mexican mountains. In attempting the arduous journey of relocation, Billy demonstrated a keen environmental consciousness, choosing not to vanquish the she-wolf (and obey the instructions of his father) but to restore her to ancestral terrain. In narrating Billy's trails across the sagebrush, McCarthy subscribed to a New Western paradigm, applying tropes of wilderness lost, multicultural identity and complex characterisation to his desert setting. In McCarthy's revisionist narrative, *Canis lupus* signified an animal with a past rather than a primordial, abstracted creation. The she-wolf was a gaunt, harried nomad who had wandered from the Sonoran Mountains in search of companionship following the capture of her mate. Ostracised from her own domain, 'She would not return to a kill. She would not cross a road or a rail line in daylight. She would not cross under a wire fence twice in the same place.' In the law of the range, the native had become alien. The wolf was a pariah, a marginalised creation that spoke of mythologies, contested boundaries, competing regional identities and the clashes between past and present in the American South-west. Meanwhile, for Billy Parham, an outsider in ranch society, the wolf represented an evocative symbol of freedom, and vibrancy. Secretly watching wolves hunting on the plains, the young cowboy iconised *Canis lupus* as both an ecological functionary and a mystical beast. From his cultural perspective, wolves possessed an appealing otherworldliness, their energy sourced directly from the wild. Billy appeared mesmerised by the graceful animals that 'twisted and turned and leapt in a silence such that they seemed of another world entire'.[42]

Unlike *Wild Animals I Have Known*, *The Call of the Wild* or *The Custer Wolf*, *The Crossing* dealt with the motivations and destiny of a human protagonist, Billy

---

41. Ibid., p. 84.
42. McCarthy, 1995, pp. 24, 4.

Parham. However, McCarthy devoted copious attention to creating the she-wolf as a powerful literary character, a non-human protagonist with voice. In writing the wolf, McCarthy, in common with his peers, focused on the specifics of animal thoughts and actions. The she-wolf displayed typical canine acumen and resilience. McCarthy also strove to impart a four-legged perspective, to imagine how visions of two-legged invaders might plague slumbering lupines, conjuring 'dreams of that malignant lesser god come pale and naked and alien to slaughter all his clan and kin and rout them from their house'. From a canine vantage, McCarthy identified human society as a malevolent and barbaric 'other', injecting a sense of misanthropy into the work that typified revisionist commentaries on wolf eradication. The wolf had been hunted out, game slaughtered and forests cut to be replaced by an anodyne landscape populated with 'awkward cattle whose stupidity and blind confusion is an affront to the wolves'. This narrative framework situated *The Crossing* as a representative text of late twentieth-century environmental advocacy, the wolf sanctified as a fairytale creature, maligned, numinous and misunderstood, the world it once inhabited somehow corroded and tamed in its absence. As Robert Rebein extrapolated, 'few people would call Cormac McCarthy an activist for the environment, but with the first section of *The Crossing*, McCarthy has written a fictional account of what many environmentalists believe about wolves – that they are mystical, that they are necessary, that they should be reintroduced in their native ranges'. [43]

According to the *New York Times*, the strength of McCarthy's work lay in its 'miracle in prose' and its mesmerising encounters between the young travellers and a procession of elder sages. *The Crossing* also reflected on interactions between the human and the non-human on the dusty trails of the American South-west. In attempting to trap, and later understand, the female wolf, McCarthy's sapient protagonists wrestled with philosophical questions over the possibility of knowing other species. Via an opulent collection of folk renditions, a stock of Western characters – trappers, drifters, gypsies and ranchers – the book offered esoteric, postmodernist, discourse on the essence of canine character. One ailing trapper analogised *Canis lupus* with 'the *copo de nieve* ... Snowflake. You catch the snowflake but when you look in your hand you don't have it no more ... If you want to see it you have to see it on its own ground.' Lying in bed at the ranch house, Billy 'tried to see the world the wolf saw. He tried to think about running in the mountains at night. He wondered if the wolf were so unknowable as the old man said.' In *The Crossing*, various people strove to comprehend the enigma of the wolf, yet all recognised the animal as her own creation, an independent spirit, unclassifiable. In this context, the 'crossing' of the title involved a pertinent exploration of the margins of the human–animal relationship. In this reading, the 'border' spoke of the separation between the human and the non-human. The wolf, in McCarthy's

43.   McCarthy, 1995, pp. 17, 24–5; Rebein, 2001, p. 191.

Karen Jones

story, possessed its own agency, roamed its own world, and could not be essential-ised. Repeatedly asked if he would sell the captured wolf, Billy explained that the animal was not his, merely entrusted into his care. *The Crossing* thereby offered a captivating narrative on (the limits to) knowing and saving other species. It also spoke of transgression. After burying the dead she-wolf in the Sonoran Mountains, Billy assumed a feral demeanour, becoming, like his canine charge, an outlaw in ancestral territory. Roaming across the borderlands, seeking stolen horses and his brother Luke, the cowboy became the renegade, hungry, and hunted. When Billy revisited civilisation, 'people passing in the street turned to look at him. Something in off the wild mesas, something out of the past. Ragged, dirty, hungry in eye and belly. Totally unspoken for.' Offering pertinent commentary on the perverse response of the human psyche towards denizens of the wild, McCarthy added, 'In that outlandish figure they beheld what they envied most and what they most reviled. If their hearts went out to him it was yet true that for very small cause they might have killed him.'[44]

While *The Crossing* narrated Billy Parham's attempt to return a persecuted wolf to her native Mexico, Asta Bowen's 1997 novel *Hungry for Home* related a lupine search for security and prosperity on the US–Canadian border. Where Mc-Carthy situated his fictional tale in a 1930s amalgam of the old and the modern West, Bowen based her lupine odyssey on the real-world story of wolf recolonisa-tion in the Northern Rockies during the 1980s and 1990s. As agents of their own recovery, the wolves in Bowen's tale displayed customary lupine zeal and resilience. The dominant wolf, Marta, was portrayed as an eco-feminist icon, a strong female character akin to the she-wolf in *The Crossing*. Marta exhibited nurturing instincts, hunting prowess, pack loyalty, individualism and, above all, stamina. Here the wolf served as totem for positive gender identity – yet remained confined by biological convention casting the female as maternal figure. Other wolves displayed similarly humanistic traits, rather like Mowat's wolf family. The embattled, aged wolf Oldtooth displayed patience and devotion while Greatfoot possessed the vigour and assured gait demanded of an alpha male. In common with the other authors in this study, Bowen's wolf society appeared an earthy, otherworldly realm, a lupo-topia where individual animals possessed distinctive personality traits and humanity existed as an eternal enemy.

Characterising the story of wolf recovery in the Rockies as a 'trail of tears' – itself a poignant reference to the plight of the Cherokee Nation in the 1830s - Bowen's fictionalised rendition of lupine restoration involved copious quantities of pain, struggle, and death. This was a damming verdict on Turnerian triumphal-ism. Here the wolf story showed a West not won but lost. In Bowen's work, the wolf emerged as a potent signifier of frontier guilt, an expression that also proved common in commentary on the wolf reintroduction programme in Yellowstone in

---

44.   McCarthy 1995, pp. 45, 51, 170; *New York Times*, 12 June 1994.

the mid-1990s. Despite the hardships endured by Marta and her pack, *Hungry for Home* nonetheless imparted a celebratory narrative that consciously reflected the successful return of wolves to the West in the latter years of the twentieth century. Individual animals certainly suffered adversity. Yet, the restoration of the species to old haunts constituted an act of environmental magnitude and attested to human magnanimity. As the 'Return of the Wolf' pamphlet issued by the US National Park Service intimated, 'wolf restoration shows that we respect the existence of other life forms, even when that may not be easy'. Species restoration signalled a renewed faith in human progress, writ in terms of ecological sustainability, wildland preservation and buoyant Sierra Club membership. In a brief epilogue that served as an exact foil to Mowat's shocking endnote, Bowen exclaimed: 'Though the deaths of so many wolves make this story tragic, for the species it ends with hope'.[45]

FROM SAVING TO KNOWING?

The alluring canine protagonists of *Wild Animals I Have Known, White Fang, The Call of the Wild, Never Cry Wolf, The Custer Wolf, Wolf of Shadows, The Crossing,* and *Hungry For Home* identify the wolf as a enduring character in North American literature and environmental history. In their canine expositions, Seton, London, Mowat, Caras, Strieber, McCarthy and Bowen employed *Canis lupus* as a signifier for wilderness. With the wolf enshrined as a totemic intermediary allowing readers to interact with wild landscapes, authors explored themes of nature versus civilisation, frontier guilt and ethical obligations. Changing ideas about nature and ecology, as well as sociological precepts, determined the shape of wolf tales. In the first wave, the likes of Seton and London cast the wolf as a Darwinian and Turnerian super-canine, all red in tooth and claw. For the writers of the 1960s, *Canis lupus* was draped in revisionist guilt at the 'winning' of the West and adorned with commentary on ecological science and family social dynamics. Issues of ecocide, species eradication and recovery, the border and ethnic identity framed wolf tales at the close of the twentieth century. Seen in this context, the wolf emerged as a powerful rhetorical device for chewing over human political, social and environmental preoccupations.

As this article has demonstrated, the storyteller emerged as a valid and effective architect of environmental advocacy, a shaper of opinion as well as a reflector of social mores. Just as Aesop crafted his animal characters to serve as four-legged instructors for human society, narrators on the lupine experience in North America configured their faunal speakers to impart sturdy environmentalist messages. Wolf tales adeptly broadcast moral judgments as to human responsibilities towards the rest of the natural world, offering the storyteller as environmental advocate, in-structor and consciousness-raiser. From the late 1800s onwards, stories heralding

---

45.   Bowen 1997, pp. 213, 211; 'The Return of the Wolf' (Yellowstone National Park Service, 1996),
       courtesy of the Yellowstone Centre for Resources.

the wolf as a four-legged hero redefined popular attitudes towards wildlife. Even pre-environmentalist works by Seton and London offered positive depictions of wolves that fostered the eventual rehabilitation of the species. Mowat and Caras participated in a social awakening to global environmental crisis and highlighted the losers in the story of America's relentless dash to supremacy. Wolf writers of the late twentieth century traded in an imaginative geography that extrapolated the trails of wolf recovery and the fictions and fixtures of the border. Throughout, these storytellers effectively used canine tales to question accustomed species hierarchies, lambast paths of progress via environmental destruction and, occasionally, to trade in misanthropy. The tales they told about wolves allowed readers to connect with the animal, in the process forging a positive wolf fairytale based around strong individual personalities and the culture of the pack. Collectively, they established a new environmental–literary paradigm that shaped popular attitudes as much as the emerging precepts of ecological science. As sociologist Ulrich Beck reminds us, 'only if nature is brought into people's everyday images, into the stories they tell, can its beauty and its suffering be seen and focused on'. The significance of literature in facilitating wolf preservation thereby situates environmental education as the vocation of the storyteller as well as the scientist. By stoking an emotional engagement between reader and wolf, fiction proved to be a powerful force in promoting inter-species empathy and ecological consciousness. [46]

Foremost wolf biologist L. David Mech freely admitted that *Never Cry Wolf* 'served to stir the public from its apathy regarding the plight of the wolf'. However, in the wider scientific community, reactions to pro-wolf stories were muted at best and often critical. Seton and London earned the slur 'nature fakers' while Mowat won a tirade of abuse from the North American wildlife community. The storyteller cut a radical presence in offering a controversial narrative that challenged prevalent societal judgements about animals and competed with the professional wildlife community for authority over the public imagination. Biological organisations keen to assert their own power as speakers on wildlife matters utilised the polarities of expert/amateur and scientist/storyteller to effectively discredit those who clothed their wolves in literary guise. A testament to the identification of science with credible expertise, many of the authors under review here felt the need to invoke a 'biological' voice in order to gain the attention and trust of the reading public. Writing in 2006, Barbara Nelson called for 'good' scientists to police the realms of wolf writing in order to ensure 'representative accuracy of the natural world'. Nelson's comment spoke of a long-standing tendency within the wildlife community to write off literature as falsehood and elevate science as above criticism or bias. I favour a different conclusion, one founded on the principle that *all* wolf tales reflect the trappings of contemporary society. As such, the focus of existing scholarship on the diametric oppositions of 'science' and 'sentiment' overlooks a

---

46. Beck 1995, p. 14.

vital point. While the charge to assimilate 'the animal's perspective' denoted an oft-touted maxim, providing a convincing rendition of lupine exigencies challenged the skills of North American novelists and wildlife managers alike. Both allowed a peek into canine ways, but necessarily from a two-legged vantage. As Barry Lopez remarked in his classic text *Of Wolves and Men:* 'in the wolf we have not so much an animal we have always known as one we have consistently imagined'. In fact, by admitting the limits to 'knowing the animal', we allow for the existence of agency in the non-human world and open up the possibility of a fuller and more provocative deconstruction of wolf tales. Such a project demands acceptance, from both storyteller and scientist, that while we might aspire to 'know' the wolf, we can never crawl beneath its skin.[47]

BIBLIOGRAPHY

Allen, D. 1979. *Wolves of Minong: Their Vital Role in a Wild Community* (Boston).

Beck, U. 1995. 'Politics in Risk Society', in Beck, *Ecological Enlightenment* (New Jersey).

Bowen, A. 1997. *Hungry for Home: A Wolf Odyssey* (New York).

Boyd, D., D. Pletscher and W. Brewster. 1993. 'Evidence of Wolves, *Canis lupus*, Burying Dead Pups'. *Canadian Field Naturalist* 10: 230–1.

Burroughs, J. 1903. 'Real and Sham Natural History', *Atlantic Monthly* XCI: 298–301.

Caras, R. 1966. *The Custer Wolf: Biography of an American Renegade* (Boston).

Catesby, M. 1985. *Birds of Colonial America*, ed. by Alan Feduccia (Chapel Hill).

Coleman, J.T. 2004. *Vicious: Wolves and Men in America* (New Haven).

Cowan, I.M. 1947. 'The Timber Wolf in the Rocky Mountains of Canada'. *Canadian Journal of Research* 25 D: 139–74.

Dunlap, T. 1988. *Saving America's Wildlife: Ecology and the American Mind, 1850–1990* (Princeton).

— 1984. 'Values for Varmints Predator Control and Environmental Ideas, 1920–39'. *Pacific Historical Review* 53 (2): 141–161.

Elton, C. 1927. *Animal Ecology* (New York).

Errington, P. 1967. *Of Predation and Life* (Ames, Iowa).

Fischer, H. 1995. *Wolf Wars* (Helena).

Foreman, D. 2000. *The Lobo Outback Funeral Home* (Boulder).

George, J.C. 1972. *Julie of the Wolves* (New York).

Hampton, B. 1997. *The Great American Wolf* (New York).

Jones, K. 2002a. *Wolf Mountains: A History of Wolves Along the Great Divide* (Calgary).

— 2002b. '"A Fierce Green Fire": Passionate Pleas and Wolf Ecology'. *Ethics, Place and Environment* 5 (1): 35–43.

---

47.   Mech 1970, pp. 339–40; Nelson 2006; Lopez 1978, p. 204.

— 2003. '"Never Cry Wolf": Science, Sentiment and the Literary Rehabilitation of *Canis lupus'*. *Canadian Historical Review* **84** (1): 65–93.

Kazin, A. 1942. *On Native Grounds* (New York)

Koiford, C. 1901. 'The Innings of the Animals'. *Dial* **XXXI**: 440.

Leopold, A. 1970 [1949]. *A Sand County Almanac* (New York).

London, J(ack). 1993 [1903, 1906]. *The Call of the Wild, White Fang, and Other Stories* (New York).

— 1910. *Revolution and Other Essays* (New York).

London, J(oan). 1939. *Jack London and His Times* (New York).

Lopez, B.H. 1978. *Of Wolves and Men* (New York).

Lutts, R. 1990. *The Nature Fakers: Wildlife, Science, and Sentiment* (Colorado).

— (ed.) 1998. *The Wild Animal Story* (Philadelphia).

McCarthy, C. 1995 [1994]. *The Crossing* (London).

McIntyre, R. (ed.) 1995. *War Against the Wolf: America's Campaign to Exterminate the Wolf* (Stillwater, MN).

Mech, L.D. 1970. *The Wolf: The Ecology and Behavior of an Endangered Species* (Minneapolis).

Mighetto, L. 1985. 'Science, Sentiment, and Anxiety: American Nature Writing at the Turn of the Century'. *Pacific Historical Review* **54**: 33–50.

Mowat, F. 1979 [1963]. *Never Cry Wolf* (Toronto).

Murie, A. 1944. *The Wolves of Mount McKinley* (Washington, DC).

Parsons, T., R Bales et al. 1955. *Family, Socialization and the Interaction Process* (New York).

Murray, J. (ed.) 1993. *Out Among the Wolves: Contemporary Writings on the Wolf* (Seattle).

Nelson, B. 2006. 'Exploiting Mexican Wolf Science and Story as Material for Wild Books'. *Interdisciplinary Studies in Literature and Environment* **13** (1): 91–111.

Phillips, M. and D. Smith. 1996. *Wolves of Yellowstone* (Stillwater, MN).

Rebein, R. 2001. *Hicks, Tribes and Dirty Realists* (Lexington).

Schullery, P. 1996. *The Yellowstone Wolf* (Worland, WY).

Seton, E.T. 1987 [1898]. *Wild Animals I Have Known* (New York).

Singer, P. 1983 [1975]. *Animal Liberation* (Wellingborough).

1995. *The Company of Wolves* (New York).

Stone, C. 1974 [1972]. *Should Trees Have Standing? Toward Legal Rights for Natural Objects* (Los Altos).

Strieber, W. 1985. *Wolf of Shadows* (New York).

Swift, G. 1983. *Waterland* (London).

Thoreau, H.D. 1864. *The Maine Woods* (Boston).

Von Bertalanffy, L. 1968. *General System Theory: Foundations, Development, Applications* (New York).

10

The Shifting Iconography of Wolves over the Twentieth Century

Linda Kalof

INTRODUCTION

For millennia, animal iconography has been a salient tracer of cultural shifts in the human valuation of other animals,[1] and no animal has been more the focus of major cultural reconfigurations in position and perceptions than the wolf. My chapter describes the iconography[2] of the wolf (*Canis lupus*) in a hundred years of the most widely read popular science magazine in the world, *National Geographic*. I explore how visual imagery is linked to the change in social discourses on wolves from detested 'varmints' in the early 1900s to a protected species and cultural icon in the late twentieth century. While much has been written about the negative image of the wolf in a wide range of popular culture narratives, including Aesop's Fables, fairytales and Christian iconography,[3] literature during the last half of the twentieth century began to paint a picture of the wolf as a gregarious family-oriented hero of the wilderness.[4] But in spite of the proliferation of both positive and negative wolf imagery in popular culture, there is little empirical documentation on the representation of the wolf in popular science outlets. That void is notable given the importance of the role of science in generating and sustaining social discourses on animals and the natural world.[5] *National Geographic* is a widely read and influential popular science magazine, and much of that renown rests on the photographs and illustrations.[6] Thus, visual imagery provides fertile ground for the historical analysis of social discourses on wolves, and popular science imagery situates historical constructions of the wolf in a social and political framework.[7] This

---

1. Kalof 2007.
2. Iconography: a) Pictorial illustration of a subject; b) The collected representations illustrating a subject.
3. For a recent overview, see Marvin 2012.
4. See, for example, Mowat 1963.
5. Haraway 1989.
6. Lutz and Collins 1993.
7. Brennen and Hardt 1999; Kalof and Amthor 2010.

chapter chronicles the social discourses on wolves using visual imagery published in *National Geographic* over the twentieth century.

BACKGROUND

A watershed in the placement of the wolf in a positive cultural context was Lois Crisler's 1956 book, *Arctic Wild*,[8] which documented the time she and her husband spent photographing the wildlife of the Brooks Range in Alaska. *Arctic Wild* catapulted the ecological value of the wolf into the consciousness of the general reader, generating wolf admirers at a time when wolf persecution was so widespread that only two US states, Alaska and Minnesota, supported wolf populations.[9] On the heels of Crisler's book, Farley Mowat published *Never Cry Wolf*,[10] in which he abandoned the objective scientific stance of a wildlife biologist in observing wildlife predatory behaviours to produce a compelling account of the social lives of an Arctic wolf pack. The wolf as an icon was born.

Backing up a few decades, it is useful to elaborate on the story of wolves as a wildlife resource in the US because it chronicles so well their shifting status in different political and cultural contexts.[11] Dunlap has described the changing social discourse on wolves and other 'varmints' from extermination to reintroduction back into ecosystems vital to the existence of predators.[12] Institutional and intellectual foundations for wildlife policy were established at the turn of the century that mandated the protection of wildlife by the government, and a change in the biological paradigm of predator–prey relations resulted in the application of principles of ecology to wildlife.[13] In the 1920s, the government's programme of poisoning predators was widely criticised, heralding a transition in the valuation of wildlife by the public. In the next decade nature education was widespread across the country and a special committee to promote ecological research and the balance of predators and prey was initiated by the government.[14] After World War Two, the social discourse on nature was in transition, with nature perceived as a fragile web capable of destruction by humans. But amid increasing opposition from the public, the predator poisoning programme continued, with the introduction of Compound 1080 and the use of strychnine and cyanide. The 'frenzy to slaughter wolves by poisoning not only killed wolves but also dogs, children and the horses

---

8. Crisler 1999.
9. Crisler 1999.
10. Mowat 1963.
11. This material is adapted from Kalof and Amthor 2010, pp. 176–7.
12. Dunlap 1988.
13. Ibid.
14. Ibid., pp. 48, 81.

who ate the grass that the wolves had salivated on as they died'.[15] The predator poisoning programme was banned in the early 1970s and the ecosystem-protection discourse gave rise to important animal protection legislation, including the Endangered Species Act and the Convention on International Trade in Endangered Species of Wild Fauna and Flora (CITES), both signed into law in 1973.[16] While the predator poisoning programme was reinstated in 1982 under political pressure by ranchers, the public continued to recognise the value of predators in ecosystems. Wolf reintroduction programmes were considered successful in the north-western US by 2007.[17] But the 'war over wolves' continues: the gray wolf has now lost protection under the Endangered Species Act in parts of the US, and there is currently a proposal before the US Fish and Wildlife Service to lift protection for all gray wolves in the lower 48 US states. While the wolf will not likely endure in the US without legal protection,[18] it is clear that his survival is also tethered to the multiplicity of social discourses on wolves.

SCIENCE AND SOCIAL DISCOURSE

It is now widely accepted that 'science is a socially-embedded activity',[19] and scientific discourses are social products that create a multiplicity of boundaries and conditions for millions of humans and other animals.[20] Popular science outlets are particularly important in this regard because they not only translate science for a lay audience, but also 'generate and transform public knowledge'.[21] For example, in recoding science for a mass audience, Donna Haraway argues that *National Geographic* made sense of women heroines in a male-dominated science by representing female primatologists such as Jane Goodall as primate 'mothers' with special attributes that allowed them to get close to nature and animals during their work in the field.[22] In addition, popular science has been found to contribute to an expanded public discourse on climate change that extends beyond the vulnerability of iconic wild megafauna to include insects and amphibians and issues facing the relationship we have with other animals, such as the widespread consumption of animals for food.[23]

15. Emel 1998, p. 98, cited in Kalof and Amthor 2010, p. 177.
16. Dunlap 1988, p. 142.
17. Busch 2007, p. 202.
18. Ibid., p. 232.
19. Gould 1996, p. 53; see also Latour and Woolgar 2013.
20. Haraway 1989, p. 289.
21. Daum 2009, p. 319.
22. Haraway 1989, p. 144.
23. Whitley and Kalof 2014.

Linda Kalof

The influence of science on the social discourse on wolves has been documented in a study of wolf narratives in Europe.[24] Two narratives were found to explain the reappearance of wolves in the French Alps and in south-eastern Norway: 1) wolves were secretly reintroduced (common among anti-wolf folks, primarily farmers); and 2) wolves are attracted to unique regional shepherding practices that do not protect livestock properly, such as leaving sheep to graze in mountains and forests (common among wolf proponents and conservationists). These two social discourses on wolves establish 'the weight gained by science … and the priority commonly attributed to the general over the particular' – farmers have a focus on local conditions and are reluctant to trust science (used to dispute the secret reintroduction theory) and pro-wolf conservationists are generalists and consider science crucial in wolf protection on a global scale.[25]

The above findings corroborate Bill Lynn's argument that social discourses on wolves 'embody divergent interpretations of wolves – who they are, what they do, and why they do it – and how human beings should respond to them'.[26] Lynn also notes that a comprehensive list of the wide range of interpretations of wolves has not yet been produced. My research will help fill that gap using wolf imagery in *National Geographic* magazine. Widely considered the 'professor of nature',[27] *National Geographic* is published in 34 languages, and has a global monthly readership of 8.2 million, five million in the United States alone.[28] As mentioned above, the photographs in *National Geographic* account for much of the magazine's popularity, and it has been reported that the vast majority of *National Geographic*'s readers look only at the photographs and their captions, giving just a cursory glance at the articles.[29] Thus, photography has considerable cultural significance, with an influence that has completely changed the visual environment and means of information exchange throughout the world.[30] Susan Sontag has argued that while non-stop imagery (television, video and film) is everywhere, we remember photographs best, and the single image serves as the basic unit for apprehending and memorising something, much like a quotation or a maxim and subject to instant recall.[31]

Nature and the meaning of wolves are not stable, unchanging concepts. Most scholars agree that representations have no determinate meaning outside the complex context in which they are situated; representations are not transparent

24. Skogen, Mauz and Krange 2006.
25. Ibid., pp. 85–6.
26. Lynn 2010, p. 82.
27. Montgomery 1993, cited in Kalof and Amthor 2010, p. 167.
28. *National Geographic* 2012.
29. Lutz and Collins 1993.
30. Gaskell 1991.
31. Sontag 2003.

images, but have 'distinctive surfaces upon which representations are inscribed'.[32] Thus, the photograph is a complex form of representation and reading photographs is a process of engaging with a series of relationships that are in fact 'hidden'.[33] For example, in a study of New Guinea photographs taken in the early 1900s, Wright argues that images that might at first blush appear to be examples of a voyeuristic colonial gaze are in fact engaged in a wider cultural history.[34] Images are like tattoos, full of multiple meanings and cultural codings.[35] In the case of wolf iconography, this multiplicity of meanings and codings comprises the range of social discourses on wolves. Thus, as a popular science magazine that has shaped ideas of exotic people, places, animals and the natural world for more than 125 years, *National Geographic* is an ideal site to examine the social discourses that emerge from the photographs of one of the most exotic, contentious and beloved wildlife species in human history – wolves.

METHOD

Using the *National Geographic* electronic archive of full issues from 1888 to 2011, I examined all wolf images, including the accompanying captions, to identify thematic categories in wolf iconography over the twentieth century. Captions are an integral part of the social construction of a discourse because photographs and captions co-constitute each other – they are in communication.[36] There were 140 images of wolves published in the magazine between 1907 (the first wolf picture published) and 2011 (the last available year in the archive). The unit of analysis was the wolf image (including photographs, paintings and drawings) and the accompanying caption. I analysed all images that depict one or more wolves (alive or dead). Feature articles on wolves were usually illustrated with multiple photographs, each with different captions and different narrative embellishments on wolves. Thus, multiple thematic categories were often present in a single article, illustrating, for example, activities of the same pack of wolves. The images were easily coded into a primary theme with no ambiguity, so the thematic categories were mutually exclusive. Eliminated from the sample were images of wolf/dog and wolf/coyote hybrids and photographs of the products of once-living wolves (such as wolf fur clothing).

32. Lynch and Woolgar 1990, p. viii.
33. Clarke 1997, p. 29.
34. Wright 2003.
35. Ibid.
36. Barthes 1977, p. 16.

RESULTS

There were five primary themes in the iconography of *Canis lupus* over the twentieth century in *National Geographic*: Hunter (33.5 per cent), Social Actor (twenty per cent) Education and Research Subjects (16.4 per cent), Subjects of Portraiture (15.7 per cent), and Objects of Extermination (ten per cent). The images that were not captured by one of the five primary themes were coded into a Miscellaneous category (9.2 per cent) which included photographs of wolf tracks and paw prints and wolves engaged in common solitary behaviours such as sleeping, stretching, resting, running and retreating.

Hunters

The wolf as hunter was, not surprisingly, the most prevalent representation of wolf imagery over the twentieth century (33.5 per cent of all photographs in the sample).

Dance of Death

Over half of the images (n=24, 51 per cent) in this category were pictures of the 'Dance of Death', during which a wolf pack surround and gradually weaken large prey. The Dance of Death was not photographed for *National Geographic* before the 1960s, but aerial photographs from the Isle Royale wolf-moose study site (the first published in 1963) made popular the images of 'life-or-death drama' in wolf–prey behaviours. The caption for the 1963 photograph of the 'dance of death' at Isle Royale was explicit in its description of the unfolding drama:

> Pack patiently awaits weakening of a moose whose wounds stain the snow. Exhaustion, shock, and stiffening muscles sap this aged cow's ability to use her battering hoofs, and the milling wolves bide their time. If she bolts, they head her off; if she lies down, they force her up, allowing her no rest. When night comes, they will make the kill.[37]

The interaction between wolf pack and moose was photographed again two years later in a feature article on wildlife at Isle Royale: 'The end is near for a moose bloodied by the largest of the island's three wolf packs'.[38]

While the early photographs of the Dance of Death were grainy aerial shots, by 1977 photographers were taking close-up pictures of the scene at ground level and with even more explicit description of the hapless victim and the resilience of the wolves in their pursuit of the prey. Instead of one panoramic photograph, tightly framed close shots of the moose and wolves were used to illustrate the drama:

> Timeless drama of predation unfolds as … [the] photographer records a moose kill in Superior National Forest. The prey, a calf with a broken leg, rests [photo 1 of

---

37. *National Geographic* (*NG*), Feb. 1963: 216.
38. *NG*, Apr. 1985: 547.

209

209

The Shifting Iconography of Wolves

mother and calf with a wolf watching the two from a short distance] while its mother stands guard – as she had all through the night before. Off and on, as the wolves closed in, the calf would hobble on its three good legs, followed by its mother, to the safety of a pond [photo 2 of mother and calf in water, two wolves advancing toward them, the wolves bodies poised, heads held low]. Trembling with cold, it would always lead her back to shore. Death came under cover of night, accompanied by terrible bellowing. The next day … [the photographer] found the pack tearing at the carcass [photo 3 of calf carcass being consumed by two wolves], already stripped of the large muscles. The cow, exhausted from innumerable charges at the advancing wolves, may have lowered her guard to feed before the fatal attack – some 24 hours after the showdown began.[39]

Ten years later, photographs of the Dance of Death again illustrated the confrontation between Arctic wolves and musk-oxen in northern Canada, but now there were twice as many photographs as action shots showing the wolves charging, chasing and catching the prey:

In an electrifying sequence, seven wolves target three musk-oxen calves guarded by 11 adults – whose hooves could crack a wolf's skull. On a flat arena the wolves casually approached their quarry. The musk-oxen bunched in a semicircle, hindquarters pressed together, protecting the calves. A long standoff deteriorated as a single ox broke ranks, and the herd scattered into small groups that grew increasingly nervous while wolves darted among them. They skirmished until finally the whole herd panicked and fled in a cloud of dust, with the wolves in hot pursuit [photo 1]. One wolf tests the group [photo 2], trying to separate a calf … from an adult. Protecting their calves, a group of oxen try to reorganize [photo 3], but to no avail. Soon the alpha male wolf closes in [photo 4], although another wolf puts on a burst of speed and grabs the calf first [photo 5]. Within a few furious moments the pack had caught and killed all three calves, including one that stirs competition among the predators [photo 6 of two wolves consuming a calf carcass, one of whom is photographed with teeth bared, ears down, protecting the carcass from a third wolf attempting to share the meal].[40]

By 2004, photographs of the Dance of Death were so sophisticated that an entire feature article was devoted to the drama, which now included not only wolves and the prey victim (a young bull moose), but also grizzly bears and ravens both of whom shared in the ensuing feast. Here I describe the major captions for the thirteen photographs that illustrated the article:

Wounded by a pack of wolves, a young bull moose confronts a foe along a river in Denali National Park and Preserve in Alaska. This face-off was part of a bloody drama rarely witnessed by humans. The bull was limping from a bloody gash on his right thigh. As a grizzly and her cubs closed in, so did the wolves. The animals were tense, hyperalert [running, leaping, pawing, pacing, snapping] and could have

---

39. *NG*, Oct. 1977: 532–3.
40. *NG*, May 1987: 572–6. The photos are not reproduced in this chapter.

killed one another. All day the wolves stalked the moose, repeatedly forcing him into the frigid river, which sapped his strength. He no longer shook his antlers at his assailants. His protruding ribs rose and fell in shallow breaths. His eyes were sunken and hollow. When a wolf closed in, hunter and prey locked eyes in … the conservation of death, a ceremonial exchange [in which] the flesh of the hunted in exchange for respect for its spirit.[41]

Prowling/Protecting/Consuming Food

Approximately 47 per cent of the wolf-as-hunter photographs were of wolves on the prowl for prey (n=10) or consuming/protecting food (n=7). While the Dance of Death photographs often focused on the desperation of the prey, the captions for the hunters were indicative of the ways that the magazine conveyed the power and strength of the wolf as hunter. For example, in describing an early drawing of a caribou surrounded by snarling Arctic wolves, an author of the early twentieth century noted that 'White wolves are the one dreaded foe Nature has given the musk-ox and the caribou in the northern wilds'.[42] In a photograph of a powerful-looking wolf running through a meadow, the caption read:

Among the fiercest of predators, a gray wolf lopes in pursuit of a meal. During bumper years for lemmings, wolves find the summer tundra a banquet table of birds and small mammals, eggs and carrion. In winter the canines run in packs and systematically harass herds of caribou, cutting out stragglers – calves, the sick, and the aged.[43]

One of the most interesting captions in the sample was a provocative invitation to the reader to come to her own conclusions as to who wolves are, based on a photograph of a wolf. The photograph was a close-up shot of an aggressive-looking wolf with teeth bared and ears flattened who crouches over the carcass of something big and bloody:

The big bad wolf. The wolf at the door. Throw him to the wolves. These are classic characterizations. Yet wildlife biologists insist that wolves are intelligent, loyal, and gregarious. So which is it? As this shot of a captive wolf [snarling while protecting his food] makes clear, it depends on your point of view.[44]

Social Actors

Twenty per cent of the images (n=28) were of wolves engaged in social behaviours, including play and dominance rituals, communal rearing of pups, curiosity and

41. *NG*, May 2004:101–10.
42. *NG*, Nov. 1916: 421–2.
43. *NG*, Mar. 1972: 334–5.
44. *NG*, May 1998: 74–5.

habituated begging. This theme did not emerge until the late 1970s, along with the increasing positive public discourse on wolves.

Social Play and Dominance Rituals

Social play and dominance images comprised 42.8 per cent of the sample of wolves as social actors. Most of the images and captions emphasised the structured nature of wolf society, a society based on clear rules that ensure the solidarity and cohesiveness of the pack. For example, in a 1977 article on wolf survival, two photographs of wolves engaged in fight/play behaviour had the following caption:

> Fangs flashing, captive wolves in Utah resolve who is top dog in highly structured wolf society. Body language normally keeps the peace. Seemingly vicious disputes [photo 1] are usually settled without bloodshed as the subordinate animal rolls over in a gesture of submission [photo 2]. Pack members that try to improve their position and fail may be the ones that leave to become lone wolves.[45]

A number of the photographs of dominance rituals included pictures of playfulness (see Figure 1), some serene, some fiercely aggressive. Serenity was the context of the photo of two female wolves interacting in a meadow of flowers, one of whom is on her back with front paws reaching toward the other: 'In summer, dominance rituals are almost playful ... But in winter, with hormones coursing, such displays become intense'.[46] Howling among wolves is considered by some wolf professionals to be primarily a joyful social occasion, and that wolves often howl just for fun.[47] While wolves howling was not a common image over the time period, the magazine occasionally published photographs of howling wolves: a pack of wolves howling in a heathery hillside ('In a wilderness concerto, the wolves awaken in the wee hours of morning and one by one life their voices to a never setting July sun'),[48] a howling pup discussed in the pup section below,[49] a close-up of a howling wolf on the cover for the March 2010 issue on Wolf Wars (no caption), and a picture of three wolves howling ('Why do wolves howl? It's their way of saying, "this is our turf", or "where's the rest of our pack?" or perhaps "we've found food"').[50] Aggressiveness was the context of a photograph of the Yellowstone Rose Creek pack, teeth bared as they 'tussle in play [and behave] like a bunch of wolves',[51] and another of juvenile gray wolves playing:

> nip and tuck ... a furious game of chase around a Minnesota lake. When wolves

---

45. *NG*, Oct. 1977: 526–7. The photos are not reproduced in this chapter.
46. *NG*, May 1987: 584–5.
47. Busch 2007; Crisler 1999.
48. *NG*, May 1987: 591.
49. *NG*, May 1987: 580.
50. *NG*, May 1998: 89.
51. Ibid.: 90–1.

212

Linda Kalof

Figure 1. Photographer Joel Sartore/National Geographic Creative, Image 513385, published May 1998, pp. 90–91.

play, their ears are usually upright. The flattened ears of these two brothers suggest aggression, but the photographer … who has observed wolves for more than 25 years, says, 'Sometimes fights can develop, but this time they just played tag for nearly two hours.' Such tireless play helps build the stamina wolves need for long chases to bring down moose and other prey.[52]

A combination of calmness and excitement provided the atmosphere for a photograph of Ethiopian wolves in ritualised greeting behaviour:

Sniffing, snapping, yipping, whimpering – wolves greet each other in a morning ritual that strengthens the solidarity of their pack while reinforcing its pecking order. Afterward they will leave the youngsters behind and set out to patrol their territory and hunt.[53]

Communal Rearing of Pups

One of the most iconic wolf social behaviours is the communal rearing and love of wolf pups, and the magazine had numerous pup-focused photographs (25 per cent of the social actor images). The captions emphasised both the strong bonds between mother and pups and between pup-sitters (adult wolves in the pack) and the young:

---

52. *NG*, Dec. 1994: 16–7.
53. *NG*, Mar. 2006: 126–7.

Doting baby-sitters, all wolves love pups – their own or another's. This wolf, raised in the Alaskan wild by naturalists …, guards a litter the couple entrusted to it. All members of wolf packs share in the upbringing of the young. Strong emotional bonds, formed early between pups and adults, become the cement of pack unity.[54]

Scruffy … was an assiduous baby-sitter. Once the author watched him awaken while the pack slept, retrieve an old fox carcass – a favorite toy – and deliver it to the pups. As they began killing it for the hundredth time, Scruffy wandered off and went back to sleep.[55]

Ears, eyes, and noses at attention, three of the pack's six pups focus on a bird outside their den in a rock outcrop. Here about seven weeks old … the pups have begun to venture short distances with the pack's seven adults. For them, the pups are the center of the universe, communally fed, reared, and defended.[56]

Small call of the wild rises as a pup practices its howl, an important part of the pack's complex social system. Vital for the pups is learning to get food. Adults sometimes deliver meat whole or in chunks but usually regurgitate partly digested meals to the young.[57]

After-dinner toy, the feather of a gull is captured by a youngster … Such play has a serious side, familiarizing the pups with the kinds of prey they will stalk on their own.[58]

Curiosity

Wolves are curious animals, and the magazine emphasised the benign nature of their curiosity with photographs of wolves in various behaviours, such as interacting with human biologists in the field, testing water from an ice floe or getting dive bombed when investigating a bird's nest (21 per cent of the social actor images). The caption for photographs of a wolf approaching and investigating humans was clear in its assertion that the stories of aggressive wolf-beasts were only myth:

How to woo a wolf: Assume a submissive posture, and the storied 'man eater' may deign to give you a sniff, as illustrated here by two naturalists in Alaska. Ordinarily wolves will flee at first sight of a human. Not one case of healthy wolves attacking people has been recorded in North America. Old accounts of marauding 'beasts' in Europe – probably embellished by legend – and now interpreted as attacks by raid wolves or wolf-dog hybrids. Nonetheless, wolves have been pursued through the ages with poisons, barbed bait, traps, and guns.[59]

54. *NG*, Oct. 1977: 524–5.
55. *NG*, May 1987: 586–7.
56. Ibid.: 567.
57. Ibid.: 580.
58. *NG*, May 1977: 592.
59. *NG*, Oct. 1977: 528–9.

Linda Kalof

While curiosity is a social behaviour that signals intelligence and inquisitiveness, wild wolf familiarity with humans has catastrophic consequences, as is noted below concerning the images of habituated wolves begging for food.

Habituated Begging

While only two images in the sample, the most haunting and disturbing photographs were of wolves habituated to humans and their food, an extreme example of the wolf as a social actor and one with severe consequences. Taken on Vargas Island near Vancouver, one photograph shows a wolf in semi-darkness, standing and staring straight ahead, head a bit lowered, looking impoverished:

> Hunter-turned beggar, a wolf accustomed to handouts on Vargas Island stares down the photographer … hoping in vain for a scrap. One of the pack later attacked a camper. Two wolves were shot as a result. (see Figure 2)[60]

Figure 2. Photographer Joel Sartore/National Geographic Creative, Image 714410, published February 2003, pp. 108–109.

Another photograph of a Vargas Island habituated wolf scavenging a tidal flat noted in the caption that the wolves face an uncertain future: as mythic beings

---

60. *NG*, Feb. 2003: 124–5.

honoured by the region's indigenous people, locals must decide whether wolves should be wild or tamed.[61]

Education and Research Subjects

Wolves were pictured as subjects of education and research in 16.4 per cent of the sample. Approximately half of the education-focused images emphasised the human connection with wolves. The photographs of the link between humans and wolves included the evolutionary history of wolf/dog domestication, excavation of the site of a wolf-human burial,[62] excavation of a site of the burial of a wolf who was adorned with jewels,[63] and excavation of a burial site of fourteen wolf heads and four male skeletons.[64] Extinct wolves were the subject of two photographs in the sample with educational value. The photograph of a stuffed Tasmanian wolf displayed among 'a who's who of extinction ... at England's Tring Zoological Museum ... experts believe that species are presently dying at the rate of 100 a day'.[65] Another photograph superimposed the skeleton of the paw of the dire wolf with the hand of a human male:

> Larger than a man's hand was the dire wolf's paw: These perfectly preserved bones of the right front foot were found in the La Brea tar pits at Los Angeles. Larger than present-day American wolves, the ferocious animals ranged over all the United States. Their massive teeth were capable of crushing big bones.[66]

Articles from the first half of the twentieth century often provided educational material on wolves, such as close descriptions of their behaviour and habits. For example, a photograph of a maned wolf had this caption:

> No real wolf is the strange Aguará-Guazú. Largest of the South American Canidae, this creature, sometimes called the red or maned wolf of Paraguay, inhabits that country and parts of Brazil and Argentina. Its prey consists of wild deer, pacas, agoutis, birds, reptiles, and some insects. Mainly nocturnal, it utters a cry sounding like its colloquial name 'A-guará'. The animal, bred to the domestic dog, has produced off-spring excellent for trailing.[67]

In a recent article supporting a captive-born wolf sanctuary, wolves were photographed as travelling ambassadors for the initiative. Pictured as they stepped off a bus in a close-up shot, one of the wolves was tethered by a heavy chain.[68]

---

61. Ibid.: 126.
62. *NG*, Jan. 2002: 4.
63. *NG*, Nov. 2010: 115.
64. *NG*, Oct. 2006: 148.
65. *NG*, Jun. 1989: 698–9.
66. *NG*, Feb. 1942: 183.
67. *NG*, Sep. 1944: 378.
68. *NG*, Jul. 2011: 44–5.

Linda Kalof

Figure 3. Photographer Joel Sartore/National Geographic Creative, Image 499197, published March 1995 (cover).

Educating the readers about the value of predators in ecosystems was the topic of an article with drawings of wolves in a lush Yellowstone ecosystem. The importance of the message requires a lengthy quote from the caption for the image:

> Yellowstone with wolves, 1995–present: Elk population has been halved ... a healthy fear of wolves also keeps elk from lingering at streamside, where it can be harder to escape attack; the number of new sprouts eaten by elk has dropped dramatically, wolf predation has reduced coyote numbers, fewer coyote attacks may be a factor in the resurgence of the park's pronghorn ... willows, cottonwoods and other riparian vegetation has begun to stabilize stream banks, helping restore natural water flow, overhanging branches again shade the water and welcome birds ... beaver colonies have risen, creating ponds and marshes supporting fish, amphibians, birds, small mammals and insects to feed them ... wolves don't cover this kill, so they boost the food supply for scavengers, notably bald and golden eagles, coyotes, ravens, magpies and bears.[69]

As research subjects, wolves were pictured as part of predator reintroduction initiatives (see Figure 3), such as the red wolf bound for a programme in Great Smoky who was photographed while huddled in the corner of a wooden crate, 'fear glinting in (her) eyes'.[70] Numerous wolves were photographed tranquilised for research purposes, such as the wolf blindfolded and carried by a volunteer 'to another pen, last stop before it lopes into the wild'.[71] In the same article, there was a compelling photograph of a frightened wolf caught with a net designed to catch salmon:

> Proceeding with caution, members of Yellowstone's wolf project use salmon nets to snag Number 27, a recent transplant from British Columbia. Upon arrival wolves were penned for ten weeks to acclimate them to their new habitat and to discourage them from bolting back home when released.[72]

In another photograph, a scientist was pictured with a very large wolf draped over his shoulders:

> Living fur collar, a tranquilized wolf rides to tests at the U.S. Navy's Arctic Research Laboratory in Barrow. How the animal's bare footpads resist freezing on Arctic ice puzzles scientists. Studies of wildlife survival secrets, they hope, may aid man in his own struggle against the cold.[73]

Subjects of Portraiture

A large number of the photographs in the sample were portrait shots of wolves (15.7 per cent): wolves yawning, crouching, sitting, standing, walking, running, sniffing

69. *NG*, Mar. 2010: 51.
70. *NG*, Oct. 1994: 38.
71. *NG*, May 1998: 83.
72. *NG*, May 1998: 83.
73. *NG*, Oct. 1971: 500.

Figure 4. Photographer Joel Sartore/National Geographic Creative, Image 1198152, published January 2009, p. 103.

flowers; full head views, side views and profile views. The one commonality among the photographs was a focus on the wolf as an individual, not just a member of a species. There were few captioning embellishments; the photographs seemed to stand alone inviting the reader to ponder the beauty and majesty of the animal (see Figure 4). When captions did accompany the wolf portraits, the words and phrases used to capture the images included 'handsome profile',[74] 'lone sentinel',[75] 'soft and serene',[76] 'drowsy',[77] 'steals through underbrush'[78] and 'cunning'.[79]

Objects of Extermination

There were relatively few images of wolves indicative of wolf-hatred or the desire to exterminate them (ten per cent). As would be expected, most of the images that fell into this category were published before 1950 and included photographs of

74. *NG*, Mar. 2006: 134.
75. *NG*, May 1987: 563.
76. Ibid.: 581.
77. Ibid.: 585.
78. *NG*, Oct. 1991: 20–1.
79. *NG*, Nov. 1988: 683.

doomed wolf pups in front of their den[80] and a timber wolf with her paw caught in a trap, 'an animal that now threatens with extinction the deer in Lake Superior region and Canada'.[81]

Many of the narratives of wolves in the early twentieth century were focused on extermination and the age-old battle between wolves and humans. For example, realistic drawings of gray wolves were described in an early article:

> Since the dawn of history Old World wolves, when hunger pressed, have not hesitated to attack men, and in wild districts have become a fearful scourge. American wolves have rarely shown this fearlessness toward man, probably owing to the abundance of fame before the advent of white men and to the general use of firearms among the pioneers. That wolves are extremely difficult to exterminate is shown by their persistence to the present day in parts of France and elsewhere in Europe. This is due both to their fecundity ... and to their keen intelligence, which they so often pit successfully against the wiles of their chief enemy – man.[82]

The caption for a photograph of a trapped wolf read:

> What could be more truculent than a wolf at Bay? It has such tremendous power in its jaws that no single dog of equal size is a match for it in a fair fight. Seldom does it slash into its prey or foe without removing some of the flesh. There are actual records of a single bite's dividing the spine of a calf and of one snap's severing a juniper limb two inches in diameter. Note the hair raised along the spine from neck to rump. This wolf was caught in a trap.[83]

A photograph of four poisoned timber wolves hanging upside down had this caption:

> Next to man, these animals are the most destructive foe of the white-tail deer in the upper lake region. Fourteen years ago, during a severe winter, when deep snows were crusted for several weeks, the wolves destroyed nearly all the deer within a ten-mile radius of Whitefish Lake. From the carcasses found it was estimated that over two thousand deer were killed in this limited area. 'A deer's fear of a wolf is only equaled by a wolf's fear of man' (see Figure 5).[84]

In an article that addressed winter activities in Minnesota, four dead wolves were pictured lying next to two single engine airplanes:

> Airmen hunt wolves from planes for a bounty of $35 each. Unused to the new peril from the air, the great gray carnivores, bane of the deer herds, often afford a good shot by running out on the ice of lakes. Now, some hunters say, the wolves are getting wiser. (see Figure 6)[85]

---

80. *NG*, Feb. 1907: 146.
81. *NG*, Jun. 1908: 423.
82. *NG*, Nov. 1916: 422–3.
83. *NG*, Sep. 1944: 365.
84. *NG*, Aug. 1921: 133.
85. *NG*, Sep. 1949: 329.

Linda Kalof

Figure 5. Photographer George Shiras/National Geographic Creative, Image 604398, published August 1921, p. 133.

A dead white wolf, shot as a trophy specimen in the Arctic, was photographed three times, once lying on the ground, once with his head held aloft for the camera and once while being skinned:

> This wolf, shot by means of the seal screen ... was larger than a good-sized dog. The white wolf is more enduring, has a wider range, and passes an easier existence than any other Arctic animal. It infests Axel Heiberg Island, where its tracks mingle with those of musk oxen and caribou.[86]

The anti-wolf iconography continues throughout the century (and beyond), albeit infrequently. In an image from the late twentieth century, four dead wolves hanging over the flat bed of a truck were photographed for a May 1998 article that described a predatory event that brought about the wolves' demise:

---

86. *NG*, Jun. 1925: 710.

The Shifting Iconography of Wolves

Figure 6. Photographer B. Anthony Stewart and Jack E. Fletcher/National Geographic Creative, Image 1126342, published September 1949, p. 329.

Razed by wolves. Two times a day, 15 year old Hayley Jolma used to bottle-feed her calf, Minnie, on the family ranch in western Montana. Then one night animals attacked and badly mauled Minnie, who had to be destroyed ... wolves were to blame ... wildlife officials shot the local pack's alpha male, and months earlier, a similar attack by the same pack prompted federal officials to kill four of its members.[87]

Finally, in a 2010 feature article on 'wolf wars' and as typical of trophy photographs in hunting magazines,[88] a dead wolf was photographed with a rifle draped across her body. The caption read:

Realtor Robert Millage's rifle lies across his trophy: the first wolf taken in Clearwater National Forest, during Idaho's 2009–2010 season. The state set a quota of 220 in its first regulated wolf hunt.[89]

---

87. *Ng*, May 1998: 94.
88. Kalof and Fitzgerald 2003.
89. *NG*, Mar. 2010: 46–7.

Linda Kalof

CONCLUSION

In the early part of the twentieth century, *National Geographic*'s iconographic cata-logue on wolves was fully engaged in promoting the social discourse of wolves as predatory opportunists, fearful scourges and life-long human enemies. The negative discourse on wolves was consistent with the social and political climate at the turn of the twentieth century that focused on the extermination of predators to preserve ungulates and livestock for human use. While most of the extermination-focused photographs were published early in the century, the role of the Fish and Wildlife Service in controlling problem predators was part of the *National Geographic* ico-nography on wolves as late as 1998, suggesting the magazine still vests in federal officials a certain level of authority in wolf control in terms of killing problem wolves.

However, over the century the theme of the demonic wolf paled in com-parison to the overwhelming presence of photographs of wolves as social actors and skilled hunters of the weak and sick among prey herds. The first photographs in the positive genre of wolves as social actors were published in 1977, reflecting the banning of the predator poisoning programme in 1972 and the post-World War Two shifting public and scientific discourse towards the belief that nature and wildlife were part of a fragile web of life that includes predators and prey as essential components in ecosystem survival. In this discourse, wolves were part of a highly structured society, immersed in ritual play and dominance behaviours and the com-munal rearing of pups. The photographs confirm that as a social species, wolves make a large investment in raising the young, they are 'highly self-regulating and social regulating' in their sexual activity (usually only the alpha male and female produce pups) and pup-rearing behaviour (most adult members of the pack assume responsibility for pup-sitting).[90]

Wolf society is also extraordinarily structured around the ever-present task of obtaining food. While pictures of wolves prowling for and protecting food were popular in the magazine, the skill required for hunting large prey was an important part of the wolf iconography in *National Geographic* in photographs of the Dance of Death. Representing a 'timeless drama of predation', these photographs emphasised the taking of weak and sick members of prey herds by patient, powerful, intelligent wolves participating in the hunt as members of a highly organised hunting pack. The Dance of Death photographs began to be published in 1977 as part of the research on wolf-moose behaviours at Isle Royale, and the popularity of photographs of this particular wolf hunting motif continued for the rest of the century.

But now the sentiment toward wolves has taken another turn along with their successful reintroduction in many parts of the US: wolves are currently off the Endangered Species List in much of the US and both hunting and trapping to control wolf populations are widely encouraged. It is interesting that this shift

---

90. Donaldson and Kymlicka 2011, pp. 145–6.

in social discourse is reflected in *National Geographic* iconography with a standard trophy photograph of the first wolf taken during Idaho's 2010 hunting season – the last photograph of a wolf trophy was published in the magazine in 1925.

It is also provocative that while the captions for the wolf photographs were usually clear in their representation of particular social discourses on wolves, there was one picture of a snarling wolf that placed the interpretation of wolves up to the reader. The caption began with the stereotypical characterisations of wolves (the big bad wolf, the wolf at the door, throw him to the wolves) and ended on the note that the interpretation of the wolf depends on one's point of view. When viewing a negative image of a wolf, it comes as no surprise that a viewer would come away with an adverse interpretation. Perhaps *National Geographic* could have considered asking the same question with a picture of a serene, playful, happy wolf, of which there were many published in the magazine (more often than photos of snarling, aggressive wolves).

Indeed, photographs of wolves in peaceful portrait shots (serene, drowsy wolves captured on film sitting, standing, walking, sniffing flowers) were very common in the magazine. These photographs encouraged viewers to consider the beauty and majesty of the wolf, showcasing her personality and individuality. It was encouraging to see that *National Geographic* began to use this kind of positive visual representation of wolves in their photographs in the last quarter of the twentieth century. In addition, given the number of positive wolf images found in this study that came from one photographer (Joel Sartore), it is undeniable that photographers play a critical role in the construction of the social discourse on wolves. I acknowledge the highly selective process that decides which photographs will be published in *National Geographic* and this process has an influence on the discourse produced. A negotiation goes on between photographers and picture editors; photographers submit their photographs, and picture editors shape the photographs into stories, often advocating for the photographer's vision.[91] Further, conservation photographers have a substantial influence on viewers' perceptions of animals. Some of my prior work has documented that exposure to animal portraiture photographs in a museum setting impacts on museum visitors' feelings about animals by increasing perceptions of kinship and animal individuality.[92]

It was surprising to have so few photographs of aggressive, menacing wolves in the sample. Some argue that, throughout the transition from the first still photographs to modern glossy technology, the basic photographic guidelines for pictures of animals and the natural world has remained the same at the magazine, showing the immutable, unchanging, innate, ahistorical and reassuring laws of nature.[93] Focusing primarily on the message of nature and the natural world he sees conveyed

---

91. Lutz and Collins 1993, pp. 84–5.
92. Kalof, Zammit-Lucia and Kelly 2011.
93. Montgomery 1993, p. 15.

in *National Geographic* photographs, Scott Montgomery argues that the magazine's animal imagery is centred on 'nature as the abode of death'.[94] Nature, according to *National Geographic*, is all about the law of survival of the fittest, and 'death is law and the law is beautiful, an inspiring subject'.[95] It has also been documented that reading time and comprehension of textual information increases with victimisation photographs in news reports.[96] It is heartening to conclude that the argument that *National Geographic* animal imagery focuses primary on blood and 'death as the law' was not supported with the data on a hundred years of wolf iconography. It may, however, be the case that 'nature, red in tooth and claw' is the prominent message in the iconography of other predatory species in the magazine: that is a question left for another study.

Finally, as was expected for a popular science magazine, there were numerous photographs of wolves in educational and research settings. Many of the education-focused pictures emphasised the connection we humans have with wolves, the value of wolves in predator–prey ecosystems and the problem of wolves going extinct in a human-dominated world – all of which are aspects of a positive discourse on wolves promoted by the magazine. Research iconography on wolves was almost entirely of wolf reintroduction programmes, yet another way that *National Geographic* has advanced a positive social discourse on wolves.

While my prior work has found that animal representations in the popular culture are usually multilayered, with single photographs falling into one or more thematic categories,[97] this was not the case with wolf iconography. The photographs examined were easily coded into one thematic category. This consistency of thematic structure is likely the result of a close study of one species, rather than multiple species in a broad topical category such as problem animals or domestic animals. This is an interesting methodological note that deserves further analysis.

It is also important that *National Geographic* has published photographs that illustrate the problem of habituated wolves and the unfortunate circumstances that arise when their habituation comes into conflict with humans. O'Connor notes that people's tolerance of large bodied animals is understandably low, and coyotes are probably at the upper end of the size range to be adaptable to humans.[98] This does not bode well for wolves, who are larger than coyotes and who are currently considered habituated in some of the US, such as Vargas Island and parts of the upper peninsula of Michigan. We humans must learn ways to avoid habituating wolves to our presence and most importantly our food; it is encouraging to see that *National Geographic* is promoting the anti-habituation message in the pages of the

---

94. Ibid., p. 30, cited in Kalof and Amthor 2010, p. 176.
95. Montgomery 1993, p. 31.
96. Zillman, Knobloch and Yu 2001.
97. Kalof and Amthor 2010.
98. O'Connor 2013, p. 78.

magazine. While focused primarily on coyotes, O'Connor argues that people and predators need to strike a compromise – predators might 'gain access to garbage, windfall apples, and rodents, yet learn avoidance of humans, so as to minimise direct conflict ... this is a matter of cultural coevolution'.[99] A quote from an essay on wolf habituation as a conservation conundrum is appropriate here:

> Although wolves adapt quickly to changing dynamics, the same is not true for the humans that dominate the landscapes wolves are recolonizing ... increasingly, wolves pass within sight of people in national parks. The denizen of the wilderness is adapting quite well to human-dominated landscapes. The conundrum is that we have managed wolf recovery so successfully that conflict situations arise more frequently and we must anticipate potential backlash by the public to avoid slipping back into an anti-wolf fervor. New efforts to educate the public about the nature of wild wolves ... are working. People are warned to take reasonable precautions, and reassured that these alone should prevent conflicts with wolves. Still, helping maintain a balanced relationship between humans and expanding wolf populations will remain a significant conservation challenge.[100]

In the end, my study confirms that *National Geographic*'s wolf iconography is linked to the change in popular perceptions of wolves from detested 'varmints' in the early 1900s to a protected species and cultural icon in the late twentieth century. Since the 1970s, the magazine has promoted a positive social discourse on wolves, emphasising their social nature, curiosity, beauty and majesty. As Scarce argues, 'social constructions are lasting, integral products of social structure, much more so than often volatile values or attitudes ... in constructing wolves, social groups also construct society'.[101]

It would be interesting to examine the influence of popular science representations on the social discourse on wolves by geographical area. A recent content analysis of news media coverage indicates that the public discourse on wolves in the northern Rocky Mountain area of the US became increasingly negative from 1999 to 2008.[102] The authors attribute these findings to differences in discourses based on geographic exposure to wolves, with areas that have experienced reintroduced wolf populations expressing more negative attitudes than areas with permanent wolf populations. In addition, it is still common for the demonic wolf genre to occupy the social discourse on wolves in popular culture, such as the 2012 film *The Grey* with the hero human, Liam Neeson, battling a pack of ferocious wild wolves.

However, in spite of the resilience of some anti-wolf narratives that swirl in the cultural domain, given *National Geographic*'s role as the most widely-read popular science periodical in the world and my documentation of their overall positive

---

99.   Ibid., p. 131.
100.   Boyd, no date.
101.   Scarce 1998, p. 44.
102.   Houston, Bruskotter and Fan 2010.

Linda Kalof

messages about wolves, I am cautiously optimistic that positive wolf imagery will prevail. Thus, considering the critical role of science in generating social discourses on animals and the natural world, there may be long-term hope for wolves after all, at least in the minds of the reader (and photographers and editors) of *National Geographic*. In explicating how popular science is inexorably linked to the historical interplay of ideology, cultural narratives and media conventions about wolves and people, my work provides a better understanding of the historical processes by which features of wolves have come to seem salient. This understanding will hopefully lead to better research on the link between animal representations in popular science and the social conditions from which they emerge and to which they contribute.

ACKNOWLEDGEMENTS

This research was funded by a grant from the National Science Foundation (Award SES-1247824).

BIBLIOGRAPHY

Barthes, R. 1977. *Image, Music, Text. Essays Selected and Translated by Stephen Heath* (London: Fontana Press).

Boyd, D.K. no date. 'Wolf Habituation as a Conservation Conundrum', in M.J. Groom, G.K. Meffe and R. Carroll (eds) *A Companion to Principles of Conservation Biology*. Third edition, http://sites.sinauer.com/groom/article.php?id=24.

Brennen, B. and H. Hardt 1999. *Picturing the Past: Media, History, and Photography* (Champaign: University of Illinois Press).

Busch, R.H. 2007. *The Wolf Almanac: A Celebration of Wolves and their World* (Guilford CT: Lyons Press).

Clarke, G. 1997. *The Photograph* (Cambridge: Oxford University Press).

Crisler, L. 1999 [1956]. *Arctic Wild: The Remarkable True Story of One Couple's Adventure Living among Wolves* (New York: The Lyons Press).

Daum, A.W. 2009. 'Varieties of Popular Science and the Transformations of Public Knowledge: Some Historical Reflections'. *Isis* **100**: 319–32.

Donaldson, S. and W. Kymlicka. 2011. *Zoopolis: A Political Theory of Animal Rights* (New York: Oxford University Press).

Dunlap, T.R. 1988. *Saving America's Wildlife* (Princeton: Princeton University Press).

Emel, J. 1998. 'Are you Man enough, Big and Bad enough? Wolf Eradication in the US', in J. Wolch and J. Emel (eds) *Animal Geographies: Place, Politics, and Identity in the Nature-Culture Borderlands* (London: Verso) pp. 91–116.

Gaskell, I. 1991. 'History of Images', in P. Burke (ed.) *New Perspectives on Historical Writing* (Cambridge: Polity Press) pp. 168–92.

Gould, S.J. 1996. *The Mismeasure of Man* (New York: Norton).

Haraway, D. 1989. *Primate Visions: Gender, Race and Nature in the World of Modern Science* (New York: Routledge).

Houston, M.J., J.T. Bruskotter and D. Fan. 2010. 'Attitudes toward Wolves in the United States and Canada: A Content Analysis of the Print News Media, 1999–2008'. *Human Dimensions of Wildlife* 15: 389–403.

Kalof, L. and R.F. Amthor. 2010. 'Cultural Representations of Problem Animals in *National Geographic*'. *Etudes rurales* 185: 165–80.

Kalof, L. 2007. *Looking at Animals in Human History* (London: Reaktion).

Kalof, L. and A. Fitzgerald. 2003. 'Reading the Trophy: Exploring the Display of Dead Animals in Hunting Magazines'. *Visual Studies* 18: 112–22.

Kalof, L., J. Zammit-Lucia and J.R. Kelly. 2011. 'The Meaning of Animal Portraiture in a Museum Setting: Implications for Conservation'. *Organization & Environment* 24 (2): 150–74.

Latour, B. and S. Woolgar. 2013 [1979]. *Laboratory Life: The Construction of Scientific Facts* (Princeton: Princeton University Press).

Lutz, C.A. and J.L. Collins. 1993. *Reading National Geographic* (Chicago: University of Chicago Press).

Lynch, M. and S. Woolgar (eds). 1990. *Representation in Scientific Practice* (Cambridge: MIT Press).

Lynn, W.S. 2010. 'Discourse and Wolves: Science, Society, and Ethics'. *Society and Animals* 18 (1): 75–92.

Marvin, G. 2012. *Wolf* (London: Reaktion).

Montgomery, S. 1993. 'Through a Lens, Brightly: The World according to *National Geographic*'. *Science as Culture* 4 (1): 7–46.

Mowat, F. 1963. *Never Cry Wolf: The Amazing True Story of Life among Arctic Wolves* (New York: Back Bay Books).

National Geographic. 2012. *About the National Geographic Society.* http://press.nationalgeographic.com/about-national-geographic (accessed 1 November 2012).

O'Connor, T. 2013. *Animals as Neighbors: The Past and Present of Commensal Species.* (East Lansing: Michigan State University Press).

Scarce, R. 1998. 'What do Wolves Mean? Conflicting Social Constructions of Canis lupus in "bordertown"'. *Human Dimensions of Wildlife* 3 (3): 26–45.

Skogen, K., I. Mauz and O. Krange. 2006. 'Wolves and Eco-power: A French-Norwegian Analysis of the Narratives on the Return of Large Carnivores'. *Journal of Alpine Research* 94 (4): 78–87.

Sontag, S. 2003. *Regarding the Pain of Others* (New York: Picador).

Whitley, C.T. and L. Kalof. 2014. 'Animal Imagery in the Discourse of Climate Change'. *International Journal of Sociology* 44 (1): 10–33.

Linda Kalof

Wright, C. 2003. 'Supple Bodies: The Papua New Guinea Photographs of Captain Francis R. Barton, 1899–1907', in C. Pinney and N. Peterson (eds) *Photography's Other Histories* (Durham: Duke University Press) pp. 146–70.

Zillmann, D., S. Knobloch and H.S. Yu. 2001. 'Effects of Photographs on the Selective Reading of News Reports'. *Media Psychology* **3** (4): 301–24

11

Alaska Wild? Wolves in America's Last Frontier

Lydia A. Dixon

The little town of Chicken, Alaska, lies about 280 miles south-east of Fairbanks. Only around fifty people live there in the summer and the population drops to just six intrepid individuals in the winter.[1] Google Maps warns that the only road into Chicken, the Taylor Highway, 'may be seasonally closed'. Once a gold-mining town, Chicken now functions more as a summer tourist stopover and a refuge for those seeking to live the Alaskan frontier dream. It is nestled in Interior Alaska, where the landscapes are wild and the winters are long. The range of the Fortymile caribou herd circles close to the town, and hunters walk the nearby hills and forests in the fall and winter looking for trophy bulls.

Chicken also lies within the borders of another wildlife management unit: the Upper Yukon-Tanana Predator Control Area. Encompassing 18,750 square miles, its sub-designation is 'Wolf Control Area'. Here, the Alaska Department of Fish and Game (ADF&G), Alaska's state wildlife management agency, oversees a programme that reduces wolf populations in order to maintain opportunities for hunters to hunt and harvest ungulates, predominantly caribou and moose. Hunting is open to both residents and non-residents of Alaska, but if moose or caribou populations drop below a certain level the hunt becomes restricted to only residents.[2] Then, predator control measures are often considered in order to protect and increase prey populations. In the Upper Yukon/Tanana region, controversy has broiled in recent years, as this Wolf Control Area is adjacent to the Yukon-Charley National Preserve, managed by the National Park Service (NPS) – a federal agency. In 2009, Defenders of Wildlife, a national non-profit organisation with an office in Alaska but headquartered in Washington, D.C., filed an injunction to halt a helicopter-control programme intended to reduce the wolf population in this area by 250 animals. In a statement posted on the Defenders of Wildlife website, Alaska representative Wade Willis asserted:

> The Board of Game is out of control. The entire Upper Yukon/Tanana program is
> an extreme, unjustified and semi-hysterical effort to meet wolf kill target numbers
> that are arbitrary and not based on sound science. The State is acting without au-

---

1. Town of Chicken, AK: About Chicken Alaska, http://townofchicken.com/about-us/, para. 3.
2. Alaska Department of Fish and Game, Division of Wildlife Conservation 2013, p. 4.

thority, without public notice, and without any regard for the integrity of Alaska's national parks. They are trying to kill hundreds of wolves before anybody has time to discover the drastic changes in this program.[3]

The NPS requested conciliatory measures from the State of Alaska in order to protect wolves whose territories fell within the Preserve. Though the State agreed to use NPS radio frequencies to avoid targeting specific resident wolf packs, they refused to establish a buffer zone around the Preserve or reconsider population control target measures.[4] Two of the radio-collared wolves that the NPS had asked to be spared were subsequently shot, despite the prior agreement between the NPS and State of Alaska.[5] Whatever the motivations behind the lethal control decisions in this case – scientific or political – it is clear that wolf control in Alaska is a contentious issue, pitting state and federal agencies against each other and embattling conservation groups.

In some ways, wolf management belies the perceptions of Alaska by outsiders, or those stakeholders and individuals who do not live and work there.[6] There are at least two prominent conceptions of place that dominate Alaska's mystique. First, it is seen as a wilderness lover's nirvana and, second, as an enticing land for intrepid modern-day settlers seeking to test their survival mettle. The latter perception is evident through Alaska's popular nickname of 'the last frontier'. When viewed from either perspective on place, however, the romantic ideals of both untrammelled landscapes and frontier self-sufficiency appear disconnected from the state practice of intensive wolf management.

WOLVES, WILDNESS, AND THE LAST FRONTIER

Wildness and, by extension, wilderness, are important components of American identity, and the wolf is often the epitomic symbol of uncontrolled wildness – for better or worse. In Barry Lopez's seminal examination of the relationships between people and wolves, *Of Wolves and Men,* he explored the myriad ways wolves have shaped the imaginations of people from very different backgrounds and cultures in North America. Lopez wrote from just north of Fairbanks on the edge between settled and wild landscapes, in a valley where the neighbourhood dogs might fall victim to a local pack of wolves – and where the opinions on how to manage wolves spanned the gamut from eradication to total protection. Lopez argued that,

> The wolf exerts a powerful influence on the human imagination. It takes your stare

---

3. Defenders of Wildlife, no date, para. 5.
4. National Park Service 2009, pp. 2–3.
5. Cockerham 2010.
6. This observation is made by a self-professed outsider, as the author has travelled minimally in Alaska and bases her observations on what she has learned through media coverage, popular culture and academic publications.

and turns it back on you … People suddenly want to explain the feelings that come over them when confronted with that stare – their fear, their hatred, their respect, their curiosity.[7]

He continues,

I remember sitting in this cabin in Alaska one evening reading over the notes of all of these encounters, and recalling Joseph Campbell, who wrote in the conclusion to Primitive Mythology that men do not discover their gods, they create them. So do they also, I thought, looking at the notes before me, create their animals.[8]

Indeed, the perception of the nature of a wolf is intimately connected to the values of the observer. It is a killing beast, devouring livestock and game animals with abandon, or a mythical and beautiful animal worthy of the highest protection of law – or perhaps a little bit of both. In her review of the wolf in North American literary tradition, Karen Jones wrote, 'In American writings on wilderness, one animal has attained a remarkable resonance – *Canis lupus*, or the grey wolf'.[9] Much has been written about the symbolism of the grey wolf in North America, but its identity as intertwined with wilderness is particularly salient in Alaska.

The Discovery Channel, a US television network, features a weekly show that capitalises on the popular culture perception of Alaska as the last frontier of the United States. 'Alaska: The Last Frontier', is now in its third season. The programme follows the life of an Alaskan family living in the bush. Episodes document their efforts to survive off the land through moose hunting, gardening and building hay sheds from recovered materials. This show is not the only one to capitalise on a popular fascination with the US's fiftieth state, however. *The New York Daily News* reported, 'Alaska may be the coldest state on the thermometer, but it's the hottest state on television', and goes on to quote a resident 'mountain man': 'It's the last unexperienced place in America … Any other place you go, it's all been mapped, logged, hiked, game-managed'.[10] Several other reality shows highlight the allure and challenges of living in Alaska, from telling the stories of modern-day gold diggers ('Gold Rush') to wilderness survival competitions ('Ultimate Survival Alaska') and even real estate transactions ('Buying Alaska').[11] This popular fascination with the idea of the 'the last frontier' and the idea that one can just disappear in Alaska – while acknowledging that a specialised set of skills is necessary to survive in its remote regions – to some degree may fulfil the romantic yearnings of armchair travellers, who watch the landscape in all of its beauty and harshness unfold from the comfort of their living rooms and a 30-inch television set. These shows take advantage of

---

7.   Lopez 1978, p. 4.
8.   Ibid, p. 5.
9.   Jones, this volume.
10. Hinckley 2013, para. 3.
11. Ibid.

Lydia A. Dixon

myths that have been intrinsic to the American psyche since westward expansion, particularly in the domination or conquering of the frontier.

Anahita and Mix argue that the idea of Alaska as a 'masculine frontier' is perpetuated through the local media and also provides a strong sense of identity for state policymakers. Alaska crafts and embraces a 'myth' of itself as 'the last frontier'.[12] In the context of wolf management, the authors analyse how this distinctly Alaskan culture shapes wolf policy, specifically the case of aerial control, despite outside pressure to abolish this practice. Alaska is widely regarded as a wild place, where men initially moved to assert their heroic natures, seen through the classic images of the 'grizzled fur trapper and rugged gold prospector'.[13] The state government clings to the lethal control programme because it supports hunting culture, which is inherently masculine. Thus, killing wolves is integrated with the idea of frontier masculinity, to which the state government policies are tied.[14] In returning to the reality television shows that showcase the ideas that frontier and wilderness are not lost in the US, however, it would be curious to see the reactions of viewers to a programme focusing on the intensive game management protocols.

Roderick Nash, a prominent environmental historian, argues that the Alaska of 1980 was reminiscent of the American West at the turn of the century; in other words, it was predominantly unexplored wilderness. In contrast to the highways, subdivisions, airports and strip malls present in much of the American West today, in Alaska, 'the matrix was wild; civilization, not wilderness, was fragile'.[15] Technological advances, particularly in the realm of aircraft, enabled people to live on some of the most remote real estate in the United States, but it still took a frontier spirit and basic survival skills to thrive.[16] In the rest of the American West, the steady frontier expansion had eroded 'wilderness' to the point where it had to be protected by legislation, in order to survive as 'Wilderness'.[17] Though both wilderness - in the sense of a place unspoiled or untrammelled by civilisation – and frontier spirit are evident in Alaska, there is tension between letting wilderness stay wild, a romantic

---

12. Anahita and Mix 2006, p. 333.
13. Ibid., p. 334.
14. Ibid., pp. 336–7.
15. Nash 1982, p. 273.
16. Ibid., p. 273.
17. The Wilderness Act of 1964 defined 'wilderness' and provided a legal designation as such for qualifying lands: 'An area of wilderness is further defined to mean in this Act an area of undeveloped Federal land retaining its primeval character and influence, without permanent improvements or human habitation, which is protected and managed so as to preserve its natural conditions and which (1) generally appears to have been affected primarily by the forces of nature, with the imprint of man's work substantially unnoticeable; (2) has outstanding opportunities for solitude or a primitive and unconfined type of recreation; (3) has at least five thousand acres of land or is of sufficient size as to make practicable its preservation and use in an unimpaired condition; and (4) may also contain ecological, geological, or other features of scientific, educational, scenic, or historical value' (16 U.S.C. 1131-1136, 78 Stat. 890).

view embraced by wilderness advocates, versus controlling wilderness in order to survive, an approach that those who live in Alaska, such as state policymakers, are more likely to take – and which can be seen in the manner in which predators and prey are managed. The increasing popularity of Alaska-focused television shows likely benefits the latter perspective.

ALASKA: PRE-STATEHOOD

In 1879, John Muir wrote, 'To the lover of pure wildness Alaska is one of the most wonderful countries in the world'.[18] However, with the gold rush, intrepid homesteaders from the lower 48 states steadily migrated northward, and imported their persistently negative attitudes towards wolves. Much has been written about the attitudes of settlers of North America towards wolves, which can be tied to the European roots (and associated culture and myths) of many Americans. As Coleman argues, wolves posed a threat to life and property, two fundamental rights guaranteed in the US Constitution.[19] It was just a matter of time before these attitudes spilled over into policy even in the most remote territory of the United States.

By the 1920s, wolves had essentially been extirpated in the US's lower 48 states. Even the National Park Service facilitated the removal of wolves from within its park boundaries. Historian Timothy Rawlson documents the early roots of and early controversy over wolf management in then-Mount McKinley National Park in his thoroughly researched *Changing Tracks*. The practice of predator removal in the US was relatively uncontroversial at the time, and stemmed from

> ignorance of the functioning of biological systems and the need to follow dominant public attitudes – and hence continue congressional appropriations. Predator control policies were economic: wolves, coyotes, and pumas had no financial value, while livestock and hunting ranges adjacent to national parks did.[20]

The story in Alaska, however, was somewhat different from that which played out in the lower 48 states. Given the vastness of the landscape, it was difficult to achieve wholesale predator eradication. Furthermore, the livestock industry, one of the constituencies that called for wolf eradication in the West, never really became established in Alaska, despite a brief stint in reindeer husbandry.[21] Though Alaskan

---

18. At this time, Alaska was a territory of the United States, having been purchased from Russia in 1867 for $7.2 million in a treaty negotiated by Secretary of the Interior William Seward. The new land acquisition was affectionately referred to as 'Seward's Folly'.

19. For a more in-depth treatment of this topic, see Coleman 2006, which chronicles the evolution of the relationship between wolves and people over time, from eradication throughout most of the lower 48 states and circling back to the social climate prompting reintroduction.

20. Rawson 2001, p. 60.

21. Ibid., pp. 88–93.

wolves appeared to have survival advantages (at least in comparison to their southern counterparts), policymakers still were not fond of their hunting competition.

In 1939, the Superintendent of Denali (then Mount McKinley) National Park, Henry Like, commissioned Adolph Murie, a renowned US ecologist and conservationist, to study the wolves within the park's boundaries. Park managers were concerned about the impacts of predators on prey species, which were also popular for hunting. Murie was tasked with evaluating the role of wolves in the park's ecosystems, and particularly how predation affected populations of Dall sheep (*Ovis dalli*).[22] Part of the impetus for the Park Service's interest in learning more about the relationships between these two resident species was pressure from hunters to reduce wolf numbers within the Park. The common perception was that the decline of sheep populations was directly correlated with the number of wolves in and around the Park.[23] Politicians and sportsmen alike saw McKinley National Park as 'a sanctuary for wolves'[24] – and this impression was not a favourable one. Despite this pressure, though, Murie recognised that the wolf still had value – both intrinsic and ecological. In the foreword to his final report, *The Wolves of Mount McKinley*, Murie wrote:

> The wolf is a powerful animal, and a cunning one, and unfortunately has run counter to the economic interests of man in settled regions … however, many persons wish to retain the wolf somewhere in the North American fauna, perhaps in the more remote parts of the continent, in wilderness areas where there will not be interferences from economic interests.[25]

Mount McKinley National Park, with its vast swathes of wilderness, could be just the place to provide a refuge for wolves and further study their role in ecosystems. Murie advocated scientific research to provide the basis for policy-making by park managers, but he was reticent about delving into policy recommendations himself. He observed the direct impacts of the wolf on ungulate populations, noting that the wolf was the 'chief check' on Dall sheep populations. Wolves also predominantly hunted caribou, though no significant impact on the viability of the caribou herds could be found at that time.[26] Murie concluded that national parks represent 'a specialised type of land use' and policies implemented 'may differ from those applicable to lands devoted to other uses'.[27] Murie likely understood that the more protective management approach implemented by the National Park Service

---

22. Murie 1985.
23. Rawson 2001, p. 126.
24. Ibid.
25. Murie 1985, p. xiv.
26. Curiously, the moose – the touchstone ungulate for much of the debate over wolf management in Alaska today – did not appear to be affected by the number of wolves in the park. In fact, the moose population appeared to increase during Murie's study period (Murie 1985, p. xiv).
27. Ibid, p. 232.

to preserve wolves in Mount McKinley National Park would probably not spill over to lands outside the park boundaries.

At the time, the idea of protecting wolves in Denali antagonised many Alaskans. Even prior to Murie's surveys, the unique preservation mandate of the Park Service arguably sparked more intensive management practices, including lethal control, by the Alaska Game Commission on state lands. In Rawson's comprehensive history of the controversy over wolves and sheep in Mount McKinley National Park, he quoted a particularly revealing editorial written in 1936 and published in the Fairbanks newspaper: 'If Alaska is to preserve her game and fur animals she – with the aid of the federal government – must wake up and carry relentless warfare into the ranks of the enemy – not tomorrow but today – not at some convenient season but in this hour of emergency'.[28] The Park Service was both geographically and politically isolated in its alternative approach to wolf management – not dissimilar to the situation that still appears to persist today.

ALASKA: POST-STATEHOOD POLICY

Many Alaskans (both Native communities and residents) depend on subsistence hunting, or harvesting wild fish and game, in order to survive. Land ownership is a factor playing a role in how hunting access and privileges have been allocated. Land ownership policies began to change in the early 1970s, beginning with the Alaska Native Claims Settlement Act (ANCSA) in 1971, which essentially resolved all native land claims. In 1978, Alaska passed a subsistence law that basically promotes human survival (in terms of access to hunted meat) above other wildlife management considerations when the Board of Game sets policy.[29] Federal land managers are also bound by a similar policy, as elaborated in the Alaska National Interest Lands Conservation Act (ANILCA), which was passed in 1980 and permits the harvesting of game species on federal lands.[30] The primary goal of ANILCA, however, is to safeguard Alaska's wilderness. 'Conservation system units', or chunks of land managed by one of several federal agencies, protected 104 million acres, though often with the input of the State of Alaska so as to defend its interests.[31] ANILCA designated 44 million acres to the national park system, 57 million acres to wilderness and 59 million acres to wildlife refuges.[32] Following ANCSA and ANILCA, both native and federal land interests in Alaska had been addressed – leaving the state 'third in line' for land claims and subsequently 'outraged'.[33] Perhaps there exists lingering

---

28. Rawson 2001, p. 129.
29. Titus 2007, pp. 367–8.
30. Ibid.
31. State participation in the policy process is mandated by the Act.
32. Nelson 2004, p. 5.
33. Gallagher and Gasbarro 1989, p. 440.

resentment over how this federal legislation and land allocation transpired, which may contribute to why wolf management today seems to be often antipathetic to the policies of the National Park Service. Granted, the debate over wolf management has existed since the birth of the National Park Service's presence in Alaska, so perhaps this landmark legislation exacerbated an already-strained relationship.[34]

LETHAL CONTROL

Alaska is remote. Few roads exist, and backcountry access is challenging. The ADF&G often relies on aircraft for wildlife management through aerial shooting, or 'taking or attempting to take an animal by discharging a firearm from an airborne aircraft', and 'land-and-shoot', where managers fly to locate the animals, but land before shooting.[35] Aerial hunting has a long history in Alaska; Rawson tells the story of an Alaskan game warden, Sam White, who piloted an aerial survey of Dall sheep in 1939 – and then suggested that if animals could easily be counted from the air, they could just as easily be shot.[36] Over time, concern over the impacts of wolves on game populations shifted away from Dall sheep to moose and caribou. Lethal wolf management became more common in the late 1940s and federal agencies were actually the first to conduct aerial control, not the state. Other tactics included bounties and poisoning. The goal then, as it remains now, was to protect ungulate populations.[37] Increased regulatory oversight occurred with the Airborne Hunting Act of 1971, which prohibited hunting from aircraft unless for the protection of wildlife, property or human life. The aerial gunning policy in Alaska is and was legally justified under the 'protection of wildlife' clause.[38]

However, in a departure from established policy and under pressure from constituents outside of Alaska, in 1994 Governor Tony Knowles suspended the lethal control programme and requested its review by the National Academy of Sciences (NAS). Their report, released in 1997, collated economic, social, scientific and political issues to try to understand what type of predator control policy (if any) would be acceptable in Alaska. The report found that it was not clear if the predator control programme helped to increase big game populations. It also suggested that predator control policies should be designed using a more participatory process and that research projects should explore economic and social factors beyond just ecological data on moose populations to create policy.[39] Based on these results,

---

34. The tension between federal and state management may be better assessed through a future qualitative, interview-based study in order to substantiate this proposition.
35. Alaska Department of Fish and Game 2007, p. 3.
36. Rawson 2001, pp. 128–9.
37. Regelin 2002.
38. Defenders of Wildlife 2011, p. 3.
39. Committee on Management of Wolf and Bear Populations in Alaska 1997, pp. 182–93.

Governor Knowles required that any management policy '(1) be based on sound science, (2) be cost-effective and (3) be broadly acceptable to the public'.[40] These directives prove to still be challenging.

There was some hope for more inclusive, publicly acceptable wildlife management decision processes. Also in 1994, a novel planning approach was piloted for the Fortymile Caribou herd. A diverse group of constituents made up the Fortymile Caribou Herd Planning Team, which held public meetings designed to capitalise on a 'wide range of experiences, wisdom, and interest in the problem to be solved. Many minds of varied viewpoints, but shared vision, developed the unique solutions in this planning effort and were able to support the recommendations.'[41] Understanding that predator management was critical to the health of the caribou herd, but also realising that lethal control would be a divisive issue, not in keeping with the intent of the group, a non-lethal management programme was proposed that focused on fertility control and translocation. Once the plan reached consensus within the group, it was presented to and approved by the necessary government organisations. Finally, and crucially, it passed muster with Governor Knowles and his aforementioned criteria, marking 'the first time in more than two decades that a predator control program in Alaska had been endorsed by both the state and federal management agencies, and state government'.[42] The Plan was in place from 1996–2001, during which the caribou population grew by 78 per cent. Wolf populations also showed signs of recovery by 2004.[43] Unfortunately, data indicated that the caribou population began to drop between 2004 and 2005 and the 2006–2012 Fortymile Caribou Herd Harvest Plan mandated that 'it [was] *absolutely* necessary to implement a lethal wolf predation control program'.[44] The success of and lessons learned from the collaborative planning process appear to have been abandoned, though exactly why is unclear.

WOLF MANAGEMENT TODAY

Today, the Alaska Department of Fish and Game (ADF&G) is directly responsible for the practical tasks related to managing wolf populations in the state. How wolves are managed, however, is determined by the Alaska Board of Game, which is a seven-member panel appointed by the governor of Alaska and confirmed by the state legislature. Informed by ecological and social data provided by the ADF&G, public input and other state agencies, the Board of Game establishes hunting seasons and protected areas and provides direction on managing wildlife for the interests

---

40. Ibid., p. 368.
41. Gronquist et al. 2005, p. 166.
42. Ibid., p. 170.
43. Ibid., p. 173.
44. Alaska Department of Fish and Game 2006, p. 3.

of different stakeholder groups.[45] Implementation and enforcement of the policies enacted by the Board of Game are the responsibility of ADF&G. The most recent Board of Game Wolf Management Policy, passed in 2011 and valid until 30 June 2016, acknowledges the range of values that people hold for wolves, as 'furbearers, big game animals, competitors for ungulate prey animals, and as subjects of enjoyment, curiosity, and study' and acknowledges that wolves have an ecological role as well.[46] Interestingly, the first three reasons listed by the Board of Game policy are those that identify a potentially adversarial relationship between wolves and people, essentially setting the context for a policy that justifies intensive management. It explicitly rationalises lethal management of wolves based on the Board of Game's understanding of the relationship between predators and prey:

> The Board also recognizes that when conflicts arise between humans and wolves over the use of prey, wolf populations may have to be managed more intensively to minimize such conflicts ... Under some conditions, it may be necessary to greatly reduce wolf numbers to aid recovery of low prey populations or to arrest undesirable reductions in prey populations. In some other areas, including national park lands, the Board also recognizes that non-consumptive uses of wolves may be considered a priority use.[47]

Not unexpectedly, the methods of wolf management are highly controversial. There are questions as to whether harvesting wolves, particularly from aircraft, is congruent with hunting ethics that advocate fair chase. These methods also seem somewhat married to tradition, hearkening to the days of wolf bounties, though now abetted by the technology of aircraft, which, as Roderick Nash pointed out, Alaska has embraced.[48] Deep-seated cultural values also shape human attitudes towards wolves. Few other species, if any, are managed with this level of violence.

Subsistence hunters and other Alaskan residents are not absent from the discussion. Brown and Decker, of Cornell's Human Dimensions Research Unit, conducted an analysis of Alaskan residents' (not hunter-specific) attitudes towards predator management in 2003 and found that many were polarised as to how and when it was appropriate to lethally-control predators. Through a public survey of households living within wolf management unit number 13 (which is located in eastern Alaska, beginning just north of Anchorage), researchers found that, in general, Alaskans like wildlife and perceive themselves to be quite knowledgeable about it. Residents tend to favour predator control to maintain subsistence-hunting opportunities, though. In fact, the authors of this study found that 'prey availability for human use is the heart of the issue for many Alaskans'.[49] This finding

---

45. Board of Fisheries and Game 2012.
46. Alaska Board of Game 2011, p. 1.
47. Ibid.
48. Nash 1982, p. 276.
49. Brown and Decker 2003, p. 4.

corroborates the goal stated in the Alaska Board of Game's wolf management policy to ensure that prey is available for people to hunt. But the authors also found that support for predator control is

> conditional ... In only one of 6 situations did a majority of statewide respondents indicate support for lethal predator control – *when predation reduces prey populations to the point that some local residents who rely on game for food are unable to find moose or caribou to hunt.*[50]

In fact, residents tended to prefer 'no action' – or no authorisation of the use of lethal control – when the impact of predators on prey populations was perceived to affect the success rate of non-resident hunters who would *not* depend on their hunt for food. This finding trumped even the fact that the local economy could be negatively affected if the number of hunters from outside the area declined.[51] Though residents do not wholeheartedly support a blanket policy to always lethally control wolves, the sentiment that the state should intervene so intensively in wildlife management in these remote areas seems somewhat contradictory to the independent, rugged individualist frontier mentality so often associated with Alaska and Alaskans.

Defenders of Wildlife remains active in Alaskan wolf management. The Defenders of Wildlife Action Fund, a political action and lobbying group that is an offshoot of its parent organisation, launched an advertising campaign in 2010 in response to the Discovery Channel's promotion of a new series, 'Sarah Palin's Alaska'. They also sponsored ads that highlighted her support of the aerial wolf hunt. Through provocative photographs of dead wolves and pithy captions,[52] the ads presented the Alaskan wolf situation to an audience unfamiliar with the duration or nuance of the controversy at a time when public interest in Sarah Palin perhaps brought a bit more attention to Alaska and its natural resource management policies. Then, in 2011, Defenders released a new report: 'Alaska's Predator Control Programs: Managing for Abundance or Abundant Mismanagement?' Defenders believes that state lawmakers largely ignore the recommendations provided by the NAS report released in 1997. The 2011 document broadly articulated the goals of the wildlife conservation stakeholder constituency, arguing that Alaskan predator control programmes (specifically for wolves) are still not scientifically sound and yet are liberally implemented.[53]

---

50. Ibid.
51. Ibid.
52. For example, ads asserted, 'Discovery just redefined obscenity on TV: Sarah Palin as an Alaskan wildlife show host' and 'You have to be pretty cold to hire someone who supports using poison gas on wolf pups'. The ads can no longer be found on the Defenders website, though they can be found through a Google image query. See Barnett 2010 for media coverage of the controversy.
53. Defenders of Wildlife 2011.

Lydia A. Dixon

To return to the National Park Service's (NPS) lands in Alaska, federal land managers are obligated to conserve natural resources. Their mandate, as declared in the Organic Act of 1916, is *'to conserve the scenery and the natural and historic objects and the wildlife therein and to provide for the enjoyment of the same in such manner and by such means as will leave them unimpaired for the enjoyment of future generations*.'[54] The problem, however, is that wolf packs do not heed political boundaries. A recent headline in the *Alaska Dispatch* illustrated this conflict: 'Has Alaska wolf-control forced park population to nosedive?' Alaska's lethal control policies in areas surrounding the Yukon-Charley Rivers National Preserve, a land area managed by the National Park Service, affected the wolves that travel between the state-managed and federally-protected lands. In fact, according to the National Park Service, wolf populations within the federally protected reserve have dropped fifty per cent since the fall of 2012.[55] The National Park Service explicitly prohibits lethal control of wolves (and other predators) on lands under their jurisdiction. The federal pre-emption doctrine establishes that federal law supersedes state law in cases where there is conflict. In this case, the intensive management law conflicts with federal mandates provided in the Alaska National Interest Lands Conservation Act (ANILCA) for managing wildlife on lands overseen by the National Park Service and the US Fish and Wildlife Service.[56] The state of Alaska, however, does not violate any legal doctrines by intensively managing wolves on the edges of federally protected lands that abut state lands, though doing so furthers conflict and adversarial relationships between state and federal land management authorities.

After the wolf control actions in this area in spring of 2013, park superintendent Greg Dudgeon said, 'We've had no formal communication from the State of Alaska on results of their helicopter and fixed-wing predator control work in the Fortymile country ... But through informal conversations we understand they were focusing efforts in the areas outside the preserve'.[57] This example illustrates an overt power play by the state to control wolves that the Park Service views as important for values other than hunting, the foremost being preservation but secondarily, and by extension, tourism and ecosystem function. The NAS report advocated increased cooperation between the managers of state and federal lands, observing, 'interagency cooperation could improve management, reduce public confusion, and eliminate unnecessary duplication'.[58] However, the State of Alaska's behaviour in this case appears to be an example of the independent, anti-federal attitude discussed earlier. Very little effort, if any, was expended to try to mitigate

---

54. The National Park Service Organic Act (16 U.S.C. 1 2 3, and 4).
55. Medred 2013, para. 1.
56. Lurman 2007, pp. 151–4.
57. Medred 2013, para. 9.
58. Committee on Management of Wolf and Bear Populations in Alaska 1997, p. 13.

the antagonism between state and federal managers. This lack of communication is problematic and adversarial.

The movement of wolves between Denali National Park and surrounding areas, particularly in the north-east region, has also been a source of conflict between state officials and federal land managers. For ten years, from 2000 to 2010, the Alaska Board of Game maintained a no-hunting, no-trapping buffer zone in two areas bordering the north-east corner of the Park. However, despite a request in 2010 for the buffer to be expanded, the Alaska Board of Game instead decided to eliminate it all together.[59] Wildlife viewing, and in particular, wolf viewing is an important draw for tourists to Denali – and, by extension, to Alaska. Visitors to Denali are keen to see charismatic megafauna, such as wolves and bears, and travel websites extol the magnificence of Denali's landscape and wildlife; National Geographic's Travel website on Denali boasts, 'The farther you go, the more you'll see, for the subarctic landscape will open up as big as the sky and the animals will move through it with wild, ancient poetry. Other North American parks have their wildlife, but none has animals as visible or diverse as Denali.'[60] However, data published by the National Park Service estimated that the number of wolves found in the Park in the spring of 2013 was the lowest since 1987.[61] An overview of an in-progress research project analysing the decline of wolf 'viewability' in the Park, available on Denali's website, says that 'more than anywhere else in Alaska, wolves in the eastern part of Denali provide significant benefits to tourism'.[62] The study, which had a publication target date of 2014, aims to explore reasons for the decline in wolf viewings, and what impact the state's policy has on wolf visibility within the Park.[63]

After the data was made public in late 2013, wolf proponents asked US Secretary of the Interior Sally Jewel and Governor of Alaska Sean Parnell to reconsider enacting a buffer zone around the periphery of this area of Denali National Park. A coalition of environmental organisations, citizens and business owners requested an easement (or similar designation) in order to eliminate trapping and hunting, and thus hopefully recover the wolf populations within the eastern region of the Park.[64] After the news regarding wolf numbers and sightings was published, the *Alaska Dispatch* reported in early December that discussion over wolf numbers and the reasons for wolf decline illustrated 'another episode of state-federal conflict in

---

59. Demer 2013.
60. National Geographic, no date, para. 2–3.
61. Denali National Park 2013a.
62. Denali National Park 2013b, para. 1.
63. Ibid. The wolf viewing index published by the authors on Denali National Park's website indicates that in 2010, 45% of visitors traveling on a Denali bus saw wolves, while in 2013, that proportion had dropped to 4%.
64. Toppenberg et al. 2013.

Alaska'.[65] The article went on to interview both Philip Hooge, Denali's assistant superintendent of resources, and the chair of the Alaska Board of Game, Ted Spraker. In their back-and-forth dialogue, it appears that the issue stems from each accusing the other of a lack of transparency and a struggle over power – issues that seem historically to permeate Alaskan wolf management. Though other potential causes for the wolf decline have been ruled out by the Park, such as reduced prey availability and disease, Spraker did not appear convinced.[66] The story of Denali's most visible wolves remains unconcluded, though Spraker is quoted advocating dialogue: 'We need to sit down and talk about it and get it out in the open'.[67] Perhaps an opportunity for a new model of co-agency wolf management is brewing, but, given the long history of animosity between federal and state agencies, it may be more difficult than Spraker admits.

Nonetheless, scientific research appears to be selectively applied by the Board of Game. The Board does not appear to want to change wolf management policies that are unpopular, and persistently pins wolves as the scapegoats for moose population decline. Other confounding factors are also at play in the relationship between moose, wolves and people; however, the Board of Game insists on boiling their management policy down to one simple conclusion with one simple solution: wolves kill moose, so wolves should be killed. Even in 2002, Wayne Regelin, the Director of the Division of Wildlife Conservation at ADF&G, acknowledged the role of public opinion in managing wolves in a presentation to the Board. He observed, 'Wolf management is complex, because sociological considerations are more influential than biological information. The majority of the American public and a sizeable proportion of the Alaskan public do not want the department to undertake wolf control'.[68] Despite pressure from various stakeholders, both inside and outside of Alaska, the political power still rests with the Board of Game.

CONCLUSIONS

For wolves, there is a fundamental tension over federal versus state management that is potent in Alaska. The 'border zones', or those areas where the State's lethal management of wolves may result in pack decline or eradication within federally protected lands, are still tough places to be wolves – or wolf managers. The State of Alaska may be reluctant to relinquish power over setting wolf policy, despite critiques from within and outside Alaska, as well as the lack of a clear justification

---

65. DeMarban 2013, para. 1.
66. A caveat here: the source is a newspaper article, and so information may have been selectively presented at the discretion of the journalist.
67. DeMarban, para. 20.
68. Regelin, 2002, p. 6.

– scientific[69] or otherwise – for the perpetuation of this controversial and resource-intensive policy. Perhaps state policymakers fear a slippery slope. If wolf management were fundamentally rethought, and a cooperative approach between federal agencies and/or local communities implemented, the potential of losing absolute power over the governance of other resources could follow as well – for better or worse, with even higher stakes.[70] It seems there could be opportunities for small pilot projects to manage wolves in a local, or borough-by-borough, manner, using a stakeholder model where all relevant parties can be included in a discussion about management objectives and tools to attain those objectives. Thus far, however, the impression through the media is that the situation today simply echoes the long-term political stagnation over resolving struggles between state and federal authority. To maintain power, the state is comfortable with the irony of heavy-handed predator (and, by extension, prey) management in a place whose wilderness and self-sufficiency are extolled in popular culture throughout the rest of the country.

These policies are emblematic of the state-centric attitudes prevalent here, as well as the notion of needing to 'take matters into one's own hands' in order to survive. Intensive predator management practices are primarily socially and culturally determined and accepted. Activism or pressure from 'outsiders' – such as environmental organisations and even the National Park Service as it is a federal agency – likely will not have much impact in changing wolf management in Alaska. Because the seven members of the Board of Game are tasked with managing Alaska's wildlife resources, any fundamental changes will have to originate from within this group. Members are appointed by the governor and must exhibit 'interest in public affairs, good judgment, knowledge, and ability in the field of action of the board, with a view to providing diversity of interest and points of view in the membership'.[71] These criteria, though important and valuable, perhaps do not encompass the necessity of having expertise in understanding scientific evidence that may not support heavy-handed wolf management across the state. Allowing that Alaska's wildlife is a national interest, and given the economic value of tourism, particularly on lands under the jurisdiction of the National Park Service, it may be worthwhile to consider allowances for less controversial wolf management tactics in places where these non-consumptive uses are prevalent.

---

69. Though not discussed extensively here, controversy exists over the rigour of scientific studies used to justify the lethal control programme as a means to bolster moose populations. Some argue (e.g. Van Ballenberghe 2006) that lethal predator control does not help moose populations; other research documents growth in calf recruitment following the removal of predators from a study area (e.g. Keech et al. 2011), though increasingly other factors are recognised as having some influence as well (e.g. Boertje et al. 2010).

70. Examples that come to mind include trophy hunting of other species, oil and gas development, timber extraction, etc.

71 Alaska Department of Fish and Game: http://www.adfg.alaska.gov/index.cfm?adfg=gameboard.main

Lydia A. Dixon

The wolf population in Alaska is probably not under any immediate threat state-wide because of the vast and remote swathes of available habitat. However, the political battle over how wolves are managed likely will continue to cause strife and ill will in Alaska and beyond among a diversity of interested stakeholders. Wolf management in Alaska, as in other places throughout the American West, has been and continues to be a struggle over values. Alaska has two advantages: wilderness and a cultural appreciation of self-reliance. Though these traits are evident in other western states as well, they are exemplified on a much grander scale here. If the historical debate over wolf management could be satisfactorily resolved through a change in policy or a reframing of the policy process – perhaps piloted first in the contested areas just outside NPS lands – the case of Alaskan wolf management could be an example and paradigm for other western states struggling with similar issues. Perhaps this change could be sparked by a few friendly phone calls and a willingness on the part of managers and policymakers to try some new tactics. Until this happens, however, wolf management in Alaska is likely to continue in the tradition of lethal control via helicopters and high-powered rifles.

BIBLIOGRAPHY

Alaska Board of Game. 2011. Board of Game Wolf Management Policy. 2011-185-BOG.

Alaska Department of Fish and Game. 2006. Fortymile Caribou Herd Harvest Plan, 2006-2012. Alaska Department of Fish and Game: Juneau, AK. Retrieved 5 May 2014 from http://www.adfg.alaska.gov/static/home/about/management/wildlifeplanning/pdfs/fortymile_harvest_plan_2006_2012.pdf

Alaska Department of Fish and Game, Division of Wildlife Conservation. 2007. Predator Management in Alaska. Alaska Department of Fish and Game: Juneau, AK.

— 2013. Annual Report to the Alaska Board of Game on Intensive Management for Moose and Caribou with Wolf Predation Control in the Upper Yukon/Tanana Rivers. Alaska Department of Fish and Game: Juneau, AK.

Alaska Department of Fish and Game. Welcome to the Alaska Board of Game. Retrieved 15 March 2014 from http://www.adfg.alaska.gov/index.cfm?adfg=gameboard.main

Anahita, S. and T.L. Mix. 2006. 'Retrofitting Frontier Masculinity for Alaska's War against Wolves'. *Gender & Society* 20 (3): 332–353.

Barnett, L. 9 April 2010. 'Wildlife Group urges Discovery to drop Sarah Palin's Docu-Series'. *Los Angeles Times*. Retrieved 28 April 2013 from http://latimesblogs.latimes.com/unleashed/2010/04/wildlife-group-urges-discovery-to-drop-sarah-palins-docuseries.html

Boards of Fisheries and Game. 2012. Alaska Statutes §16.05.221.

Boertje, Rodney D., M.A. Keech and T.F. Paragi. 2010. 'Science and Values influencing Predator Control for Alaska Moose Management'. *Journal of Wildlife Management* 74 (5): 917–28.

Brown, T.L. and D.J. Decker. 2003. 'Alaska Residents' Attitudes toward Predator Management Statewide and in Unit 13: Executive Summary'. HDRU Publ. 03-4. Department of Natural Resources, N.Y.S. College of Agriculture and Life Sciences (Ithaca: Cornell University).

Cockerham, S. 18 March 2010. 'Collared Wolves killed During Aerial Predator Control'. *Anchorage Daily News*. http://www.adn.com/2010/03/18/1189910/collared-wolves-killed-in-predator.html

Coleman, J.T. 2006. *Vicious: Wolves and Men in America* (New Haven: Yale University Press).

Committee on Management of Wolf and Bear Populations in Alaska. 1997. *Wolves, Bears, and their Prey in Alaska: Biological and Social Challenges in Wildlife Management* (Washington, D.C.: National Academy Press).

Defenders of Wildlife. 2011. *Alaska's Predator Control Programs: Managing for Abundance or Abundant Mismanagement?* (Washington D.C.: Defenders of Wildlife).

— no date. Wildlife conservation group moves to block illegal Upper Yukon/Tanana Wolf Killing Program, http://www.defenders.org/press-release/wildlife-conservation-group-moves-block-illegal-upper-yukontanana-wolf-killing-program

DeMarban, A. 3 December 2013. 'Alaska, Federal Officials Spar over Decline in Denali Wolf Sightings. Alaska Dispatch'. http://www.alaskadispatch.com/article/20131203/alaska-federal-officials-spar-over-decline-denali-wolf-sightings

Demer, L. 17 May 2013. 'Where have all the Denali wolves gone?' *Anchorage Daily News*. Accessed on 4 November 2013 at http://www.adn.com/2013/05/17/2906539/where-have-all-the-denali-wolves.html

Denali National Park. 2013a. 'Wolf Survey Data, Spring (approx. 15 March), Denali National Park and Preserve, 1986–2013'. http://www.nps.gov/dena/naturescience/upload/Wolf-Survey-Data-Spring-1986to2013.pdf

— 2013b. 'Wolf Viewing Project'. http://www.nps.gov/dena/naturescience/wolfviewing.htm

Gallagher, T.J. and A.F. Gasbarro. 1989. 'The Battles for Alaska: Planning in America's last Wilderness'. *Journal of the American Planning Association* 55 (4): 433–44.

Gronquist, R.M., T.L. Haynes and C. Gardner. 2005. 'Rebuilding the Fortymile Caribou Herd: A Model of Cooperative Management Planning'. *Rangifer* 16: 163–75.

Hinckley, D. 15 December 2013. 'The Unexplored Regions of Alaska have been a Magnet for Reality Television Shows'. *New York Daily News*. http://www.nydailynews.com/entertainment/tv-movies/alaska-magnet-reality-television-article-1.1545928

Keech, M.A., M.S. Lindberg, R.D. Boertje, P. Valkenburg, B.D. Taras, T.A. Boudreau and K.B. Beckman. 2011. 'Effects of Predator Treatments, Individual Traits, and Environment on Moose Survival in Alaska'. *Journal of Wildlife Management* 75 (6): 1361–80.

Lopez, B. 1978. *Of Wolves and Men* (New York: Charles Scribner's Sons).

Lurman, J. and S.P. Rabinowitch. 2007. 'Preemption of State Wildlife Law in Alaska: Where, When, and Why'. *Alaska Law Review* 24: 145–71.

Medred, C. 11 April 2013. 'Has Alaska Wolf-Control forced Park Population to Nosedive?' *Alaska Dispatch*. Retrieved from http://www.alaskadispatch.com/article/20130411/has-alaskas-wolf-control-efforts-forced-nosedive-yukon-charley-population

Murie, A. 1985. *The Wolves of Mount McKinley* (Seattle: University of Washington Press).

Nash, R. 1982. *Wilderness and the American Mind* (New Haven: Yale University Press).

National Geographic. no date. 'Denali National Park'. http://travel.nationalgeographic.com/travel/national-parks/denali-national-park/

National Park Service. 2009. 'Briefing Statement. Issue: ADF&G shooting wolves from helicopters adjacent to YUCH'. Retrieved from: http://www.wolfsongnews.org/news/wolf_kill/YUCH%20Wolf%20Control%20Briefing%20Statement%203-15-09.pdf

Nelson, D. 2004. Northern Landscapes: The Struggle for Wilderness Alaska. Resources for the Future (Washington, D.C).

Rawson, T. 2001. *Changing Tracks: Predators and Politics in Mount McKinley National Park* (Fairbanks: University of Alaska Press).

Regelin, W. 2002. 'Wolf Management in Alaska with an Historic Perspective. Presentation to the Alaska Board of Game'. Retrieved online at http://www.adfg.alaska.gov/index.cfm?adfg=intensivemanagement.historicwolf

Titus, K. 2007. 'Intensive Management of Wolves and Ungulates in Alaska'. Transactions of the North American Wildlife and Natural Resources Conference (Portland: Wildlife Management Institute).

Toppenberg, J. et al. 27 November 2013. 'Re: Denali National Park wildlife buffer conservation easement exchange or purchase between the State of Alaska and the United States'. Letter to Honorable Sally Jewel, Secretary, U.S. Dept. of Interior, and Honorable Sean Parnell, Governor, State of Alaska. http://bloximages.newyork1.vip.townnews.com/newsminer.com/content/tncms/assets/v3/editorial/3/ef/3efbd5e6-57d1-11e3-b091-0019bb30f31a/5296a4c964b77.pdf

Van Ballenberghe, V. 2006. 'Predator Control, Politics, and Wildlife Conservation in Alaska'. *Alces* 42: 1–11.

12

Not an Easy Road to Success: The History of Exploitation and Restoration of the Wolf Population in Poland after World War Two

Robert W. Mysłajek and Sabina Nowak

INTRODUCTION

In Poland, as in many other European countries, the wolf (*Canis lupus*) has always aroused extreme emotions. On the one hand, it was treated as a pest and ruthlessly exterminated and, on the other hand, people found this species extremely fascinating. The author of the first Polish popular science monograph on the species, published in 1926, wrote with nostalgia: 'The wolf adds a peculiar charm to the forest and arouses fear in the eyes of the mob. So, when the last of these predators dies, our forests will ultimately lose their aureole of remote wilderness.'[1] Without a doubt, however, the pro-nature sentiments were dimmed by an aversion to this predator, leading to incessant attempts of extermination, interrupted only when people focused on fighting their own species, at times of rebellion and war. An analysis of archival data from the Białowieża Primeval Forest in the nineteenth and twentieth centuries shows that periods of high wolf densities occurred after wars and national uprisings.[2] The same thing could be seen in Poland after the Second World War, where the number of wolves increased and their range expanded. At the turn of the 1940s and the 1950s, they inhabited most forests throughout the country[3] and their numbers reached 1,000 individuals.[4] A favourable condition for wolves in post-war Poland was the massive migration and forced deportation of people, which led to the abandonment of most of the villages in the eastern part of the Polish Carpathians near the border with the Ukraine,[5] a region that became

---

1. Świętorzecki 1926, p. 118.
2. Jędrzejewska et al. 1996.
3. Wolsan et al. 1992.
4. Okarma 1992, pp. 12–4.
5. Soja 2008, p. 82.

Robert W. Mysłajek and Sabina Nowak

an important refuge for the wolf population in the following decades. This also happened in many of the former lands of East Prussia and Germany.[6]

A Regulation of the President of the Republic of Poland on the Hunting Law from 1927 was still in force in Poland after World War Two.[7] According to this law, the wolf was considered as game, and could be hunted throughout the year. In fact, under the guise of wildlife management, wolves were being eradicated. The hunting press routinely featured articles urging the absolute destruction of this species[8] and forest services were obligated to meticulously record its presence. The clear objective of such actions was pointed out by phrases such as 'discovery of wolf tracks in the area should be used for their extirpation'.[9] It is symptomatic that the second Polish monograph on wolves, published in 1953, was devoted not so much to the predator itself as to ways to eradicate it.[10]

The main arguments used by hunters for exterminating wolves involved the losses hunting clubs suffered due to wolf predation of wild ungulates. Authors of articles also tried to encourage reader beliefs about the exceptional threat from these predators to humans. Colourful descriptions of wolves attacking villagers and foresters were commonly seen in articles in hunting magazines. They often ended with dramatic appeals to take direct action. It was explicitly indicated that 'the last bell has rung to start the extermination of wolves'.[11] These appeals were approved by the communist authorities, and soon a real crusade against wolves started.

THE WAR WITH WOLVES

The meeting of the Bureau of the Polish Government on 29 January 1955 was of great significance for Polish wolves, as the constant lobbying of hunters prompted the authorities to adopt a resolution for eradicating these predators. As a result, the wolf was excluded from the list of game animals[12] and the Minister of Forestry issued a detailed order governing their extermination.[13] All forces were deployed to the front of the battle against wolves. Special officials were appointed as responsible for carrying out the campaign: the Chief Commissioner for the Eradication of Wolves and relevant provincial and county commissioners. It was allowed not

---

6. Davies 2005, pp. 392–8.
7. Rozporządzenie Prezydenta Rzeczypospolitej z dnia 3 grudnia 1927 r. o prawie łowieckim.
8. Żebrowski 1952.
9. Wrocławski Okręg Lasów Państwowych we Wrocławiu. Unpublished letter from 10 Oct. 1953. Signature TU-273/W.
10. Kowalski 1953a, pp. 1–57.
11. Kowalski 1953b, p. 5.
12. Rozporządzenie Ministerstwa Leśnictwa z dnia 6 grudnia 1955 r. w sprawie wyłączenia wilka ze spisu dzikich zwierząt łownych.
13. Zarządzenie Ministra Leśnictwa z dnia 26 lutego 1955 r. w przedmiocie wykonania uchwały nr 75 Prezydium Rządu z dnia 29 stycznia 1955 r. w sprawie tępienia wilków.

only to kill wolves using firearms, but also to poison them and to remove pups from dens. The majority of wolves were simply shot during individual or group hunts. Individual hunts were conducted mostly from hunting towers in front of which bait (usually the carcass of large livestock) was placed to attract the wolf. The most popular group hunt on wolves was organised using a special device called a '*fladry*'. *Fladry* are simply strips of red fabric, approximately ten by fifty centimetres, attached every forty centimetres to a single long string. Wolves avoid crossing such a barrier; however the mechanism underlying this behaviour is still not fully understood. During snow-tracking, after finding wolves resting in the forest, hunters would quickly and quietly surround the area with a *fladry*. The animals were driven by beaters into a bottleneck formed using the *fladry*, at the end of which hunters waited with guns. This method allowed all members of a pack to be killed in a single hunt.[14]

Awards were paid for wolves which had been killed over the entire country: 1,000 złotys for killing a wolf on an individual hunt, 500 złotys for killing a wolf on a group hunt and 200 złotys for removing a pup from the den. These were significant amounts, considering the fact that during this period the average monthly salary was 1,008 złotys.[15] To receive the award, one had to present the skin and skull of the killed animal to a special commission, which sometimes gathered many months afterwards. A protocol number was stamped on the skin and the skull was crashed. Destroying skulls was not accepted by the hunters because it deprived them of the opportunity to present these trophies in competitions or exhibitions. In reaction to complaints the rules changed, and both the wolf's skin and the skull could be kept by the person who killed the wolf.[16] The rewards steadily increased, so in 1960 they amounted to 1,200 złotys, and in 1964 to 1,500 złotys. In some counties in the Carpathian Mountains, an extra award of 500 złotys was paid per wolf. Poisoning was banned only in 1973, but high bounties were still paid until 1975. In the Rzeszów province (SE Poland) the awards reached 3,000 złotys,[17] when the average monthly salary was 2,789 złotys.[18]

From the 1950s to late 1960s there were regular articles in hunting magazines reporting the results of the anti-wolf campaign. Detailed recommendations concerning various methods of hunting these carnivores[19] and using poison[20] were also published. Mistakes and failures in the campaign were eagerly criticised,

14. Okarma and Jędrzejewski 1997.
15. Polish Central Statistical Office: http://www.stat.gov.pl/gus/5840_1630_PLK_HTML.htm
16. Zarządzenie Ministra Leśnictwa i Przemysłu Drzewnego z dnia 6 czerwca 1960 r. w sprawie tępienia wilków.
17. Okarma 1992.
18. Polish Central Statistical Office: http://www.stat.gov.pl/gus/5840_1630_PLK_HTML.htm.
19. Stadion-Rzyszczewski 1967, pp. 6–7.
20. Siedlecki 1958.

forcing provincial and district authorities to increase efforts to eradicate wolves.[21] Since the rewards were very attractive, the commissioners also had to be prepared for possible scams and frauds. Particularly difficult was an unequivocal identification of species killed because of lack of clear characteristics to distinguish between skulls of wolves and dogs.[22]

Though there were some local failures, the campaign to eradicate wolves was carried out very efficiently. In 1959, just four years after the start of the campaign, the size of the wolf population in Poland was estimated to be 250 individuals, and the author of one of the articles commented it with pride: 'Wolf's plague under control'.[23] However, wolves were still being exterminated until 1975, when they were re-entered onto the list of game animals.[24] The ruthless eradication conducted in 1954–1975 caused the death of more than 3,300 wolves across Poland.[25]

AWAKENING AWARENESS

In 1975 the number of wolves in the country was estimated at less than 100 individuals.[26] The remnants survived in forests of the Carpathian Mountains and the north-eastern and very eastern parts of the country.[27] During the campaign, however, some scientists called for restraint in this systematic eradication.[28] Knowledge about wolf ecology and awareness of the positive role of large predators in the natural environment has started to be more common amongst scientists but also in society.[29] The new hunting law apparently took the voices of scientists into account. From 1975 the Regulation on Hunting Seasons for Game Animals established a protection season for the wolf from 1 April to 31 July.[30] However, it was not in force in the provinces of Krosno (eastern Carpathians), Nowy Sącz (central part of Polish Carpathians) and Przemyśl (Carpathian foothills), where wolves could be hunted throughout the year. In fact, the protection season was introduced only in regions where wolves did not live or appeared only occasionally, and they were hunted year-round in the areas where they were still present. A unified hunting season for this species, covering the entire country, was not introduced until the

---

21. Sikorski 1957.
22. Sumiński 1969.
23. Siedlecki 1959.
24. Rozporządzenie Ministra Leśnictwa i Przemysłu Drzewnego z dnia 17 listopada 1975 r. w sprawie uznania wilka i piżmaka za zwierzęta łowne.
25. Sumiński 1975, p. 49; Okarma 1992, p. 13.
26. Okarma 1992, pp. 12–14.
27. Wolsan et al. 1992.
28. Sumiński 1970; Klarowski 1973.
29. Wołk 1974.
30. Rozporządzenie Ministra Leśnictwa i Przemysłu Drzewnego z dnia 17 listopada 1975 r. w sprawie okresów polowań na zwierzęta łowne.

end of 1981.[31] In 1980–1990 the hunting of wolves was based on a hunting census that was conducted yearly and on fixed hunting quotas. The culls, however, were still very high, especially in the source populations: in the Carpathian Mountains and in north-eastern Poland. A comparison of the number of wolves shot in the easternmost part of the Carpathians (Krosno province) in 1980–1990[32] and those killed during the anti-wolf campaign[33] in the same region showed that the regular hunting differed from the deliberate persecution by only twelve per cent per year (73 wolves versus 83 wolves on average). In western Poland, just after wolves began to recolonise the forests where they had been killed years before, hunters increased their interest in wolf hunts. Wherever wolves appeared and established a pack, they were hunted almost at once. It happened that even if wolves were not recorded in a hunting ground, a hunting quota was set to allow shooting in case they appeared during the following winter. This caused great instability in the few packs living in western Poland, resulting in a very low wolf population density in the region, which, according to a habitat suitability model for Polish wolves, is able to host many more wolves than eastern Poland.

The 1980s brought the decline of communism and the beginning of the systemic changes that dramatically altered the political system in the whole of Central and Eastern Europe. After 1989 these democratic changes have also significantly influenced the fate of wolves in Poland. They helped to stimulate civic activity in Poland and enabled the creation of hundreds of Non-Governmental Organisations (NGOs), many of which became involved in environmental protection. Several aimed to change the legal status of the wolf and the lynx from game to protected species,[34] an idea also supported by scientists.[35] The Nature Conservation Act introduced at the time allowed protection of species not only nationally, but also in particular provinces, and so the activities of conservationists could be carried out at both the national and provincial level. The campaign made its first achievements in the early 1990s, when wolves became protected in Poznań province in 1992, and in 1994 the hunting season for wolves in Bielsko-Biała province (south Poland, the westernmost part of the Carpathians) was shortened to one day only. In 1995 the Minister of the Environment changed the regulation on the protection of animal species and introduced protection for the wolf in most of Poland, with the exception of the provinces of Krosno, Przemyśl and Suwałki (north-east Poland). At the same time, however, governors of the Przemyśl and Suwałki provinces protected wolves under their own regulations, so the species could only be

---

31. Rozporządzenie Ministra Leśnictwa i Przemysłu Drzewnego z dnia 30 grudnia 1981 r. w sprawie okresów polowań na zwierzęta łowne.
32. Okarma 1989; Okarma 1992, pp. 12–14.
33. Brewczyński 2013.
34. Nowak 1996.
35. Bereszyński and Mizera 1992.

Robert W. Mysłajek and Sabina Nowak

hunted in the province of Krosno. The campaign achieved its main goal in 1998 when the wolf became protected in the entire country. Thus, Poland became the only state in Eastern Europe to protect populations of large carnivores before its accession to the European Union and prior to adopting such obligations under the Habitats Directive.

It is worth noting that the wolf in Poland was not placed under protection because of its low population or restricted distribution, but because of its role in the forest ecosystem. The legal justification for the act stated that, 'The wolf plays an important role in maintaining the ecological balance in the environment and is a natural regulator of the population number and health status of game ungulates'.[36] After achieving their goal, NGOs focused on building a system of compensation for damage to livestock caused by wolves, on promotion of various measures to prevent wolf depredation,[37] monitoring of the wolf population,[38] education of society, etc.

The formal protection of the species itself, however, was not enough to solve the problems associated with the negative effects of Poland's rapid urbanisation and economic growth on the natural environment. In the twenty-first century the wolf has had to face new challenges.

SUCCESS ... AND WHAT NEXT?

Currently, wolves in Poland are under strict protection. It is prohibited to kill, injure, capture or keep them as pets, to destroy wolf dens or disturb animals during denning, as well as to store and sell skins or other parts of dead individuals without proper authorisation. In special cases (e.g. scientific projects, elimination of individuals posing threat to humans), permission for capturing or killing wolves can be obtained from the General Director for Environmental Protection and the regional directorates for environmental protection. Violation of this law is punishable by jail or a fine. The Regulation of the Minister of the Environment on the Protection of Animal Species also allows for protection zones to be created, with a diameter of 500 m around the breeding sites of wolves, from 1 April to the end of August.[39] Zones can be designated or repealed by the regional director for environmental protection by way of administrative decision.

After Poland's accession to the European Union the wolf also became protected under Council Directive 92/43/EEC for the conservation of natural habitats and of wild fauna and flora (the Habitats Directive). The reservation submitted during the negotiation of the Treaty of Accession resulted in moving the Polish wolf population from Annex IV to V, which covers species of community interest whose

36. Bereszyński 1998, pp. 125–6.
37. Nowak and Mysłajek 2006, pp. 1–55.
38. Nowak and Mysłajek 2011, pp. 1–75.
39. Rozporządzenie Ministra Środowiska z dnia 6 października 2014 r., w sprawie ochrony zwierząt.

taking from the wild may be subject to management measures. However, the wolf in Poland has remained in Annex II among priority species for which, in order to protect their habitats, it is necessary to designate special areas of conservation as part of the 'Natura 2000' network.

Wolves currently inhabit all the major forests of the north-eastern and eastern parts of the country, the Carpathians and the larger forests of western Poland. There are also reports of their presence in the Sudety Mountains (south-west Poland). Since the wolf became protected, a systematic increase in the range and number of its population has been reported.[40] These predators usually choose to live in areas with high forest coverage and minimum fragmentation, a small share of human settlements and the lowest density of roads and railway lines.[41]

Even the biggest forest complexes in Poland are not large enough to house a wolf population capable of functioning over a long period of time, independently of the neighbouring subpopulations. Furthermore, the connection between forest tracts may be hampered or impossible, for example due to the presence of large agricultural areas, continuous building development, fenced roads and railway lines, water reservoirs or tourism and industry infrastructure.[42] The obstacles to free movement of wolves from one forest complex to another weaken the exchange of individuals between subpopulations. Isolated populations are thus exposed to inbreeding. It is extremely important for the survival of large carnivores to maintain connectivity between forests; they also need to move freely within each forest.[43] In 2005, the Ministry of the Environment commissioned a project of ecological corridors in Poland.[44] It was later widely used when deciding on the location of wildlife crossing structures at newly built motorways, which according to Polish law have to be fenced along the whole route. In this way it was possible to minimise the negative impact of transport infrastructure on animals.[45]

As in other countries, illegal culling and snaring are important factors in the mortality of large carnivores. Hunters are primarily responsible for the intentional culling of wolves; however, snares are used by poachers for killing wild ungulates and large predators are trapped accidently. Local assessment of the impact of poaching on the population of large carnivores was possible by marking individuals with collars fitted with transmitters. It revealed that in the Białowieża Primeval Forest fifty per cent of wolves monitored by radio-telemetry were killed in snares or with firearms.[46] However, it is difficult to extrapolate these results to the whole

---

40. Nowak and Mysłajek 2011.
41. Jędrzejewski et al. 2004; Jędrzejewski et al. 2005a.
42. Huck et al. 2010, pp. 177–92.
43. Huck et al. 2011, pp. 91–101.
44. Jędrzejewski et al. 2005b, pp. 1–78.
45. Nowak and Mysłajek 2010.
46. Theuerkauf et al. 2003.

Robert W. Mysłajek and Sabina Nowak

of Poland, as the economic situation of local societies and poaching 'traditions' varies between regions.

Poland shares its wolf population with neighbouring countries. Wolves are being killed in Russia, Lithuania, Belarus, Ukraine and Slovakia. Because there are extensive forests inhabited by wolves along border areas, and a significant portion of Polish wolf packs cover cross-border territories, the killing of wolves in neighbouring countries has a negative impact on the protected Polish population.[47] In the Polish border areas, a number of 'Natura 2000' sites have been created to, among other things, protect the habitat of large predators. Intensive hunting in neighbouring countries adversely affects the protection status of species in these areas. This is a significant problem for Poland, due to its need to fulfil commitments to the European Commission. International cooperation in the monitoring and management of shared cross-border populations of large carnivores is therefore extremely important.

Collisions with vehicles are another result of human activity that causes high mortality in wolf populations. This mainly concerns the deaths of animals hit by cars, but individuals killed by trains were also reported. The significance of such mortalities to the wolf population depends on the area: in western Poland, where the wolf population is still small, each wolf capable of reproduction and contribution to the gene pool of the population, or of helping with rearing pups, is extremely important.

FUTURE PERSPECTIVES

Assessments based on the habitat suitability model for wolves in Poland showed that 1,220–1,720 individuals may live in the country, with the most probable population size being 1,450–1,540 individuals.[48] Strict protection of species favours the return of wolves to the areas from which they were previously eradicated. Thanks to this protection, the population of wolves is growing in western Poland,[49] and wolves from the Polish population are settling in Germany[50]. The level of wolf damage to livestock in 2004–2011 ranged between 800 and 1,200 animals, but financial compensation is paid by the state. Damage assessment and compensation are made in every province by the regional directorates for environmental protection, and inside national parks by the director of the park. Compensation covers the value of animals killed and other costs, such as veterinary treatment of injured livestock or disposal of cadavers. However, it is not paid if livestock is left unprotected on a remote pasture overnight. NGOs and regional directorates for environmental

47.   Jędrzejewski et al. 2005c; Nowak et al. 2008.
48.   Jędrzejewski et al. 2008.
49.   Nowak et al. 2011, pp. 709–15.
50.   Czarnomska et al. 2013.

protection conduct projects supporting farmers, supplying them with livestock guard dogs, electric fences and sets of *fladry*, which are used for livestock protection. Throughout the country there are more than seventy 'Natura 2000' areas that protect the habitats of wolves. Numerous educational campaigns about this species have also been conducted. It would seem that its future is certain, but this is not necessarily the case.

Voices calling for a return of hunting this species in Poland do not go unheard. The hunting lobby, as if unaware of the change in the public perception of the killing of wild animals, still returns to economic arguments, promoting a vision of the wolf as a species causing great harm to wildlife management.[51] However, scientific studies indicate more and more examples of environmental functions and services provided by wolves. These include the positive impact of wolves on the number[52] and behaviour of wild ungulates,[53] in particular on the regeneration and renewal of forests,[54] as well as on the state of protection of other endangered species.[55] The future of wolves is largely dependent on whether such knowledge of the subject will break through into public awareness.

ACKNOWLEDGEMENTS

RWM postdoctoral internship was funded by the National Science Centre (Poland), grant number DEC-2014/12/ S/NZ8/00624. This work was also supported by EuroNatur (Germany), the International Fund for Animal Welfare (USA) and the Wolves and Humans Foundation (UK).

BIBLIOGRAPHY

Archival Sources

Rozporządzenie Prezydenta Rzeczypospolitej z dnia 3 grudnia 1927 r. o prawie łowieckim. Dziennik Ustaw, 110, poz. 934.

Rozporządzenie Ministerstwa Leśnictwa z dnia 6 grudnia 1955 r. w sprawie wyłączenia wilka ze spisu dzikich zwierząt łownych. Dziennik Ustaw, 45, poz. 303.

Rozporządzenie Ministra Leśnictwa i Przemysłu Drzewnego z dnia 17 listopada 1975 r. w sprawie okresów polowań na zwierzęta łowne. Dziennik Ustaw, 38, poz. 208.

Rozporządzenie Ministra Leśnictwa i Przemysłu Drzewnego z dnia 17 listopada 1975 r. w sprawie uznania wilka i piżmaka za zwierzęta łowne. Dziennik Ustaw, 38, poz. 207.

---

51. Brewczyński 2013.
52. Ripple and Beschta 2012.
53. Kuijper et al. 2013.
54. Beschta and Ripple 2010.
55. Ripple et al. 2014.

Rozporządzenie Ministra Leśnictwa i Przemysłu Drzewnego z dnia 30 grudnia 1981 r. w sprawie okresów polowań na zwierzęta łowne. Dziennik Ustaw, 2, poz. 17.

Rozporządzenie Ministra Środowiska z dnia 6 października 2014 r., w sprawie ochrony zwierząt. Dziennik Ustaw z 2014, poz. 1348.

Wrocławski Okręg Lasów Państwowych we Wrocławiu. Pismo z dn. 10 października 1953 r. Zn. spr. TU-273/W.

Zarządzenie Ministra Leśnictwa z dnia 26 lutego 1955 r. w przedmiocie wykonania uchwały nr 75 Prezydium Rządu z dnia 29 stycznia 1955 r. w sprawie tępienia wilków. Monitor Polski, 24, poz. 242.

Zarządzenie Ministra Leśnictwa i Przemysłu Drzewnego z dnia 6 czerwca 1960 r. w sprawie tępienia wilków. Monitor Polski, 55, poz. 266.

Research Literature

Bereszyński, A. 1998. *Wilk (Canis lupus Linnaeus, 1758) w Polsce i jego ochrona. Wydawnictwo Akademii Rolniczej w Poznaniu* (Poznań: Wydawnictwo Akademii Rolniczej w PoznaniuWydawnictwo Akademii Rolniczej w Poznaniu).

Bereszyński, A. and T. Mizera. 1992. 'Chrońmy wilka'. *Przegląd Leśniczy* 6: 12.

Beschta, R.L. and W.J. Ripple. 2010. 'Recovering Riparian Plant Communities with Wolves in Northern Yellowstone, USA'. *Restoration Ecology* 18 (3): 380–9.

Brewczyński, P. 2013. 'Ochrona wilka a gospodarka łowiecka w Polsce – konflikt nieunikniony?' *Chrońmy Przyrodę Ojczystą* 69 (3): 204–20.

Czarnomska, S.D., B. Jędrzejewska, T. Borowik, M. Niedziałkowska, A.V. Stronen, S. Nowak, R.W. Mysłajek, H. Okarma, M. Konopiński, M. Pilot, W. Śmietana, R. Caniglia, E. Fabbri, E. Randi, C. Pertoldiand W. Jędrzejewski. 2013. 'Concordant Mitochondrial and Microsatellite DNA Structuring between Polish Lowland and Carpathian Mountain Wolves'. *Conservation Genetics* 14 (3): 573–88.

Davies, N. 2005 [1979]. *God's Playground. A History of Poland. Vol. II. 1795 to the Present* (Oxford, New York: Oxford University Press).

Huck, M., W. Jędrzejewski, T. Borowik, M. Miłosz-Cielma, K. Schmidt, B. Jędrzejewska, S. Nowak and R.W. Mysłajek. 2010. 'Habitat Suitability, Corridors and Dispersal Barriers for Large Carnivores in Poland'. *Acta Theriologica* 55 (2): 177–92.

Huck, M., W. Jędrzejewski, T. Borowik, B. Jędrzejewska, S. Nowak and R.W. Mysłajek. 2011. 'Analyses of Least Cost Paths for Determining Effects of Habitat Types on Landscape Permeability: Wolves in Poland'. *Acta Theriologica* 56 (1): 91–101.

Jędrzejewska, B., W. Jędrzejewski, A.N. Bunevich, L. Miłkowski and H. Okarma. 1996. 'Population Dynamics of Wolves *Canis lupus* in Białowieża Primeval Forest (Poland and Belarus) in Relation to Hunting by Humans, 1847–1993'. *Mammal Review* 26 (2–3): 103–26.

Jędrzejewski, W., M. Niedziałkowska, S. Nowak and B. Jędrzejewska. 2004. 'Habitat Variables Associated with Wolf (*Canis lupus*) Distribution and Abundance in Northern Poland'. *Diversity and Distributions* 10 (3): 225–33.

Jędrzejewski, W., M. Niedziałkowska, R.W. Mysłajek, S. Nowak and B. Jędrzejewska. 2005a. 'Habitat Selection by Wolves *Canis lupus* in the Uplands and Mountains of Southern Poland'. *Acta Theriologica* **50** (3): 417–28.

Jędrzejewski, W., S. Nowak, K. Stachura, M. Skierczyński, R.W. Mysłajek, K. Niedziałkowski, B. Jędrzejewska, J.M. Wójcik, H. Zalewska and M. Pilot. 2005b. *Projekt korytarzy ekologicznych łączących Europejską Sieć Natura 2000 w Polsce.* (Białowieża: Zakład Badania Ssaków PAN.).

Jędrzejewski, W., W. Branicki, C. Veit, I. Medugorac, M. Pilot, A.N. Bunevich, B. Jędrzejewska, K. Schmidt, J. Theuerkauf, H. Okarma, R. Gula, L. Szymura and M. Förster. 2005c. 'Genetic Diversity and Relatedness Within Packs in an Intensely Hunted Population of Wolves *Canis lupus*'. *Acta Theriologica* **50** (1): 1–22.

Jędrzejewski, W., B. Jędrzejewska, B. Zawadzka, T. Borowik, S. Nowak and R.W. Mysłajek. 2008. 'Habitat Suitability Model for Polish Wolves *Canis lupus* based on Long-Term National Census'. *Animal Conservation* **11** (5): 377–90.

Klarowski, R. 1973. 'Wilkowi grozi wymarcie'. *Chrońmy Przyrodę Ojczystą* **29** (6): 66–70.

Kowalski, Z. 1953a. *Wilk i jego zwalczanie* (Warszawa: Państwowe Wydawnictwo Rolnicze i Leśne).

— 1953b. 'Ogłaszam alarm wilczy'. *Łowiec Polski* **1**: 4–5.

Kuijper, D.P.J., C. de Kleine, M. Churski, P. van Hooft, J. Bubnicki and B. Jędrzejewska. 2013. 'Landscape of Fear in Europe: Wolves Affect Spatial Patterns of Ungulate Browsing in Białowieża Primeval Forest, Poland'. *Ecography* **36** (12): 1263–75.

Nowak, S. 1996. 'Dzikie jest piękne – kampania na rzecz objęcia ochroną gatunkową rysia i wilka w całej Polsce'. *Biuletyn Informacyjny X Ogólnopolskiego Spotkania Ruchów Ekologicznych Kolumna* 1996: 110–111.

Nowak, S. and R.W. Mysłajek. 2006. *Poradnik ochrony zwierząt hodowlanych przed wilkami* (Twardorzeczka: Stowarzyszenie dla Natury 'Wilk').

— 2011. *Wilki na zachód od Wisły* (Twardorzeczka: Stowarzyszenie dla Natury 'Wilk').

Nowak, S. and R.W. Mysłajek. 2010. 'Existing Experiences and Background Information from Poland', in K. Heller and A. Spangenberg (eds) *TEWN Manual. Recommendations for the Reduction of Habitat Fragmentation caused by Transport Infrastructure Development* (Euro Natur: Radolfzell) pp. 65–8.

Nowak, S., R.W. Mysłajek and B. Jędrzejewska. 2008. 'Density and Demography of Wolf *Canis lupus* Population in the Western-Most Part of the Polish Carpathian Mountains, 1996–2003'. *Folia Zoologica* **57** (4): 392–402.

Nowak, S., R.W. Mysłajek, A. Kłosińska and G. Gabryś. 2011. 'Diet and Prey Selection of Wolves *Canis lupus* Recolonising Western and Central Poland'. *Mammalian Biology* **76** (6): 709–15.

Okarma, H. 1989. 'Distribution and Numbers of Wolves in Poland'. *Acta Theriologica* **34** (35): 497–503.

— 1992. *Wilk. Monografia przyrodniczo-łowiecka* (Białowieża: Nakładem Autora).

Okarma, H. and W. Jędrzejewski. 1997. 'Livetrapping Wolves with Nets'. *Wildlife Society Bulletin* **25** (1): 78–82.

Ripple, W.J. and R.L. Beschta. 2012. 'Large predators limit herbivore densities in northern forest ecosystems'. *European Journal for Wildlife Resources* **58**: 733–42.

Ripple, W.J., R.L. Beschta, J.K. Fortin and C.T. Robbins. 2014. 'Trophic Cascades from Wolves to Grizzly Bears in Yellowstone'. *Journal of Animal Ecology* **83** (1): 223–33.

Siedlecki, L. 1958. 'Zastosowanie luminalu w walce z wilkami'. *Łowiec Polski* **23**: 6–7.

— 1959. 'Plaga wilcza opanowana'. *Łowiec Polski* **14**: 4–5.

Sikorski, A. 1957. 'Zwalczanie wilków w okresie letnim'. *Łowiec Polski* **7–8**: 8.

Soja, M. 2008. *Cykle rozwoju ludności Karpat Polskich w XIX i XX wieku*. Instytut Geografii i Gospodarki Przestrzennej Uniwersytetu Jagiellońskiego (Kraków).

Stadion-Rzyszczewski J. 1967. 'Fladrowanie wilków'. *Łowiec Polski* **3**: 6–7, 10.

Sumiński, P. 1969. 'Wilk czy pies? (Czy można odróżnić czaszkę wilka od czaszki psa)'. *Łowiec Polski* **20**: 12.

— 1970. 'Jeszcze raz w obronie wilka'. *Chrońmy Przyrodę Ojczystą* **21** (5): 59–61.

Sumiński, P. 1975. 'The Wolf in Poland', in D.H. Pimlott (ed.) *Wolves. Proceedings of the First Working Meeting of Wolf Specialists and of the First International Conference on Conservation of the Wolf*. International Union for Conservation of Nature and Natural Resources (Morges, Switzerland) pp. 44–52.

Świętorzecki, B. 1926. *Wilk* (Warszawa: Nakładem Myśliwskiej Spółki Wydawniczej).

Theuerkauf, J., W. Jędrzejewski, K. Schmidt and R. Gula. 2003. 'Spatiotemporal Segregation of Wolves from Humans in the Białowieża Forest (Poland)'. *Journal of Wildlife Management* **67** (4): 706–16.

Wolsan, M., M. Bieniek and T. Buchalczyk. 1992. 'The History of Distributional and Numerical Changes of the Wolf *Canis lupus* L. in Poland', in B. Bobek, K. Perzanowski and W.L. Regelin (eds) *Global Trends in Wildlife Management*. Trans. 18th IUGB Congress, Krakow 1987 (Krakow, Warszawa: Wydawnictwo Świat Press) pp. 375–80.

Wołk, E. 1974. 'O roli wilka w biocenozach'. *Łowiec Polski* **7**: 7.

Żebrowski, B. 1952. 'Sprawa wilcza'. *Łowiec Polski* **9**: 7–8.

13

If You Wander in Winter, They Will Eat You: Local Knowledge, Wolves and Justice in Central Asia

Adam Pérou Hermans

INTRODUCTION

Until the 8 November 2005 death of Kenton Carnegie in Saskatchewan, not a single fatal wolf attack was authenticated in North America.[1] The attack surprised many North Americans. Decades of work by wolf biologists had shown them that wolves are rarely dangerous to humans. Public sentiment differs in Central Asia, where locals perceive their wolves as very dangerous. Central Asians' histories of human–wolf interactions fundamentally differ from those in North America and from accounts of human–wolf conflict familiar to the West. Central Asian anecdotes of wolf attacks abound. Whether they are folk tales or facts is difficult to determine. Local communities lack access to the scientific resources needed to document and prove their accounts. If the wolves in Central Asia are unusually dangerous, locals' inability to prove as much raises serious concern for the communities' welfare, human–wolf relations, and wolf conservation. North American and Western European discourses on human–wolf relationships dominate knowledge about wolves. They are abundant and often hold scientific authority. Framed in transnational and public terms, Western accounts of Western wolves become default global knowledge on wolves. Central Asian discourses, not framed for consumption or supported by science, are comparatively invisible. In remote regions, locals may not think to raise or promote their discourse; they are not even part of the conversation. The dominance of Western accounts may obscure the complexity of human–wolf conflict by overlooking distinctions in less visible regions such as Central Asia. Granted, Westerners long held beliefs describing vicious wolves as well.[2] Sorting out such complexity requires navigating cultural preconceptions (folk truth), careful science (fact truth) and the space between.

---

1. Graves and Geist 2007.
2. Coleman 2004, Lopez 2004.

260

Adam Pérou Hermans

Figure 1. Darshaydarra, Wakhan Valley, High Pamir, Tajikistan, June 2012. (Photograph: Adam Pérou Hermans).

WOLF ATTACKS IN CENTRAL ASIA

The Pamir Mountains span eastern Tajikistan, the north-eastern finger of Afghanistan, and western edges of China and Pakistan. The far Afghan–Tajik border is bifurcated by the Wakhan branch of the Ab-e-Panj River. Approximately 10,800 people live in the 2,200 square kilometres of the Wakhan Valley.[3] Most of these people are Wakhi pastoralists, grazing their goats, sheep and yak in mountain meadows during the summer and enduring long winters nestled in the valley.

The Pamir boast a range of wildlife including Siberian ibex (*Capra sibirica*), markhor (*Capra falconeri*), argali (*Ovis ammon polii*), snow leopards (*Uncia uncia*) and the Tibetan wolf (*Canis lupus chanco*). The Tibetan wolves, in particular, seem to be a problem in the Pamir. Children sleep with stock at pasture, keeping a fire stoked to deter the wolves.[4] Old men tell of wolves picking up sheep, tossing them over their backs and carrying them away.[5] Locals claim the Wakhan has many wolves and that these wolves are unusually hungry in December and January. Many dare not venture out in deep snow during the winter for fear wolves might eat them.[6]

3. United Nations Environmental Programme 2003.
4. Matrob Matrobov, personal communication, 2012.
5. Davlatjon, personal communication, 2012.
6. This information was obtained informally through casual conversation but repeated by Davlatjon, his wife Bibibimo and Matrob Matrobov. My fieldwork is limited to a few conversations

If You Wander in Winter, They Will Eat You

One may be inclined to attribute such concern to familiar folk fears of wolves rather than knowledge of actual attacks. Wild, healthy wolves rarely attack people. At least, wolves rarely attack people in North America.

While still rare, wolf attacks in Eurasia are more common.[7] A comprehensive review by Linnell et al. describes attacks across the region, from Spain to India.[8] The authors categorise the attacks into three types: rabid, defensive or predatory. Most attacks come from rabid wolves. Defensive attacks – protecting pups, self-defence in a trap – follow. Predatory attacks are the least common. The attackers are often wolf-dog hybrids, less afraid of humans and more likely to live nearby human settlements.[9]

This chapter does not address the problem of attacks by rabid wolves. Rabies alone does not adequately explain the claims of attacks in Central Asia. The disease poses a risk of conflation in local accounts – attacks sometimes do come from rabid wolves[10] – but this is not all the Pamiri describe. Their stories describe wild wolves *hunting* them: predatory attacks.

North America has only two official records of fatal wolf attacks by non-rabid wolves: Kenton Carnegie and Candice Berner near Chignik Lake, Alaska, in 2010.[11] This of course does not mean that wolves did not kill Native Americans or do not attack contemporary North Americans (Native or otherwise) – much evidence exists to the contrary, including two 2013 reports on wolf attacks in Minnesota and the Yukon respectively.[12] By comparison, in 2005 in Central Asia,

---

in the Wakhan. I cannot prove these claims; I can only present records of Central Asian wolf attacks from obscure journalism and a peripheral book of Russian and Soviet accounts of wolves translated by a Russian linguist for the US Air Force. I have no other evidence that these attacks occurred. Yet this difficulty in verification is, in part, the subject of this chapter. I seek to address what to make of these claims when the science necessary to authenticate them is not available or perhaps even possible. I address wolf attacks in particular because they raise important questions for wildlife conservation, social and environmental justice and the collision of the two, namely: how are concerns of justice and wildlife conservation to be remedied in the face of uncertainty?

7. Mech and Boitani 2010.
8. Linnell et al. 2002.
9. Mech and Boitani 2010.
10. Clarke 1971. In a review of the history of wolf attacks across Europe and Central Asia, Clark argues that most involved rabid or hybrid wolves.
11. Butler et al. 2011.
12. Linnell et al. 2002 provide documentation of a series of attacks in North America during the twentieth century; Mader 2007 offers perhaps the most extensive account. Granted, Mader is an independent scholar and the Research Director for Abundant Wildlife Society of North America: 'A private wildlife research organization dedicated to the preservation of the Great North American Traditions of Hunting, Fishing and Trapping'. Please see also, Angulo 1947; Jenness 1985; McNay and Mooney 2005; McNay 2002, Mech and Boitani 2010. The Minnesota and Yukon cases both come from local news sources (CBC News 2013; Orrick 2013). As such, they are not yet authenticated. Lacking nuance, such accounts may be exaggerated, fictional or wrong interpretations of behaviour. Please see Linnell et al. 2002 for more on this concern, and Boyd 2006.

wolves reportedly killed six people in Afghanistan[13], two in Uzbekistan[14] and one in Iran.[15] Local newspapers report wolf attacks across the region.[16] Wolves attacked six Tajik Pamiri in the winter of 2012.[17] These reports all come from journalists so they are not considered verified but they are only recent cases from the region. Russian and Soviet records offer huge numbers – e.g. in Russia, wolves reportedly killed 376 people between 1849 and 1851 and 1,445 people in the 49 provinces of European Russia between 1870 and 1887[18] – but these records do not always note when the wolves were rabid. Pavlov, too, describes hundreds of wolf attacks in the former Soviet Union.[19] He considered it his duty to report cases of wolf aggression towards humans, fearing increased study of wolves risked 'disorient[ing] society' and leading to communities forgetting the man-eating wolves of the past. This agenda leaves his work suspect but biologists note that many of his records appear reasonable when checked against medical records and cross-checked by careful Russian biologists.

The scant scholarship on wolves in the region is not decisive. Two accounts from neighbouring north-west Pakistan describe little fear of wolves and offer no reports of attacks.[20] By contrast, of far western China, Richard Harris writes: 'And although attacks on humans are extremely rare, in China, unlike in North America, there is documentation of wolves killing people within living memory'.[21] To the south, India provided authenticated accounts of numerous attacks on children, albeit many of which were by a single, bold wolf.[22] For Central Asia, such accounts remain limited to somewhat obscure journalism and a line in a 2002 World Wide Fund for Nature Central Asia report on the Tajik Pamir: 'Some cases of wolf attack

13. Newman 2005.
14. Blua 2005.
15. Iran Focus 2005.
16. Barrand 2003; Blua 2005; Graves and Geist 2007; Newman 2005.
17. Radio Free Europe 2012.
18. Graves and Geist 2007, pp. 21, 29; Shaw 2009. Graves is also an independent scholar and not a wolf biologist but a Russian linguist for the US Air Force. An ungulate (not wolf) biologist and professor emeritus, Valerius Geist, offers his authority as editor of Graves' book and author of the foreword and an appendix. Shaw, a wildlife biologist, reviewed the book and noted that Geist's authority 'improves the book's value' but also that the book suffers from its author's lack of expertise. This concern is not unfounded. Graves mentions in the Foreword that he was inspired to begin translating when '[he] became disgusted with all of the highly pro-wolf – misleading and often inaccurate – Western literature about wolves'. His acknowledgements to the editor of *Hunting and Game Management*, a technical editor of *American Rifleman* magazine, the president of the Montana Shooting Sports Association and the chairman of the Yellowstone Elk Herd Inc, among others, make one wary of his information as well (p. 15–7). Geist also seems to hold a drastically different perspective on the canids from that held by those who study them.
19. Pavlov 1982.
20. Abbas et al. 2013.
21. Harris 2008.
22. Jhala and Sharma 1997.

If You Wander in Winter, They Will Eat You

Figure 2. The Davlatjon family at their compound in Darshaydarra, Kūhistoni Badakhshon, Tajikistan. Their accounts, and my corresponding concern for their safety, inspired this chapter. (Photograph: Adam Pérou Hermans).

on man were registered in winter'.[23] In the wilder areas of the region, wolves may threaten not just one's livestock or livelihood but one's very life.

Nearby, Iran's Hamedan province has seen an unusual spate of wolf attacks; researchers recorded 47 attacks from 2001 to 2010, many resulting in fatalities.[24] Tests for rabies and hybridisation came up negative, leading the researchers to describe the conflict as 'predatory attacks made by hungry wolves'.[25] While scientifically-verified reports do not exist for Central Asia, such reports from the region suggest that human–wolf conflict in Central Asia could radically differ from human–wolf conflict in North America.[26]

WHY ARE WOLF ATTACKS A PROBLEM OF JUSTICE?

The field of environmental justice arose in response to concerns that certain groups suffer disproportionate environmental costs.[27] Classic cases referred to the environ-

23. Pereladova 2002.
24. Behdarvand et al. 2014.
25. Ibid., p. 157.
26. Graves and Geist 2007; Shaw 2009.
27. Bullard 2005.

ment where people live and work rather than the more wild landscapes focused on by other environmental agendas. Environmental justice advocates are less concerned with protecting wildlife or ecosystems than with ensuring safe, healthy environments for all. The injustice they address is that certain communities bear disproportionate burdens stemming from an unhealthy, if not dangerous, environment.[28] Initially the movement addressed distributive injustice, arguing that environmental costs should be more fairly distributed and not imposed upon certain groups. This concept of justice can be taken into consideration when siting polluting factories but it is less applicable to dangerous animals. Institutions do not (usually) place or distribute dangerous animals.[29] Thus the case of wolf attacks on the Wakhi may not appear to be an example of environmental injustice. The Wakhi may be suffering disproportionately but no institution put this suffering upon them. Rather, the Wakhi live among wolves. Wolves 'cause' the suffering but wolves, of course, do not discriminate. This challenges a description of the wolf attacks as an environmental injustice – nature cannot be described as acting unjustly.

Tragic events stemming from nature are considered bad but not wrong. Governments respond to storms with humanitarian aid not retribution. Again, at first glance, environmental justice may not seem to help in cases of environmentally-caused problems, despite its effectiveness in addressing costs relating to environmental problems caused by institutions. Yet political ecologists show how such cases are exactly problems of environmental justice in at least two ways. First, they illustrate that environmentally-caused (i.e. 'natural') problems are not independent of human influence. They contest the human–nature binary and do not accept that events can be attributed to 'nature' alone. For example, wolf behaviour may be a response to human activity and use of the landscape; Tibetan wolves do not live in an environment devoid of human impact.[30] Second, political ecologists explain how certain people suffer more from nature – be it a hurricane, an earthquake or Tibetan wolves – because of marginalisation, discrimination and various other ways in which they are more vulnerable to nature. These vulnerabilities come not from nature itself but from institutions treating these people differently and thus leaving, or even making, them more exposed to certain risks.[31]

---

28. Kiniyalocts 2000.
29. Wolf reintroduction is a possible exception. The siting of a national park or conservation effort, too, may provide both a population of dangerous animals and protection for those animals. Local communities may feel this places unfair environmental burdens on them, as the animals threaten their livelihood yet remain protected. See Adams and Hutton 2007; Geisler 2003; West et al. 2006.
30. See, Wilbert 2006, for an especially good explanation.
31. Robbins 2011.

If You Wander in Winter, They Will Eat You

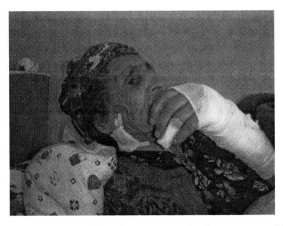

Figure 3. Radio Free Europe/Radio Liberty reports: 'Eighty-nine-year-old Ozodamoh Saidnurulloeva was being attacked by a wolf in her yard before a neighbor scared it away'. Navobod, Tajikistan, January 2012. www.rferl.org © 2014. RFE/RL, Inc. Reprinted with the permission of Radio Free Europe/Radio Liberty, 1201 Connecticut Ave NW, Ste 400, Washington DC 20036.

KNOWLEDGE, POWER AND JUSTICE

One way the Wakhi may be made more vulnerable is by an inability to authenticate their accounts of wolf attacks. Many scholars address the bias favouring knowledge developed by Western science.[32] Harding describes how science must be 'undressed' or contextualised so that it is understood as a certain kind of knowledge rather than presented as an objective account.[33] Only once it is situated can it be compared and contrasted more fairly with other ways of understanding the world. Terms for knowledges seen as existing outside science vary but accounts such as the Wakhi's may be diminished as 'local knowledge', situated in a certain place, culture and experience. By contrast, Western science often claims objectivity and separation from the standpoint of the researcher in its production.[34] However, Western science is situated as well.[35] Research on wolves is influenced by many factors: funding, previous studies, the researchers' countries of origin. Wolf biologists are not as widely distributed as wolves. Inevitably, their research is limited. Collective, accepted knowledge of wolves becomes generalised from the areas in which wolves are well-studied. The limits of science result in a limit of authenticated knowledge. Local

---

32. Agrawal 1995; Haraway 1988; Jasanoff and Martello 2004.
33. Harding 2011.
34. Apffel-Marglin 1996; Goldman 2007.
35. Haraway 1988.

observations, accounts and often distinctly different human–wolf relations may be missed simply due to lack of study. Nadasdy notes that understanding other types of knowledge offers both empirical upshots – e.g. better understanding of wolves – and normative upshots: local knowledges may help outsiders better understand how they can, could and even *should* relate to nature, including dangerous animals such as wolves.[36]

Local and scientific knowledge can also be produced in similar ways.[37] Rather than distinguishing between knowledge as scientific and 'local', such claims could be parsed out along lines of deduction and induction. A Wakhi shepherd may deduce that a wolf killed a goat by assessing evidence: wolf tracks, wolf bite marks in the goat's neck. A villager may accept that her friend was attacked if her friend shows her bite marks in his leg and clumps of wolf fur he grabbed in fending off the attack. Like science, local knowledge can be informed by evidence and careful deduction. Yet outsiders often construe local knowledge as induction, i.e. a story of one wolf attack becomes a general fact that wolves attack, even with only scant evidence. Folk stories, such as of wolves killing all 147 attendants at a wedding in Ukraine,[38] lead to induction that wolves are vicious, bloodthirsty creatures. This 'knowledge' is not deduced from evidence but induced from stories: therein lies the difficulty in incorporating anecdotal accounts into other (essentially rationalist) discourses about the wolf, especially when folk tales have served to demonise the wolf in the past. While testimonies may be evidence (when presented by a witness to the event), stories are testimonies repeated to the point of exaggeration, alteration, even re-creation. When science conflicts with deduced local knowledge, different evidence may be the source of contention, not necessarily different levels of intellectual rigour.

The prioritisation of scientific knowledge in describing the natural world belies an injustice in knowledge production: unequal distribution of the tools needed to study, document and publish accounts; unequal participation of various communities in scientific study;[39] and unequal use or recognition of various knowledges in describing and responding to nature.[40] The injustice stems from different access. The Wakhi do not have the resources to produce scientific accounts of their relations with wolves. It is difficult to authenticate a wolf attack. The only 'authenticated' wolf attacks in North America come from cases in which

---

36. Nadasdy 1999.
37. Goldman 2007.
38. Shaw 2009.
39. A lack of science is a problem across Tajikistan, not just for the Wakhi. Tajik science relies on fragments of Soviet heritage. Little support is granted to invest in the training or equipping of new scientists. The Pamirs are the most literate and educated region in the country, thanks to support from the Aga Khan foundation (Rosen, personal communication, 2013).
40. Foucault 1972; Foucalt 1980.

contemporary North Americans were attacked. Proof of the 2010 wolf attack in Alaska came by way of a forty-page report.[41]

CARE AND CONCERN WITH KNOWLEDGE CLAIMS

Wolf biologists have good reason to remain sceptical when folk claims vary from their studies and documentation, especially when these claims may serve other interests such as in obtaining weapons, conserving game or protecting livestock. The lack of adequate evidence and research supporting local claims makes them difficult to verify. As noted by Linnell et al.:

> In any such study based on summarising historical records, newspaper and magazine accounts, traditional literature, etc., there are many potential sources of error that appear. These errors can result from problems with translation, recording error, exaggeration ('journalistic license'), ignorance, or wilful distortion of the truth to cover up events.[42]

The review further lists common causes of such errors: problems with oral tradition, fake attacks, confusion about names and mistaken identity,[43] conflation of killings with scavenging, euphemisms, exaggeration and superstition.[44] These make local accounts difficult to trust.

Wolf biologists' knowledge can be critiqued and situated as well. For example, much of their knowledge comes from studies conducted in North America.[45] Biologists are also not free of bias – as revealed by how they justify their pursuit of clarification and accuracy. In describing the danger of habituation and the 'conservation conundrum'[46] it causes, Boyd writes: 'the challenge is to avoid creating public fear of wolves, yet paint a realistic picture of wolf behaviour in hopes of reducing

---

41.   Butler et al. 2011. All knowledge producers are limited by some restraints. Just as Pamiri may not have the means to scientifically study their wolves, Western biologists do not have the means to conduct their research and science everywhere. Here, again, local knowledge can offer insights as to how much wolf behaviour in different regions either echoes or varies from that of wolves in better-studied areas.

42.   Linnell et al. 2002, p. 9.

43.   For example, a conservationist working in Tajikistan believes the attack mentioned at the beginning of this chapter was 'very likely caused by a stray dog' (Rosen, personal communication, 2013).

44.   Linnell et al. 2002.

45.   Today most wolves remain only in the vast northern regions. Northern North America, from Montana and Minnesota north through Canada to Alaska, boasts a long, careful and close history of wolf study. Ecologically similar regions of the former Soviet Union, while home to even larger populations and higher densities of wolves, do not share the same bounty of research. Thus scientific knowledge of wolves is based more on studies of the populations in North America than elsewhere. This affects how well wolves outside North America are understood.

46.   The conundrum: protecting wolves seems to make them more dangerous to people – hunting and persecution keep wolves afraid and thus keep people safe.

human-wolf conflicts and subsequent wolf mortality'.[47] This is not problematic in itself but her concern with protecting wolves reveals a position perhaps not shared and an agenda (wolf conservation) that may taint the attempted detached approach of science.[48] Wolves are not endangered in Central Asia.[49] Conservation of non-endangered species such as the Tibetan wolf can simply mean that eradication of the wolves is not an acceptable solution to problems of conflict. Here conservation can be construed *as coexistence*. More often the term conservation refers to conservation *as control*, e.g. international conservation projects for snow leopards, argali and other rare, endangered species eliciting agencies, regulations and projects to protect the animals. Fear of wolves presents a challenge to conservation as coexistence – yet fear is an appropriate and justifiable response to knowledge that wolves attack people. Conservationists may be tempted to challenge such fear as unwarranted due to their own, well-founded, fear of wolf persecution. If this concern becomes mixed up in the research, they may continue to see attacks as not just rare, but also the result of unusual circumstances—rabies, hybridisation, a wild pack habituating to humans, even an abnormal jaw.[50] If studies imply these attacks are outside the realm of natural wolf behaviour, then they, in a sense, add a moral element to the description of the wolves: wolves are inherently good, they attack when something is wrong.

Western biologists hold great power in claiming authority on wolf behaviour. They write books and papers on the topic. They are consulted as experts in cases of wolf conflict. Their knowledge is the most widely disseminated and the most influential. Local knowledge holds less power and may be marginalised in the interests of conservation, resulting in policy that may overlook local claims and concerns. For example, despite similar accounts of wolf attacks in Afghanistan,[51] wolves were protected across the country in 2009.[52] Conservation organisations helped draft the environmental legislation for the post-Taliban government and maintain a presence in the region.[53]

Conservationists may be understood as having a certain 'philosophy of nature'.[54] They see nature as inherently good, and thus worth conserving. This normative element differs from the objective orientation of biology. Discussing the return of wolves to the French Alps, Buller shows how to some this is biodiversity

---

47. Boyd 2006; Linnell et al. 2002.
48. Haraway 1988.
49. Mech and Boitani 2010b.
50. Orrick 2013.
51. Newman 2005.
52. Mech and Boitani 2010.
53. Smallwood et al. 2011.
54. Thompson 2002.

enhancement.[55] A missing species has returned; the environment is now more natural and more complete. Akin to many Wakhi, to French pastoralists, Buller argues, the wolves' return may be seen as a threat to biosecurity. The environment in which they live and raise their children, herds and flocks is no longer considered safe. The pastoralists see this as unjust.[56] Different 'philosophies of nature' and knowledge claims will have to be carefully considered by all relevant parties if goals of both environmental justice and biodiversity conservation are to be met. The Wakhi and other Pamiri[57] have few means to offer their accounts of the natural world to the larger epistemic communities now wielding power over the Pamir.

THE UNUSUALLY DANGEROUS TIBETAN WOLF?

Even if Wakhi accounts of attacks are accepted by the government or conservation organisations, apolitical ecological explanations for the wolves' behaviour may still lead to injustice by obscuring the causes of the attacks. For example, one explanation may be that Tibetan wolves are just more aggressive than other subspecies.[58]

Though one must be careful with folk accounts, folk stories of wolves differ dramatically between the regions. Crudely, Russian, Eastern European and Central Asian folktales describe the big bad wolf, while Athabascan, Cheyenne and other Native American accounts and stories tend more to mythologise noble, admirable canids.[59] Further, folk accounts often seem to track wolf behaviour. Walker shows how Japanese tales of wolves adapted to changes in both Japanese society and in wolf behaviour.[60] Prior to modernisation, the Japanese honoured wolves as the 'Large-Mouthed Pure God'. Upon encountering a wolf they would greet it: 'O lord wolf, what do you say? How about chasing the deer from our fields?'[61] They cherished wolves as protectors of their grain as wolves preyed upon the deer and boar that devastated the crops. With the introduction of horses and ranching, wolves and humans came into conflict and the wolves started to fall from grace. Then rabies arrived on the islands in the early eighteenth century and dramatically

---

55. Buller 2008.

56. Ibid., p. 1590.

57. The term Pamiri describes the people living across the region of the Pamir Mountains. Wakhi describes the people living in the Wakhan valley.

58. This is probably not a subspecies issue. Again, a report describing the Tibetan wolf nearby in Pakistan describes little fear of wolves and no reports of attacks. Abbas et al. 2013.

59. For Soviet examples, see Graves and Geist 2007, pp. 141–70; for European, see, Clark 1996, p. 134; for Native American, Lopez 2004, pp. 114–34. Lopez is careful to note that, in North America, woodland tribes were more afraid of wolves (as they'd come upon the wolves by accident in the forest, rather than being able to watch them from a safe distance across open expanses) and that all Native Americans were wary of wolves, particularly rabid individuals (p. 123). This is only a rough parsing out. Mongolians, for example, have a wolf totem, and cherish the canids (Rong 2008).

60. Walker 2005.

61. Ibid., pp. 69, 79.

changed accounts of the wolf in Japanese culture. Rabies created unusually violent wolves and perceptions of the canids quickly changed. In folk stories, wolves went from Gods to demons.[62]

Beyond folk accounts, the contrast of North American and Eurasian wolves is supported by the drastically different statistics of wolf attacks cited across the continent. Moriceau describes thousands of attacks in France from the fifteenth to twentieth centuries, with the most occurring between the 1560s and the early 1800s.[63] Kruuk notes similar contrast between wolf attacks in Europe and North America, focusing on surprising records of attacks from Belarus, Estonia and even nineteenth century Holland.[64] Turkey also has documentation of attacks.[65] Linnell et al.'s comprehensive review of wolf attacks on humans supports these accounts, describing drastically higher numbers of attacks for Europe, India, Iran and Russia than for North America across the past three centuries.[66].

These differences in behaviour may represent different wolf 'cultures'. Subspecies specifics (e.g. size) may matter less than learned behaviour. A concept of wolf cultures offers a feasible explanation for how and why wolves behave differently in different regions. Both Seton and Walker describe wolves (in North America and Japan, respectively) learning to avoid traps and passing along this knowledge to pups.[67] Wolves display not just learned behaviour but also transmission of this behaviour across generations.[68] Perhaps wolves in North America simply did not learn to hunt humans the way Central Asian and Russian wolves did. Pavlov describes how, following a spate of attacks, Russians would kill the perpetrating wolves and their litters and the attacks would stop.[69] If hunting humans is a learned behaviour, not a trait specific to certain subspecies, such attacks can become a problem anywhere. In 'An American Wolf Pack Turns Russian', Geist offers a behavioural progression via habituation of wolves 'learning' to overcome fear and then to attack humans.[70]

Many Central Asians were and remain pastoral. They do not just entice wolves with their livestock but also associate themselves with prey. The wolves may

62. Ibid, p. 108.
63. Smith 2009.
64. Kruuk 2002.
65. Emsen 2007; Turkmen et al. 2012. Emsen claims wolf attacks in Turkey are 'not uncommon'. Turkmen et al. describe them as 'rare'.
66. Linnell et al. 2002: see Tables 9 and 40. Mech and Boitani describe the discrepancy between North America and Eurasia as well (Mech and Boitani 2010).
67. Seton 1974, p. 765; Walker 2005, p. 105.
68. Haber 2005; Haber 2007. For example, certain wolf packs train their cubs to overcome a fear of heights and then use cliffs to hunt Dall sheep (*Ovis dalli*). Neighbouring packs, despite being in the same environment, lack this skill (Alexander Lee, Denali Education Center, personal communication, 2013).
69. Pavlov 1982.
70. Graves and Geist 2007.

not distinguish the shepherds as in a different category – i.e. not prey – from the livestock, especially as many shepherds are children. The wolves may hunt flock and child together. Many old Soviet accounts describe children being attacked while tending their flocks.[71] This could explain both how such hunting behaviour arose and why it continues. On the contrary, most Native American tribes were not pastoralists but hunters like the wolves. Wolves had less reason to encroach and may have recognised Native Americans more as fellow predators than as prey. Predators command a certain level of respect if not fear. Again the loss of fear, i.e. habituation, can lead to attacks on humans.[72]

If habituation makes wolves dangerous, perhaps wolves need to be taught fear and kept afraid. The danger of habituation alludes to the source of the problem not lying in the natural environment (i.e. a space void of human influence or responsibility) or in some inherent, violent inclination of the Tibetan wolf subspecies. Instead the wolves' behaviour is a response to human actions. Certain policies or people may be creating or allowing habituated, dangerous wolves.

Another apolitical ecological explanation is simply the amount of snow.[73] Every twelve or thirteen years winter hits the Pamir extra hard, resulting in unusually deep snow.[74] Deep snowpack stresses wildlife, including wolves. Conservationists note that this is when the wolves turn to hunting argali. Locals say that this is when the wolves come after them.[75] Apolitical ecological explanations confuse responsibility for the problem. By placing the conflicts' causes in the natural world, such explanations make no one responsible. The injustice is not in the deep snow stressing the wolves but that when wolves are stressed, the Wakhi are left to deal with dangerous animals and do not have the means to do so. Justice may require empowering the Wakhi and leaving them less vulnerable.

CREATING DANGEROUS NATURE

The government claims the attacks happen because it stopped funding the wolf-culling programme.[76] This claim may show an interest in continued power in the region (and a potential problem as the Pamirs fall within the Gorno-Badakhshan Auton-

---

71. Ibid.
72. Ibid., Linnell et al. 2002.
73. Radio Free Europe 2012.
74. Pereladova 2002.
75. Wolf biologists may contest such accounts. They argue that, statistically, wolf attacks peak from June to August (Linnell et al. 2002). They speculate that, in the summer, more people are out foraging and herding and that the wolves are unusually stressed by needing to provide for their pups (Rootsi 2001). In the Pamirs wolves are high up in the alpine meadows during the summer. They tend not to come down to the valleys, and thus villages, until they are following their prey down in the winter (Pereladova 2002).
76. Radio Free Europe 2012.

omous Oblast [GBAO] region, an ethnically and religiously distinct part of the country) but it also shows concern for the people. The government acknowledged the Pamiri's claims after locals sent a special request to the Environmental Protection Department for armed specialists to come cull the wolves.[77] Whether or not this will solve the problem (the government claimed they hoped to settle it in three days) or address the injustice adequately rather than just for the moment is another question. At least the Pamiri are being heard and their problem is being addressed.

Though the renewal of culling may be a just response, it may not be an adequate solution to maintain both justice *and* wildlife conservation. Rangers shoot two to 25 wolves a year but they claim this is not enough.[78] Wolf-culling programmes in a region with little wolf research risk, oddly, either eradicating the wolves or being ineffectual. Not knowing specific wolf numbers[79] causes arbitrary and uninformed culling quotas. Random culling is an unacceptable solution for remedying concerns of conservation and justice. Culling is expensive and near impossible to accomplish by hunting. Traps and poison may offer better chances of success but they pose huge risks to other wildlife, particularly species of conservation concern such as snow leopards.

Some explanations for wolf attacks actually attribute the *cause* of the wolf attacks to people and politics instead of to nature. Here the injustice is not obscured by any ecological confusion and may be akin to more familiar cases of environmental justice. Certain people, pursuing their own interests at the expense of others, make the environment more dangerous.

A group of Japanese geographers argue that the wolves are more prone to attack people because trophy hunters and soldiers have depleted the wolves' prey throughout the Pamir.[80] Border guards, especially, reduce local game as the guards' numbers increase with unrest in Afghanistan and as they hunt for food.[81] Neither trophy nor subsistence hunting represents discrimination, per se. The hunters and guards do not shoot the ungulates to send wolves after the Wakhi but they do gain dinner or trophies, i.e. benefits, while potentially putting the Wakhi at risk with their behaviour.[82]

---

77. Ibid.
78. Pereladova 2002.
79. The best available is a rough estimate of 250–275 (2002 WWF survey) to 1,300 (European Commission, 2007) (Pereladova 2002; Saidov 2007).
80. Watanabe et al. 2010. Albeit their claims refer to wolf attacks on livestock – they do not officially explain attacks on humans. Phrases such as 'According to one local hunter, wolves gradually began to "ignore" people after the collapse of the Soviet Union. They became more aggressive, especially since around 2002-2003' could be describing the situation with attacks on humans as well. This also echoes an account of conflict with wolves arising in Japan after great slaughters of deer; see Walker 2005, p. 148.
81. Schaller 2007.
82. Though not necessarily – Tatjana Rosen writes that some concessions manage the ungulate populations sustainably and their land actually supports high snow leopard populations and she

Soldiers may be more difficult to implicate than trophy hunters. Their employer, the State, could be charged with not providing its workers with adequate food or support, and thus assigned some responsibility in creating dangerous conditions for the Wakhi and other Pamiri. This also adds complexity to the culling programme. If the State is creating the problem by sending soldiers out to compete with the wolves for prey then shooting wolves in attempt to quell Pamiri concerns is neither addressing the real source of the problem nor considering concerns for conservation (of a variety of species: wolves and those animals the soldiers hunt for food).

Trophy hunting presents a different problem. Trophy hunters hunt argali. Tibetan wolves also hunt argali. Hunting is big business – hunters pay $25,000 per animal: $9,000 for a permit and at least $16,000 more for guiding, lodging and other expenses.[83] Trophy hunters and their fixers shoot wolves to protect the argali.[84] If these groups' agenda – protecting argali – becomes conflated with Wakhi communities' claims, the Wakhi's concerns may be challenged by outsiders as invalid in yet another way. More importantly, stressing wolves by reducing their prey may cause attacks on people and livestock. In the Pamir, Tibetan wolves feed mostly on red marmots (*Marmota caudata*). In the winter, when the marmots are hibernating, the wolves turn to tolai hare (*Lepus tolai*), argali and occasionally Siberian ibex.[85] Hunters shoot the prey that the wolves need when stressed; this corresponds to the villagers' claims that wolf attacks occur in the winter. This is an example of Western science helping to describe the injustice. Wolf biology supports local accounts, verifying their concerns. When the research is available, science and local knowledge can be mutually reinforcing, adding depth and detail to local claims.

Injustice here stems also from policy working in the interests of hunting businesses and not of the marginalised Wakhi. Argali hunting is managed by private enterprises holding concessions to large areas of land in the Pamir.[86] It is heavily regulated but the laws are designed to assure the conservation of the argali. Thus justice may require not just restrictions on hunting by the soldiers but also stricter quotas or regulations on trophy hunting.[87] Justice may also require protection of the villagers – and not just the argali – from wolves. This observation echoes more classic cases of environmental justice in which calls are made to protect those left vulnerable by policies working in the interest of empowered institutions at the expense of local communities.

---

suspects high wolf populations as well (personal communication, 2013).

83.   Schaller 2007; Rosen, personal communication, 2013.

84.   Saidov 2007.

85.   Hepter et al. 1988.

86.   Schaller 2007.

87.   The official quota is actually small given the population of the sheep, but some concessions operate without permits (Rosen, personal communication, 2013).

INJUSTICE ALL AROUND

The Pamiri argue that wolves attack them because they cannot protect themselves. This disarmament explanation also appears in literature on wolf attacks in Russia.[88] Some scholars argue that, up until 1991, the Soviets supplied the Wakhi and other Pamiri with guns and ammunition. Wolf numbers have increased since.[89] Others claim the Soviets denied accounts of wolf attacks as an excuse to keep the populace unarmed.[90] Either way rural Central Asians remain unarmed. Graves describes encountering a shepherd in Kazakhstan armed only with 'a long iron rod' to protect himself and his flock from wolves.[91] In Mainwad, Afghanistan, Din Mohammad, a seventy-year-old Kuchi sheep owner with twelve children and 36 grandchildren, says life in the camp is now a nightly terror.

> 'We are afraid of the wolves. They are very big, they come up to a man's waist.[92] Yesterday a wolf bit a boy on the leg during the night, but the child struggled so the wolf snatched a sheep that was also in the tent. We launched a hunt party to get the sheep back, but by the time we found it, the wolves had devoured it. We have only sticks to defend ourselves, so we couldn't even kill the wolves. They just loped back to their desert lair. We are keeping vigil at night and we have posted watchmen, but we dare not sleep at night ... We need guns to defend ourselves', says Din Mohammad. 'Until we can do that we are sitting ducks for the wolves'.[93]

The Tajiks' situation is also dire. They are explicit in expressing their vulnerability: Locals in the Sijd and Rivak villages told RFE/RL they have pitchforks and shovels to fight wolves when necessary. Law enforcement officers told RFE/RL that a special request has been sent to the Environmental Protection Department to send armed specialists to help reduce the wolf population in the area.[94]

Akin to the Soviets in the past, those holding power in the region have many reasons to be reluctant to arm the populace.[95] In fact many herders did own shotguns to protect their herds but the guns were confiscated following unrest in the summer of 2012.[96] The Wakhi may not just need weapons to protect themselves but also to prevent the wolves from habituating. Similar arguments explain why wolves do not attack people in North America and justify Maasai hunting lions.[97]

---

88. Graves and Geist 2007.
89. Watanabe et al. 2010.
90. Pavlov 1982.
91. Graves and Geist 2007, p. 21.
92. This is probably an exaggeration. Heptner et al. (1988) note that the Tibetan wolf is a small subspecies.
93. Barrand 2003.
94. Radio Free Europe 2012.
95. Again, the Pamir falls in the Gorno Badakhshan Autonomous Oblast [GBAO] of Tajikistan, a semi-autonomous, ethnically and religiously-distinct region that borders Afghanistan.
96. Rosen, personal communication, 2013.
97. Graves and Geist 2007; Boyd 2006; Goldman et al. 2013.

The Wakhi's vulnerability to the wolves creates a feedback loop, perpetuating the danger and thus injustice of their environment.

Wolves attack livestock across the world.[98] In the Pamir, pastoral communities own little more than their livestock. Much scholarship, particularly in the wake of the fall of the Soviet Union and now in conjunction with the war in Afghanistan, describes the difficulties facing many Pamiri.[99] In the region losing one's livestock is often losing one's livelihood. Economic loss and hardship are also concerns for justice but these are questions of distributive justice and solutions are available. The government can compensate Pamiri for economic losses due to wolves. These costs could be distributed in a fair way, e.g. by considering wolf-caused losses a public problem and thus sharing the costs.[100] Other options are available, too. For example, if it is determined that argali hunting is causing wolf attacks, portions of the hunting profits could be returned to the community and used to better protect the people and their livestock.[101] Still, distributive justice does not address the fear or harm of attacks on humans. One cannot be adequately compensated for a lost person. Fear cannot be better distributed. Wolves can cause great emotional distress to rural communities.[102] Better governance cannot spread wolf-fear more fairly nor should it.

CONCLUSION: REMEDYING JUSTICE AND CONSERVATION IN THE WAKHAN

Adequate recognition of knowledge and participation in governance can be considered elements of environmental justice.[103] Some argue that injustice among these elements actually causes the unjust distribution that other theories of justice seek to address.[104] Others note that they represent another form of injustice. Either way, both describe potential injustice to the Wakhi. The Wakhi are made vulnerable by not being able to participate in the production of knowledge about wolves. If their wolves are different, the Wakhi lack the means and power to describe these differences (assuming that scientific recognition would lead to better protection). They are made even more vulnerable by their lack of participation in the govern-

---

98. For example, Watanabe et al. 2010; Namgail et al. 2007.

99. Breu and Hurni 2003; Kassam 2009; Kerven et al. 2012; Kleinn 2005; Kreutzmann 2003; Kreutzmann 2005; Kreutzmann 2010; Ostrowski 2007; Pak and Rambaut 2003; Robinson and Guenther 2007; Robinson et al. 2010; Stucker 2009, Strong and Squires 2012.

100. Shafqat Hussain's work in Pakistan remedying conflict with snow leopards offers a prime example: see Hussain 2000.

101. A portion of the cost of permits is already supposed to return to local communities, but they rarely receive the funds due to corruption (Rosen, personal communication, 2013).

102. Buller 2008.

103. Schlosberg 2004.

104. Young 1990.

ance of their valley. They cannot help better regulate argali hunting or redistribute its benefits. They do not conduct culling programmes or set wolf quotas. They do not invite the border guards or determine the number of rangers on patrol. This is the result of other social injustice stemming from regional politics.

People in other parts of the world may more easily coexist with wolves (and even more dangerous carnivores) because their communities have recognition – i.e. their concerns are better heard and addressed and they participate in determining how dangerous, local animals are managed. For example, wolf conflict is dealt with differently in the United States. Even when wolves were listed as endangered following their reintroduction to Yellowstone National Park in 1995, the 10(j) rule deemed them an 'experimental' population, which allowed managers flexibility to address problems specifically to livestock producers.[105] Today, in places where wolves are federally delisted and not protected by state regulations, such as Idaho and Montana, livestock producers are typically permitted to lethally remove wolves that threaten or kill livestock. Furthermore, both Montana and Idaho have established hunting seasons that permit the taking of wolves as trophy game animals. In North America, local stakeholders make claims about wolves – e.g. that wolves kill their livestock or reduce game for hunting – and these claims are heard and addressed in various ways. In some areas, wolves are even culled by government agencies to protect wild game.[106] The reason why these communities are heard and the Wakhi and other Central Asians are not does not necessarily have to do with better science. Instead this may be a testament to democracy or varying degrees of recognition and participation granted to rural North Americans but not Central Asians.

Addressing injustice stemming from lack of participation and recognition may simply require a focus on process. Local knowledge can be invited and incorporated into governance and decision-making. Even better, explicit discussions of values between stakeholders and the relevant communities can help clearly define all goals and concerns. Locally-generated policy can offer the most palatable, appropriate and just solutions. Including Wakhi in the process of addressing this conflict may offer the best chance for a successful solution: conserving wildlife and achieving justice.

Environmental justice asks: are all relevant and concerned groups, especially those living in this environment, helping to decide what sort of environment this is? If the Wakhi are part of determining their surroundings they will be able to address how vulnerable they are to wolf attacks. Central Asia, including the Pamir, supports an unusually high density of wolves.[107] About 1,300 wolves wander the Pamir and their numbers are increasing.[108] This need not be a bad thing so long as

---

105. Federal Register 2008.
106. See for example Dixon, this volume.
107. Pereladova 2002.
108. Saidov 2007.

the Pamiri have the power and means to safely coexist. If so and if they feel secure and empowered, justice will be met and conservation can follow.

BIBLIOGRAPHY

Abbas, F., T.P. Rooney and A. Mian. 2013. 'Grey wolf in Gilgit-Baltistan, Pakistan: Distribution, abundance, and persecution'. *Canid Biology & Conservation* 16 (6): 18–24.

Adams, W.M. and J. Hutton. 2007. 'People, Parks and Poverty: Political Ecology and Biodiversity Conservation'. *Conservation and Society* 5 (2): 147–83.

Apffel-Marglin, F. 1996. 'Introduction: Rationality and the World', in F. Apffel-Marglin and S.A. Marglin (eds) *Decolonizing Knowledge: From Development to Dialogue* (Oxford: Oxford University Press) pp. 1–39.

Agrawal, A. 1995. 'Dismantling the Divide Between Indigenous and Scientific Knowledge'. *Development and Change* 26 (3): 413–39.

Angulo, J.J. 1947. 'A Record of a Timber Wolf Attacking a Man'. *Journal of Mammalogy* 28 (3): 294–9.

Barrand, J. 2003. 'In Maiwand, South of Kandahar, Cordaid Beneficiaries Live in Fear of their Lives'. *Wolf Song of Alaska*. July. http://www.vargfakta.se/wp-content/uploads/2012/03/The-Killer-Wolves-of-Maiwand.pdf

Behdarvand, N., M. Kaboli, M. Ahmadi, E. Nourani, A.S. Mahini and M.A. Aghbolaghi. 2014. 'Spatial risk model and mitigation implications for wolf–human conflict in a highly modified agroecosystem in western Iran'. *Biological Conservation* 177: 156–164.

Blua, A. 2005. 'Central Asia: Cohabitation of Wolves, Humans Proves Difficult'. *Radio Free Europe/ Radio Liberty*, 15 March. http://www.rferl.org/content/article/1057987.html

Boyd, D.K. 2006. 'Article 17: (Case Study) Wolf Habituation as a Conservation Conundrum', in M.J. Groom, G.K. Meffe and C.R. Carroll (eds) *Principles of Conservation Biology* (Sunderland: Sinauer Associates).

Breu, T. and H. Hurni. 2003. *The Tajik Pamirs: Challenges of Sustainable Development in an Isolated Mountain Region* (Berne: Centre for Development and Environment (CDE), University of Berne).

Bullard, R.R.D (ed.) 2005. *The Quest for Environmental Justice: Human Rights and the Politics of Pollution* (San Francisco: Sierra Club Books).

Buller, H. 2008. 'Safe from the Wolf: Biosecurity, Biodiversity, and Competing Philosophies of Nature'. *Environment and Planning A* 40 (7): 1583–97.

Butler, L., B. Dale, K. Beckmen and S. Farley. 2011. 'Findings Related to the March 2010 Fatal Wolf Attack near Chignik Lake, Alaska'. *Wildlife Special Publication*, ADF&G/ DWC/WSP-2011-2 (Palmer, Alaska).

CBC News. 2013. 'Wolf chases Cyclist on Alaska Highway in Yukon'. *CBC News North*. 10 July. http://www.cbc.ca/news/canada/north/wolf-chases-cyclist-on-alaska-highway-in-yukon-1.1393925

Clarke, C.D.H. 1971. 'The beast of Gevauden'. *Natural History* 80: 44–51, 66–73.

Clark, T.W. 1996. *Tales of the Wolf: Fifty-One Stories of Wolf Encounters in the Wild* (Moose Homestead Publishers).

Coleman, J.T. 2004. *Vicious: Wolves and Men in America* (New Haven: Yale University Press).

Emsen, I.M. 2007. 'Panfascial (craniomaxillomandibular) Trauma by Animal Bite: A Wolf Attack'. *Plastic and Reconstructive Surgery* **119** (1): 438–9.

Foucault, M. 1972. *The Archaeology of Knowledge* (New York: Harper and Row).

— 1980. *Power/Knowledge: Selected Interviews and Other Writings 1972–1977* (New York: Pantheon Books).

Geisler, C. 2003. 'A New Kind of Trouble: Evictions in Eden'. *International Social Science Journal* **55** (175): 69–78.

Goldman, M.J. 2007. Tracking Wildebeest, Locating Knowledge: Maasai and Conservation Biology Understandings of Wildebeest Behavior in Northern Tanzania. *Environment and Planning D: Society and Space* **25**: 307–31.

Goldman, M.J., J.R. de Pinho and J. Perry. 2013. 'Beyond Ritual and Economics: Maasai Lion Hunting and Conservation Politics'. *Oryx* **44** (3): 1–11.

Graves, W.N. and V. Geist. 2007. *Wolves in Russia: Anxiety through the Ages* (Calgary: Detselig Enterprises).

'Gray Wolf (*Canis lupus*)'. 2008. Federal Register 73:239. Rules and Regulations. 11 December: 75361-75371. http://www.fws.gov/mountain-prairie/species/mammals/wolf/Enclosure%20(10j%20rules).pdf

Haber, G. 2005. 'Behavior and Conservation of Wolves in Alaska'. *Alaska Wolves*. http://www.alaskawolves.org/Reports.html

Haber, G.C. 2007. 'Wolf Foraging and Related Social Variations in Denali National Park'. *Alaska Park Science* **6**(2): 73–7.

Haraway, D. 1988. 'Situated Knowledges: The Science Question in Feminism and the Privilege of Partial Perspective'. *Feminist Studies* **14** (3): 575–99.

Harding, S. (ed.) 2011. *The Postcolonial Science and Technology Studies Reader* (Durham: Duke University Press).

Harris, R.B. 2008. *Wildlife Conservation in China: Preserving the Habitat of China's Wild West* (London: M.E. Sharpe).

Hepter, V.G., A.A. Nasimovich, A.G. Bannikoc and R.S. Hoffman. 1988. *Mammals of the Soviet Union Vol II, Part 1a: Sinenia and Carnivora (sea cows, wolves and bears)* (Washington DC: Smithsonian Institute and the National Science Foundation).

Hussain, S. 2000. 'Protecting the Snow Leopard and Enhancing Farmers' Livelihoods: A Pilot Insurance Scheme in Baltistan'. *Mountain Research and Development* **20** (3): 226–31.

Iran Focus 2005. 'Homeless man eaten by wolves in Iran. January 4th'. http://www.iranfocus.com/en/index.php?option=com_content&task=view&id=1150

Jasanoff, S. and M. Martello (ed.) 2004. *Earthly Politics: Local and Global in Environmental Governance* (Cambridge, MA: MIT Press).

Jenness, S.E. 1985. 'Arctic Wolf Attacks Scientist – A Unique Canadian Incident'. *Arctic* **38** (2): 129–32.

Jhala, Y.V. and D.K. Sharma. 1997. 'Child-lifting by wolves in eastern Uttar Pradesh, India'. *Journal of Wildlife Research* 2 (2): 94–101.

Kassam, K.A. 2009. 'Viewing Change through the Prism of Indigenous Human Ecology: Findings from the Afghan and Tajik Pamirs'. *Human Ecology* 37 (6): 677–90.

Kerven, C., B. Steimann, C. Dear and L. Ashley. 2012. 'Researching the Future of Pastoralism in Central Asia's Mountains: Examining Development Orthodoxies'. *Mountain Research and Development* 32 (3): 368–77.

Kiniyalocts, M. 2000. *Environmental Justice: Avoiding the Difficulty of Proving Discriminatory Intent in Hazardous Waste Siting Decisions.* Land Tenure Center. (University of Wisconsin-Madison).

Kleinn, E. 2005. 'Paper 4: Development Initiatives versus Environmental Protection?' In *Strategies for Development and Food Security in the Mountainous Areas of Central Asia.* International Workshop Sponsored by Inwnet, AKF, and GTZ. Dushanbe, Tajikistan: 6–10 June.

Kreutzmann, H. 2003. 'Ethnic Minorities and Marginality in the Pamirian Knot: Survival of Wakhi and Kirghiz in a Harsh Environment and Global Contexts'. *The Geographical Journal* 169 (3): 215–35.

— 2005. 'June. Paper 2: The Significance of Geopolitical Issues for Development of Mountainous Areas of Central Asia', in *Strategies for Development and Food Security in the Mountainous Areas of Central Asia.* International Workshop Sponsored by Inwnet, AKF, and GTZ. Dushanbe, Tajikistan: 6–10 June.

— 2010. 'Pluralism, Resilience, and the Ecology of Survival: Case studies from the Pamir Mountains of Afghanistan'. *Ecology and Society* 15 (2): 8.

Kruuk, H. 2002. *Hunter and Hunted: Relationships between Carnivores and People* (Cambridge: Cambridge University Press).

Linnell, J.D.C., R. Andersen, Z. Andersone, L. Balciauskas, J.C. Blanco, L. Boitani, S. Brainerd, U. Breitenmoser, I. Kojola, O. Liberg, J. Løe, H. Okarma, H.C. Pedersen, C. Promberger, H. Sand, E.J. Solberg, H. Valdmann and P. Wabakken. 2002. *The Fear of Wolves: A Review of Wolf Attacks on Humans* (NINA Norsk institutt for naturforskning).

Lopez, B. 2004 [1978]. *Of Wolves and Men* (New York: Scribner Book Company).

Mader, T.R. 2007. 'Wolf Attacks on Humans'. Abundant Wildlife Society of North America: Beresford, South Dakota.

McNay, M.E. and P.W. Mooney 2005. 'Attempted Predation of a Child by a Gray Wolf, Canis lupus, near Ice Bay, Alaska'. *Canadian Field Naturalist* 119: 197–201.

McNay, M.E. 2002. 'Wolf-Human Interactions in Alaska and Canada: A Review of the Case History'. *Wildlife Society Bulletin* 30 (3): 831–43.

Mech, L.D. and L. Boitani. 2010. *Wolves: Behavior, Ecology, and Conservation.* (Chicago: University of Chicago Press).

Mech, L.D. and L. Boitani. 2010b. 'Canis lupus'. IUCN 2012. IUCN Red List of Threatened Species. Version 2012.2. www.iucnredlist.org [Accessed 1 Mar. 2013].

Nadasdy, P. 1999. 'The Politics of TEK: Power and the "Integration" of Knowledge'. *Arctic Anthropology* **36** (1–2): 1–18.

Namgail, T., J.L. Fox and Y.V. Bhatnagar. 2007. 'Carnivore-Caused Livestock Mortality in Trans-Himalaya'. *Environmental Management* **39** (4): 490–6.

Newman, S. 2005. 'Afghan Wolf Attacks'. *Earthweek: A Diary of our Planet.* Universal Press Syndicate. 27 Mar. http://www.wolfsongalaska.org/Afghan_Wolf_Attacks

Orrick, D. 2013. 'Teen Recovering After Apparent Wolf Attack at Northern Minnesota Campground'. *Twin Cities: Pioneer Press.* 26 Aug. http://www.twincities.com/localnews/ci_23947833/apparent-wolf-attack-hurts-teen-northern-minnesota-campground

Ostrowski, S. 2007. 'Wakhi Livestock in Big Pamir in 2006'. WCS Ecosystem Health Project. January. http://pdf.usaid.gov/pdf_docs/PNADJ571.pdf

Pak, N.K. and P.O. Rambaut. 2003. 'Mountains of Tajikistan: Problems of Sustainable Development', in N.K. Pak and P.C. Rambaut (eds) *The Integration of Science and Technology Systems of the Central Asian Republics Into the Western World* (Amsterdam: IOS Press).

Pavlov, M.P. 1982. *The Wolf in Game Management* (Moscow: Agropromizdat).

Pereladova, O. (ed.) 2002. *Potential Management and Use of Wildlife Game Species Inhabiting Gorno.* Badakhshan Autonomous Oblast (GBAO) of the Republic of Tajikistan. World Wide Fund for Nature [WWF].

Radio Free Europe. 2012. 'Tajik Granny Escapes Wolf's Jaws'. *Radio Free Europe Radio Liberty, Radio Ozodi* [RFE/RL], 20 Jan. http://www.rferl.org/content/tajikistan_wolf_attacks/24457676.html

Robbins, P. 2011 [2004]. *Political Ecology* (Malden: Wiley).

Robinson, S. and T. Guenther. 2007. 'Rural Livelihoods in Three Mountainous Regions of Tajikistan'. *Post-Communist Economies* **19** (3): 359–78.

Robinson, S., M. Whitton, S. Biber-Klemm and N. Muzofirshoev. 2010. 'The Impact of Land-Reform Legislation on Pasture Tenure in Gorno-Badakhshan: From Common Resource to Private Property?' *Mountain Research and Development* **30** (1): 4–13.

Rong, J. 2008. *Wolf Totem* (New York: Penguin).

Rootsi, I. 2001. 'Man-Eater Wolves in the 19th Century Estonia'. *Proceedings of the Baltic Large Carnivore Initiative Symposium. Human Dimensions of Large Carnivores in Baltic Countries*, pp. 77–91.

Saidov, A. 2007. *PATCA Report: the Survey of Mammals Pamir-Alai Transboundary Conservation Area.* European Commission on the Establishment Pamir-Alai Transboundary Conservation Area between Tajikistan and Kyrgyzstan (Europe Aid/122639/C/SER/Multi) (Dushanbe).

Schaller, G.B. 2007. 'A Proposal for a Pamir International Peace Park'. *USDA Forest Service Proceedings RMRS* **49**: 227–31.

Schlosberg, D. 2004. 'Reconceiving Environmental Justice: Global Movements and Political Theories'. *Environmental Politics* **13**: 517–40.

Seton, E.T. 1974. *Life-Histories of Northern Animals: An Account of the Mammals of Manitoba,* Vol. 2 (New York: Arno Press, Doubleday and Co).

Shaw, J.H. 2009. 'Review: Wolves in Russia: Anxiety through the Ages'. *Journal of Wildlife Management* 73 (6): 1025–6.

Smallwood, P., C. Shank, A. Dehgan and P. Zahler. 2011. 'Wildlife Conservation in Afghanistan?' *BioScience* 61 (7): 506–11.

Smith, J.M. 2009. 'History of the Big Bad Wolf: 3000 Attacks on Men in France, XVth-XXth Century'. *Journal of Modern History* 81: 165–7.

Strong, P.J. and V. Squires. 2012. 'Rangeland-Based Livestock: A Vital Subsector Under Threat in Tajikistan', in V.R. Squires (ed.) *Rangeland Stewardship in Central Asia. Balancing Improved Livelihoods, Biodiversity Conservation and Land Protection* (Dordrecht: Springer) pp. 213–35.

Stucker, D. 2009. 'Environmental Injustices, Unsustainable Livelihoods, and Conflict: Natural Capital Inaccessibility and Loss among Rural Households in Tajikistan', in J. Agyeman and Y. Ogneva-Himmelberger (eds) *Environmental Justice and Sustainability in the Former Soviet Union* (Cambridge: MIT Press) pp. 237–74.

Thompson, Ch. 2002. 'When Elephants Stand for Competing Philosophies of Nature: Amboseli National Park, Kenya', in J. Law and A. Mol (eds) *Complexities: Social Studies of Knowledge Practices* (Durham: Duke University Press) pp. 166–90.

Turkmen, S., A. Sahin, M. Gunaydin, O. Tatli, Y. Karaca, S. Turedi and A. Gunduz. 2012. 'A Wild Wolf Attack and Its Unfortunate Outcome: Rabies and Death'. *Wilderness & Environmental Medicine* 23: 248–50.

United Nations Environmental Programme [UNEP]. 2003. *Afghanistan Wakhan Mission Technical Report*. Geneva. http://postconflict.unep.ch/publications/WCR.pdf

Walker, B.L. 2005. *The Lost Wolves of Japan* (Seattle, London: University of Washington Press).

Watanabe, T., S. Izumiyama, L. Guanavinaka and M. Anarbaev. 2010. 'Wolf Depredation on Livestock in the Pamir'. *Geographical Studies* 85: 26–36. http://www.ihdp.unu.edu/file/get/8402.pdf

West, P., J. Igoe and D. Brockington. 2006. 'Parks and Peoples: The Social Impact of Protected Areas'. *Annual Review of Anthropology* 35: 251–77.

Wilbert, C. 2006. 'What is Doing the Killing? Animal Attacks, Man-Eaters, and the Shifting Boundaries and Flows of Human-Animal Relations', in The Animal Studies Group (ed.) *Killing Animals* (Chicago: University of Illinois Press) pp. 30–49.

Young, I.M. 1990. *Justice and the Politics of Difference* (Princeton: Princeton University Press).

14

Hierarchy, Intrusion and the Anthropomorphism of Nature: Hunter and Rancher Discourse on North American Wolves

Jessica Bell

BACKGROUND

A Particularly Symbolic Animal

The reintroduction of wolves to wild areas where they had been formerly extirpated is one of the most controversial conservation initiatives in the United States. This issue is particularly pressing given the federal de-listing of the wolf and the transition to state management of wolves.[1] Numerous studies have examined attitudes toward wolves and wolf restoration in the United States and Europe and have demonstrated that such attitudes are often correlated with demographic factors such as age, gender, level of educational attainment and urban or rural residence, as well as distance from wolves and knowledge of wolves.[2] Hunters and ranchers are two populations that often have antagonistic attitudes toward wolves and support lethal control of the species.[3] Yet opposition to wolf conservation is not uniform between and within these groups. One meta-analysis of wolf attitudinal studies demonstrated that, although attitudes toward wolves had a negative correlation with ranching and farming occupations, hunters were more positive toward wolves than the general population.[4] A second longitudinal study in Utah found that, although hunters were less positive toward wolves than urban residents, the majority of hunters still had a positive view of wolves.[5]

---

1. Treves and Bruskotter 2011.
2. Skogen and Thrane 2007; Kellert 1985; Williams, Ericsson and Heberlein 2002; Browne-Nunez and Taylor 2002.
3. Browne-Nunez and Taylor 2002; Kellert 1985; Bruskotter, Vaske and Schmidt 2009.
4. Williams, Ericsson and Heberlein 2002.
5. Bruskotter, Schmidt and Teel 2007.

However, in Wisconsin, bear hunters[6] were more likely than livestock producers, who were in turn more likely than the general rural population, to favour reducing or eliminating Wisconsin's wolf population.[7] And, although hunters may have more favourable attitudes than the general public toward wolves in certain areas of the United States, a small minority with strong anti-predator biases can exert a disproportionately harmful impact on predator populations.[8] Although programmes exist to compensate ranchers and hunters for wolf-related losses of livestock and hunting dogs, these compensation programmes often have little effect on tolerance for wolves, suggesting that attitudes toward wolves are not purely a matter of economics but are 'deep rooted and value laden and are connected to individual lifestyles and views of the place of humans in nature'.[9]

Wolves have been and continue to be 'particularly symbolic animals',[10] animals upon whom larger ideological issues are superimposed.[11] Their presence in religious parables, folklore and literature has made them symbols of both evil and redemption, of the savage beast and noble wilderness.[12] Wolves are integrated into numerous ideological conflicts over ways of knowing the world, states' rights, property rights, the urban–rural divide, social change and social constructions of nature. To opponents of wolf reintroduction, wolf conservation symbolises the privileging of expert, scientific knowledge over lay, practical knowledge[13] and the destruction of personal freedom and self-determination at the hands of a powerful and controlling federal government.[14] In the United States, the issue of states' rights is intertwined with property rights, with wolf opponents claiming that the federal government's real objective in introducing wolves is to eject people from the Western landscape by undermining rural livelihoods and placing restrictive environmental regulations on private property.[15] Within this framework, wolf reintroduction is viewed as ignoring and threatening powerless rural communities. Ridiculing scientific knowledge about wolves, circulating rumours about secretive government plans and opposing wolf conservation may thus be ways of exercising cultural resistance against scientific and governmental institutions seen as unjustly powerful.[16]

---

6. According to a study by Naughton-Treves, Grossberg and Treves (2003), bear hunters are concerned about losing their valuable hunting dogs to predation by wolves.
7. Naughton-Treves, Grossberg and Treves 2003.
8. Kellert, Black, Rush and Bath 1996.
9. Naughton-Treves, Grossberg and Treves 2003, p. 1508.
10. Lynn 2010, p. 82.
11. Figari and Skogen 2011; Nie 2001; Lopez 1978.
12. Marvin 2012; Jones, this volume.
13. Scarce 1998; Skogen and Krange 2003; Skogen 2001.
14. Nie 2001; Clark and Rutherford 2005; Wilmot and Clark 2005.
15. Wilson 1997.
16. Skogen, Mauz and Krange 2008; Skogen and Thrane 2007; Skogen 2001; Wilson 1997.

Wolf reintroduction is also ideologically intertwined with the urban–rural divide and, in the United States, the division between Eastern and Western residents.[17] Wolf opponents see wolves as animals reintroduced and protected by urban outsiders who do not understand or empathise with the needs of rural life; 'wolves thus symbolize attacks on the community not from encroaching wilderness, as one might believe, but from cities'.[18] Wolves become representatives of processes of social change, such as urbanisation and migration, which alter communities and threaten traditionalist worldviews.[19]

Finally, wolves represent various ideological conceptualisations of nature and the human–nature relationship. In the United States, the pioneers who settled the West had an antipathy towards wilderness and large predators. Subjugation of the wilderness and extermination of wolves were seen as necessary and moral steps towards transforming the land from a Godless wasteland into useful economic space.[20] Since many rural occupations in the United States continue to be nature-extractive, rural residents often hold utilitarian attitudes toward the natural environment;[21] within this framework, wolves may be viewed as value-less.[22] Carnivore management is thus often a conflict between people with dominionistic and utilitarian belief systems, in which satisfaction is derived from mastery over animals and attention is given to animals' material value; and those with moralistic and ecologistic belief systems, in which concerns about the exploitation of animals and the environment as a whole are primary.[23] These different value systems inform ideological assumptions about how nature should be used.[24] Wolf opponents see nature primarily as a resource for humans and favour production-oriented, extractive approaches to land management; in the United States, this viewpoint is known as the 'wise use movement'.[25] In contrast, wolf proponents often see nature as an ecosystem rather than a tool, in need of protection from human overuse and worthwhile for its aesthetic properties.[26] Integral to these different conceptualisations of nature are contrasting ideologies about the 'natural order' and whether humans are viewed as *managers of* nature or *part of* nature.[27] Aldo Leopold, a key figure in the American movement to preserve predators, changed his stance on wolves in favour of protec-

17. Nie 2001; Wilmot and Clark 2005.
18. Skogen and Krange 2003, p. 320.
19. Scarce 2005; Skogen and Thrane 2007.
20. Kellert et al. 1996.
21. Kellert 1986.
22. Chavez, Gese and Krannich 2005.
23. Clark and Rutherford 2005; Kellert 1985.
24. Wilmot and Clark 2005.
25. Nie 2001, p. 4.
26. Sheridan 2007; Skogen 2001; Campion-Vincent 2005.
27. Van Horn 2012, p. 205.

tion; this was linked to a shift from viewing humans as the 'conqueror' of nature to seeing humankind as a 'plain member and citizen' of the biotic community.[28]

These ideological constructions have a powerful impact on whether or not wolves are viewed as natural and legitimate parts of the landscape. In cultures where human space is not seen as a realm separate from and opposed to wilderness, wolves are not viewed as intruders and are thus tolerated and even revered.[29] In landscapes that are humanised, or seen as primarily or exclusively for human use, the presence of wild wolves can lead to a 'symbolic mismatch', leading wolves to be viewed as 'unnatural' and thus illegitimate.[30] These constructions can also change over time. For example, as the Adirondack region of New York became defined as a landscape of leisure by a growing urban-based ideology focused on recreational tourism, the untamed wilderness and the wolf became 'out of place' and de-legitimised.[31]

Discourse and the Perpetuation of Ideology

Discourse is one primary way in which the ideological foundations that shape representations of wolves are perpetuated. Discourse conveys information about the legitimacy of particular relationships between humans, animals and nature. Several authors have explored how overarching ideologies of anthropocentrism and speciesism are replicated through discourse.[32] Turner traced how the ideology of anthropocentrism is produced and perpetrated through discourse that objectifies and commodifies animals, privileges the human perspective and encourages ownership and domination.[33] Both Stibbe and Yates argued that speciesism is perpetuated through such linguistic practices as referring to animals as 'it', using animal references or characteristics as derogatory terms to insult humans and using misleading terminology or euphemisms to refer to practices that abuse animals.[34]

In the realm of wildlife issues in particular, discourse can convey information about the intrinsic versus utilitarian value of wildlife,[35] frame particular species as invaders in need of punishment,[36] use ethical and environmental terminology to disguise and legitimate violence toward animals[37] and influence approaches to wildlife policy.[38] Several scholars have used content analyses of newspapers to

---

28. Leopold 1989, p. 204.
29. Marvin 2012.
30. Figari and Skogen 2011, p. 328.
31. Brownlow 2000.
32. Dunayer 2001; Goatly 2002.
33. Turner 2009.
34. Stibbe 2001; Yates 2010.
35. Stibbe 2001.
36. Potts 2009.
37. Kheel 1995.
38. Lynn 2010.

examine the public discourse on various North American predators, including wolves,[39] cougars,[40] Florida panthers,[41] coyotes,[42] black bears,[43] cormorants[44] and sharks.[45] The public discourse on these animals conveys important ideological notions about risk, responsibility and criminality. The risks that predators pose to humans were in some cases exaggerated[46] and in other cases emphasised over the risks that humans pose to predators.[47] For some species, a rise in negative human–wildlife interactions led to predators increasingly being framed as 'perpetrators' of risk (rather than victims) or even 'criminals'. These discursive frames often carried implicit moral judgments. For example, in the case of cougars, negative terms such as 'serial killers' implied that cougars exhibit premeditated criminal behaviour and delivered implicit messages about how 'criminals' should be dealt with, namely without mercy. Over time, cougar attacks were increasingly attributed to cougar personality and morality, leading the animal's 'moral worthiness' of legal protection to be called into question.[48]

Of the two content analyses focused on wolves, one found that newspapers in states with either new or anticipated wolf populations had significantly more negative expressions per article than areas with no or permanent wolf populations.[49] The authors suggest that, 'even absent wolves, the anticipated presence of wolf populations can increase negative discourse about the predator, which in turn could promote changes in attitudes, especially among people with little knowledge or experience with wolves'.[50] The other content analysis found that support of wolf control is linked to what the authors call retro frontier masculinity, an ideology that promotes a particular form of masculinity by casting wolf hunters as paternalist protectors, feminising opponents of wolf hunting and reifying the masculine family provider role.[51] Although these studies are useful for examining how discourse on wolves is influenced by gender and familiarity with wolves, they examine *public* discourse, or mainstream media, rather than the discourse of particular stakeholder populations.

In this chapter, I use Critical Discourse Analysis to examine discursive representations of wolves in hunter and rancher online forums. Critical Discourse

---

39. Houston, Bruskotter and Fan 2010; Anahita and Mix 2006.
40. Wolch, Gullo and Lassiter 1997.
41. Jacobson et al. 2012.
42. Alexander and Quinn 2011.
43. Siemer, Decker and Shanahan 2007.
44. Muter, Gore and Riley 2009.
45. Muter et al. 2013.
46. Alexander and Quinn 2011.
47. Muter et al. 2013.
48. Wolch, Gullo and Lassiter 1997.
49. Houston, Bruskotter and Fan 2010.
50. Ibid., p. 400.
51. Anahita and Mix 2006.

Analysis is a theoretical and methodological approach that views discourse as a social and ideological practice.[52] Discourse is a social practice in that it both reflects and constructs social relations. As an ideological practice, discourse serves to replicate particular power relationships and ideological assumptions. A major function of dominant discourse, the discourse of those in power, is to legitimate a particular ideological viewpoint and to naturalise the existing social order.[53] When the dominant discourse is extensively pervasive (and alternative discourses are diminished or absent), this discourse is viewed as *common sense* or *natural*. In other words, the ideological underpinnings become invisible and the reality constructed by the dominant discourse becomes both inevitable and ideal. In online forums, respondents who disagree with the dominant discourse are often marginalised through being sent several highly negative and emotionally charged replies and/or being given low comment ratings by their online peers.[54] Analysing online forums can illuminate how the power relations and ideological assumptions perpetuated by discourse influence representations of wildlife.

I analysed the articles, blog posts and discussion threads retrieved by the search term 'wolves' on the online versions of the magazines *Beef Magazine*, *Cattle Today*, *American Hunter* and *Outdoor Life Magazine*. *Beef Magazine* and *Cattle Today* are two of the leading online sites for members of the United States cattle industry. *Beef Magazine* reports an annual draw of two million page views; *Cattle Today* hosts nine forums on various topics related to cattle rearing and rural life, with the number of posts per forum ranging from 8,000 to over 20,000 comments. Of the numerous hunting magazines published in the United States, *American Hunter* and *Outdoor Life Magazine* have two of the highest circulation figures, with a reported 898,044 and 753,394 subscribers respectively.[55] The only hunting magazine that has a higher circulation is *American Rifleman*, which had no articles or blog posts about wolves on its online archive and was thus excluded from analysis. The posting dates of my sample ranged from 1999 to 2013 and yielded a sample of 1,187 articles, blog posts and discussion threads. The discourse in these forums clustered around three themes: hierarchy, intrusion and the anthropomorphism of nature.

The dominant discourse portrays 'man' as the top predator in an environment that is inherently hierarchical. This notion of hierarchy is couched in religious language that evokes the Christian concept of dominion. Wolves are also framed as invaders who symbolise the intrusive presence of certain human groups, namely environmentalists and employees of the federal government. The dominant discourse derides environmentalists and animal activists for anthropomorphising animals

52. Fairclough 1989.
53. Van Dijk 1993.
54. Miller 2005.
55. These circulation figures were reported by the Alliance for Audited Media for its Fishing and Hunting Division as of 30 June 2012.

through false sentiment that doesn't adequately represent nature. However, the ranchers and hunters use anthropomorphism themselves by transplanting human conceptualisations of ethics onto the behaviour of wolves, leading to the image of wolves as 'inhumane' predators. I argue that these discursive representations serve to naturalise, legitimise and perpetuate particular ideological conceptualisations of the social structure of the United States and human-animal relationships. From within these ideological frameworks, wolves are viewed as threatening the social and natural order. Finally, I examine how non-dominant discourses that emerge in these online forums offer alternative ideological perspectives that might promote wolf conservation in the United States.

DISCURSIVE THEMES

Wolves and Hierarchical Conceptions of Nature

According to the dominant discourse, man is the apex predator in an environment that is intrinsically construed in a hierarchical manner. For example, one commentator notes, 'The wolf is entitled to be a wolf and when they start becoming a problem then the *top predator* will do what he has to do'.[56] Another writes, 'Coyotes need to be killed as a matter of course and so do wolves. This makes man the *top predator as he always has been historically* and is *healthier* for deer and elk and every other creature that depends on human beings to act intelligently for their continued existence.' This discourse also communicates the notion that nature is a hierarchy that only allows for one apex predator: man. This arrangement is described as a) rooted in tradition and b) healthy and necessary. Describing this arrangement as traditional and healthy serves to legitimate and naturalise this particular ideological conceptualisation of nature. The notion of man as the sole and necessary apex predator leads to the idea that nature cannot be balanced without the intervention of man. In a comment typical of the dominant discourse, one commentator states, '*The wolves in themselves can't add balance* because there is no predator controlling the wolves!!!!! ... There can be no short-term balance in nature without man's intervention.'

A hierarchical view of nature yields resistance to the concept, espoused by many wildlife biologists and environmentalists, that the reintroduction of non-human predators can bring balance to nature. Within this ideology of hierarchical human–animal relationships, nature is seen as *already balanced* and man is viewed as the *only species* that can maintain balance. As an animal that preys on species that are valuable and desired by hunters and ranchers, the wolf is portrayed as 'not respecting' the core tenet of this hierarchical ideology: the supremacy of man. This yields the notion that wolves are unruly and destructive creatures who must

---

56. Throughout this chapter, the italicised emphasis has been added.

learn their subordinate place in nature; for example, one hunter writes, 'Now it's winter again, and the remnants of that blood thirsty bunch [of wolves] are going to get another *lesson in respect, and their place in the food chain* with yours truly!!!' Another hunter describes how wolves and other predators need 'a good dose of leadicillin' (to be shot with lead bullets) in order to learn to respect and fear man. The almost exclusive use of 'man' and masculine pronouns imply that this hier-archical conceptualisation of nature is gendered. Other scholars have suggested that a construction of masculinity that is predicated upon mastery and control of nature is linked to the history of wolf eradication in the United States and to the continuation of anti-wolf sentiment.[57]

In addition to appealing to social tradition to legitimise this hierarchical conceptualisation of nature, many hunters and ranchers also use religious tradition to support the dominant discourse. Typical comments include: 'If you believe in Creationism it doesn't matter who was here first. Man was given dominion over all creatures', 'God gave us dominion over birds and animals', and 'We were cre-ated in GOD'S image not an animal's'. This discourse appeals to religious tradi-tion to legitimise and naturalise two ideological concepts: a) the right of humans to maintain hierarchical control over nature and b) a strict qualitative boundary between humans and other animals. Within this framework, humans are viewed as the managers of nature and animals are primarily viewed as objects and resources. This is reflected in the use of possessive pronouns to describe wildlife, such as '*our* elk herds', '*your* deer', or '*my* turkey population'. Wildlife species are viewed as *belonging* to humans. By hunting 'game' populations, wolves are committing the criminal act of theft.[58] The dominant discourse thus constructs 'natural behavior' in a particular way congruent with a hierarchical ideology of human–animal relations. Wolf predatory behaviour is de-naturalised and painted as destructive and criminal, whereas human predatory behaviour is naturalised and portrayed as ecologically healthy and necessary.

The de-naturalisation of wolf predatory behaviour leads to the concept of the wolf as an animal who, by upsetting man's hierarchy and possession of nature, destroys ecosystems. Wolves are described as 'over-dominant predator[s]' who 'kill anything in their path' and 'pose a serious threat to wildlife'. A commonly expressed sentiment is that wolves, if not controlled by humans, will 'wipe out' 'to almost extinction' all other wildlife species. Anti-wolf sentiment is often framed as trying to 'save' other wildlife species, especially ungulate species and 'native' wildlife. Like the representations of wolves as intrusive and inhumane (discussed later in this chapter), the representation of wolves as destroyers of ecosystems reflects an ideology in which wolves are viewed as a uniquely destructive species. For example, in responding to a federal government statement that described the wolf's recovery as a success story

---

57. Emel 1998; Anahita and Mix 2006; Antonio 1995.
58. For an exploration of the criminal identity of wolves, see Marvin 2012, p. 89.

similar to the rebound of whooping cranes and pelicans, one rancher notes, 'Of course, whooping cranes and pelicans have never torn apart a 100-pound elk calf or a rancher's cattle'. The wolf's behaviour is framed as unnaturally detrimental, which reinforces the notion that human interventions to control wolves are necessary to preserve ecosystems. The insinuation is that, without a hierarchical model of human–animal relationships in which humans subdue wolves, the result would be ecological chaos and destruction.

The Anthropomorphism of Nature

Another theme that emerged in the sample was anthropomorphic characterisations of nature and wildlife. The dominant discourse claims that environmental and animal advocates perpetuate an inaccurate, idealistic version of nature. For example, one hunter claims that, 'the environmentalists base their opinions on emotion alone *they do not use fact* or reason in their logic. They romanticise a wolf howling at the moon on a hilltop.' One commentator notes that, 'Wolves are not the compassionate family creatures that they are portrayed to be, and projecting human characteristics on an animal [is] an *inaccurate view of nature*'. The environmentalist or anti-hunting viewpoint is termed 'anthropomorphic', 'sugar-coated fantasy/spam' that does not acknowledge 'the reality of the woods'. The dominant discourse aims to align one particular ideological viewpoint, the belief that wolves are destructive and brutal, with reality or common sense. This serves to marginalise alternative discourses and to present the wolf conflict as a matter of reality versus fiction, not one of differing opinions.

Although the dominant discourse condemns anthropomorphism, there are frequent examples of this discourse transplanting human conceptualisations and benchmarks of ethics onto the behaviour of wolves. A common claim is that wolves kill for 'sport' rather than for food. Representative comments include: 'Wolves kill just to kill', 'they kill just because they can just like a *sadistic killer* going into the woods blasting anything that moves', 'we have seen the wolves in our area *kill for sport*', 'a wolf pack kills deer and elk *for fun*', and 'they [wolves] *thrill kill*'. One extended piece of discourse describes how wolves 'deliberately' seek out dogs to kill for sport and then 'lure' dogs into the woods to kill them; another comment labels a wolf as a 'serial killer'. This discourse is interesting for multiple reasons. First, although ascribing compassion to wolves is described as anthropomorphic, ascribing malice and sadism is not seen as anthropomorphic. Second, many of the commenters themselves hunt for sport, and defend sport hunting as ethical, yet they condemn wolves for supposedly committing this same behaviour.

This discourse reflects an ideology that simultaneously judges wolves by human ethical standards while considering wolves to be inherently unethical. For example, one hunter writes, 'The wolves eat only a small amount of meat off of the elk. They also *inhumanely* kill the animal. *Humans humanely kill the animal* and eat a lot more meat than the wolf.' This comment simultaneously applies human conceptualisations of ethics to an animal's natural behaviour (by definition, only humans can be 'humane' or 'inhumane') and finds wolves to be incapable of fulfilling this ethical standard. This discursive strategy appears often in the dominant discourse. Another comment reads: 'They [wolves] kill elk and deer up here and just eat the womb and the calf inside, leaving the carcass. *If hunters were to do that* there would be big static.' Again, the implications are that the predatory behaviours of wolves and humans can be judged according to the same ethical standards and that, unlike humans, wolves are unethical killers. Frequently, wolves are portrayed as 'remorseless killers', which insinuates that wolves should (but don't) feel remorse for natural behaviour, a clear example of placing human ethical standards onto wolves while finding them lacking. Other scholars have documented this image of wolves as excessive and immorally violent.[59]

Another common theme was to characterise wolf predation with terms such as 'horrific', 'gut-wrenching', 'graphic' and 'stomach-turning'. Describing wolf predation behaviour with these terms serves to de-naturalise it. Instead of being viewed as part of the natural cycle of life between predator and prey, the behaviour becomes something monstrous, disturbing and unnatural, something that should be stopped. One editor's note for a photo essay warns: 'Some of the photos in this gallery show wolves killing and eating game animals, please read on at your own discretion'. The same warning is not placed on images of human hunters with the animals they have killed, indicating that the kills of wolves are being discursively framed as more grisly and violent than the kills of humans. This discourse perpetuates the image of man as the only ethical killer, which serves to legitimate a system in which man is the sole apex predator.

The Intrusive Wolf

A third discursive theme that appeared in the sample was the representation of wolves as intrusive. One way in which wolves are portrayed as intrusive is through the discourse of states' rights and property rights. Wolves symbolise the intrusion of the federal government in the ability of states and property owners to defend their livelihoods and interests. For example, in discussing legislation to remove wolves from the Endangered Species Act, one rancher links the de-listing of wolves with the return of 'authority to the states where it rightly belongs'; another rancher notes that, 'many ranchers feel wolf reintroduction was a taking of private property by the federal government'.

The dominant discourse frames wolves and their advocates as being intruders who threaten the social and economic stability of rural Western communities. One rancher comments, 'This maneuver [wolf reintroduction] by the federal government

---

59. Marvin 2012, p. 43; Van Horn 2012, p. 207.

is stealing from me, my children, and our future. It may destroy our livelihood, and our entire lifestyle is also in jeopardy.' Frequently, wolf advocates are characterised as urbanites from liberal cities 'back East' who 'seem to know what we want/need BETTER than those of us that live out here in the West'. The dominant discourse describes wolf advocates (and, by proxy, wolves) as outsiders who don't belong in the Western landscape; typical comments include: 'I think they [wolves] should be reintroduced to California, Massachusetts, Chicago, Washington DC and other liberal meccas', 'Stupid treehuggers. Go back to where you came from and leave our states alone for us to manage', 'Let's release about 6 breeding pairs in all the eastern states and it won't take long for the attitudes to change', and 'These tree huggers and animal huggers are ruining everything. They need to go back under the rock they came from and mind their own business. I wonder what they would say if it was their livestock or their pet that was killed by wolves, would they want to save them then. They should have never restocked those wolves, they have done more damage than good.'

Within this ideological framework, opposing wolf reintroduction is aligned with a) preserving Western culture and independence and b) remedying the social injustice in which the segments of society that benefit from wolf reintroduction (urbanites, liberals, the federal government, East-Coasters) do not have to suffer the costs of this conservation initiative.

The dominant discourse also portrays wolves as intrusive by arguing that the reintroduced wolves are actually a non-native species. For example, one commentator notes, 'The Feds call it a reintroduction except the grey wolf was *never here in the first place.* A mess made by people who have no idea, in areas they don't even live.' In other remarks made by ranchers and hunters, wolves are described as 'introduced' (as opposed to *re*-introduced), 'non-native' and 'transplants'. A common belief is that the wolves used in reintroduction programmes belong to a different species from the wolves that originally lived in the United States. Whether or not this rumour is factually correct or not, its perpetuation reveals truths about the social reality espoused by the dominant discourse.[60] These 'Canadian wolves' are seen as a) more destructive and inhumane than their American cousins and b) the cause of the extinction of the American wolf. A moral dichotomy is created between the good native wolves, who 'didn't bother our livestock' and 'never over-populated their areas and did not kill for fun' and the evil introduced wolves, who are 'more aggressive' and have 'upset the balance'. The dominant discourse promotes the idea that, prior to the introduction of these new wolves, 'we actually still had native wolves', but that the arrival of these new wolves (not the actions of humans) 'decimated' the native population.

This discourse serves to a) promote the ideology that wolf conservation is an intrusion rather than a restoration and b) de-legitimise the presence of the wolf.

---

60. Campion-Vincent 2005.

By describing wolves as introduced, as opposed to re-introduced, the dominant discourse places wolves in the socially constructed category of 'invasive species' or 'varmint'. For example, one commentator notes that, 'The new invasive species of wolf in Montana has driven the native population completely extinct and *should be handled like any invasive species, such as knapweed*'; another comment reads, 'In my opinion grey wolves *should be considered varmints because they were never native to the US*'. The terms of 'invasive species' and 'varmint' carry ideological connotations. These terms perpetuate the notions that wolves 'don't belong here', that wolves are detrimental to ecosystems and that lethal control or extermination is not only acceptable, but also necessary.

Wolves, the Social Structure of the United States, and Human–Animal Relationships

The discursive representations of wolves mentioned thus far serve to naturalise, legitimise and perpetuate particular ideological conceptualisations of human–animal relationships and the social structure of the United States. The dominant discourse communicates the notion that nature is a hierarchy that only allows for one apex predator: man. This ideological conceptualisation of nature is legitimised and naturalised through appeals to social and religious tradition and through describing man as the only ethical predator and the only species who can maintain nature's balance. Representations of wolves and their advocates as intrusive and detrimental to ecological flourishing promote the notion that defending the Western way of life requires combatting wolf reintroduction. Wolf reintroduction is portrayed as a social injustice in which the portion of the population that approves of wolf conservation does not have to bear its detrimental effects.

From within this ideological framework, wolves are viewed as threatening the natural and social order. The wolf is seen as not respecting the supremacy of man and wolf predatory behaviour is de-naturalised and portrayed as destructive and criminal. Hunting wolves is deemed necessary not only to preserve other wildlife, but also to maintain the human–animal boundary and human supremacy over nature. Commentators advocate hunting wolves so that the wolf will 'have its fear of man restored' and 'will quickly learn to respect humans and will soon learn the boundaries'. Lethally controlling wolves is linked with the reassertion of man's right to be the sole apex predator. Arguments for the hunting of wolves include, '*I like being the apex predator* in the woods', 'We simply want to do the same thing the wolf does to other wolves, bears, coyotes and lions-*challenge their position as the top predator*'; and 'I for one recognize that *I am on top of the food chain* and I will not accept that I need to get along with or tolerate the current wolf levels'.

In addition to being portrayed as ecologically detrimental and a danger to the sustainability of other wildlife, the wolf is construed as a threat to the basic tenets of society in the Western United States. In addition to being linked to the intrusion of outside and unwanted social groups, namely environmentalists and employees of the federal government, wolves are viewed as a threat to social order. They are described as 'destroying peace of mind' and endangering the public's right to security and safety. From this ideological viewpoint, letting wolves remain 'unchecked' (un-hunted) will lead to the breakdown of social order and civilisation and will perhaps even culminate, as many commenters claim, in wolves 'finding us on their food chain' and 'eating humans because there will be nothing more to eat in their natural habitat if wolf populations are left unchecked'.

The notion of wolves as threatening the social order is linked to a particular conceptualisation of the history and values of the United States. The dominant discourse portrays the elimination of wolves as a necessary and worthy accomplishment of the European settlers who founded the United States. For example, one hunter notes, 'there is a reason our forefathers eradicated the wolves in the West'; a rancher comments, 'After settling our country, farmers, ranchers, and trappers got rid of almost all of the grey wolves. Along came the Endangered Species Act and now we have more than 6,000 wolves preying on our livestock; *Wolves were almost exterminated for a good reason. I say go back to the old ways.*'

The dominant discourse also ties the reintroduction of wolves to the erosion of 'freedoms that we as Americans cherish', such as the 'right to defend our own property against predators', hunting rights and gun ownership rights. From within this ideological framework, the wolves threaten the values, lifestyle and economy of the Western United States, leading one commentator to exclaim, 'the wolves have seen to it that *our Western heritage is gone forever!*' Wolves are represented as causing not only material destruction (of livestock and wild ungulates) but also *social destruction.*

As discussed in this chapter and in the work of other scholars, views on wolf conservation are linked to ideologies about a) how humans fit in nature and relate to other animals and b) the defence of social communities.[61] Although resistance to wolf reintroduction is often framed as the protection of rural communities, it is 'equally a defence of a more dominance-oriented understanding of the human being'.[62] At stake are notions of animality, humanity and the relationship between the two. Opposition to wolf reintroduction can be seen as the defence of the human identity as the rightful manager of a hierarchically ordered nature.

An Alternative Discourse

Although the dominant discourse in this sample promoted this particular notion of human–animal relationships, an alternative discourse emerged that challenged the prevalent representations of wolves. This alternative discourse was less frequent

61. Van Horn 2012, p. 222; Scarce 2005, p. 142; Marvin 2012, p. 178.
62. Van Horn 2012, p. 222.

and comments that endorsed this ideology tended to be rated lower by online peers. However, several hunters and ranchers advocated this ideology, suggesting that, although the dominant discourse represents the views of those in power in these communities, representations of wolves among hunters and ranchers are not monolithic.

The alternative discourse disputes a hierarchical view of nature. One hunter notes, 'Nature has managed to keep a system of checks and balances for … oh let's see … millions of years. Hubris and ignorance have caused the extinction of so many species at the hands of humans who feel that the earth is our property. *We are part of a web*, not the oligarchs who choose what should live and what should die.' Humans are viewed as 'not the only master' but rather '*just another big link* in the chain' who are 'part of the food chain'. This promotes the notions that a) 'true wilderness [is] where *man is not the only top predator*' and b) man's control is not necessary to maintain nature's balance. Rather, humans should 'let nature take its course'.

Within an ideological framework that sees nature as a web rather than a hierarchy, competition between wolves and humans is perceived as natural and not something to be eliminated. One hunter writes, 'When I hunt where there are wolves and bears and coyotes, *it is just competition. Hunters should not feel it is their right to kill*. It is their right to hunt'; another comments, 'wolves have the right to hunt along side humans or in their own packs'.

Whereas the dominant discourse stresses the need to teach wolves to respect human authority, the alternative discourse promotes the notion of mutual respect between humans and wolves. For example, one hunter notes, 'Wolves are better hunters that we. *Let's show some respect*'; another hunter comments, 'Just because you guys can't out smart a wolf when it comes to hunting doesn't mean you need to get rid of them … they are part of the ecosystem and they are beautiful animals … *have some respect!*' Within this alternative framework, wolves are seen as *belonging to* and *benefitting* ecosystems. Wolves are described as being 'in Montana/Utah/Wyoming *long before* you or any of your ancestors were there'. Another commentator notes, 'Who was here first? Them or us? Seems like we're taking more of *their territory*.' Humans, not wolves, are seen as responsible for disrupting ecosystems. As one hunter comments, 'When white men came to America, there were wolves, deer, elk and everything else *living in balance*, do you really expect me to blame the wolf for what *you are destroying* by building your house in the elk's backyard?' By eliminating wolves and other predators, 'bad things happen' and you 'throw nature out of whack'. These appeals to the historical presence of wolves and biological principles serve to legitimise and naturalise wolf conservation.

This representation of wolves is in stark contrast to the dominant discourse, which portrays wolves as destructive invaders. The alternative discourse does not attempt to de-naturalise wolf predatory behaviour. This challenges the representation of wolves as 'inhumane predators'. One commentator notes, 'A comment was made above that sometimes the wolves kill just for sport. Excuse me, but the human race also does the same thing. At least the wolves hunt in open spaces. How many hunters hunt in a contained fenced area that has been stocked with deer or other wildlife?' This alternative discourse refutes the notion, endorsed by the dominant discourse, that man is the only ethical and humane hunter. Overall, the alternative discourse challenges the notions (perpetuated by the dominant ideology) that nature is a hierarchy, that wolves are introduced invaders and inhumane predators and that wolves destroy ecosystems.

Whereas the dominant discourse promotes the idea that lethal control is the best (or only) method for controlling wolf behaviour, the alternative discourse offers solutions that involve humans altering their behaviours. For example, one rancher comments, 'My herd does not have trouble with wolves. The wolves cross my property all the time but they leave the cows alone. People keep asking what that is? The answer: I keep heifers based on their mother instincts. I keep heifers that are close friends.' Another rancher describes how, as a result of rotating cows between small paddocks, 'We have no predator losses'.

DISCUSSION

Hierarchical Conceptions of Nature

Cultures that use a hierarchical schema to organise the world do so in various ways. Some view humans as superior to all other animals, while others rank beings by characteristics other than species-membership or place nature above humankind.[63] A hierarchical view of nature that places all humans above all animals is often linked to the concepts of human exceptionalism and the 'naturalness' of human dominion over animals.[64] Although human uniqueness and power can be used as arguments for humans' ethical obligations toward animals and stewardship of nature,[65] historically these concepts have also provided justification for animal mistreatment. The notion of the great chain of being (or *scala naturae*), a hierarchical conception of nature in which 'man' is beneath God and animals are beneath humanity, has profoundly shaped Western philosophy, culture and science.[66] This concept emerged from the work of Plato and Aristotle; in the seventeenth and eighteenth centuries, several theologians and philosophers combined this notion with the Christian concept of dominion to claim that other species existed purely for the good and use of humankind. The influential eighteenth century botanist and zoologist Carl

---

63. Descola 2013; Ingold 1994.
64. Thomas 1983; DeMello 2012.
65. Linzey 1987; Preece and Fraser 2000.
66. Lovejoy 1936; Clutton-Brock 1995.

Linnaeus echoed this ideology when he agreed with Aristotle that nature advances 'through Minerals, Vegetables and Animals and finishes with Man' and that these other kingdoms of nature existed *for* man.[67] This hierarchical conceptualisation of nature in Western philosophy and science has historically been used to justify the consumption of animals, vivisection, the moral and cognitive inferiority of animals and the exploitation of natural resources.[68] As in the dominant discourse discussed in this chapter, appeals to religious and social tradition were used to legitimate this ideology toward animals.[69]

The link between a hierarchical conceptualisation of nature and utilitarian attitudes and behaviour towards wildlife can be examined through the lens of Social Dominance Theory, which postulates that people high in Social Dominance Orientation prefer a hierarchically stratified society and use legitimating myths to justify their superior place in the hierarchy.[70] Although this theory was originally developed to explain prejudice among humans, one study found that Social Dominance Orientation was predictive of endorsement of the use of animals for human purposes.[71] Many wolf opponents see wolves as threatening 'man's' mastery over nature. Perpetuating through discourse the notion that ecosystems and communities can only flourish when man is the sole apex predator serves to legitimate human's superior position in the 'natural' hierarchy.

The Anthropomorphism of Nature

There are multiple forms of anthropomorphism and how exactly to define anthropomorphism is a matter of ongoing debate in the scientific community.[72] My focus here is on the ascription of human characteristics to nonhuman animals *for ideological purposes*. In other words, I am not concerned with proving decisively whether or not wolves hunt for 'sport' like humans but rather in exploring the ideological purpose of describing wolves in this manner. The attribution of human traits to nonhuman animals can in some instances enhance ecological consciousness and empathy for animals by helping humans acknowledge areas of human–animal similarity.[73] In the case of wolves, literature that described wolf society in human terms played an important role in the development of an environmental ethic sympathetic to wolves.[74] While a moderate application of anthropomorphism that acknowledges the emotional, cognitive, and behavioural similarities between human and nonhuman

67. Clutton-Brock 1995, p. 434.
68. Thomas 1983; Clutton-Brock 1995.
69. Thomas 1983.
70. Hyers 2006.
71. Ibid.
72. Mitchell 1997.
73. Bekoff 2007.
74. Jones 2003.

animals can be useful in encouraging support for animal welfare and conservation, if anthropomorphism is taken too far, it can 'excessively subsume animals into a human model' and eliminate animals' distinctive attributes and needs.[75]

This form of anthropomorphism has been used for the ideological purposes of a) making animals complicit in their own use and b) projecting onto animals aspects of the human condition that are seen as undesirable or immoral. When circuses and marine mammal parks ascribe human characteristics to their animals, they conceal the domination of animals necessary to their industries and create the illusion that animals 'consent' to their use.[76] Animal agriculture uses anthropomorphism to manufacture the consent of farmed animals; advertisements in which cows promote milk and pigs sell pork disseminate the notion that farmed animals approve of their own consumption.[77] In the case of wolves, discourse that transplants human conceptualisations of ethics onto wolves by referring to them as 'serial killers' or 'sadistic' serves the ideological purpose of making wolves complicit in their own lethal management. In other words, this discourse promotes the notion that it is the wolves' *own immoral behaviour* that makes it necessary to lethally control or exterminate them. Like journalists who portray California cougars as 'morally' deficient and thus unworthy of protection,[78] wolf opponents paint wolves as complicit and criminally responsible for their own lethal management.

This representation of wolves is facilitated by a long history of projecting onto wolves the darkest aspects of human nature. As Marvin writes, 'wolves become perceived and represented as creatures of dangerous and wicked intention because humans need an image for their own wickedness and wrongdoing'.[79] Wolves are a common symbol of evil and threat in Christian Scriptures; the 'wolf in sheep's clothing', Jesus' metaphor for false prophets, attributed not only danger, but also duplicity and immorality, to wolves.[80] The ascription of immorality to wolves is often interrelated with representations of them as *intruders*. For example, in Albania, shepherds describe wolves as 'a thief, a raider, a murderer, a vicious killer, a violator and a dishonourable animal'; the wolf is so labelled because he intrudes upon private property, which in the mountain villages of Albania is synonymous with dishonour.[81]

---

75. Malamud 1998, p. 37.
76. Schwalm 2007; Desmond 1999.
77. Glenn 2004.
78. Wolch, Gullo and Lassiter 1997.
79. Marvin 2012, p. 45.
80. Ibid.
81. Marvin 2010, p. 68.

CONCLUSION

Uncovering how representations of wolves reflect ideological assumptions about the social and natural order illuminates both the challenges and opportunities for wolf conservation in the United States. A core challenge is the deep-rooted ideological underpinnings of opposition to wolf reintroduction. Congruent with previous research, representations of wolves in this sample were intertwined with numerous ideological conflicts over ways of knowing the world, states' rights, property rights, the urban/rural divide, social change and social constructions of nature. These are deep-rooted issues connected to issues of community, identity and worldview, and education or economic compensation may not address these underlying ideological concerns. Yet this analysis indicates that hunter and rancher discourse is not monolithic. Although the dominant discourse appears to oppose wolf introduction, an alternative discourse emerged that seems to promote wolf–human co-existence.

The core limitation of this study is that I cannot determine what percentage of hunters and ranchers post on these online discussion forums. In other words, the discourse on these forums may not be representative of the American hunter and rancher populations as a whole. However, this analysis is about the *dominance* of particular representations of wolves rather than their frequency. Online wildlife forums tend to coalesce around particular representations of animals as a result of dissenters from the dominant ideology being marginalised or pressured into silence.[82] In the online forums I examined, negative ratings and comments were used to chastise those who expressed the willingness to co-exist with wolves. This can be seen as an attempt to naturalise the dominant anti-wolf discourse, so that it appears to be the only 'common sense' worldview, and to encourage conformity within the community. A topic for further research is the power relations within rancher and hunter communities that lead to particular representations of wolves being privileged over others. Understanding the ideological roots of attitudes towards wolves, and the role of discourse and power in sustaining or challenging dominant ideologies, is essential for ensuring a sustainable future for wolves in the United States.

BIBLIOGRAPHY

Alexander, S.M. and M.S. Quinn. 2011. 'Coyote (*Canis latrans*) Interactions with Humans and Pets reported in the Canadian Print Media (1995–2010)'. *Human Dimensions of Wildlife* 16 (5): 345–59.

Anahita, S. and T.L. Mix. 2006. 'Retrofitting Frontier Masculinity for Alaska's War against Wolves'. *Gender and Society* 20 (3): 332–53.

---

82. Miller 2005.

Jessica Bell

Antonio, D. 1995. 'Of Wolves and Women', in C.J. Adams and J. Donovan (eds) *Animals and Women: Feminist Theoretical Explanations* (Durham, London: Duke University Press) pp. 213–30.

Bekoff, M. 2007. 'Wild Justice and Fair Play: Cooperation, Forgiveness, and Morality in Animals', in L. Kalof and A. Fitzgerald (eds) *The Animals Reader* (New York: Berg) pp. 72–90.

Browne-Nunez, Ch. and J.G. Taylor. 2002. *Americans' Attitudes toward Wolves and Wolf Reintroduction: An Annotated Bibliography.* Information Technology Report USGS/BRD/ITR-2002-0002. (Denver: U.S. Government Printing Office).

Brownlow, A. 2000. 'A Wolf in the Garden: Ideology and Change in the Adirondack Landscape', in C. Philo and C. Wilbert (eds) *Animal Spaces, Beastly Places* (New York: Routledge) pp. 141–58.

Bruskotter, J.T., R.H. Schmidt and T.L. Teel. 2007. 'Are Attitudes toward Wolves changing? A Case Study in Utah'. *Biological Conservation* 139: 211–8.

Bruskotter, J.T., J.J. Vaske and R.H. Schmidt. 2009. 'Social and Cognitive Correlates of Utah Residents' Acceptance of the Lethal Control of Wolves'. *Human Dimensions of Wildlife* 14 (2): 119–32.

Campion-Vincent, V. 2005. 'The Restoration of Wolves in France: Story, Conflicts and Use of Rumor', in A. Herda-Rapp and T.L. Goedeke (eds) *Mad about Wildlife: Looking at Social Conflict over Wildlife* (Leiden, Boston: Brill) pp. 99–122.

Chavez, A.S., E.M. Gese and R.S. Krannich. 2005. 'Attitudes of Rural Landowners toward Wolves in Northwestern Minnesota'. *Wildlife Society Bulletin* 33 (2): 517–27.

Clark, T.W. and M.B. Rutherford. 2005. 'Coexisting with Large Carnivores: Orienting to the Problems', in T.W. Clark, M.B. Rutherford and D. Casey (eds) *Coexisting with Large Carnivores: Lessons from Greater Yellowstone* (Washington, Covelo, London: Island Press) pp. 3–27.

Clutton-Brock, J. 1995. 'Aristotle, the Scale of Nature and Modern Attitudes to Animals'. *Social Research* 62 (3): 421–40.

DeMello, M. 2012. *Animals and Society: An Introduction to Human-Animal Studies* (New York: Columbia University Press).

Descola, P. 2013. *Beyond Nature and Culture* (Chicago: The University of Chicago Press).

Desmond, J.C. 1999. *Staging Tourism: Bodies on Display from Waikiki to SeaWorld* (Chicago: The University of Chicago Press).

Dunayer, J. 2001. *Animal Equality: Language and Liberation* (Derwood: Ryce).

Emel, J. 1998. 'Are you Man enough, Big and Bad enough? Wolf Eradication in the US', in J. Wolch and J. Emel (eds) *Animal Geographies: Place, Politics and Identity in the Nature-Culture Borderlands* (London: Verso) pp. 91–118.

Fairclough, N. 1989. *Language and Power* (London: Longman).

Figari, H. and K. Skogen. 2011. 'Social Representations of the Wolf'. *Acta Sociologica* 54 (4): 317–32.

Glenn, C. 2004. 'Constructing Consumables and Consent: A Critical Analysis of Factory Farm Industry Discourse'. *Journal of Communication Inquiry* 28 (1): 63–81.

Goatly, A. 2002. 'The representation of nature on the BBC world service'. *Text* 22 (1): 1–27.

Houston, M.J., J.T. Bruskotter and D. Fan. 2010. 'Attitudes toward Wolves in the United States and Canada: A Content Analysis of the Print News Media, 1999–2008'. *Human Dimensions of Wildlife* 15 (5): 389–403.

Hyers, L.L. 2006. 'Myths Used to Legitimate the Exploitation of Animals: An Application of Social Dominance Theory'. *Anthrozoos* 19 (3): 194–210.

Ingold, T. 1994. 'From Trust to Domination: An Alternative History of Human-Animal Relations', in A. Manning and J. Serpell (eds) *Animals and Human Society: Changing Perspectives* (London: Routledge) pp. 1–22.

Jacobson, S.K., C. Langin, J.S. Carlton and L.L. Kaid. 2012. 'Content Analysis of Newspaper Coverage of the Florida Panther'. *Conservation Biology* 26 (1): 171–9.

Jones, K. 2003. 'Never Cry Wolf: Science, Sentiment and the Literary Rehabilitation of *Canis Lupus*'. *The Canadian Historical Review* 84: 1–16.

Kellert, S. 1986. 'The Public and the Timber Wolf in Minnesota'. *Transactions of the North American Wildlife and Natural Resource Conference* 51: 193–200.

1985. 'Public Perceptions of Predators, Particularly the Wolf and Coyote'. *Biological Conservation* 31: 167–89.

Kellert, S.R., M. Black, C.R. Rush and A.J. Bath. 1996. 'Human Culture and Large Carnivore Conservation in North America'. *Conservation Biology* 10 (4): 977–90.

Kheel, M. 1995. 'License to Kill: An Ecofeminist Critique of Hunters' Discourse', in C.J. Adams and J. Donovan (eds) *Animals and Women: Feminist Theoretical Explanations* (Durham, London: Duke University Press) pp. 85–125.

Leopold, A. 1989. *A Sand County Almanac, and Sketches Here and There* (New York: Oxford University Press).

Linzey, A. 1987. *Christianity and the Rights of Animals* (London: SPCK).

Lopez, B. 1978. *Of Wolves and Men* (New York: Charles Scribner's and Sons).

Lovejoy, A.O. 1936. *The Great Chain of Being: A Study of the History of an Idea* (New York: Harper & Brothers).

Lynn, W.S. 2010. 'Discourse and Wolves: Science, Society and Ethics'. *Society & Animals* 18: 75–92.

Malamud, R. 1998. *Reading Zoos: Representations of Animals in Captivity* (New York: New York University Press).

Marvin, G. 2010. 'Wolves in Sheep's (and Others') Clothing', in D. Brantz (ed.) *Beastly Natures. Animals, Humans, and the Study of History* (Charlottesville, London University of Virginia Press) pp. 59–80.

2012. *Wolf* (London: Reaktion Books).

Miller, C.D. 2005. 'Virtual Deer: Bagging the Mythical "Big One" in Cyberspace', in A. Herda-Rapp and T.L. Goedeke (eds) *Mad about Wildlife: Looking at Social Conflict over Wildlife* (Leiden, Boston: Brill) pp. 51–72.

Jessica Bell

Mitchell, R.W. 1997. 'Anthropomorphism and Anecdotes: A Guide for the Perplexed', in R.W. Mitchell, N.S. Thompson and H.L. Miles (eds) *Anthropomorphism, Anecdotes and Animals* (Albany: State University of New York Press) pp. 407–28.

Muter, B.A., M.L. Gore, K.S. Gledhill, Ch. Lamont and Ch. Huveneers. 2013. 'Australian and U.S. News Media Portrayal of Sharks and their Conservation'. *Conservation Biology* 27 (1): 187–96.

Muter, B.A., M.L. Gore and S.J. Riley. 2009. 'From Victim to Perpetrator: Evolution of Risk Frames Related to Human-Cormorant Conflict in the Great Lakes'. *Human Dimensions of Wildlife* 14 (5): 366–79.

Naughton-Treves, L., R. Grossberg and A. Treves. 2003. 'Paying for Tolerance: Rural Citizens' Attitudes toward Wolf Depredation and Compensation'. *Conservation Biology* 17 (6): 1500–11.

Nie, M.A. 2001. 'The Sociopolitical Dimensions of Wolf Management and Restoration in the United States'. *Human Ecology Review* 8 (1): 1–12.

Potts, A. 2009. 'Kiwis against Possums: A Critical Analysis of Anti-Possum Rhetoric in Aotearoa New Zealand'. *Society & Animals* 17: 1–20.

Preece, R. and D. Fraser. 2000. 'The Status of Animals in Biblical and Christian Thought: A Study in Colliding Values'. *Society & Animals* 8 (3): 245–63.

Scarce, R. 1998. 'What do wolves mean? Conflicting Social Constructions of *Canis lupus* in "Bordertown"'. *Human Dimensions of Wildlife* 3 (3): 26–45.

2005. 'More than mere Wolves at the Door: Reconstructing Community amidst a Wildlife Controversy', in A. Herda-Rapp and T.L. Goedeke (eds) *Mad about Wildlife: Looking at Social Conflict over Wildlife* (Leiden, Boston: Brill) pp. 123–46.

Schwalm, T. 2007. 'No Circus without Animals? Animal Acts and Ideology in the Virtual Circus', in L. Simmons and Ph. Armstrong (eds) *Knowing Animals* (Leiden, Boston: Brill) pp. 79–104.

Sheridan, T.F. 2007. 'Embattled Ranchers, Endangered Species and Urban Sprawl: The Political Ecology of the New American West'. *Annual Review of Anthropology* 36: 121–38.

Siemer, W.F., D.J. Decker and J. Shanahan. 2007. 'Media Frames for Black Bear Management Stories during Issue Emergence in New York'. *Human Dimensions of Wildlife* 12 (2): 89–100.

Skogen, K. 2001. 'Who's afraid of the Big, Bad Wolf? Young People's Responses to the Conflicts over Large Carnivores in Eastern Norway'. *Rural Sociology* 66 (2): 203–226.

Skogen, K. and O. Krange. 2003. 'Wolf at the Gate: The Anti-Carnivore Alliance and the Symbolic Construction of Community'. *Sociologia Ruralis* 43 (3): 309–25.

Skogen, K., I. Mauz and O. Krange. 2008. 'Cry Wolf! Narratives of Wolf Recovery in France and Norway'. *Rural Sociology* 73 (1): 105–33.

Skogen, K. and Ch. Thrane. 2007. 'Wolves in Context: Using Survey Data to situate Attitudes within a wider Cultural Framework'. *Society & Natural Resources* 21 (1): 17–33.

Stibbe, A. 2001. 'Language, Power, and the Social Construction of Animals'. *Society and Animals* 9 (2): 145–61.

Thomas, K. 1983. *Man and the Natural World: A History of the Modern Sensibility* (New York: Pantheon Books).

Treves, A. and J.T. Bruskotter. 2011. 'Gray Wolf Conservation at a Crossroads'. *BioScience* **61** (8): 584–5.

Turner, R. 2009. 'The Discursive Construction of Anthropocentrism'. *Environmental Ethics* **31**: 183–201.

Van Dijk, T.A. 1993. 'Principles of Critical Discourse Analysis'. *Discourse & Society* **4** (2): 249–83.

Van Horn, G. 2012. 'The Making of a Wilderness Icon: Green Fire, Charismatic Species and the Changing Status of Wolves in the United States', in A. Gross and A. Vallely (eds) *Animals and the Human Imagination* (New York: Columbia University Press) pp. 203–37.

Williams, Ch.K., G. Ericsson and T.A. Heberlein. 2002. 'A Quantitative Summary of Attitudes toward Wolves and their Reintroduction (1972–2000)'. *Wildlife Society Bulletin* **30** (2): 575–84.

Wilson, M.A. 1997. 'The Wolf in Yellowstone: Science, Symbol or Politics? Deconstructing the Conflict between Environmentalism and Wise Use'. *Society & Natural Resources* **10** (5): 453–68.

Wilmot, J. and T.W. Clark. 2005. 'Wolf Restoration: A Battle in the War over the West', in T.W. Clark, M.B. Rutherford and D. Casey (eds) *Coexisting with Large Carnivores: Lessons from Greater Yellowstone* (Washington, Covelo, London: Island Press) pp. 138–73.

Wolch, J.R., A. Gullo and U. Lassiter. 1997. Changing Attitudes toward California's Cougars. *Society & Animals* **5** (2): 95–116.

Yates, R. 2010. 'Language, Power and Speciesism'. *Critical Society* **3**: 11–9.

Author Biographies

Julien Alleau is a historian, and received all his education, Bachelors, Masters and Doctoral degrees, from the University of Caen Basse-Normandie in France. His Ph.D. Thesis 'Keeping the distance: a history of the relationship between humans and wolves in the western Alps (sixteenth to eighteenth centuries)' was completed in 2011. The thesis focused on archival studies of cases of wolf attacks on humans and wolf hunting, but interpreted these within the changing social and ecological context of the region. From 2011 to 2013 he was a post-doctoral fellow at the Norwegian Institute for Nature Research in Trondheim, Norway.

Jessica Bell is a Ph.D. student in Sociology, specialising in Animal Studies, Environmental Science and Policy and Conservation Criminology, at Michigan State University. Jessica's research interests include scientific representations of animal behaviour and mind, the impact of visual and discursive representations of wildlife on conservation, the sociopolitical dynamics of conservation initiatives and conservation crime (e.g. wildlife poaching). Her upcoming publications include an article on the conservation claims and repercussions of circuses (in press with *Society & Animals*) and a book chapter on elephant tourism and the ivory trade in Thailand (in *Conservation Criminology: The Nexus of Crime, Risk and Natural Resources*, 2015, Wiley-Blackwell). She has presented her work at numerous international conferences, including the International Society of Anthrozoology, the American Sociological Association, the International Wolf Symposium and the Australian Animal Studies Group.

Roger Bergström has worked as a visiting professor in wildlife ecology and as a researcher at Swedish Association for Hunting and Wildlife Management, Forestry Research Institute of Sweden and Department of Wildlife, Fish and Environmental Studies, SLU. His focus of research has been plant–animal interactions, but is now history of wildlife populations and game management in Sweden.

Kjell Danell is professor emeritus in wildlife ecology at the Swedish University of Agricultural Sciences at Umeå. He is a field ecologist with main interests in ecology of populations and communities in tundra, boreal forest and savanna biomes. A recent interest is history of natural resources and their use in a wider sense.

Karin Dirke is a senior lecturer in History of Ideas at the Department of Culture and Aesthetics, Stockholm University. Her research interests concern the historic relationship between humans and other animals, both wild and domestic.

Lydia A. Dixon is a Ph.D. Candidate in the Environmental Studies Program at the University of Colorado Boulder. She previously earned a Masters in Environmental Management from the Yale School of Forestry and an A.B. in Environmental Studies from Dartmouth College. In her research, she studies conflicts between people over living with large carnivores as well as how local knowledge can contribute to effective policy-making processes. Her dissertation explores these issues in the context of wolf management in Wyoming, where she lived for nearly a decade prior to beginning her doctorate.

José María Fernández-García is a wildlife conservation officer and consultant working for public administration in Spain. As a project manager, he has been involved in planning and implementation of population monitoring of endangered species, and identification of important sites to preserve biodiversity.

Adam Pérou Hermans is a Ph.D. candidate at the University of Colorado, studying environmental philosophy. His academic work seeks to describe, explore, and address conflicts between international wildlife conservation and social justice. Pérou Hermans moonlights as a filmmaker. His films span six continents and have featured in festivals around the world. For his dissertation he co-produced a series of dramatic narrative films with and for local communities in Nigeria and Cameroon. The series, *Gorilla Folk Films From the Cross River Headwaters*, retells local stories to offer alternative conceptions of gorilla conservation.

Karen Jones is Senior Lecturer in History at the University of Kent and editor of *Environment and History*. Her books include *Wolf Mountains: The History of Wolves Along the Great Divide* (2002) – a comparative study of the biology, mythology and culture surrounding wolves in national parks in the Rockies and *The Invention of the Park* (2005) – a survey of the park idea from the Garden of Eden to British landscape parks and beyond. She has published on national parks and transnational nature conservation (*Civilizing Nature* (2012)), co-edited a collection on guns and empire in the nineteenth century (*A Cultural History of Firearms in the Age of Empire* (2013)) and written on hunting and photography (*Wild Things: Nature and the Social Imagination* (2013)).

Linda Kalof is Professor of Sociology, Animal Studies and Environmental Science and Policy, and founding director of Michigan State University's interdisciplinary doctoral specialisation in Animal Studies. Her current research examines animal iconography in popular science and is funded by the National Science Foundation.

Alexander Kling studied German Literature at the University of Bayreuth. In 2009 he received his Magister degree. Since 2009 he has been teaching and researching at the University of Wuerzburg. His Ph.D. is focused on a literary and cultural history of the wolves between the Thirty Years' War and the French Revolution.

His main topics of research are Animal Studies, Cultural and Political Theory and the Literature of the 17th and 18th Century. Furthermore he is co-organiser of the young researchers' network for Cultural and Literary Animal Studies (CLAS).

John Linnell has a background in zoology, but has increasingly worked on inter-disciplinary projects that explore the complex relationships between humans and wildlife. His work mainly focuses on large carnivores and large herbivores, and he has run projects in many parts of Europe, in addition to India, Brazil and Myanmar. He is based at the Norwegian Institute for Nature Research in Trondheim, Norway.

Patrick Masius is a Post-doctoral researcher at Göttingen University, Germany. His research focuses on natural hazards and dangerous animals. In 2010, he received his Ph.D. at Göttingen University with a historical study on politics of natural disasters in the German Empire. Previously, he studied Geography and Social Anthropology at the Universities of Bayreuth and Sussex.

Robert W. Mysłajek holds a Master's degree from the Agricultural University in Kraków, Poland; he also completed postgraduate studies in molecular biology at the Jagiellonian University, Poland. He earned his Ph.D. in biology at the Institute of Nature Conservation, Polish Academy of Sciences. He is a postdoctoral research fellow in the Institute of Genetics and Biotechnology at the Faculty of Biology, University of Warsaw. He is also a vice-president of the Association for Nature, 'Wolf'.

Sabina Nowak graduated from the Silesian University in Katowice. She completed her Ph.D. in biology at the Institute of Nature Conservation, Polish Academy of Sciences, doing research on the ecology of the wolf population in the Carpathian Mountains. She is a member of the Large Carnivore Initiative IUCN, and the State Council of Nature Conservation – an advisory body for the Polish Ministry of Sciences. She also serves as an expert for the Polish–German wolf working group. She is a president of the Association for Nature, 'Wolf', Poland.

Martin Rheinheimer studied history and classical philology at the universities of Kiel (Germany) and Thessaloniki (Greece) and received his Dr. phil. for a thesis on the medieval crusader principality of Galilee. His Dr. habil. was achieved with a thesis on village bylaws in the early modern duchy of Schleswig. Since 1999, he has been a Professor in maritime and regional history at the University of Southern Denmark, first at the campus in Esbjerg and, from 2013, in Odense. His main field of interest is the social and economic history of the North Sea and Baltic Region. Among recent publications are *Der Kojenmann. Mensch und Natur im Wattenmeer 1860–1900* (2007) and *Der fremde Sohn. Hark Olufs' Wiederkehr aus der Sklaverei* (2001, 3rd ed. 2007).

Steven Rodriguez researches the development of national parks and environmental movements in Indonesia, Vietnam, and Cambodia.

Author Biographies

Jana Sprenger is a Post-doctoral researcher at Göttingen University. She researches the persecution and extirpation of wolves in early modern and modern Germany. In 2011, she received her Ph.D. at Göttingen University with a study about the perception, damage and control of insect pests in forestry and agriculture in Prussian Brandenburg. Previously, she studied Biology, focusing on biodiversity, at Kassel University.

Index

A

Abbey, Edward 175
actor–network theory 6, 21. 32
administration 82, 85, 91–4, 98, 122–5,
    131–3, 137, 166, 172, 252
  colonial 10, 163, 165, 169
  national 59
  provincial 166, 168, 169
aerial shooting 11, 232, 236, 239
Aesop 175, 199, 203
aesthetic 35, 17, 284
Afghanistan 260, 262, 268, 272, 274, 275,
agriculture 3, 28, 59, 96, 104, 119, 121, 143,
    165, 169, 171, 253, 298
Alaska 11, 175, 181–4, 204, 209, 213, 229–46,
    261, 267
Albania 5, 298
Alleau, Julien 8, 9, 79–100
Alps 20, 21, 79, 81, 88, 93, 156, 206, 268
America, North *see also* Canada; United States
    72, 81, 157, 163, 171, 175–202,
    203–29, 229–46, 259, 261–3, 266–7,
    270, 274, 276, 282–303
American Indian *see* Native American
animal rights 76, 181, 184, 189
anthropomorphism 4, 5, 181, 188, 190, 191,
    282–303
apocalypse 23. 27, 84, 194–5
appetite 66
archaeology 71, 143, 146
archive 32, 81–9, 92–3, 97–8, 101–02, 145,
    158, 207, 247, 287,
argali 260, 268, 271, 273, 275–6
aristocracy *see* nobility
Aristotle 296–7
Asia 8, 163–74
  Central 259–81
  East 69
  South 124
Asturias 148, 149, 151
Atlantic 141, 155
atom bomb *see* nuclear
attack (by wolves) 2, 3, 5, 8–10, 13, 29, 30,
    40, 41, 43, 81–100, 105–15, 119–20,
    122, 135, 164–6, 169–72, 209, 213,
    214, 217, 219, 221, 248, 259–81, 284

B

Bacon, Francis 19
bait 63–73, 104, 124–6, 137, 148, 213, 249
Bas-Dauphiné 81–6, 93, 98
Basque Country 146, 153, 155, 157
battue *see also* driving 8, 39, 49, 57, 64–7, 73,
    75, 85, 91–3
bear 75, 103, 114, 241, 283, 293, 295
  black 286
  brown 64, 66, 74, 120, 152, 217
  grizzly 209
Beaufort, François de 134
Beaujolais, beast of 86
beauty (of wolves) 188, 200, 218, 223, 225,
    231, 295
Beck, Ulrich 200
behaviour (of wolves) 5–7, 9, 66–7, 86–9, 98,
    106, 109, 110, 120, 143, 158, 171,
    172, 180, 181, 183, 185, 191, 192,
    204, 208, 210–15, 222, 249, 264,
    267–72, 288–91, 293, 295–8
Bell, Jessica 11, 12, 282–303
Bergh, Henry 184
Bergström, Roger 9, 57–78
Berlin 126, 128, 129,
Berne Convention 10, 135
bestial 176, 183
Białowieża Primeval Forest 247, 253
bible; biblical 2, 23, 26, 28, 33
Bihar 169, 172
Birckholtz, Melchior 69
Black, Max 20
boar, wild 25, 41, 97, 136, 157, 158, 164, 269
borders
  territorial; administrative 58, 102, 106, 123,
    127, 132, 196, 198, 200, 242, 254,
    260
  metaphorical 13, 112, 194, 197, 199
bounty 10, 50–1, 74–6, 88, 93–4, 102, 110,
    114, 122–4, 126, 132, 144, 158,
    168–9, 171–2, 219, 249–50
Bowen, Asta 176, 198–9
Bozenhart, Johannes 23, 30–1, 35–6
Brandenburg 9, 119–40
British India 163–74
Brummer, Magnus Hendric 72

Index

brutality
  (of humans) 39, 47
  (of wolves)175, 183–4, 290
Buck 182–5, 188, 191, 195
Burroughs, John 181, 185–6,

C

Canada 11, 209, 219
cannibalism 26, 46
Cantabria 141, 146, 150, 151
Caras, Roger 176, 186, 191–3, 199, 200
caribou 187, 190, 210, 220, 229, 234, 236–7,
       239
carnivore 1, 7, 10–12, 57, 61–2, 66–7, 75,
       86–8, 91, 102–04, 108, 111, 165–6,
       168, 180–1, 184, 186, 192, 193, 219,
       249, 252–4, 276, 284
Carpathian Mountains 247, 249, 250–1, 253
carrion 26, 32, 33, 34, 87, 97, 180, 210
Castilla 154, 156
Catholicism 24, 81–4, 143
cattle 27, 29, 40–1, 46, 49, 50, 70, 91, 97,
       103–04, 111, 122, 134, 137, 155,
       159, 165, 168, 178–80, 192, 197,
       287, 290
Charlemagne 9, 92, 120
child *see also* infant vii, 8–10, 26, 40, 42, 46,
       82–3, 86–7, 89–92, 97–9, 105, 109–
       12, 119, 135, 145, 159, 163–4, 170,
       171, 204, 260, 262, 269, 271, 274
Christianity 3, 28, 43, 83, 203, 287, 296, 298
chronicle 19–38, 84, 121, 143, 146, 152
Civil War
  English 19
  Spanish 146
civilisation 3, 12, 26–8, 33–5, 135, 180,
       182–4, 187, 189, 190, 198, 199, 232,
       294
climate 49, 64, 141, 205
coercion 73–4, 188
cohabitation 13
Coleman, Jon T. 176, 233
communication vii, 6, 30, 35, 64, 72, 126, 179,
       187–8, 194, 195, 207, 241, 288
compensation 131, 136, 157, 252, 254, 275,
       283, 299
conservation 1, 11, 76, 79, 154, 156, 171, 186,
       190, 191, 193, 206, 210, 223, 225,
       230, 234, 239, 251–3, 259, 267–9,
       271–3, 275, 277, 282, 283, 288,
       292–5, 298–9

construction; constructedness (cultural) 4, 6,
       20, 22, 36, 58, 85, 201, 203, 207,
       223, 225, 283, 285, 287, 289, 293,
       299
controversy 1, 8, 11, 19, 59, 81, 107, 156, 191,
       200, 229, 233, 235, 238, 243, 282
Cooper, James Fenimore 175
corridor, ecological 253
cosmology 30
cougar 286, 298
court
  law 48
  royal 62, 64, 69, 70
cowardice (imputed to wolves) 67, 120, 163,
       164, 169
coyote 207, 217, 224, 225, 233, 286, 288,
       293, 295
criminality
  of humans 5, 10, 43, 46
  of wolves vii, 5, 9, 43, 57, 176, 286, 289,
       293, 298
crisis
  environmental 200
  socio-political 19, 22–3, 26, 36, 92
Crisler, Lois 204
Critical Discourse Analysis 286
cub *see also* whelp 64, 66, 72, 131–2, 181, 183,
       193, 195, 209
culling 128–9, 251, 253, 271–3, 276
culture
  human vii, 1–5, 7, 8, 10–14, 20–3, 26, 28–9,
       32, 35, 47, 52, 120, 136, 137, 152,
       158, 176, 177, 182, 185, 188, 193,
       196, 203–04, 206–07, 224–6, 230,
       231–3, 238, 243–4, 259, 265, 270,
       283, 285, 292, 296,
  wolf 200
curiosity
  human 238, 177
  wolf 182, 210, 213, 214, 225, 231
Custer Wolf 191–3, 196, 199
cyanide 189, 204

D

Dance of Death 208–10, 222
Danell, Kjell 9, 57–78
danger vii, 7, 8, 10, 28, 30, 39, 40, 42, 49, 91,
       98, 103–05, 107–08, 115, 119, 120,
       145, 165–6, 168–71, 179, 259, 264,
       266, 267, 269, 271–3, 275–6, 293,
       294, 298

Index

Dante 2

Danube, R. 31

Darwin, Charles 179, 184

Darwinism 179, 183, 199

Dauphiné, beast of 8, 79–101

death 2, 3, 6, 13, 41–3, 46, 47, 49–53, 82–4, 89, 110, 112, 113, 163–4, 166, 170, 172, 180, 185, 198, 208–10, 224, 250, 254, 259,

debate *see also* controversy 14, 62 79, 107, 156, 164, 165, 170, 176, 177, 182, 185, 190, 196, 236, 244, 297

deconstruction *see* construction (cultural)

deer 13, 41, 61, 62, 123, 157, 189, 215, 219, 269, 288, 289–91, 295–6

red 88, 97, 136, 157

roe 61, 76, 97, 136, 157, 158, 168

white-tail 219

Defenders of Wildlife 229, 239

deforestation 143, 171

demography *see also* population

human 81, 142, 143, 157

wolf 156

demon 3, 43–5, 47, 49, 175, 185, 222, 225, 266, 270

Denali National Park *see also* Mount McKinley National Park 209, 234–5, 241–2

Denmark 40

Derrida, Jacques 4, 20–1, 32

destabilisation *see also* crisis 3

Dirke, Karin 2, 9, 57–78, 101–18

discourse 1, 10, 12, 13, 58, 101, 108, 113, 179, 186, 189, 197, 203–07, 211, 222–6, 259, 266, 282–303

disorder *see* order

dispersal (of wolves) 153–7

Dixon, Lydia 11, 229–46

dog 6, 25, 26, 29, 32, 33, 34, 67, 69, 87, 88, 102, 106, 112, 114, 136, 144, 164, 170, 181, 184, 185, 204, 207, 213, 215, 219, 220, 230, 250, 255, 261, 283, 290

dogma 156, 175, 180, 184

dominance 1, 12, 13, 25, 62, 107, 108, 115, 143, 176, 180, 184, 188, 195, 198, 205, 210, 211, 222, 224, 225, 230, 232, 233, 259, 285, 287–99

dominion 284, 287, 289, 296

drama 106, 107,109, 112–15, 178, 179, 190, 208–09, 222,

driving (of wolves) *see also* battue 7, 9, 50, 52, 65, 66, 70, 111, 122, 124, 126, 128, 137, 144, 249

Dunlap, Thomas 176, 204

E

Early Modern 3, 7, 9, 19, 40, 44, 82, 83, 85, 88, 89, 92, 97, 122

eating

by humans 25–6, 62

by wolves 8, 62, 79–100, 110, 137, 163, 171, 184, 210–13, 260, 262, 290, 291, 294

Ebro, R. 141, 152

ecology 99, 135, 142, 156–8, 175–7, 184, 186, 188, 189, 191, 192, 193, 194, 196, 199, 200, 204, 234, 236–8, 250, 252, 253, 269, 271, 284, 289, 290, 293, 297

political 264

economy; economic 1, 3, 12, 59, 70, 74, 79, 81, 85, 103, 143–4, 157–8, 165, 184, 192, 233, 234, 236, 239, 243,252, 254, 255, 275, 283, 284, 291, 294, 299

ecosystem 1, 13, 141, 142, 157–8, 204–05, 217, 222, 224, 234, 240, 252, 264, 284, 289, 290, 293, 295–7

education 61, 63, 69, 72, 182, 189, 190, 200, 204, 215, 217, 224, 225, 252, 255, 282, 299

elephant 164, 166, 169,

Elton, Charles 186, 188

emotion 1, 79, 102, 113–15, 176, 178, 181, 185, 192, 200, 213, 247, 275, 287, 290, 297

empathy 179, 181, 182, 187, 188, 189, 192, 193, 195, 200, 284, 297

encounter (human–wolf) 1, 7, 13, 21, 22, 27–36, 102, 108, 112, 114, 163, 185, 195, 197, 231, 269, 274

Endangered Species Act (ESA), United States 11, 202, 222, 291, 294

endangered status (of wolves) 10, 11, 137, 154, 158, 255, 268, 276

Enlightenment 4

environmentalism *see also* conservation 176, 186, 194, 197, 199, 200, 287, 288, 290, 294

eradication (of wolves) *see* extermination

Erasmus 19

Estonia 67, 87, 98, 270
ethics; the ethical 10, 74, 137, 158, 163, 177,
	180, 186, 199, 238, 285, 288, 290–1,
	293, 296, 298
ethnography 146, 152
Europe 2, 3, 4, 7, 8, 10, 13, 79, 81, 104, 105,
	141, 142, 152, 175, 206, 213, 219,
	270, 282
	Central 2, 13
	Eastern 13, 107, 127, 137, 142, 157, 251,
		252, 269
	Northern 13
	Southern 13, 107
	Western 85, 99, 142, 259
European Union 252
evil 1, 2, 5, 9, 13, 27, 28, 43, 46–7, 49, 53,
	104, 166, 283, 298
extermination 1, 3, 7, 9, 10, 26, 33, 35, 39–56,
	57–9, 61–3, 66–76, 93, 94, 101–04,
	115, 119–40, 123, 125, 144, 146,
	153, 156–8, 163–74, 192, 197, 199,
	204, 208, 218–19, 222, 230, 233,
	242, 247–50, 254, 268, 272, 284,
	287, 293, 294, 298

F

fable 2, 20, 21, 175, 187, 190, 195, 203
fairytale vii, 1, 2, 13, 20, 52, 137, 175, 197,
	200, 203
family 5, 186, 188, 190, 194, 198–9, 203,
	231, 286
farming *see also* agriculture 10, 11, 12, 22, 26,
	40, 50, 73, 108, 135–6, 143, 155,
	206, 255, 282, 294
fear 1, 5, 8, 12, 25, 31, 32, 35, 40, 47, 49, 52,
	79, 91, 103, 105–07, 109, 112, 114,
	115, 165, 175, 183–4, 217, 219, 231,
	247, 260, 261, 262, 267, 268, 270,
	271, 275, 289, 293
Fernández-García, José María 10, 141–62
figurative 20–2, 36, 177
film 52–3, 190, 193, 206, 223, 225
Finland 57, 58, 106, 109, 110, 111
fire 10, 27, 34, 46, 69, 81, 122, 143, 182, 260
firearm 8, 24, 92, 103, 112, 213, 219, 236,
	249, 253, 274, 294
food *see also* eating 6, 7, 12, 13, 24, 25–8, 33,
	42, 66, 84, 97, 99, 103, 119, 121,
	157, 192, 195, 205, 210–14, 217,
	222, 224, 239, 272–3, 289, 290,
	293–5

forest 3, 26, 28, 31, 39–41, 52, 66, 68, 75,
	86–8, 91–2, 96–7, 99, 106, 110, 119,
	121, 127, 128, 135, 141,163, 164,
	169, 195, 197, 206, 229, 247–55,
forester; forestry 9, 50, 61–5, 69, 70, 72, 92,
	103–04, 120, 122, 124, 126, 132, 137
forum, online 282–303
fox 25, 65, 69, 109, 131, 144, 164, 213
France 8, 9, 12, 46, 79–100, 105, 106, 128,
	134, 137, 219, 270,
fraud 129, 131, 134, 250
Friesenegger, Maurus 23–30
frontier *see also* border 20, 179, 180, 183, 191,
	193, 194, 198, 199, 229–32, 239, 286

G

gallows 5, 39–40, 43
game 10, 28, 49, 51, 59, 61–2, 64, 70–1, 75,
	87, 99, 103, 119, 128, 136, 144, 152,
	165, 197, 231, 232, 235, 239, 248,
	250, 251, 252, 267, 272, 276, 289,
	291
Germany vii, 8, 9, 19–38, 39–56, 69, 106,
	119–40, 248, 254
Gevaudan, beast of 8, 86, 92, 105, 111
gluttony (of wolves) *see* greed
Goodall, Jane 205
government *see also* administration 3, 7, 9, 67,
	107, 120, 124, 126, 128, 129, 131,
	136, 144, 163, 166, 168, 170, 187,
	189, 204, 232, 235, 237, 248, 264,
	268, 269, 271–2, 275, 276, 283, 287,
	289, 291, 292, 294
Goubert, Pierre 81
greed 58, 66, 88, 104
Grimmelshausen, Hans Jakob Christoffel von
	33–6
gun *see* firearm

H

habitat vii, 3, 7, 11, 12, 41, 119, 136, 156,
	157, 163, 217, 244, 251, 253–5, 294
Habitats Directive 10, 135, 252
habituation 211, 214, 224–5, 267, 268, 270–1,
	274
hanging *see also* gallows 5, 39, 43–4
Haraway, Donna 21, 205
hazard, natural 3, 9
heath 41, 91, 92, 96, 136
Heberle, Hans 23–30, 36

Index

Helsinki 106
Hermans, Adam Pérou 8, 259–81
hero; heroism 178–80, 182–6, 190–2, 200, 203, 225, 232
hierarchy 22, 184, 188, 200, 282–303
history of ideas 4
Hobbes, Thomas 19–20, 25, 33
Holocene 141–2, 158
hostility 3, 104, 176, 183, 195
house 5, 24, 29, 30, 32, 34, 35, 43, 50, 91, 197, 295
hunting
  by humans see also aerial shooting, battue, driving vii, 7, 9–10, 12, 27–8, 30, 36, 39, 42, 44, 49–50, 52, 57–78, 85, 87, 88, 91–8, 102–04, 108, 111, 113–15, 119–40, 144, 146, 150–3, 157, 158, 164–5, 168–70, 176–7, 188, 191, 197, 208, 219, 221, 222, 223, 229, 231–41, 248–55, 272, 274–6, 282–303
  by wolves 2, 120, 163, 176, 178, 179, 180, 182, 183, 188, 190, 192, 195–6, 198, 208, 210, 212, 214, 222, 261, 270–1
hyena 105, 170, 171
hysteria 49, 169, 229

I

Iberia 10, 141–62
ibex, Siberian 260, 273
iconography 184, 191, 203–28
ideology 11, 226, 282–303
image; imagery 1, 2, 8, 19–21, 25, 33–6, 43–4, 47, 88, 104, 106, 135, 137, 176, 183, 188, 191, 193, 200, 203–28, 232, 288, 289, 291, 298
imagination; imaginary 1, 3, 31–3, 36, 42–8, 58, 113–14, 175, 183, 194, 197, 200, 201, 230
imperialism 108, 165
India 8, 10, 69, 89, 163–74, 261, 262, 270
infant see also child 89, 164
Ingold, Tim 6
injustice see justice
intelligence, wolf 6, 135, 176, 181, 186, 210, 214, 219, 222
interaction vii, 1, 4, 6, 7, 14, 20–1, 25, 79, 97, 158, 171–2, 187, 188, 197, 208, 211, 213, 259, 286

invasion (by wolves) 26, 29, 58, 285, 287, 293, 295–6
Iran 262, 263, 270
irrationality see rationality
Italy 8, 93, 111

J

jackal 170
Japan 2, 10, 269–70
journalism see also media; newspaper 105, 112, 115, 262, 298
judiciary; judicial see also law 8, 48
justice 72, 82, 84, 259–81, 292–3

K

kinship 180, 196, 223
Kipling, Rudyard 135
Kling, Alexander 2, 19–38
knowledge 31, 104, 141, 143, 156, 192, 195, 238, 243, 255, 282–3, 286
  historical 79
  local 259–81
  production of vii, 259–81
  scientific 39, 205, 250, 283
Koblenz 119, 120, 124, 129, 131–2

L

Lagerlöf, Selma 113
landscape 3, 4, 7, 11, 12, 91–2, 96–8, 143, 146, 178, 179, 183, 185, 186, 188–190, 192, 195–7, 199, 225, 229–31, 233, 241, 264, 283, 285, 292,
  cultural 136, 137
landownership 62, 144, 235, 291
language 6, 20–1, 32, 66, 73, 181, 195, 196, 206, 287
Lascaux cave 2
Latour, Bruno 6, 22
law; legal; legislation 1, 5, 39, 48–9, 57, 59, 61–2, 73–4, 81–3, 92, 97, 120, 144, 150, 166, 205, 231, 232, 235, 236, 239, 240, 248, 250, 251–3, 268, 273, 274, 286, 291
León 142, 149, 150, 151, 156, 159
leopard 10, 163, 164, 165, 166, 168, 169, 171
  snow 260, 268, 272
Leopold, Aldo 13, 186, 284,
Lindgren, Astrid 109

Linnaeus 64, 67, 297
Linnell, John 8, 9, 79–100, 261, 267, 270,
literature 44–6, 48, 52, 28, 66, 109, 113, 135,
    137, 146, 158, 175–202, 203, 267,
    283, 297
  research; scientific 156, 274
Little Red Riding Hood (Little Red Cap) vii, 2,
    79, 89, 108, 120, 190
livestock *see also* cattle, sheep 3, 7, 9, 10, 12,
    13, 24, 29, 30, 34, 59, 61, 66, 73,
    74–6, 79, 91–2, 94, 97–8, 119, 121,
    126, 136, 143, 155, 157, 206, 222,
    231, 233, 249, 252, 254–5, 263, 267,
    270–1, 273, 275–6, 283, 292, 294
Lobo 7, 178–81, 185, 191
London, Jack 176–7, 181–8, 190, 192, 194,
    196, 199, 200
Lopez, Barry 2, 201, 230
louveterie 9, 92, 94–5
'*lupus cervarius*' 87–8
Lutts, Ralph 177, 186
Lynn, Bill 206
lynx 69, 75, 88, 93, 103, 108, 111, 121, 182,
    251
Lyonnais, beast of 86

M

magic 2, 40, 43–9, 51
Malleus Maleficarum 44
management vii, 1, 11, 12–14, 66, 70, 76, 98,
    120, 136, 201, 225, 229–46, 248,
    253–5, 273, 276, 282, 284, 289, 294
manpower 59, 61, 64, 66, 129
marginalisation 196, 264, 268, 273, 287, 290,
    299
Marta 198–9
Marvin, Gary 5, 298
masculinity 66, 179, 183, 186, 232, 286, 289
Masius, Patrick 1–18, 119–40
mastery *see also* dominion, dominance 284,
    289, 297
materiality 4, 7, 20–3, 32, 35, 36, 59, 178,
    186, 284
McCarthy, Cormac 176, 196–9
meat 62, 103, 146, 184, 195, 213, 235, 290,
    291
Mech, L. David 177, 200
media *see also* film; journalism; newspaper;
    television 2, 11, 52, 101, 225–6, 232,
    243, 286

medicine 45, 83
medieval 2, 62, 121, 143, 144, 146, 150, 175
Mediterranean 141, 146, 152, 153
metaphor *see also* figurative 2, 19–22, 32, 35–6,
    84, 182, 298
metaphysics 30, 178
Mexico 198
mice 25–6, 28, 34, 190
migration
  of humans 144, 194, 196, 233, 247, 284
  of wolves *see also* dispersal 127–8, 132,
    134–5, 137, 157
military *see also* soldier 9, 24, 59, 61, 63, 67,
    70, 75, 84, 95, 164, 165
Minnesota 194, 204, 211, 219, 261
monastery 23, 24, 27, 28
Montaigne, Michel de 19
Montgomery, Scott 224
moose 61, 64, 71, 76, 208–12, 222, 229, 231,
    236, 239, 242
morality 4, 5, 33, 35, 67, 104–05, 109, 143,
    175, 178–80, 182–4, 190, 199, 268,
    284, 286, 291–2, 297–8
Mount McKinley National Park *see also* Denali
    National Park 177, 233–5
movie *see* film
Mowat, Farley 176, 186–93, 196, 198–200,
    204
Muir, John 180, 192, 233
murder; murderousness 8, 46, 82, 187, 298
Murie, Adolph 177, 186, 193, 234–5
Mysłajek, Robert 10, 247–58
myth 2, 3, 5, 8, 20, 42, 43, 49, 79, 88, 98, 108,
    175, 176, 191, 192, 196, 213, 214,
    231–3, 269, 297

N

Nagel, T. 4
Napoleonic
  cadasters 96
  wars 132, 134 137
narrative 4, 5, 6, 13, 22, 29–32, 36, 84, 85,
    101–18, 176, 177, 178, 180, 183–90,
    192–200, 203, 206, 207, 219, 225,
    226
Nash, Roderick 232, 238
National Geographic 203–28, 241
National Park Service (US) 199, 229, 233, 234,
    236, 240, 241, 243
Native American 2, 261, 269, 271

Index

Natura 2000 253–5
naturalist 154, 163, 170, 175, 178, 179–81, 184, 186, 189, 190, 192, 193, 213
Nature 3, 4, 5, 7, 12, 14, 19–38, 42–3, 47, 62, 107–08, 114, 115, 135, 137, 175–202, 204–06, 210, 222–5, 247, 264, 266, 268–9, 272, 283–303
Nelson, Barbara 200
New Mexico 178–9, 196
newspaper *see also* journalism; media vii, 73, 76, 101–18, 120, 127, 179, 235, 262, 267, 285, 286
NGO 251, 252, 254
nobility 59, 61, 62, 63, 88, 104, 144
North-West Provinces, India 166, 169, 170
Norway 12, 58, 76, 112, 206
Nowak, Sabine 10, 247–58
nuclear 188, 194–5

O

O'Connor, T. 224–5
Odin 2, 42, 43
oral (tradition) 52, 267
order 3, 9, 22–7, 35–6, 178, 180–1, 284, 287, 288, 293–4, 299
Orrelius, Magnus 58, 105
outlaw 5, 43, 178–80, 191–2, 198

P

pack 9, 12, 27, 32, 33, 72, 97, 123, 124, 128, 132, 137, 154, 155, 164, 177, 179–81, 183, 186–90, 193–5, 198–200, 204, 207–14, 221–2, 225, 230, 240, 242, 249, 251, 254, 268, 290, 295
paleozoology 141
Pamir Mountains 269–81
parable *see also* fable 183, 189, 196, 283
parish register 81–7, 112
parliament 59, 61–3, 69, 70, 73, 102–04
pasture 96, 119, 144, 151, 157, 154, 260
peasant 23–6, 29–30, 33, 40–2, 50, 57, 59, 61–6, 68–70, 73, 74, 94, 103–04, 122, 124, 164
pelt 30, 164, 168
perception 1, 3, 9, 10, 12, 14, 20, 22–6, 28, 31, 35, 58, 119, 120, 134–5, 137, 158, 186, 187, 203, 223, 225, 230–1, 234, 255, 270
periodical 101, 225

pest *see also* varmint 1, 3, 62–3, 69, 88, 124, 144, 247
pestilence 26, 32
Peter and the Wolf 108
pharmacy 63, 66, 69
philosophy 4, 5, 186, 197, 268–9, 296–7,
photography 108, 190, 203–28, 239
pioneer 3, 4, 175, 177, 179, 183, 192, 219, 284
pitfall trap 70–3, 148
plague *see also* pestilence 23, 25–8, 104
Plautus 19
playing 97, 164, 190, 210–13, 222, 223
Pleistocene 142
Poetic Edda, The 19
poison 63, 66–70, 73, 75, 124–6, 137, 145–6, 156, 158, 168, 181, 194, 204–05, 213, 219, 222, 236, 249, 272,
Poland 10, 128, 135, 137, 247–58
policy 14, 93, 95, 145, 163, 204, 232–44, 268, 273, 276, 285
politics vii, 1, 2, 19–20, 25, 32, 81, 92, 95, 97, 119, 122, 137, 143, 144, 158, 184, 194, 199, 203, 204, 205, 222, 230, 234–6, 239–40, 242–4, 251, 272, 276,
population *see also* demography
  human 10, 24, 25, 29, 33, 64, 72, 102, 152, 155
  wolf vii, 7, 10, 11, 22, 27, 28, 75–6, 79, 92, 97, 98, 112, 113, 115, 120, 121–4, 127–9, 132, 134–7, 142–3, 145, 146, 153–8, 171, 172, 204, 22, 225, 229–30, 234, 237–44, 247–58, 274, 276, 282, 283, 286, 292–4
popular (belief, culture, thinking) 13, 40, 43, 45, 46, 49, 51, 66, 107, 135, 137, 176, 184, 185, 187, 190, 193, 194, 200, 203, 205, 206, 207, 224–6, 231, 233, 243, 247
portent 27, 115
Portugal 149, 151
post-modern 5
power (political) 6, 25, 52, 59, 61–6, 73–5, 82, 94, 108, 179, 184, 189, 200, 240, 242, 243, 265, 268–9, 271, 273–7, 283, 287, 295, 299
predator vii, 1–4, 7, 9–13, 21, 57–9, 61, 66, 73–4, 76, 88, 91, 98, 104, 109–10, 119–23, 127, 136–7, 144, 157, 158, 169, 176, 178–80, 184, 186–8, 192,

204–05, 209–10, 217, 220, 222,
224–5, 229, 233–40, 243, 247–8,
250, 253–4, 261, 263, 271, 283–4,
286–91, 293–7
management of *see* management
Preis, Caspar 23–4, 29–31, 35, 36
prejudice 176–7, 187, 297
priest 45, 61, 81–8, 91
propaganda 59, 61, 63, 72
Protestant 24, 44, 81, 82
Provence 92–3
Prussia 3, 9, 121–9, 132, 248
psychology 44–5, 98, 192
Pyrenees 20–1, 88, 141 153, 156

R

rabies 2, 85, 89, 98, 99, 105–06, 108, 109,
115, 261, 263, 268, 269, 270
Ragnarök 43
rancher 11, 12, 180, 191, 197, 205, 282–303
rationality 1, 4, 8, 42, 45, 48–9, 51–2, 137,
187, 191, 266
Rawlson, Timothy 233
reindeer 71, 233
reintroduction 11, 193, 197, 198, 204–06,
217, 222, 224–5, 276, 283–4, 288,
291–4, 299
religion 74, 82–3, 143, 175, 272, 283, 287,
289, 293, 297
reproduction 6, 119, 123, 129, 132, 135, 137,
157, 172, 254
restoration (of wolves) 193, 196, 198–9,
247–58, 282, 292
reward *see* bounty
Rheinheimer, Martin 3, 5, 8, 9, 39–56
rhetoric 3, 20, 22–3, 32–3, 35–6, 58, 59, 61,
194, 199
Rhineland 119–37
Riehl, Wilhelm Heinrich 135
rights *see also* animal rights 12, 62, 76, 82, 88,
94, 95, 181, 184, 189, 233, 283, 291,
294, 299
Ritvo, Harriet 4
Rocky Mountains 11, 198, 225
Rodriguez, Steven 8, 10, 163–74
Romans 2, 42, 89, 143, 146
romanticism 3, 177, 179, 183, 184, 189, 192,
230, 231, 232, 290
Roosevelt, Theodore 181, 185, 186

rural 1, 11, 12, 13, 29, 79, 81, 98, 122, 126,
144, 157, 274, 275, 276, 282–4, 287,
291, 294, 299
Russia 2, 8, 58, 106, 112–13, 254, 262, 269,
270, 274

S

Sami 108
sanctuary, wolf 215, 234
Sartore, Joel 223
Schleswig-Holstein 9, 39–56
Schönberg, Anders 64–5, 67, 69
science; scientist *see also* knowledge, scientific
vii, 1, 3, 6, 10, 14, 39, 45, 66, 69, 83,
136, 166, 176–93, 199–201, 203–07,
217, 222, 224–6, 229, 230, 234, 236,
237, 242–3, 247, 250–2, 255, 259,
261, 265–8, 273–6, 283, 296–7,
self
-assertion 30–1, 36
-perception 25–6
semiotic 4, 19–38
sentimentality 113, 181, 188, 189, 193
Seton, Ernest Thompson 176–82, 185–7, 190,
194, 199–200
Sewell, Anna 184
sexuality 46, 66
sheep 2, 22, 29, 91, 119, 238, 136, 143–4,
155, 157, 158, 180, 206, 234, 234–6,
260, 274
Dall 206, 234–6
shepherd 9, 89, 91, 97, 99, 11, 120, 144, 159,
206, 266, 271, 274, 298
snake 10, 163, 166,
snare *see also* trap 146, 253
snow 25, 64, 112, 122, 124, 182, 208, 219,
249, 260, 268, 271,
society
human 5, 7, 47, 49, 57, 144, 157, 176, 177,
178, 182, 184, 185, 189, 192, 194,
196, 197, 199, 200, 252, 262, 269,
292, 293, 297
wolf 188, 195, 198, 211, 222, 225, 297
soldier 24–5, 29–30, 34, 59, 106, 272–3
Sontag, Susan 206
Soviet 262, 271, 274, 275
Spain 13, 141–62, 261
Spencer, Herbert 178, 183, 184, 185
spirituality 82, 83, 177, 179, 187

sport 164, 165, 168, 171, 183, 189, 234, 290, 296, 297
Sprenger, Jana 1–18, 119–40
stakeholder 10, 11, 13, 79, 230, 238, 239, 242, 243, 244, 276, 286
starvation 85, 170
state, the 7, 9, 59, 64, 72–3, 82, 101, 126, 137, 189, 192, 221, 254, 273
Stockholm 64, 66, 67, 113, 114
story *see also* fable; myth, narrative vii, 6, 33, 46, 83, 85, 102, 105–15, 175–202, 204, 236, 242, 266
Strieber, Whitley 176, 194–5, 199
strychnine 10, 69, 124, 145, 156, 204
subconscious 1, 182
subsistence 178, 235, 238, 272
subspecies 141, 143, 163, 269–71
Sudety Mountains 253
survival 23, 10, 13, 127, 129, 153, 154, 170, 178, 182, 184, 186, 188, 192, 194, 195, 196, 211, 217, 222, 224, 230, 231–5, 243, 253
Sweden 12, 57–78, 101–18
Swift, Graham 176
symbolism 1, 3, 12, 42–3, 51–3, 59, 62, 79, 88, 108, 136, 143, 175, 179, 192, 194, 196, 230, 231, 282–5, 287, 291, 298

T

Tajikistan 259–81
tax 41–2, 59
taxonomy 88, 143
technology 27, 63, 135,137, 143, 223, 232, 238
television 7, 206, 231–3
Thirty Years' War 2, 19–38, 40, 49, 63, 95, 121, 125
Thomas, Keith 4
Thoreau, Henry David 175
tiger 10, 135, 163–9, 171, 172
Tlingit [people] 175
totem 176, 185, 187, 194, 198, 199
Touraine, beast of 86
tourism 157, 229, 240–3, 253, 285
transport 72, 164, 165 253
trap; trapping *see also* pitfall trap 7, 57, 64, 67, 70–3, 94, 103–04, 109, 122, 125–7, 132, 137, 144–52, 157, 168, 178, 180, 197, 213, 219, 222, 232, 241, 261, 270, 272, 294

Treves 122–6, 129–34
trophy 108, 165, 220, 221, 223, 229, 272–3, 276

U

Ukraine 247, 254, 266
ungulate 97, 146, 157, 222, 229, 234, 236, 238, 248, 252, 253, 255, 272, 289, 294
United Kingdom (UK) 13, 166
United States (US) 2, 3, 7, 10, 11, 126, 175–246, 276, 282–303
urban; urbanisation; urbanite 7, 11, 79, 157, 177, 190, 252, 282, 283–4, 285, 292, 299
Uzbekistan 262

V

values, cultural/ethical 62, 283–5, 176, 177, 187, 192, 225, 231, 238, 240, 244, 276, 294
varmint 176, 203, 204, 225, 293
Victorian 176, 178
village 5, 24, 29, 33–5, 39, 40, 50, 71, 119, 120, 121, 145, 150, 164–5, 170, 247, 248, 266, 273–4, 298
visual *see also* iconography; image 176, 188, 190, 203, 204, 206, 223
von Aken, Frans Joachim 69
von Aken, Frans Mikael 69
von Greiff, Johan Ludwig 70, 103
von Liewen, Berndt 67–9, 73
Vosges 127, 132
vulnerability 9, 91, 97–8, 205, 264–5, 271, 273–6
vulture 32, 33, 145

W

Wakhi [people] 259–81
war vii, 2, 7, 9, 19–38, 41–2, 47, 49, 57, 59, 61, 95, 122, 132, 137, 143, 194, 247, 275
werewolf 5, 43, 46–8, 88, 105
West (American) 3, 178, 183, 185, 191–4, 196, 198–9, 232, 233, 244, 292–4
whelp 122, 129–32
White Fang 135, 181–5, 191, 193
Wildlife Service, Canadian 189, 191
witch; witchcraft 40, 44–9

Index

wilderness 1, 3–4, 12, 33, 135, 175–6, 179–80, 182–4, 187, 189–90, 193, 196, 199, 203, 211, 225, 230–5, 243–4, 247, 283–5, 295
Wodan *see* Odin
wolf
  gray (*Canis lupus*) 158, 175, 231, 292
  Indian (*Canis lupus pallipes*) 163–74
  Tibetan (*Canis lupus chanco*) 260, 268–9, 271
Wolf and the Seven Young Goats, The 120
Wolf of Shadows 194–5, 199

World War Two 8, 10, 204, 222, 248

Y

Yellowstone National Park 13, 176, 185, 193, 198, 211, 217, 276

Z

zoo 7, 52, 108, 194, 215
zoology 20, 28, 66, 181, 296

CPSIA information can be obtained at www.ICGtesting.com
Printed in the USA
LVOW06*1944191115

463340LV00010B/130/P